Praise for the earlier editions of *Programming in Scala*

Programming in Scala is probably one of the best programming books
I've ever read. I like the writing style, the brevity, and the thorough explanations. The book seems to answer every question as it enters my mind—it's
always one step ahead of me. The authors don't just give you some code
and take things for granted. They give you the meat so you really understand
what's going on. I really like that.

- Ken Egervari, Chief Software Architect

Programming in Scala is clearly written, thorough, and easy to follow.
It has great examples and useful tips throughout. It has enabled our organi-
zation to ramp up on the Scala language quickly and efficiently. This book
is great for any programmer who is trying to wrap their head around the
flexibility and elegance of the Scala language.

- Larry Morroni, Owner, Morroni Technologies, Inc.

The *Programming in Scala* book serves as an excellent tutorial to the
Scala language. Working through the book, it flows well with each chapter
building on concepts and examples described in earlier ones. The book takes
care to explain the language constructs in depth, often providing examples
of how the language differs from Java. As well as the main language, there
is also some coverage of libraries such as containers and actors.

I have found the book really easy to work through, and it is probably
one of the better written technical books I have read recently. I really would
recommend this book to any programmer wanting to find out more about the
Scala language.

- Matthew Todd

i

I am amazed by the effort undertaken by the authors of *Programming in Scala*. This book is an invaluable guide to what I like to call Scala the Platform: a vehicle to better coding, a constant inspiration for scalable software design and implementation. If only I had Scala in its present mature state and this book on my desk back in 2003, when co-designing and implementing parts of the Athens 2004 Olympic Games Portal infrastructure!

To all readers: No matter what your programming background is, I feel you will find programming in Scala liberating and this book will be a loyal friend in the journey.

- Christos KK Loverdos, Software Consultant, Researcher

Programming in Scala is a superb in-depth introduction to Scala, and it's also an excellent reference. I'd say that it occupies a prominent place on my bookshelf, except that I'm still carrying it around with me nearly everywhere I go.

- Brian Clapper, President, ArdenTex, Inc.

Great book, well written with thoughtful examples. I would recommend it to both seasoned programmers and newbies.

- Howard Lovatt

The book *Programming in Scala* is not only about *how*, but more importantly, *why* to develop programs in this new programming language. The book's pragmatic approach in introducing the power of combining object-oriented and functional programming leaves the reader without any doubts as to what Scala really is.

- Dr. Ervin Varga, CEO/founder, EXPRO I.T. Consulting

This is a great introduction to functional programming for OO programmers. Learning about FP was my main goal, but I also got acquainted with some nice Scala surprises like case classes and pattern matching. Scala is an intriguing language and this book covers it well.

There's always a fine line to walk in a language introduction book between giving too much or not enough information. I find *Programming in Scala* to achieve a perfect balance.

- Jeff Heon, Programmer Analyst

I bought an early electronic version of the *Programming in Scala* book, by Odersky, Spoon, and Venners, and I was immediately a fan. In addition to the fact that it contains the most comprehensive information about the language, there are a few key features of the electronic format that impressed me. I have never seen links used as well in a PDF, not just for bookmarks, but also providing active links from the table of contents and index. I don't know why more authors don't use this feature, because it's really a joy for the reader. Another feature which I was impressed with was links to the forums ("Discuss") and a way to send comments ("Suggest") to the authors via email. The comments feature by itself isn't all that uncommon, but the simple inclusion of a page number in what is generated to send to the authors is valuable for both the authors and readers. I contributed more comments than I would have if the process would have been more arduous.

Read *Programming in Scala* for the content, but if you're reading the electronic version, definitely take advantage of the digital features that the authors took the care to build in!

- Dianne Marsh, Founder/Software Consultant, SRT Solutions

Lucidity and technical completeness are hallmarks of any well-written book, and I congratulate Martin Odersky, Lex Spoon, and Bill Venners on a job indeed very well done! The *Programming in Scala* book starts by setting a strong foundation with the basic concepts and ramps up the user to an intermediate level & beyond. This book is certainly a must buy for anyone aspiring to learn Scala.

- Jagan Nambi, Enterprise Architecture, GMAC Financial Services

Programming in Scala is a pleasure to read. This is one of those well-written technical books that provide deep and comprehensive coverage of the subject in an exceptionally concise and elegant manner.

The book is organized in a very natural and logical way. It is equally well suited for a curious technologist who just wants to stay on top of the current trends and a professional seeking deep understanding of the language core features and its design rationales. I highly recommend it to all interested in functional programming in general. For Scala developers, this book is unconditionally a must-read.

- Igor Khlystov, Software Architect/Lead Programmer, Greystone Inc.

The book *Programming in Scala* outright oozes the huge amount of hard work that has gone into it. I've never read a tutorial-style book before that accomplishes to be introductory yet comprehensive: in their (misguided) attempt to be approachable and not "confuse" the reader, most tutorials silently ignore aspects of a subject that are too advanced for the current discussion. This leaves a very bad taste, as one can never be sure as to the understanding one has achieved. There is always some residual "magic" that hasn't been explained and cannot be judged at all by the reader. This book never does that, it never takes anything for granted: every detail is either sufficiently explained or a reference to a later explanation is given. Indeed, the text is extensively cross-referenced and indexed, so that forming a complete picture of a complex topic is relatively easy.

- Gerald Loeffler, Enterprise Java Architect

Programming in Scala by Martin Odersky, Lex Spoon, and Bill Venners: in times where good programming books are rare, this excellent introduction for intermediate programmers really stands out. You'll find everything here you need to learn this promising language.

- Christian Neukirchen

Programming in Scala

Fifth Edition

Programming in Scala
Fifth Edition

Martin Odersky, Lex Spoon, Bill Venners,
and Frank Sommers

artima
ARTIMA PRESS
WALNUT CREEK, CALIFORNIA

Programming in Scala
Fifth Edition

Martin Odersky is the creator of the Scala language and a professor at EPFL in Lausanne, Switzerland. Lex Spoon worked on Scala for two years as a post-doc with Martin Odersky. Bill Venners is president of Artima, Inc. Frank Sommers is president of Autospaces, Inc.

Artima Press is an imprint of Artima, Inc.
2070 N Broadway Unit 305, Walnut Creek, California 94597

First edition published as PrePrint™ eBook 2007
First edition published 2008
Second edition published 2010
Third edition published 2016
Fourth edition published 2019
Fifth edition published 2021
Build date of this impression April 4, 2023
Produced in the United States of America

27 26 25 24 23   4 5 6 7 8
ISBN-10: 0-9971480-0-4
ISBN-13: 978-0-9971480-0-8

Library of Congress Control Number: 2021903968

to Nastaran - M.O.
to Fay - L.S.
to Siew - B.V.
to Jungwon - F.S.

Overview

Contents

Contents

Contents

List of Figures

List of Figures

List of Tables

List of Listings

Foreword

Watching the birth of a new programming language is a funny thing. To anyone who uses a programming language—whether you are dabbling with programming for the first time or are a grizzled career software engineer—programming languages just seem to exist. Like a hammer or axe, a programming language is a tool, already there, that enables us to perform our trade. We seldom think of how that tool came to be, what the process was to design it. We might have opinions about its design, but beyond that, we usually just put up with it and push forward.

Being there as a programming language is created, however, brings a totally different perspective. The possibilities for what could be seem endless. Yet at the same time, the programming language must satisfy what seems like an infinite list of constraints. It's an odd tension.

New programming languages are created for many reasons: a personal desire to scratch a niggling itch, a profound academic insight, technical debt, or the benefit of hindsight of other compiler architectures—even politics. Scala 3 is a combination of some of these.

Whatever combination it may be, it all started when Martin Odersky disappeared one day, emerging a few days later to announce in a research group meeting that he had begun experimenting with bringing the DOT calculus to life by writing a new compiler from scratch.[1] Here we were, a group of PhD students and postdocs who had until recently been a big part of the development and maintenance of Scala 2. At the time, Scala was reaching what felt like unfathomable heights of success, especially for an esoteric and academic programming language from a school with a funny-sounding name in Switzerland. Scala had recently taken off among startups in the Bay Area, and Typesafe, later named Lightbend, had recently been formed to support,

---

[1]DOT, or *dependent object types*, calculus is a series of formalizations attempting to characterize the essence of Scala's type system.

maintain, and manage releases of Scala 2. So why all of a sudden a new compiler and possibly a new and different programming language? Most were skeptical. Martin was undeterred.

Months passed. Like clockwork, at twelve noon every day, the entire lab would gather in the hallway connecting all of our offices. After a fair number of us and Martin had assembled, we'd venture together to one of EPFL's many cafeterias, grab lunch, and later, an after-lunch coffee. Each day during this ritual, ideas for this new compiler were a recurrent theme. Discussions would ping pong about, anywhere from focusing on something "150%" compatible with Scala 2 (to avoid a Python 2 versus Python 3 debacle), to creating new language with full-spectrum dependent types.

One by one, the skeptics in the research group seemed to become sold by some appealing aspect of Scala 3, be it streamlining the implementation of the typechecker, the brand new compiler architecture, or the powerful additions to the type system. Over time, much of the community also came around to the idea of Scala 3 being a marked improvement over Scala 2. Different people had different reasons for this. For some, it was the improvements in readability via the decision to make braces and parentheses around conditions in conditionals optional. For others, it was improvements to the type system; for example, match types for improved type-level programming. The list went on.

Rather than blindly steaming ahead on the design of Scala 3 based on hunch alone, I can confidently assert that Scala 3 is the result of much learning from design decisions of the past, and years of conversation with the EPFL research group and the Scala community. And there was no way but to start from a clean slate, and build on clean foundations. With this from-scratch approach, what emerged is, at its core, a new programming language.

Scala 3 is a new programming language. Sure, it might be compatible with Scala 2, and it might sound like the third major release of an already-existing programming language. But don't let that fool you. Scala 3 represents a substantial streamlining of many of the experimental ideas pioneered in Scala 2.

Perhaps what is most uniquely "Scala" about Scala 3 is what happened to implicits. Scala, since its inception, has been used by clever programmers to achieve functionality that few thought was even possible given Scala's feature set, let alone something Scala was designed for. The feature previously-known as implicits is perhaps the most well-known feature of Scala that has been exploited to bend Scala 2 in unexpected ways. Example use cases of

Figure 1 · What was intended.   Figure 2 · What we got.

implicits include retroactively adding a method to a class, without extending and re-compiling that class. Or, given a type signature used in some context, automatically selecting the right implementation for that context. This is just the tip of the iceberg—we even wrote a research paper attempting to catalog the multitude of ways in which developers have used implicits.[2]

This is like providing a user with knobs and levers and leaving it to them to build a smoothly-functioning piece of machinery, like the mechanical calculator shown in Figure 1. But often, what comes out instead is something that looks more like a kinetic sculpture of Theo Jansen, such as the one shown in Figure 2, than anything with an obvious use.[3] Simply put, you give a programming community something as basic as a lever and a knob, and the intrepid will seek to find creative ways to use it. It's human nature. But perhaps here, Scala 2's mistake was the idea to provide something as general-purpose as something like knobs and levers in the first place.

The point here is that in Scala 2, there was this endless array of possibilities for what implicits could be used for, which necessitated an entire research paper, and which the community generally couldn't agree upon how to sanely use. No language feature should have such a murky purpose for being. And yet, here they were—implicits were seen by many as the unique and powerful feature of Scala that essentially no other language had, and by many others as a mysterious and often frustrating mechanism that would invasively rewrite code that you had written to be something else.

---

[2]Krikava, *et al.*, *Scala implicits are everywhere*. [Kri19]

[3]For a more dynamic depiction of the kinetic sculptures of Theo Jansen, which are collectively entitled *Strandbeest*, see https://www.youtube.com/watch?v=LewVEF2B_pM.

Foreword

You may have heard the oft-repeated mantra that in many ways, Scala 3 represents a simplification of the Scala that came before it. The story of implicits is an excellent example. Cognizant of the back flips programmers were doing with implicits in an attempt to realize broader programming patterns like typeclass derivation, Martin, with the help of many others, came to the conclusion that we should not focus on implicits as a mechanism for people to use in the most general case. Rather, we should focus on what programmers want to *do* with implicits, and make that easier and more performant. This is where the mantra, "Scala 3 focuses on intent rather than mechanism," comes from.

With Scala 3, rather than focus on the generality of implicits as a mechanism, the decision was made to focus on specific use-cases that developers had in mind when choosing to use implicits in the first place, and to make these patterns more direct to use. Examples include passing context or configuration information to methods implicitly, without the programmer having to explicitly thread through repetitive arguments; retroactively adding methods to classes; and converting between types, like `Ints` and `Doubles` during arithmetic. Now, Scala 3 makes these use cases available to programmers without needing to understand some "deep" intuition about how the Scala compiler resolves implicits. You can instead just focus on tasks like "add a method `foo` to class `Bar` without having to recompile it." No PhD required. Just replace the previous notion of "implicit" with other more direct keywords that correspond to specific use cases, such as `given` and `using`. See Chapters 21 and 22 for more on this.

This story of "prioritizing intent over mechanism" doesn't stop at the revamping of implicits. Rather, the philosophy goes on to touch upon most every aspect of the language. Examples include additions and streamlining of many aspects of Scala's type system, from union types, to enums, to match types—or even the cleanups to Scala's syntax: optional braces to improve readability, and more readable "quiet" syntax for `if`s, `else`s, and `while`s, resulting in conditionals that look much more English-like.

Don't take my word for it. Whether you're a newcomer to Scala, or an experienced Scala developer, I hope you find many of the new design ideas that have entered Scala 3 to be as refreshing and straightforward as I do!

Heather Miller
Lausanne, Switzerland
June 1, 2021

Acknowledgments

Many people have contributed to this book and to the material it covers. We are grateful to all of them.

Scala itself has been a collective effort of many people. The design and the implementation of version 1.0 was helped by Philippe Altherr, Vincent Cremet, Gilles Dubochet, Burak Emir, Stéphane Micheloud, Nikolay Mihaylov, Michel Schinz, Erik Stenman, and Matthias Zenger. Phil Bagwell, Antonio Cunei, Iulian Dragos, Gilles Dubochet, Miguel Garcia, Philipp Haller, Sean McDirmid, Ingo Maier, Donna Malayeri, Adriaan Moors, Hubert Plociniczak, Paul Phillips, Aleksandar Prokopec, Tiark Rompf, Lukas Rytz, and Geoffrey Washburn joined in the effort to develop the second and current version of the language and tools.

Gilad Bracha, Nathan Bronson, Caoyuan, Aemon Cannon, Craig Chambers, Chris Conrad, Erik Ernst, Matthias Felleisen, Mark Harrah, Shriram Krishnamurti, Gary Leavens, David MacIver, Sebastian Maneth, Rickard Nilsson, Erik Meijer, Lalit Pant, David Pollak, Jon Pretty, Klaus Ostermann, Jorge Ortiz, Didier Rémy, Miles Sabin, Vijay Saraswat, Daniel Spiewak, James Strachan, Don Syme, Erik Torreborre, Mads Torgersen, Philip Wadler, Jamie Webb, John Williams, Kevin Wright, and Jason Zaugg have shaped the design of the language by graciously sharing their ideas with us in lively and inspiring discussions, by contributing important pieces of code to the open source effort, as well as through comments on previous versions of this document. The contributors to the Scala mailing list have also given very useful feedback that helped us improve the language and its tools.

George Berger has worked tremendously to make the build process and the web presence for the book work smoothly. As a result this project has been delightfully free of technical snafus.

Many people gave us valuable feedback on early versions of the text. Thanks goes to Eric Armstrong, George Berger, Alex Blewitt, Gilad Bracha,

William Cook, Bruce Eckel, Stéphane Micheloud, Todd Millstein, David Pollak, Frank Sommers, Philip Wadler, and Matthias Zenger. Thanks also to the Silicon Valley Patterns group for their very helpful review: Dave Astels, Tracy Bialik, John Brewer, Andrew Chase, Bradford Cross, Raoul Duke, John P. Eurich, Steven Ganz, Phil Goodwin, Ralph Jocham, Yan-Fa Li, Tao Ma, Jeffery Miller, Suresh Pai, Russ Rufer, Dave W. Smith, Scott Turnquest, Walter Vannini, Darlene Wallach, and Jonathan Andrew Wolter. And we'd like to thank Dewayne Johnson and Kim Leedy for their help with the cover art, and Frank Sommers for his work on the index.

We'd also like to extend a special thanks to all of our readers who contributed comments. Your comments were very helpful to us in shaping this into an even better book. We couldn't print the names of everyone who contributed comments, but here are the names of readers who submitted at least five comments during the eBook PrePrint™ stage by clicking on the Suggest link, sorted first by the highest total number of comments submitted, then alphabetically. Thanks goes to: David Biesack, Donn Stephan, Mats Henricson, Rob Dickens, Blair Zajac, Tony Sloane, Nigel Harrison, Javier Diaz Soto, William Heelan, Justin Forder, Gregor Purdy, Colin Perkins, Bjarte S. Karlsen, Ervin Varga, Eric Willigers, Mark Hayes, Martin Elwin, Calum MacLean, Jonathan Wolter, Les Pruszynski, Seth Tisue, Andrei Formiga, Dmitry Grigoriev, George Berger, Howard Lovatt, John P. Eurich, Marius Scurtescu, Jeff Ervin, Jamie Webb, Kurt Zoglmann, Dean Wampler, Nikolaj Lindberg, Peter McLain, Arkadiusz Stryjski, Shanky Surana, Craig Bordelon, Alexandre Patry, Filip Moens, Fred Janon, Jeff Heon, Boris Lorbeer, Jim Menard, Tim Azzopardi, Thomas Jung, Walter Chang, Jeroen Dijkmeijer, Casey Bowman, Martin Smith, Richard Dallaway, Antony Stubbs, Lars Westergren, Maarten Hazewinkel, Matt Russell, Remigiusz Michalowski, Andrew Tolopko, Curtis Stanford, Joshua Cough, Zemian Deng, Christopher Rodrigues Macias, Juan Miguel Garcia Lopez, Michel Schinz, Peter Moore, Randolph Kahle, Vladimir Kelman, Daniel Gronau, Dirk Detering, Hiroaki Nakamura, Ole Hougaard, Bhaskar Maddala, David Bernard, Derek Mahar, George Kollias, Kristian Nordal, Normen Mueller, Rafael Ferreira, Binil Thomas, John Nilsson, Jorge Ortiz, Marcus Schulte, Vadim Gerassimov, Cameron Taggart, Jon-Anders Teigen, Silvestre Zabala, Will McQueen, and Sam Owen.

We would also like to thank those who submitted comments and errata after the first two editions were published, including Felix Siegrist, Lothar Meyer-Lerbs, Diethard Michaelis, Roshan Dawrani, Donn Stephan,

William Uther, Francisco Reverbel, Jim Balter, and Freek de Bruijn, Ambrose Laing, Sekhar Prabhala, Levon Saldamli, Andrew Bursavich, Hjalmar Peters, Thomas Fehr, Alain O'Dea, Rob Dickens, Tim Taylor, Christian Sternagel, Michel Parisien, Joel Neely, Brian McKeon, Thomas Fehr, Joseph Elliott, Gabriel da Silva Ribeiro, Thomas Fehr, Pablo Ripolles, Douglas Gaylor, Kevin Squire, Harry-Anton Talvik, Christopher Simpkins, Martin Witmann-Funk, Jim Balter, Peter Foster, Craig Bordelon, Heinz-Peter Gumm, Peter Chapin, Kevin Wright, Ananthan Srinivasan, Omar Kilani, Donn Stephan, Guenther Waffler.

Lex would like to thank Aaron Abrams, Jason Adams, Henry and Emily Crutcher, Joey Gibson, Gunnar Hillert, Matthew Link, Toby Reyelts, Jason Snape, John and Melinda Weathers, and all of the Atlanta Scala Enthusiasts for many helpful discussions about the language design, its mathematical underpinnings, and how to present Scala to working engineers.

A special thanks to Dave Briccetti and Adriaan Moors for reviewing the third edition, and to Marconi Lanna for not only reviewing, but providing motivation for the third edition by giving a talk entitled "What's new since *Programming in Scala.*"

Bill would like to thank Gary Cornell, Greg Doench, Andy Hunt, Mike Leonard, Tyler Ortman, Bill Pollock, Dave Thomas, and Adam Wright for providing insight and advice on book publishing. Bill would also like to thank Dick Wall for collaborating on our *Stairway to Scala* course, which is in great part based on this book. Our many years of experience teaching *Stairway to Scala* helped make this book better. Lastly, Bill would like to thank Darlene Gruendl and Samantha Woolf for their help in getting the third edition completed.

Finally, we would like to thank Julien Richard-Foy for his work to bring the fourth edition of this book up to date with Scala 2.13, in particular the new collections redesign.

Introduction

This book is a tutorial for the Scala programming language, written by people directly involved in the development of Scala. Our goal is that by reading this book, you can learn everything you need to be a productive Scala programmer. All examples in this book compile with Scala version 3.0.0.

Who should read this book

The main target audience for this book is programmers who want to learn to program in Scala. If you want to do your next software project in Scala, then this is the book for you. In addition, the book should be interesting to programmers wishing to expand their horizons by learning new concepts. If you're a Java programmer, for example, reading this book will expose you to many concepts from functional programming as well as advanced object-oriented ideas. We believe learning about Scala, and the ideas behind it, can help you become a better programmer in general.

General programming knowledge is assumed. While Scala is a fine first programming language, this is not the book to use to learn programming.

On the other hand, no specific knowledge of programming languages is required. Even though most people use Scala on the Java platform, this book does not presume you know anything about Java. However, we expect many readers to be familiar with Java, and so we sometimes compare Scala to Java to help such readers understand the differences.

How to use this book

Because the main purpose of this book is to serve as a tutorial, the recommended way to read this book is in chapter order, from front to back. We have tried hard to introduce one topic at a time, and explain new topics only in terms of topics we've already introduced. Thus, if you skip to the back to get an early peek at something, you may find it explained in terms of concepts you don't quite understand. To the extent you read the chapters in order, we think you'll find it quite straightforward to gain competency in Scala, one step at a time.

If you see a term you do not know, be sure to check the glossary and the index. Many readers will skim parts of the book, and that is just fine. The glossary and index can help you backtrack whenever you skim over something too quickly.

After you have read the book once, it should also serve as a language reference. There is a formal specification of the Scala language, but the language specification tries for precision at the expense of readability. Although this book doesn't cover every detail of Scala, it is quite comprehensive and should serve as an approachable language reference as you become more adept at programming in Scala.

How to learn Scala

You will learn a lot about Scala simply by reading this book from cover to cover. You can learn Scala faster and more thoroughly, though, if you do a few extra things.

First of all, you can take advantage of the many program examples included in the book. Typing them in yourself is a way to force your mind through each line of code. Trying variations is a way to make them more fun and to make sure you really understand how they work.

Second, keep in touch with the numerous online forums. That way, you and other Scala enthusiasts can help each other. There are numerous mailing lists, discussion forums, a chat room, a wiki, and multiple Scala-specific article feeds. Take some time to find ones that fit your information needs. You will spend a lot less time stuck on little problems, so you can spend your time on deeper, more important questions.

Finally, once you have read enough, take on a programming project of your own. Work on a small program from scratch or develop an add-in to a larger program. You can only go so far by reading.

EBook features

This book is available in both paper and PDF eBook form. The eBook is not simply an electronic copy of the paper version of the book. While the content is the same as in the paper version, the eBook has been carefully designed and optimized for reading on a computer screen.

The first thing to notice is that most references within the eBook are hyperlinked. If you select a reference to a chapter, figure, or glossary entry, your PDF viewer should take you immediately to the selected item so that you do not have to flip around to find it.

Additionally, at the bottom of each page in the eBook are a number of navigation links. The Cover, Overview, and Contents links take you to the front matter of the book. The Glossary and Index links take you to reference parts of the book. Finally, if you find a typo, or something you think could be explained better, please click on the Suggest link, which will take you to an online web application where you can give the authors feedback.

Although the same pages appear in the eBook as in the printed book, blank pages are removed and the remaining pages renumbered. The pages are numbered differently so that it is easier for you to determine PDF page numbers when printing only a portion of the eBook. The pages in the eBook are, therefore, numbered exactly as your PDF viewer will number them.

Typographic conventions

The first time a *term* is used, it is italicized. Small code examples, such as x + 1, are written inline with a mono-spaced font. Larger code examples are put into mono-spaced quotation blocks like this:

```
def hello() =
  println("Hello, world!")
```

When interactive shells are shown, responses from the shell are shown in a lighter font:

```
scala> 3 + 4
val res0: Int = 7
```

Content overview

- Chapter 1, "A Scalable Language," gives an overview of Scala's design as well as the reasoning, and history, behind it.

- Chapter 2, "First Steps in Scala," shows you how to do a number of basic programming tasks in Scala, without going into great detail about how they work. The goal of this chapter is to get your fingers started typing and running Scala code.

- Chapter 3, "Next Steps in Scala," shows you several more basic programming tasks that will help you get up to speed quickly in Scala. After completing this chapter, you should be able to start using Scala for simple scripting tasks.

- Chapter 4, "Classes and Objects," starts the in-depth coverage of Scala with a description of its basic object-oriented building blocks and instructions on how to compile and run a Scala application.

- Chapter 5, "Basic Types and Operations," covers Scala's basic types, their literals, the operations you can perform on them, how precedence and associativity works, and what rich wrappers are.

- Chapter 6, "Functional Objects," dives more deeply into the object-oriented features of Scala, using functional (*i.e.*, immutable) rational numbers as an example.

- Chapter 7, "Built-in Control Structures," shows you how to use Scala's built-in control structures: `if`, `while`, `for`, `try`, and `match`.

- Chapter 8, "Functions and Closures," provides in-depth coverage of functions, the basic building block of functional languages.

- Chapter 9, "Control Abstraction," shows how to augment Scala's basic control structures by defining your own control abstractions.

- Chapter 10, "Composition and Inheritance," discusses more of Scala's support for object-oriented programming. The topics are not as fundamental as those in Chapter 4, but they frequently arise in practice.

- Chapter 11, "Traits," covers Scala's mechanism for mixin composition. The chapter shows how traits work, describes common uses, and explains how traits improve on traditional multiple inheritance.

- Chapter 12, "Packages and Imports," discusses issues with programming in the large, including top-level packages, import statements, and access control modifiers like `protected` and `private`.

- Chapter 13, "Pattern Matching," introduces twin constructs that support you when writing regular, non-encapsulated data structures. Case classes and pattern matching are particularly helpful for tree-like recursive data.

- Chapter 14, "Working with Lists," explains in detail lists, which are probably the most commonly used data structure in Scala programs.

- Chapter 15, "Working with Other Collections," shows you how to use the basic Scala collections, such as lists, arrays, tuples, sets, and maps.

- Chapter 16, "Mutable Objects," explains mutable objects and the syntax Scala provides to express them. The chapter concludes with a case study on discrete event simulation, which shows some mutable objects in action.

- Chapter 17, "Scala's Hierarchy," explains Scala's inheritance hierarchy and discusses its universal methods and bottom types.

- Chapter 18, "Type Parameterization," explains some of the techniques for information hiding introduced in Chapter 13 by means of a concrete example: the design of a class for purely functional queues. The chapter builds up to a description of variance of type parameters and how it interacts with information hiding.

- Chapter 19, "Enums and ADTs," describes enums, a new feature of Scala 3 that enables you to concisely define enumerated and algebraic data types.

- Chapter 20, "Abstract Members," describes all kinds of abstract members that Scala supports; not only methods, but also fields and types, can be declared abstract.

- Chapter 21, "Givens," describes Scala's feature that helps you work with contextual parameters to functions. Passing in all contextual information is simple, but can entail a lot of boilerplate. Givens help you reduce that boilerplate.

- Chapter 22, "Extension Methods," describes Scala's mechanism for making it *appear* as if a function is defined as a method on a class, when it is really defined outside the class.

- Chapter 23, "Typeclasses," introduces context bounds, and describes and gives several examples of typeclasses.

- Chapter 24, "Collections in Depth," gives a detailed tour of the collections library.

- Chapter 25, "Assertions and Tests," shows Scala's assertion mechanism and gives a tour of several tools available for writing tests in Scala, focusing on ScalaTest in particular.

Resources

At `https://www.scala-lang.org`, the main website for Scala, you'll find the latest Scala release and links to documentation and community resources. For a more condensed page of links to Scala resources, visit this book's website: `https://booksites.artima.com/programming_in_scala_5ed`.

Source code

You can download a ZIP file containing the source code of this book, which is released under the Apache 2.0 open source license, from the book's website: `https://booksites.artima.com/programming_in_scala_5ed`.

Errata

Although this book has been heavily reviewed and checked, errors will inevitably slip through. For a (hopefully short) list of errata for this book, visit `https://booksites.artima.com/programming_in_scala_5ed/errata`. If you find an error, please report it at the above URL, so that we can fix it in a future printing or edition of this book.

Programming in Scala
Fifth Edition

`"Hello, reader!"`

Chapter 1

A Scalable Language

The name Scala stands for "scalable language." The language is so named because it was designed to grow with the demands of its users. You can apply Scala to a wide range of programming tasks, from writing small scripts to building large systems.[1]

Scala is easy to get into. It runs on the standard Java and JavaScript platforms and interoperates seamlessly with all platform libraries. It's quite a good language for writing scripts that pull together existing libraries. But it can apply its strengths even more when used for building large systems and frameworks of reusable components.

Technically, Scala is a blend of object-oriented and functional programming concepts in a statically typed language. The fusion of object-oriented and functional programming shows up in many different aspects of Scala; it is probably more pervasive than in any other widely used language. The two programming styles have complementary strengths when it comes to scalability. Scala's functional programming constructs make it easy to build interesting things quickly from simple parts. Its object-oriented constructs make it easy to structure larger systems and adapt them to new demands. The combination of both styles in Scala makes it possible to express new kinds of programming patterns and component abstractions. It also leads to a legible and concise programming style. And because it is so malleable, programming in Scala can be a lot of fun.

This initial chapter answers the question, "Why Scala?" It gives a high-level view of Scala's design and the reasoning behind it. After reading the chapter you should have a basic feel for what Scala is and what kinds of

---

[1] Scala is pronounced *skah-lah*.

3

tasks it might help you accomplish. Although this book is a Scala tutorial, this chapter isn't really part of the tutorial. If you're eager to start writing some Scala code, you should jump ahead to Chapter 2.

1.1 A language that grows on you

Programs of different sizes tend to require different programming constructs. Consider, for example, the following small Scala program:

```
var capital = Map("US" -> "Washington", "France" -> "Paris")
capital += ("Japan" -> "Tokyo")
println(capital("France"))
```

This program sets up a map from countries to their capitals, modifies the map by adding a new binding ("Japan" -> "Tokyo"), and prints the capital associated with the country France.[2] The notation in this example is high level, to the point, and not cluttered with extraneous semicolons or type annotations. Indeed, the feel is that of a modern "scripting" language like Perl, Python, or Ruby. One common characteristic of these languages, which is relevant for the example above, is that they each support an "associative map" construct in the syntax of the language.

Associative maps are very useful because they help keep programs legible and concise, but sometimes you might not agree with their "one size fits all" philosophy because you need to control the properties of the maps you use in your program in a more fine-grained way. Scala gives you this fine-grained control if you need it, because maps in Scala are not language syntax. They are library abstractions that you can extend and adapt.

In the above program, you'll get a default Map implementation, but you can easily change that. You could for example specify a particular implementation, such as a HashMap or a TreeMap, or with Scala's parallel collections module, invoke the par method to obtain a ParMap that executes operations in parallel. You could specify a default value for the map, or you could override any other method of the map you create. In each case, you can use the same easy access syntax for maps as in the example above.

---

[2]Please bear with us if you don't understand all the details of this program. They will be explained in the next two chapters.

This example shows that Scala can give you both convenience and flexibility. Scala has a set of convenient constructs that help you get started quickly and let you program in a pleasantly concise style. At the same time, you have the assurance that you will not outgrow the language. You can always tailor the program to your requirements, because everything is based on library modules that you can select and adapt as needed.

Growing new types

Eric Raymond introduced the cathedral and bazaar as two metaphors of software development.[3] The cathedral is a near-perfect building that takes a long time to build. Once built, it stays unchanged for a long time. The bazaar, by contrast, is adapted and extended each day by the people working in it. In Raymond's work the bazaar is a metaphor for open-source software development. Guy Steele noted in a talk on "growing a language" that the same distinction can be applied to language design.[4] Scala is much more like a bazaar than a cathedral, in the sense that it is designed to be extended and adapted by the people programming in it. Instead of providing all constructs you might ever need in one "perfectly complete" language, Scala puts the tools for building such constructs into your hands.

Here's an example. Many applications need a type of integer that can become arbitrarily large without overflow or "wrap-around" of arithmetic operations. Scala defines such a type in library class `scala.math.BigInt`. Here is the definition of a method using that type, which calculates the factorial of a passed integer value:[5]

```
def factorial(x: BigInt): BigInt =
  if x == 0 then 1 else x * factorial(x - 1)
```

Now, if you call `factorial(30)` you would get:

```
265252859812191058636308480000000
```

`BigInt` looks like a built-in type because you can use integer literals and operators such as `*` and `-` with values of that type. Yet it is just a class that

---

[3] Raymond, *The Cathedral and the Bazaar*. [Ray99]

[4] Steele, "Growing a language." [Ste99]

[5] `factorial(x)`, or `x!` in mathematical notation, is the result of computing $1 * 2 * \ldots * x$, with 0! defined to be 1.

5

happens to be defined in Scala's standard library.[6] If the class were missing, it would be straightforward for any Scala programmer to write an implementation, for instance, by wrapping Java's class `java.math.BigInteger` (in fact that's how Scala's `BigInt` class is implemented).

Of course, you could also use Java's class directly. But the result is not nearly as pleasant, because although Java allows you to create new types, those types don't feel much like native language support:

```
import java.math.BigInteger

def factorial(x: BigInteger): BigInteger =
  if x == BigInteger.ZERO then
    BigInteger.ONE
  else
    x.multiply(factorial(x.subtract(BigInteger.ONE)))
```

`BigInt` is representative of many other number-like types—big decimals, complex numbers, rational numbers, confidence intervals, polynomials—the list goes on. Some programming languages implement some of these types natively. For instance, Lisp, Haskell, and Python implement big integers; Fortran and Python implement complex numbers. But any language that attempted to implement all of these abstractions at the same time would simply become too big to be manageable. What's more, even if such a language were to exist, some applications would surely benefit from other number-like types that were not supplied. So the approach of attempting to provide everything in one language doesn't scale very well. Instead, Scala allows users to grow and adapt the language in the directions they need by defining easy-to-use libraries that *feel* like native language support.

Growing new control constructs

The previous example demonstrates that Scala lets you add new types that can be used as conveniently as built-in types. The same extension principle also applies to control structures. This kind of extensibility is illustrated by the `AnyFunSuite` style of ScalaTest, a popular testing library for Scala.

As an example, here is a simple test class that contains two tests:

---

[6]Scala comes with a standard library, some of which will be covered in this book. For more information, you can also consult the library's Scaladoc documentation, which is available in the distribution and online at `https://www.scala-lang.org`.

```
class SetSpec extends AnyFunSuite:
  test("An empty Set should have size 0") {
    assert(Set.empty.size == 0)
  }
  test("Invoking head on an empty Set should fail") {
    assertThrows[NoSuchElementException] {
      Set.empty.head
    }
  }
```

We don't expect you to fully understand the `AnyFunSuite` example at this point. Rather, what's significant about this example for the topic of scalability is that neither the `test` construct nor the `assertThrows` syntax are built-in operations in Scala. Even though the both may look and act very much like a built-in control constructs, they are in fact methods defined in the ScalaTest library. Both of these constructs are completely independent of the Scala programming language.

This example illustrates that you can "grow" the Scala language in new directions even as specialized as software testing. To be sure, you need experienced architects and programmers to do this. But the crucial thing is that it is feasible—you can design and implement abstractions in Scala that address radically new application domains, yet still feel like native language support when used.

1.2 What makes Scala scalable?

Scalability is influenced by many factors, ranging from syntax details to component abstraction constructs. If we were forced to name just one aspect of Scala that helps scalability, though, we'd pick its combination of object-oriented and functional programming (well, we cheated, that's really two aspects, but they are intertwined).

Scala goes further than all other well-known languages in fusing object-oriented and functional programming into a uniform language design. For instance, where other languages might have objects and functions as two different concepts, in Scala a function value *is* an object. Function types are classes that can be inherited by subclasses. This might seem nothing more than an academic nicety, but it has deep consequences for scalability. This section gives an overview of Scala's way of blending object-oriented and functional concepts.

Scala is object-oriented

Object-oriented programming has been immensely successful. Starting from Simula in the mid-60s and Smalltalk in the 70s, it is now available in more languages than not. In some domains, objects have taken over completely. While there is not a precise definition of what object-oriented means, there is clearly something about objects that appeals to programmers.

In principle, the motivation for object-oriented programming is very simple: all but the most trivial programs need some sort of structure. The most straightforward way to do this is to put data and operations into some form of containers. The great idea of object-oriented programming is to make these containers fully general, so that they can contain operations as well as data, and that they are themselves values that can be stored in other containers, or passed as parameters to operations. Such containers are called objects. Alan Kay, the inventor of Smalltalk, remarked that in this way the simplest object has the same construction principle as a full computer: it combines data with operations under a formalized interface.[7] So objects have a lot to do with language scalability: the same techniques apply to the construction of small as well as large programs.

Even though object-oriented programming has been mainstream for a long time, there are relatively few languages that have followed Smalltalk in pushing this construction principle to its logical conclusion. For instance, many languages admit values that are not objects, such as the primitive values in Java. Or they allow static fields and methods that are not members of any object. These deviations from the pure idea of object-oriented programming look quite harmless at first, but they have an annoying tendency to complicate things and limit scalability.

By contrast, Scala is an object-oriented language in pure form: every value is an object and every operation is a method call. For example, when you say 1 + 2 in Scala, you are actually invoking a method named + defined in class Int. You can define methods with operator-like names that clients of your API can then use in operator notation.

Scala is more advanced than most other languages when it comes to composing objects. An example is Scala's *traits*. Traits are like interfaces in Java,

---

[7]Kay, "The Early History of Smalltalk." [Kay96]

but they can also have method implementations and even fields.[8] Objects are constructed by *mixin composition*, which takes the members of a class and adds the members of a number of traits to them. In this way, different aspects of classes can be encapsulated in different traits. This looks a bit like multiple inheritance, but differs when it comes to the details. Unlike a class, a trait can add some new functionality to an unspecified superclass. This makes traits more "pluggable" than classes. In particular, it avoids the classical "diamond inheritance" problems of multiple inheritance, which arise when the same class is inherited via several different paths.

Scala is functional

In addition to being a pure object-oriented language, Scala is also a full-blown functional language. The ideas of functional programming are older than (electronic) computers. Their foundation was laid in Alonzo Church's lambda calculus, which he developed in the 1930s. The first functional programming language was Lisp, which dates from the late 50s. Other popular functional languages are Scheme, SML, Erlang, Haskell, OCaml, and F#. For a long time, functional programming has been a bit on the sidelines—popular in academia, but not that widely used in industry. However, in recent years, there has been an increased interest in functional programming languages and techniques.

Functional programming is guided by two main ideas. The first idea is that functions are first-class values. In a functional language, a function is a value of the same status as, say, an integer or a string. You can pass functions as arguments to other functions, return them as results from functions, or store them in variables. You can also define a function inside another function, just as you can define an integer value inside a function. And you can define functions without giving them a name, sprinkling your code with function literals as easily as you might write integer literals like 42.

Functions that are first-class values provide a convenient means for abstracting over operations and creating new control structures. This generalization of functions provides great expressiveness, which often leads to very legible and concise programs. It also plays an important role for scalability. As an example, the ScalaTest testing library offers an `eventually` construct that takes a function as an argument. It is used like this:

---

[8] Starting with Java 8, interfaces can have default method implementations, but these do not offer all the features of Scala's traits.

9

```
val xs = 1 to 3
val it = xs.iterator
eventually { it.next() shouldBe 3 }
```

The code inside `eventually`—the assertion, `it.next() shouldBe 3`—is wrapped in a function that is passed unexecuted to the `eventually` method. For a configured amount of time, `eventually` will repeatedly execute the function until the assertion succeeds.

The second main idea of functional programming is that the operations of a program should map input values to output values rather than change data in place. To see the difference, consider the implementation of strings in Ruby and Java. In Ruby, a string is an array of characters. Characters in a string can be changed individually. For instance you can change a semicolon character in a string to a period inside the same string object. In Java and Scala, on the other hand, a string is a sequence of characters in the mathematical sense. Replacing a character in a string using an expression like `s.replace(';', '.')` yields a new string object, which is different from `s`. Another way of expressing this is that strings are immutable in Java whereas they are mutable in Ruby. So looking at just strings, Java is a functional language, whereas Ruby is not. Immutable data structures are one of the cornerstones of functional programming. The Scala libraries define many more immutable data types on top of those found in the Java APIs. For instance, Scala has immutable lists, tuples, maps, and sets.

Another way of stating this second idea of functional programming is that methods should not have any *side effects*. They should communicate with their environment only by taking arguments and returning results. For instance, the `replace` method in Java's `String` class fits this description. It takes a string and two characters and yields a new string where all occurrences of one character are replaced by the other. There is no other effect of calling `replace`. Methods like `replace` are called *referentially transparent*, which means that for any given input the method call could be replaced by its result without affecting the program's semantics.

Functional languages encourage immutable data structures and referentially transparent methods. Some functional languages even require them. Scala gives you a choice. When you want to, you can write in an *imperative* style, which is what programming with mutable data and side effects is called. But Scala generally makes it easy to avoid imperative constructs when you want because good functional alternatives exist.

10

1.3 Why Scala?

Is Scala for you? You will have to see and decide for yourself. We have found that there are actually many reasons besides scalability to like programming in Scala. Four of the most important aspects will be discussed in this section: compatibility, brevity, high-level abstractions, and advanced static typing.

Scala is compatible

Scala doesn't require you to leap backwards off the Java platform to step forward from the Java language. It allows you to add value to existing code—to build on what you already have—because it was designed for seamless interoperability with Java.[9] Scala programs compile to JVM bytecodes. Their run-time performance is usually on par with Java programs. Scala code can call Java methods, access Java fields, inherit from Java classes, and implement Java interfaces. None of this requires special syntax, explicit interface descriptions, or glue code. In fact, almost all Scala code makes heavy use of Java libraries, often without programmers being aware of this fact.

Another aspect of full interoperability is that Scala heavily re-uses Java types. Scala's Ints are represented as Java primitive integers of type `int`, `Floats` are represented as `floats`, `Booleans` as `booleans`, and so on. Scala arrays are mapped to Java arrays. Scala also re-uses many of the standard Java library types. For instance, the type of a string literal `"abc"` in Scala is `java.lang.String`, and a thrown exception must be a subclass of `java.lang.Throwable`.

Scala not only re-uses Java's types, but also "dresses them up" to make them nicer. For instance, Scala's strings support methods like `toInt` or `toFloat`, which convert the string to an integer or floating-point number. So you can write `str.toInt` instead of `Integer.parseInt(str)`. How can this be achieved without breaking interoperability? Java's `String` class certainly has no `toInt` method! In fact, Scala has a very general solution to solve this tension between advanced library design and interoperability. Scala lets you define rich extensions, which are always applied when non-

---

[9]Originally, there was an implementation of Scala that ran on the .NET platform, but it is no longer active. More recently, an implementation of Scala that runs on JavaScript, Scala.js, has become increasingly popular.

existing members are selected.[10] In the case above, when looking for a `toInt` method on a string, the Scala compiler will find no such member of class `String`, but it will find an implicit conversion that converts a Java `String` to an instance of the Scala class `StringOps`, which does define such a member. The conversion will then be applied implicitly before performing the `toInt` operation.

Scala code can also be invoked from Java code. This is sometimes a bit more subtle, because Scala is a richer language than Java, so some of Scala's more advanced features need to be encoded before they can be mapped to Java. The details will be explained in *Advanced Programming in Scala*.

Scala is concise

Scala programs tend to be short. Scala programmers have reported reductions in number of lines of up to a factor of ten compared to Java. These might be extreme cases. A more conservative estimate would be that a typical Scala program should have about half the number of lines of the same program written in Java. Fewer lines of code mean not only less typing, but also less effort at reading and understanding programs and fewer possibilities of defects. There are several factors that contribute to this reduction in lines of code.

First, Scala's syntax avoids some of the boilerplate that burdens Java programs. For instance, semicolons are optional in Scala and are usually left out. There are also several other areas where Scala's syntax is less noisy. As an example, compare how you write classes and constructors in Java and Scala. In Java, a class with a constructor often looks like this:

```
class MyClass { // this is Java

    private int index;
    private String name;

    public MyClass(int index, String name) {
        this.index = index;
        this.name = name;
    }
}
```

---

[10]In 3.0.0, the standard rich extensions are implemented via *implicit conversions*. In later releases of Scala these will be replaced by *extension methods*.

In Scala, you would likely write this instead:

```
class MyClass(index: Int, name: String)
```

Given this code, the Scala compiler will produce a class that has two private instance variables, an `Int` named `index` and a `String` named `name`, and a constructor that takes initial values for those variables as parameters. The code of this constructor will initialize the two instance variables with the values passed as parameters. In short, you get essentially the same functionality as the more verbose Java version.[11] The Scala class is quicker to write, easier to read, and most importantly, less error prone than the Java class.

Scala's type inference is another factor that contributes to its conciseness. Repetitive type information can be left out, so programs become less cluttered and more readable.

But probably the most important key to compact code is code you don't have to write because it is done in a library for you. Scala gives you many tools to define powerful libraries that let you capture and factor out common behavior. For instance, different aspects of library classes can be separated out into traits, which can then be mixed together in flexible ways. Or, library methods can be parameterized with operations, which lets you define constructs that are, in effect, your own control structures. Together, these constructs allow the definition of libraries that are both high-level and flexible to use.

Scala is high-level

Programmers are constantly grappling with complexity. To program productively, you must understand the code on which you are working. Overly complex code has been the downfall of many a software project. Unfortunately, important software usually has complex requirements. Such complexity can't be avoided; it must instead be managed.

Scala helps you manage complexity by letting you raise the level of abstraction in the interfaces you design and use. As an example, imagine you have a `String` variable `name`, and you want to find out whether or not that `String` contains an upper case character. Prior to Java 8, you might have written a loop, like this:

---

[11]The only real difference is that the instance variables produced in the Scala case will be final. You'll learn how to make them non-final in Section 10.6.

```
boolean nameHasUpperCase = false;   // this is Java
for (int i = 0; i < name.length(); ++i) {
    if (Character.isUpperCase(name.charAt(i))) {
        nameHasUpperCase = true;
        break;
    }
}
```

Whereas in Scala, you could write this:

```
val nameHasUpperCase = name.exists(_.isUpper)
```

The Java code treats strings as low-level entities that are stepped through character by character in a loop. The Scala code treats the same strings as higher-level sequences of characters that can be queried with *predicates*. Clearly the Scala code is much shorter and—for trained eyes—easier to understand than the Java code. So the Scala code weighs less heavily on the total complexity budget. It also gives you less opportunity to make mistakes.

The predicate _.isUpper is an example of a function literal in Scala.[12] It describes a function that takes a character argument (represented by the underscore character) and tests whether it is an upper case letter.[13]

Java 8 introduced support for *lambdas* and *streams*, which enable you to perform a similar operation in Java. Here's what it might look like:

```
boolean nameHasUpperCase =    // This is Java 8 or higher
    name.chars().anyMatch(
        (int ch) -> Character.isUpperCase((char) ch)
    );
```

Although a great improvement over earlier versions of Java, the Java 8 code is still more verbose than the equivalent Scala code. This extra "heaviness" of Java code, as well as Java's long tradition of loops, may encourage many Java programmers in need of new methods like exists to just write out loops and live with the increased complexity in their code.

On the other hand, function literals in Scala are really lightweight, so they are used frequently. As you get to know Scala better you'll find more and more opportunities to define and use your own control abstractions.

---

[12] A function literal can be called a *predicate* if its result type is Boolean.
[13] This use of the underscore as a placeholder for arguments is described in Section 8.5.

You'll find that this helps avoid code duplication and thus keeps your programs shorter and clearer.

Scala is statically typed

A static type system classifies variables and expressions according to the kinds of values they hold and compute. Scala stands out as a language with a very advanced static type system. Starting from a system of nested class types much like Java's, it allows you to parameterize types with *generics*, to combine types using *intersections*, and to hide details of types using *abstract types*.[14] These give a strong foundation for building and composing your own types, so that you can design interfaces that are at the same time safe and flexible to use.

If you like dynamic languages, such as Perl, Python, Ruby, or Groovy, you might find it a bit strange that Scala's static type system is listed as one of its strong points. After all, the absence of a static type system has been cited by some as a major advantage of dynamic languages. The most common arguments against static types are that they make programs too verbose, prevent programmers from expressing themselves as they wish, and make impossible certain patterns of dynamic modifications of software systems. However, often these arguments do not go against the idea of static types in general, but against specific type systems, which are perceived to be too verbose or too inflexible. For instance, Alan Kay, the inventor of the Smalltalk language, once remarked: "I'm not against types, but I don't know of any type systems that aren't a complete pain, so I still like dynamic typing."[15]

We hope to convince you in this book that Scala's type system is far from being a "complete pain." In fact, it addresses nicely two of the usual concerns about static typing: Verbosity is avoided through type inference, and flexibility is gained through pattern matching and several new ways to write and compose types. With these impediments out of the way, the classical benefits of static type systems can be better appreciated. Among the most important of these benefits are verifiable properties of program abstractions, safe refactorings, and better documentation.

---

[14]Generics are discussed in Chapter 18; intersections (*e.g.*, A & B & C) in Section 17.5; and abstract types in Chapter 20.

[15]Kay, in an email on the meaning of object-oriented programming. [Kay03]

Verifiable properties. Static type systems can prove the absence of certain run-time errors. For instance, they can prove properties like: Booleans are never added to integers; private variables are not accessed from outside their class; functions are applied to the right number of arguments; only strings are ever added to a set of strings.

Other kinds of errors are not detected by today's static type systems. For instance, they will usually not detect non-terminating functions, array bounds violations, or divisions by zero. They will also not detect that your program does not conform to its specification (assuming there is a spec, that is!). Static type systems have therefore been dismissed by some as not being very useful. The argument goes that since such type systems can only detect simple errors, whereas unit tests provide more extensive coverage, why bother with static types at all? We believe that these arguments miss the point. Although a static type system certainly cannot *replace* unit testing, it can reduce the number of unit tests needed by taking care of some properties that would otherwise need to be tested. Likewise, unit testing cannot replace static typing. After all, as Edsger Dijkstra said, testing can only prove the presence of errors, never their absence.[16] So the guarantees that static typing gives may be simple, but they are real guarantees of a form no amount of testing can deliver.

Safe refactorings. A static type system provides a safety net that lets you make changes to a codebase with a high degree of confidence. Consider for instance a refactoring that adds an additional parameter to a method. In a statically typed language you can do the change, re-compile your system, and simply fix all lines that cause a type error. Once you have finished with this, you are sure to have found all places that need to be changed. The same holds for many other simple refactorings, like changing a method name or moving methods from one class to another. In all cases a static type check will provide enough assurance that the new system works just like the old.

Documentation. Static types are program documentation that is checked by the compiler for correctness. Unlike a normal comment, a type annotation can never be out of date (at least not if the source file that contains it has recently passed a compiler). Furthermore, compilers and integrated development environments (IDEs) can make use of type annotations to provide

---

[16]Dijkstra, "Notes on Structured Programming." [Dij70]

better context help. For instance, an IDE can display all the members available for a selection by determining the static type of the expression on which the selection is made and looking up all members of that type.

Even though static types are generally useful for program documentation, they can sometimes be annoying when they clutter the program. Typically, useful documentation is what readers of a program cannot easily derive by themselves. In a method definition like:

```
def f(x: String) = ...
```

it's useful to know that f's argument should be a String. On the other hand, at least one of the two annotations in the following example is annoying:

```
val x: HashMap[Int, String] = new HashMap[Int, String]()
```

Clearly, it should be enough to say just once that x is a HashMap with Ints as keys and Strings as values; there's no need to repeat the same phrase twice.

Scala has a very sophisticated type inference system that lets you omit almost all type information that's usually considered annoying. In the previous example, the following two less annoying alternatives would work just as well:

```
val x = new HashMap[Int, String]()
val x: Map[Int, String] = new HashMap()
```

Type inference in Scala can go quite far. In fact, it's not uncommon for user code to have no explicit types at all. Therefore, Scala programs often look a bit like programs written in a dynamically typed scripting language. This holds particularly for client application code, which glues together prewritten library components. It's less true for the library components themselves, because these often employ fairly sophisticated types to allow flexible usage patterns. This is only natural. After all, the type signatures of the members that make up the interface of a reusable component should be explicitly given, because they constitute an essential part of the contract between the component and its clients.

1.4 Scala's roots

Scala's design has been influenced by many programming languages and ideas in programming language research. In fact, only a few features of Scala are genuinely new; most have been already applied in some form in other languages. Scala's innovations come primarily from how its constructs are put together. In this section, we list the main influences on Scala's design. The list cannot be exhaustive—there are simply too many smart ideas around in programming language design to enumerate them all here.

At the surface level, Scala adopts a large part of the syntax of Java and C#, which in turn borrowed most of their syntactic conventions from C and C++. Expressions, statements, and blocks are mostly as in Java, as is the syntax of classes, packages and imports.[17] Besides syntax, Scala adopts other elements of Java, such as its basic types, its class libraries, and its execution model.

Scala also owes much to other languages. Its uniform object model was pioneered by Smalltalk and taken up subsequently by Ruby. Its idea of universal nesting (almost every construct in Scala can be nested inside any other construct) is also present in Algol, Simula, and, more recently, in Beta and gbeta. Its uniform access principle for method invocation and field selection comes from Eiffel. Its approach to functional programming is quite similar in spirit to the ML family of languages, which has SML, OCaml, and F# as prominent members. Many higher-order functions in Scala's standard library are also present in ML or Haskell. Scala's implicit parameters were motivated by Haskell's type classes; they achieve analogous results in a more classical object-oriented setting. Scala's main actor-based concurrency library, Akka, was heavily inspired by Erlang.

Scala is not the first language to emphasize scalability and extensibility. The historic root of extensible languages that can span different application areas is Peter Landin's 1966 paper, "The Next 700 Programming Lan-

---

[17]The major deviation from Java concerns the syntax for type annotations: it's "variable: Type" instead of "Type variable" in Java. Scala's postfix type syntax resembles Pascal, Modula-2, or Eiffel. The main reason for this deviation has to do with type inference, which often lets you omit the type of a variable or the return type of a method. Using the "variable: Type" syntax is easy—just leave out the colon and the type. But in C-style "Type variable" syntax you cannot simply leave off the type; there would be no marker to start the definition anymore. You'd need some alternative keyword to be a placeholder for a missing type (C# 3.0, which does some type inference, uses var for this purpose). Such an alternative keyword feels more ad-hoc and less regular than Scala's approach.

guages."[18] (The language described in this paper, Iswim, stands beside Lisp as one of the pioneering functional languages.) The specific idea of treating an infix operator as a function can be traced back to Iswim and Smalltalk. Another important idea is to permit a function literal (or block) as a parameter, which enables libraries to define control structures. Again, this goes back to Iswim and Smalltalk. Smalltalk and Lisp both have a flexible syntax that has been applied extensively for building internal domain-specific languages. C++ is another scalable language that can be adapted and extended through operator overloading and its template system; compared to Scala it is built on a lower-level, more systems-oriented core.

Scala is also not the first language to integrate functional and object-oriented programming, although it probably goes furthest in this direction. Other languages that have integrated some elements of functional programming into object-oriented programming (OOP) include Ruby, Smalltalk, and Python. On the Java platform, Pizza, Nice, Multi-Java—and Java 8 itself—have all extended a Java-like core with functional ideas. There are also primarily functional languages that have acquired an object system; examples are OCaml, F#, and PLT-Scheme.

Scala has also contributed some innovations to the field of programming languages. For instance, its abstract types provide a more object-oriented alternative to generic types, its traits allow for flexible component assembly, and its extractors provide a representation-independent way to do pattern matching. These innovations have been presented in papers at programming language conferences in recent years.[19]

1.5 Conclusion

In this chapter, we gave you a glimpse of what Scala is and how it might help you in your programming. To be sure, Scala is not a silver bullet that will magically make you more productive. To advance, you will need to apply Scala artfully, and that will require some learning and practice. If you're coming to Scala from Java, the most challenging aspects of learning Scala may involve Scala's type system (which is richer than Java's) and its support for functional programming. The goal of this book is to guide you gently up Scala's learning curve, one step at a time. We think you'll find it a rewarding

---

[18]Landin, "The Next 700 Programming Languages." [Lan66]

[19]For more information, see [Ode03], [Ode05], and [Emi07] in the bibliography.

intellectual experience that will expand your horizons and make you think differently about program design. Hopefully, you will also gain pleasure and inspiration from programming in Scala.

In the next chapter, we'll get you started writing some Scala code.

Chapter 2

First Steps in Scala

It's time to write some Scala code. Before we start on the in-depth Scala tutorial, we put in two chapters that will give you the big picture of Scala, and most importantly, get you writing code. We encourage you to actually try out all the code examples presented in this chapter and the next as you go. The best way to start learning Scala is to program in it.

To run the examples in this chapter, you should have a standard Scala installation. To get one, go to `https://www.scala-lang.org/download` and follow the directions for your platform. This page describes several ways to install or try Scala. For the steps in this chapter, we'll assume you've installed the Scala binaries and added them to your path.[1]

If you are a veteran programmer new to Scala, the next two chapters should give you enough understanding to enable you to start writing useful programs in Scala. If you are less experienced, some of the material may seem a bit mysterious to you. But don't worry. To get you up to speed quickly, we had to leave out some details. Everything will be explained in a less "fire hose" fashion in later chapters. In addition, we inserted quite a few footnotes in these next two chapters to point you to later sections of the book where you'll find more detailed explanations.

Step 1. Learn to use the Scala REPL

The easiest way to get started with Scala is by using the Scala REPL,[2] an interactive "shell" for writing Scala expressions and programs. The REPL,

---

[1]We tested the examples in this book with Scala version 3.0.0.
[2]REPL stands for Read, Evaluate, Print, Loop.

which is called scala, will evaluate expressions you type and print the resulting value. You use it by typing scala at a command prompt:[3]

```
$ scala
Starting Scala REPL...
scala>
```

After you type an expression, such as 1 + 2, and hit enter:

```
scala> 1 + 2
```

The REPL will print:

```
val res0: Int = 3
```

This line includes:

- the keyword val, which declares a variable,

- an automatically generated or user-defined name to refer to the computed value (res0, which means result 0),

- a colon (:), followed by the type of the expression (Int),

- an equals sign (=),

- the value resulting from evaluating the expression (3).

The type Int names the class Int in the package scala. Packages in Scala are similar to packages in Java: They partition the global namespace and provide a mechanism for information hiding.[4] Values of class Int correspond to Java's int values. More generally, all of Java's primitive types have corresponding classes in the scala package. For example, scala.Boolean corresponds to Java's boolean. scala.Float corresponds to Java's float. And when you compile your Scala code to Java bytecodes, the Scala compiler will use Java's primitive types where possible to give you the performance benefits of the primitive types.

The resX identifier may be used in later lines. For instance, since res0 was set to 3 previously, res0 * 3 will be 9:

---

[3]If you're using Windows, you'll need to type the scala command into the "Command Prompt" DOS box.

[4]If you're not familiar with Java packages, you can think of them as providing a full name for classes. Because Int is a member of package scala, "Int" is the class's simple name, and "scala.Int" is its full name. The details of packages are explained in Chapter 12.

```
scala> res0 * 3
val res1: Int = 9
```

To print the necessary, but not sufficient, Hello, world! greeting, type:

```
scala> println("Hello, world!")
Hello, world!
```

The println function prints the passed string to the standard output, similar to System.out.println in Java.

Step 2. Define some variables

Scala has two kinds of variables, vals and vars. A val is similar to a final variable in Java. Once initialized, a val can never be reassigned. A var, by contrast, is similar to a non-final variable in Java. A var can be reassigned throughout its lifetime. Here's a val definition:

```
scala> val msg = "Hello, world!"
val msg: String = Hello, world!
```

This statement introduces msg as a name for the string "Hello, world!". The type of msg is java.lang.String, because on the JVM Scala strings are implemented by Java's String class.

If you're used to declaring variables in Java, you'll notice one striking difference here: neither java.lang.String nor String appear anywhere in the val definition. This example illustrates *type inference*, Scala's ability to figure out types you leave off. In this case, because you initialized msg with a string literal, Scala inferred the type of msg to be String. When the Scala REPL (or compiler) can infer types, it is often best to let it do so rather than fill the code with unnecessary, explicit type annotations. You can, however, specify a type explicitly if you wish, and sometimes you probably should. An explicit type annotation can both ensure the Scala compiler infers the type you intend, as well as serve as useful documentation for future readers of the code. In contrast to Java, where you specify a variable's type before its name, in Scala you specify a variable's type after its name, separated by a colon. For example:

```
scala> val msg2: java.lang.String = "Hello again, world!"
val msg2: String = Hello again, world!
```

23

Or, since `java.lang` types are visible with their simple names[5] in Scala programs, simply:

```
scala> val msg3: String = "Hello yet again, world!"
msg3: String = Hello yet again, world!
```

Going back to the original `msg`, now that it is defined, you can use it as you'd expect, for example:

```
scala> println(msg)
Hello, world!
```

What you can't do with `msg`, given that it is a `val`, not a `var`, is reassign it.[6] For example, see how the REPL complains when you attempt the following:

```
scala> msg = "Goodbye cruel world!"
1 |msg = "Goodbye cruel world!"
  |^^^^^^^^^^^^^^^^^^^^^^^^^^^^^
  |Reassignment to val msg
```

If reassignment is what you want, you'll need to use a `var`, as in:

```
scala> var greeting = "Hello, world!"
var greeting: String = Hello, world!
```

Since `greeting` is a `var` not a `val`, you can reassign it later. If you are feeling grouchy later, for example, you could change your `greeting` to:

```
scala> greeting = "Leave me alone, world!"
greeting: String = Leave me alone, world!
```

   To enter something into the REPL that spans multiple lines, just keep typing after the first line. If the code you typed so far is not complete, the REPL will respond with a vertical bar on the next line.

```
scala> val multiLine =
     |    "This is the next line."
multiLine: String = This is the next line.
```

---

[5]The simple name of `java.lang.String` is `String`.

[6]In the REPL, however, you can *define* a new `val` with a name that was already used before. This mechanism is explained in Section 7.7.

If you realize you have typed something wrong, but the REPL is still waiting for more input, you can use the arrow keys to move up, down, left, or right to fix the mistakes. If you want to abort your entry completely, you can escape by pressing enter twice:

```
scala> val oops =
     |
     |
You typed two blank lines.  Starting a new command.
scala>
```

In the rest of the book, we'll usually leave out the scala prompt, vertical bars, and REPL output on successful input to make the code easier to read (and easier to copy and paste from the PDF eBook into the REPL).

Step 3. Define some functions

Now that you've worked with Scala variables, you'll probably want to write some functions. Here's how you do that in Scala:

```
def max(x: Int, y: Int): Int =
  if x > y then x
  else y
```

Function definitions start with def. The function's name, in this case max, is followed by a comma-separated list of parameters in parentheses. A type annotation must follow every function parameter, preceded by a colon, because the Scala compiler (and REPL, but from now on we'll just say compiler) does not infer function parameter types. In this example, the function named max takes two parameters, x and y, both of type Int. After the close parenthesis of max's parameter list you'll find another ": Int" type annotation. This one defines the *result type* of the max function itself.[7] Following the function's result type is an equals sign and an indented block that defines the body of the function. In this case, the body contains a single if expression, which selects either x or y, whichever is greater, as the result of the max function. As demonstrated here, Scala's if expression can result in a

---

[7]In Java, the type of the value returned from a method is its return type. In Scala, that same concept is called *result type*.

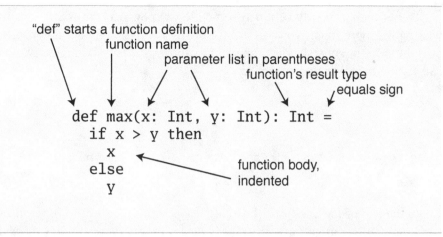

Figure 2.1 · The basic form of a function definition in Scala.

value, similar to Java's ternary operator. For example, the Scala expression "if x > y then x else y" behaves similarly to "(x > y) ? x : y" in Java. The equals sign that precedes the body of a function hints that in the functional world view, a function defines an expression that results in a value. The basic structure of a function is illustrated in Figure 2.1.

Sometimes the Scala compiler will require you to specify the result type of a function. If the function is *recursive*,[8] for example, you must explicitly specify the function's result type. In the case of max, however, you may leave the result type off and the compiler will infer it.[9] Also, if a function consists of just one statement, you can optionally write the function entirely on one line. Thus, you could alternatively write the max function like this:

```
def max(x: Int, y: Int) = if x > y then x else y
```

Once you have defined a function, you can call it by name, as in:

```
val bigger = max(3, 5) // 5
```

Here's the definition of a function that takes no parameters and returns no interesting result:

---

[8]A function is recursive if it calls itself.

[9]Nevertheless, it is often a good idea to indicate function result types explicitly, even when the compiler doesn't require it. Such type annotations can make the code easier to read, because the reader need not study the function body to figure out the inferred result type.

```
scala> def greet() = println("Hello, world!")
def greet(): Unit
```

When you define the `greet()` function in the REPL, it will respond with `def greet(): Unit`. "greet" is, of course, the name of the function. The empty parentheses indicate the function takes no parameters. And `Unit` is `greet`'s result type. A result type of `Unit` indicates the function returns no interesting value. Scala's `Unit` type is similar to Java's `void` type; in fact, every `void`-returning method in Java is mapped to a `Unit`-returning method in Scala. Methods with the result type of `Unit`, therefore, are only executed for their side effects. In the case of `greet()`, the side effect is a friendly greeting printed to the standard output.

In the next step, you'll place Scala code in a file and run it as a script. If you wish to exit the REPL, you can do so by entering `:quit`.

```
scala> :quit
$
```

Step 4. Write some Scala scripts

Although Scala is designed to help programmers build very large-scale systems, it also scales down nicely to scripting. A script is just a Scala source file that includes a top-level function annotated as `@main`. Put this into a file named `hello.scala`:

```
@main def m() =
  println("Hello, world, from a script!")
```

then run:

```
$ scala hello.scala
```

And you should get yet another greeting:

```
Hello, world, from a script!
```

In this example, the function marked with `@main` is named `m` (for main), but that name doesn't matter for running the script. You run a script, regardless of the name of its main function, by running `scala` and specifying the name of the script file that contains the main function.

27

You can access command line arguments passed to your script by taking them as parameters to your main function. For example, you could accept string arguments by taking a parameter with a special type annotation, String*, which means zero to many repeated parameters of type String.[10] Inside the main function, the parameter will have type Seq[String], which is a sequence of strings. In Scala, sequences are zero based, and you access an element by specifying an index in parentheses. So the first element in a Scala sequence named steps is steps(0). To try this out, type the following into a new file named helloarg.scala:

```scala
@main def m(args: String*) =
  // Say hello to the first argument
  println("Hello, " + args(0) + "!")
```

then run:

```
$ scala helloarg.scala planet
```

In this command, "planet" is passed as a command line argument, which is accessed in the script as args(0). Thus, you should see:

```
Hello, planet!
```

Note that this script included a comment. The Scala compiler will ignore characters between // and the next end of line and any characters between /* and */. This example also shows Strings being concatenated with the + operator. This works as you'd expect. The expression "Hello, " + "world!" will result in the string "Hello, world!".

Step 5. Loop with while; decide with if

To try out a while, type the following into a file named printargs.scala:

```scala
@main def m(args: String*) =
  var i = 0
  while i < args.length do
    println(args(i))
    i += 1
```

---

[10]Repeated parameters are described in Section 8.8.

> **Note**
> Although the examples in this section help explain while loops, they do
> not demonstrate the best Scala style. In the next section, you'll see better
> approaches that avoid iterating through sequences with indexes.

This script starts with a variable definition, var i = 0. Type inference
gives i the type Int, because that is the type of its initial value, 0. The while
construct on the next line causes the *block* (the two lines of code beneath it)
to be repeatedly executed until the boolean expression i < args.length
is false. args.length gives the length of the args sequence. The block
contains two statements, each indented two spaces, the recommended indentation style for Scala. The first statement, println(args(i)), prints out
the ith command line argument. The second statement, i += 1, increments
i by one. Note that Java's ++i and i++ don't work in Scala. To increment
in Scala, you need to say either i = i + 1 or i += 1. Run this script with the
following command:

```
$ scala printargs.scala Scala is fun
```

And you should see:

```
Scala
is
fun
```

For even more fun, type the following code into a new file with the name
echoargs.scala:

```
@main def m(args: String*) =
  var i = 0
  while i < args.length do
    if i != 0 then
      print(" ")
    print(args(i))
    i += 1
  println()
```

In this version, you've replaced the println call with a print call, so that
all the arguments will be printed out on the same line. To make this readable,
you've inserted a single space before each argument except the first via the

29

if i != 0 then construct. Since i != 0 will be `false` the first time through the `while` loop, no space will get printed before the initial argument. Lastly, you've added one more `println` to the end, to get a line return after printing out all the arguments. Your output will be very pretty indeed. If you run this script with the following command:

```
$ scala echoargs.scala Scala is even more fun
```

You'll get:

```
Scala is even more fun
```

Note that in Scala, unlike in Java, you need not put the boolean expression for a `while` or an `if` in parentheses. Another difference from Java is that you can optionally leave off the curly braces on a block, even if it has more than one statement, so long as you indent each line appropriately. And although you haven't seen any of them, Scala does use semicolons to separate statements as in Java, except that in Scala the semicolons are very often optional, giving some welcome relief to your right little finger. If you had been in a more verbose mood, therefore, you could have written the `echoargs.scala` script more in a Java style as follows:

```
@main def m(args: String*) = {
  var i = 0;
  while (i < args.length) {
    if (i != 0) {
      print(" ");
    }
    print(args(i));
    i += 1;
  }
  println();
}
```

As of Scala 3, the indentation-based style, called "quiet syntax," is recommended over the curly brace style. Scala 3 also introduced *end markers*, to make it easier to see where larger indented regions end. End markers consist of the keyword end followed by a *specifier token*, which is either an identifier or a keyword. An example is shown in Listing 10.9.

Step 6. Iterate with foreach and for-do

Although you may not have realized it, when you wrote the while loops in the previous step, you were programming in an *imperative* style. In the imperative style, which is the style you normally use with languages like Java, C++, and Python, you give one imperative command at a time, iterate with loops, and often mutate state shared between different functions. Scala enables you to program imperatively, but as you get to know Scala better, you'll likely often find yourself programming in a more *functional* style. In fact, one of the main aims of this book is to help you become as comfortable with the functional style as you are with imperative style.

One of the main characteristics of a functional language is that functions are first class constructs, and that's very true in Scala. For example, another (far more concise) way to print each command line argument is:

```
@main def m(args: String*) =
  args.foreach(arg => println(arg))
```

In this code, you call the foreach method on args and pass in a function. In this case, you're passing in a *function literal* that takes one parameter named arg. The body of the function is println(arg). If you type the above code into a new file named pa.scala and execute with the command:

```
$ scala pa.scala Concise is nice
```

You should see:

```
Concise
is
nice
```

In the previous example, the Scala compiler infers the type of arg to be String, since String is the element type of the sequence on which you're calling foreach. If you'd prefer to be more explicit, you can mention the type name. But when you do, you'll need to wrap the argument portion in parentheses (which is the normal form of the syntax anyway):

```
@main def m(args: String*) =
  args.foreach((arg: String) => println(arg))
```

31

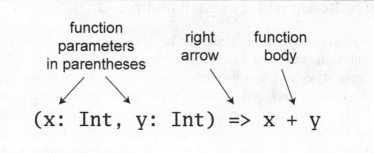

Figure 2.2 · The syntax of a function literal in Scala.

Running this script has the same behavior as the previous one.

If you're in the mood for more conciseness instead of more explicitness, you can take advantage of a special shorthand in Scala. If a function literal consists of one statement that takes a single argument, you need not explicitly name and specify the argument.[11] Thus, the following code also works:

```
@main def m(args: String*) =
  args.foreach(println)
```

To summarize, the syntax for a function literal is a list of named parameters, in parentheses, a right arrow, and then the body of the function. This syntax is illustrated in Figure 2.2.

Now, by this point you may be wondering what happened to those trusty for loops you have been accustomed to using in imperative languages, such as Java or Python. In an effort to guide you in a functional direction, only a functional relative of the imperative for (called a *for expression*) is available in Scala. While you won't see their full power and expressiveness until you reach (or peek ahead to) Section 7.3, we'll give you a glimpse here. In a new file named forargs.scala, type the following:

```
@main def m(args: String*) =
  for arg <- args do
    println(arg)
```

---

[11]This shorthand, called a *partially applied function*, is described in Section 8.6.

32

Between "for" and "do" is "arg <- args".[12] To the right of the <- symbol is the familiar `args` sequence. To the left of <- is "`arg`", the name of a `val`, not a `var`. (Because it is always a `val`, you just write "`arg`" by itself, not "`val arg`".) Although `arg` may seem to be a `var`, because it will get a new value on each iteration, it really is a `val`: `arg` can't be reassigned inside the body of the `for` expression. Instead, for each element of the `args` array, a *new* `arg` `val` will be created and initialized to the element value, and the body of the `for` will be executed.

If you run the `forargs.scala` script with the command:

```
$ scala forargs.scala for arg in args
```

You'll see:

```
for
arg
in
args
```

Scala's `for` expression can do much more than this, but this example is enough to get you started. We'll show you more about `for` in Step 12 of Chapter 3, Section 7.3, and in *Advanced Programming in Scala*.

Conclusion

In this chapter, you learned some Scala basics and, hopefully, took advantage of the opportunity to write a bit of Scala code. In the next chapter, we'll continue this introductory overview and get into more advanced topics.

---

[12]You can say "in" for the <- symbol. You'd read for `arg` <- `args` do, therefore, as "for arg in args do."

Chapter 3

Next Steps in Scala

This chapter continues the previous chapter's introduction to Scala. In this chapter, we'll introduce some more advanced features. When you complete this chapter, you should have enough knowledge to enable you to start writing useful scripts in Scala. As with the previous chapter, we recommend you try out these examples as you go. The best way to get a feel for Scala is to start writing Scala code.

Step 7. Parameterize arrays with types

In Scala, you can instantiate objects, or class instances, using new. When you instantiate an object in Scala, you can *parameterize* it with values and types. Parameterization means "configuring" an instance when you create it. You parameterize an instance with values by passing objects to a constructor in parentheses. For example, the following Scala code instantiates a new `java.math.BigInteger` and parameterizes it with the value "12345":

```
val big = new java.math.BigInteger("12345")
```

You parameterize an instance with types by specifying one or more types in square brackets. An example is shown in Listing 3.1. In this example, `greetStrings` is a value of type `Array[String]` (an "array of string") that is initialized to length 3 by parameterizing it with the value 3 in the first line of code. If you run the code in Listing 3.1 as a script, you'll see yet another `Hello, world!` greeting. Note that when you parameterize an instance with both a type and a value, the type comes first in its square brackets, followed by the value in parentheses.

```
val greetStrings = new Array[String](3)

greetStrings(0) = "Hello"
greetStrings(1) = ", "
greetStrings(2) = "world!\n"

for i <- 0 to 2 do
  print(greetStrings(i))
```

Listing 3.1 · Parameterizing an array with a type.

Note

Although the code in Listing 3.1 demonstrates important concepts, it does not show the recommended way to create and initialize an array in Scala. You'll see a better way in Listing 3.2 on page 39.

Had you been in a more explicit mood, you could have specified the type of greetStrings explicitly like this:

```
val greetStrings: Array[String] = new Array[String](3)
```

Given Scala's type inference, this line of code is semantically equivalent to the actual first line of Listing 3.1. But this form demonstrates that while the type parameterization portion (the type names in square brackets) forms part of the type of the instance, the value parameterization part (the values in parentheses) does not. The type of greetStrings is Array[String], not Array[String](3).

The next three lines of code in Listing 3.1 initialize each element of the greetStrings array:

```
greetStrings(0) = "Hello"
greetStrings(1) = ", "
greetStrings(2) = "world!\n"
```

As mentioned previously, arrays in Scala are accessed by placing the index inside parentheses, not square brackets as in Java. Thus the zeroth element of the array is greetStrings(0), not greetStrings[0].

These three lines of code illustrate an important concept to understand about Scala concerning the meaning of val. When you define a variable with val, the variable can't be reassigned, but the object to which it refers could potentially still be changed. So in this case, you couldn't reassign greetStrings to a different array; greetStrings will always point to the same Array[String] instance with which it was initialized. But you *can* change the elements of that Array[String] over time, so the array itself is mutable.

The final two lines in Listing 3.1 contain a for expression that prints out each greetStrings array element in turn:

```
for i <- 0 to 2 do
  print(greetStrings(i))
```

The first line of code in this for expression illustrates another general rule of Scala: if a method takes only one parameter, you can call it without a dot or parentheses. The to in this example is actually a method that takes one Int argument. The code 0 to 2 is transformed into the method call 0.to(2).[1] Note that this syntax only works if you explicitly specify the receiver of the method call. You cannot write "println 10", but you can write "Console println 10".

Scala doesn't technically have operator overloading, because it doesn't actually have operators in the traditional sense. Instead, characters such as +, −, *, and / can be used in method names. Thus, when you typed 1 + 2 into the Scala interpreter in Step 1, you were actually invoking a method named + on the Int object 1, passing in 2 as a parameter. As illustrated in Figure 3.1, you could alternatively have written 1 + 2 using traditional method invocation syntax, 1.+(2).

Another important idea illustrated by this example will give you insight into why arrays are accessed with parentheses in Scala. Scala has fewer special cases than Java. Arrays are simply instances of classes like any other class in Scala. When you apply parentheses surrounding zero, one, or more values to a variable, Scala will transform the code into an invocation of a method named apply on that variable. So greetStrings(i) gets transformed into greetStrings.apply(i). Thus accessing an element of an array in Scala is simply a method call like any other. This principle is not restricted to arrays: any application of an object to some arguments in parentheses will be transformed to an apply method call. Of course this will

---

[1]This to method actually returns not an array but a different kind of sequence, containing the values 0, 1, and 2, which the for expression iterates over. Sequences and other collections will be described in Chapter 15.

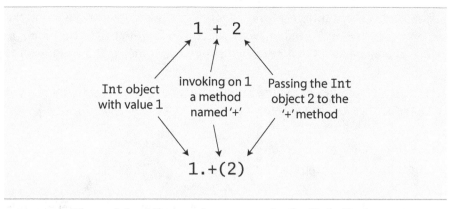

Figure 3.1 · All operations are method calls in Scala.

compile only if that type of object actually defines an `apply` method. So it's not a special case; it's a general rule.

Similarly, when an assignment is made to a variable to which parentheses and one or more arguments have been applied, the compiler will transform that into an invocation of an `update` method that takes the arguments in parentheses as well as the object to the right of the equals sign. For example:

```
greetStrings(0) = "Hello"
```

will be transformed into:

```
greetStrings.update(0, "Hello")
```

Thus, the following is semantically equivalent to the code in Listing 3.1:

```
val greetStrings = new Array[String](3)

greetStrings.update(0, "Hello")
greetStrings.update(1, ", ")
greetStrings.update(2, "world!\n")

for i <- 0.to(2) do
  print(greetStrings.apply(i))
```

Scala achieves a conceptual simplicity by treating everything, from arrays to expressions, as objects with methods. You don't have to remember special cases, such as the differences in Java between primitive and their corresponding wrapper types, or between arrays and regular objects. Moreover, this uniformity does not incur a significant performance cost. The Scala compiler uses Java arrays, primitive types, and native arithmetic where possible in the compiled code.

Although the examples you've seen so far in this step compile and run just fine, Scala provides a more concise way to create and initialize arrays that you would normally use (see Listing 3.2). This code creates a new array of length three, initialized to the passed strings, "zero", "one", and "two". The compiler infers the type of the array to be Array[String], because you passed strings to it.

```
val numNames = Array("zero", "one", "two")
```

Listing 3.2 · Creating and initializing an array.

What you're actually doing in Listing 3.2 is calling a factory method, named apply, which creates and returns the new array. This apply method takes a variable number of arguments[2] and is defined on the Array *companion object*. You'll learn more about companion objects in Section 4.3. If you're a Java programmer, you can think of this as calling a static method named apply on class Array. A more verbose way to call the same apply method is:

```
val numNames2 = Array.apply("zero", "one", "two")
```

Step 8. Use lists

One of the big ideas of the functional style of programming is that methods should not have side effects. A method's only act should be to compute and return a value. Some benefits gained when you take this approach are that methods become less entangled, and therefore more reliable and reusable. Another benefit (in a statically typed language) is that everything that goes into and out of a method is checked by a type checker, so logic errors are more likely to manifest themselves as type errors. Applying this functional philosophy to the world of objects means making objects immutable.

As you've seen, a Scala array is a mutable sequence of objects that all share the same type. An Array[String] contains only strings, for example.

---

[2]Variable-length argument lists, or *repeated parameters*, are described in Section 8.8.

Although you can't change the length of an array after it is instantiated, you can change its element values. Thus, arrays are mutable objects.

For an immutable sequence of objects that share the same type you can use Scala's List class. As with arrays, a List[String] contains only strings. Scala's List differs from Java's java.util.List type in that Scala Lists are always immutable (whereas Java Lists can be mutable). More generally, Scala's List is designed to enable a functional style of programming. Creating a list is easy, and Listing 3.3 shows how:

```
val oneTwoThree = List(1, 2, 3)
```

Listing 3.3 · Creating and initializing a list.

The code in Listing 3.3 establishes a new val named oneTwoThree, initialized with a new List[Int] with the integer elements 1, 2, and 3.[3] Because Lists are immutable, they behave a bit like Java strings: when you call a method on a list that might seem by its name to imply the list will mutate, it instead creates and returns a new list with the new value. For example, List has a method named ':::' for list concatenation. Here's how you use it:

```
val oneTwo = List(1, 2)
val threeFour = List(3, 4)
val oneTwoThreeFour = oneTwo ::: threeFour
```

After executing this code, oneTwoThreeFour will refer to List(1, 2, 3, 4), but oneTwo will still refer to List(1, 2) and threeFour to List(3, 4). Neither of the operand lists are mutated by the concatenation operator, :::, which returns a *new list* with the value List(1, 2, 3, 4).

Perhaps the most common operator you'll use with lists is '::', which is called "cons." Cons prepends a new element to the beginning of an existing list and returns the resulting list. For example, if you run this code:

```
val twoThree = List(2, 3)
val oneTwoThree = 1 :: twoThree
```

The value of oneTwoThree will be List(1, 2, 3).

---

[3] You don't need to say new List because "List.apply()" is defined as a factory method on the scala.List *companion object*. You'll read more on companion objects in Section 4.3.

Note

In the expression "1 :: twoThree", :: is a method of its *right* operand,
the list, twoThree. You might suspect there's something amiss with the
associativity of the :: method, but it is actually a simple rule to
remember: If a method is used in operator notation, such as a * b, the
method is invoked on the left operand, as in a.*(b)—unless the method
name ends in a colon. If the method name ends in a colon, the method is
invoked on the *right* operand. Therefore, in 1 :: twoThree, the :: method
is invoked on twoThree, passing in 1, like this: twoThree.::(1).
Operator associativity will be described in more detail in Section 5.9.

Given that a shorthand way to specify an empty list is Nil, one way to
initialize new lists is to string together elements with the cons operator, with
Nil as the last element.[4] For example, using the following way to initialize the oneTwoThree variable will give it the same value as the previous
approach, List(1, 2, 3):

```
val oneTwoThree = 1 :: 2 :: 3 :: Nil
```

Scala's List is packed with useful methods, many of which are shown in
Table 3.1. The full power of lists will be revealed in Chapter 14.

Why not append to lists?

Class List does offer an "append" operation—it's written :+ and is
explained in Chapter 24—but this operation is rarely used, because
the time it takes to append to a list grows linearly with the size of the
list, whereas prepending with :: takes constant time. If you want to
build a list efficiently by appending elements, you can prepend them
and when you're done call reverse. Or you can use a ListBuffer, a
mutable list that does offer an append operation, and when you're done
call toList. ListBuffer will be described in Section 15.1.

---

[4]The reason you need Nil at the end is that :: is defined on class List. If you try to just
say 1 :: 2 :: 3, it won't compile because 3 is an Int, which doesn't have a :: method.

Table 3.1 · Some List methods and usages

What it is	What it does
List.empty or Nil	The empty List
List("Cool", "tools", "rule")	Creates a new List[String] with the three values "Cool", "tools", and "rule"
val thrill = "Will" :: "fill" :: "until" :: Nil	Creates a new List[String] with the three values "Will", "fill", and "until"
List("a", "b") ::: List("c", "d")	Concatenates two lists (returns a new List[String] with values "a", "b", "c", and "d")
thrill(2)	Returns the element at index 2 (zero based) of the thrill list (returns "until")
thrill.count(s => s.length == 4)	Counts the number of string elements in thrill that have length 4 (returns 2)
thrill.drop(2)	Returns the thrill list without its first 2 elements (returns List("until"))
thrill.dropRight(2)	Returns the thrill list without its rightmost 2 elements (returns List("Will"))
thrill.exists(s => s == "until")	Determines whether a string element exists in thrill that has the value "until" (returns true)
thrill.filter(s => s.length == 4)	Returns a list of all elements, in order, of the thrill list that have length 4 (returns List("Will", "fill"))
thrill.forall(s => s.endsWith("l"))	Indicates whether all elements in the thrill list end with the letter "l" (returns true)
thrill.foreach(s => print(s))	Executes the print statement on each of the strings in the thrill list (prints "Willfilluntil")

Table 3.1 · continued

`thrill.foreach(print)`	Same as the previous, but more concise (also prints `"Willfilluntil"`)
`thrill.head`	Returns the first element in the `thrill` list (returns `"Will"`)
`thrill.init`	Returns a list of all but the last element in the `thrill` list (returns `List("Will", "fill")`)
`thrill.isEmpty`	Indicates whether the `thrill` list is empty (returns `false`)
`thrill.last`	Returns the last element in the `thrill` list (returns `"until"`)
`thrill.length`	Returns the number of elements in the `thrill` list (returns 3)
`thrill.map(s => s + "y")`	Returns a list resulting from adding a `"y"` to each string element in the `thrill` list (returns `List("Willy", "filly", "untily")`)
`thrill.mkString(", ")`	Makes a string with the elements of the list (returns `"Will, fill, until"`)
`thrill.filterNot(s => s.length == 4)`	Returns a list of all elements, in order, of the `thrill` list *except those* that have length 4 (returns `List("until")`)
`thrill.reverse`	Returns a list containing all elements of the `thrill` list in reverse order (returns `List("until", "fill", "Will")`)
`thrill.sortWith((s, t) => s.charAt(0).toLower < t.charAt(0).toLower)`	Returns a list containing all elements of the `thrill` list in alphabetical order of the first character lowercased (returns `List("fill", "until", "Will")`)
`thrill.tail`	Returns the `thrill` list minus its first element (returns `List("fill", "until")`)

Step 9. Use tuples

Another useful container object is the *tuple*. Like lists, tuples are immutable, but unlike lists, tuples can contain different types of elements. Whereas a list might be a List[Int] or a List[String], a tuple could contain both an integer and a string at the same time. Tuples are very useful, for example, if you need to return multiple objects from a method. Whereas in Java you would often create a JavaBean-like class to hold the multiple return values, in Scala you can simply return a tuple. And it is simple: To instantiate a new tuple that holds some objects, just place the objects in parentheses, separated by commas. Once you have a tuple instantiated, you can access its elements individually with a zero-based index in parentheses. An example is shown in Listing 3.4:

```
val pair = (99, "Luftballons")
val num = pair(0)  // type Int, value 99
val what = pair(1) // type String, value "Luftballons"
```

Listing 3.4 · Creating and using a tuple.

In the first line of Listing 3.4, you create a new tuple that contains the integer 99 as its first element and the string "Luftballons" as its second element. Scala infers the type of the tuple to be Tuple2[Int, String], and gives that type to the variable pair as well.[5] In the second line, you access the first element, 99, by its index, 0.[6] The result type of pair(0) is Int. In the third line, you access the second element, "Luftballons", by its index, 1. The result type of pair(1) is String. This demonstrates that tuples keep track of the individual types of each of their elements.

The actual type of a tuple depends on the number of elements it contains and the types of those elements. Thus, the type of (99, "Luftballons") is Tuple2[Int, String]. The type of ('u', 'r', "the", 1, 4, "me") is Tuple6[Char, Char, String, Int, Int, String].[7]

---

[5]The Scala compiler uses a syntactic sugar form for tuple types that looks like a tuple of types. For example, Tuple2[Int, String] is represented as (Int, String).

[6]Note, prior to Scala 3, you accessed the elements of a tuple using one-based field names, such as _1 or _2.

[7]As of Scala 3, you can create tuples of any length.

Step 10. Use sets and maps

Because Scala aims to help you take advantage of both functional and imperative styles, its collections libraries make a point to differentiate between mutable and immutable collections. For example, arrays are always mutable; lists are always immutable. Scala also provides mutable and immutable alternatives for sets and maps, but uses the same simple names for both versions. For sets and maps, Scala models mutability in the class hierarchy.

For example, the Scala API contains a base *trait* for sets, where a trait is similar to a Java interface. (You'll find out more about traits in Chapter 11.) Scala then provides two subtraits, one for mutable sets and another for immutable sets.

As you can see in Figure 3.2, these three traits all share the same simple name, Set. Their fully qualified names differ, however, because each resides in a different package. Concrete set classes in the Scala API, such as the HashSet classes shown in Figure 3.2, extend either the mutable or immutable Set trait. (Although in Java you "implement" interfaces, in Scala you "extend" or "mix in" traits.) Thus, if you want to use a HashSet, you can choose between mutable and immutable varieties depending upon your needs. The default way to create a set is shown in Listing 3.5:

```
var jetSet = Set("Boeing", "Airbus")
jetSet += "Lear"
val query = jetSet.contains("Cessna") // false
```

Listing 3.5 · Creating, initializing, and using an immutable set.

In the first line of code in Listing 3.5, you define a new var named jetSet and initialize it with an immutable set containing the two strings, "Boeing" and "Airbus". As this example shows, you can create sets in Scala similarly to how you create lists and arrays: by invoking a factory method named apply on a Set companion object. In Listing 3.5, you invoke apply on the companion object for scala.collection.immutable.Set, which returns an instance of a default, immutable Set. The Scala compiler infers jetSet's type to be the immutable Set[String].

To add a new element to an immutable set, you call + on the set, passing in the new element. The + method will create and return a new immutable set with the element added. Although mutable sets offer an actual += method,

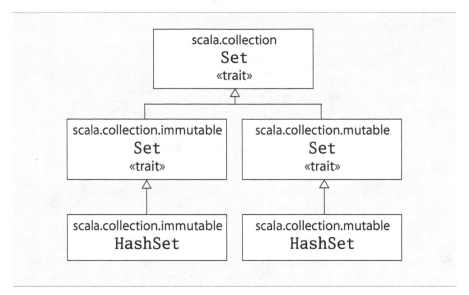

Figure 3.2 · Class hierarchy for Scala sets.

immutable sets do not.

In this case, the second line of code, "jetSet += "Lear"", is essentially a shorthand for:

```
jetSet = jetSet + "Lear"
```

Thus, in the second line of Listing 3.5, you reassign the jetSet var with a new set containing "Boeing", "Airbus", and "Lear". Finally, the last line of Listing 3.5 determines whether or not the set contains the string "Cessna". (As you'd expect, it evaluates to false.)

If you want a mutable set, you'll need to use an *import*, as shown in Listing 3.6:

```
import scala.collection.mutable

val movieSet = mutable.Set("Spotlight", "Moonlight")
movieSet += "Parasite"
// movieSet now contains: "Spotlight", "Moonlight", "Parasite"
```

Listing 3.6 · Creating, initializing, and using a mutable set.

The first line of Listing 3.6 imports `scala.collection.mutable`. An import statement allows you to use a simple name instead of the longer, fully qualified name. As a result, when you say `mutable.Set` on the third line, the compiler knows you mean `scala.collection.mutable.Set`. On that line, you initialize `movieSet` with a new mutable set that contains the strings `"Spotlight"` and `"Moonlight"`. The subsequent line adds `"Parasite"` to the mutable set by calling the `+=` method on the set, passing in the string `"Parasite"`. As mentioned previously, `+=` is an actual method defined on mutable sets. Had you wanted, instead of writing `movieSet += "Parasite"`, you could have written `movieSet.+=("Parasite")`.[8]

Although the default set implementations produced by the mutable and immutable `Set` factory methods shown thus far will likely be sufficient for most situations, occasionally you may want an explicit set class. Fortunately, the syntax is similar. Simply import that class you need, and use the factory method on its companion object. For example, if you need an immutable `HashSet`, you could do this:

```
import scala.collection.immutable.HashSet

val hashSet = HashSet("Tomatoes", "Chilies")
val ingredients = hashSet + "Coriander"
// ingredients contains "Tomatoes", "Chilies", "Coriander"
```

Another useful collection trait in Scala is `Map`. As with sets, Scala provides mutable and immutable versions of `Map`, using a class hierarchy. As you can see in Figure 3.3, the class hierarchy for maps looks a lot like the one for sets. There's a base `Map` trait in package `scala.collection`, and two subtrait `Map`s: a mutable `Map` in `scala.collection.mutable` and an immutable one in `scala.collection.immutable`.

Implementations of `Map`, such as the `HashMap`s shown in the class hierarchy in Figure 3.3, extend either the mutable or immutable trait. You can create and initialize maps using factory methods similar to those used for arrays, lists, and sets.

For example, Listing 3.7 shows a mutable map in action. On the first line of Listing 3.7, you import the mutable `Map`. You then define a `val` named

---

[8]Because the set in Listing 3.6 is mutable, there is no need to reassign `movieSet`, which is why it can be a `val`. By contrast, using `+=` with the immutable set in Listing 3.5 required reassigning `jetSet`, which is why it must be a `var`.

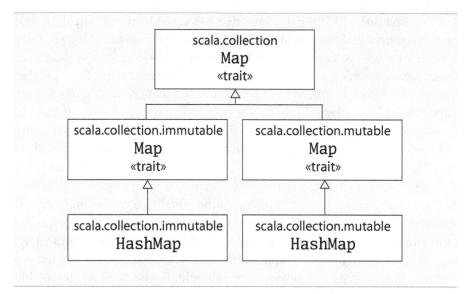

Figure 3.3 · Class hierarchy for Scala maps.

```
import scala.collection.mutable

val treasureMap = mutable.Map.empty[Int, String]
treasureMap += (1 -> "Go to island.")
treasureMap += (2 -> "Find big X on ground.")
treasureMap += (3 -> "Dig.")
val step2 = treasureMap(2) // "Find big X on ground."
```

Listing 3.7 · Creating, initializing, and using a mutable map.

treasureMap, and initialize it with an empty mutable Map that has integer keys and string values. The map is empty because you invoke the factory method named empty and specify Int as the key type and String as the value type.[9] On the next three lines you add key/value pairs to the map using the -> and += methods. As illustrated previously, the Scala compiler transforms a binary operation expression like 1 -> "Go to island." into

---

[9]The explicit type parameterization, "[Int, String]", is required in Listing 3.7 because without any values passed to the factory method, the compiler is unable to infer the map's type parameters. By contrast, the compiler can infer the type parameters from the values passed to the map factory shown in Listing 3.8, thus no explicit type parameters are needed.

(1).->("Go to island."). Thus, when you say 1 -> "Go to island.", you are actually calling a method named -> on an integer with the value 1, passing in a string with the value "Go to island." This -> method, which you can invoke on any object in a Scala program, returns a two-element tuple containing the key and value.[10] You then pass this tuple to the += method of the map object to which `treasureMap` refers. Finally, the last line looks up the value that corresponds to the key 2 in the `treasureMap`. After you run this code, the `step2` variable will refer to Find big X on ground."

If you prefer an immutable map, no import is necessary, as immutable is the default map. An example is shown in Listing 3.8:

```
val romanNumeral = Map(
  1 -> "I", 2 -> "II", 3 -> "III", 4 -> "IV", 5 -> "V"
)
val four = romanNumeral(4) // "IV"
```

Listing 3.8 · Creating, initializing, and using an immutable map.

Given there are no imports, when you say `Map` in the first line of Listing 3.8, you'll get the default: a `scala.collection.immutable.Map`. You pass five key/value tuples to the map's factory method, which returns an immutable `Map` containing the passed key/value pairs. If you run the code in Listing 3.8 the `four` variable will refer to "IV".

Step 11. Learn to recognize the functional style

As mentioned in Chapter 1, Scala allows you to program in an imperative style, but encourages you to adopt a more functional style. If you are coming to Scala from an imperative background—for example, if you are a Java programmer—one of the main challenges you may face when learning Scala is figuring out how to program in the functional style. We realize this style might be unfamiliar at first, and in this book we try hard to guide you through the transition. It will require some work on your part, and we encourage you to make the effort. If you come from an imperative background, we believe that learning to program in a functional style will not only make you

---

[10]The Scala mechanism that allows you to invoke methods, like ->, on objects that don't declare them directly is called *extension methods*. These will be covered in Chapter 22.

a better Scala programmer, it will expand your horizons and make you a better programmer in general.

The first step is to recognize the difference between the two styles in code. One telltale sign is that if code contains any vars, it is probably in an imperative style. If the code contains no vars at all—*i.e.*, it contains *only* vals—it is probably in a functional style. One way to move towards a functional style, therefore, is to try to program without vars.

If you're coming from an imperative background, such as Java, C++, or C#, you may think of var as a regular variable and val as a special kind of variable. On the other hand, if you're coming from a functional background, such as Haskell, OCaml, or Erlang, you might think of val as a regular variable and var as akin to blasphemy. The Scala perspective, however, is that val and var are just two different tools in your toolbox, both useful, neither inherently evil. Scala encourages you to lean towards vals, but ultimately reach for the best tool given the job at hand. Even if you agree with this balanced philosophy, however, you may still find it challenging at first to figure out how to get rid of vars in your code.

Consider the following while loop example, adapted from Chapter 2, which uses a var and is therefore in the imperative style:

```
def printArgs(args: List[String]): Unit =
  var i = 0
  while i < args.length do
    println(args(i))
    i += 1
```

You can transform this bit of code into a more functional style by getting rid of the var, for example, like this:

```
def printArgs(args: List[String]): Unit =
  for arg <- args do
    println(arg)
```

or this:

```
def printArgs(args: List[String]): Unit =
  args.foreach(println)
```

This example illustrates one benefit of programming with fewer vars. The refactored (more functional) code is clearer, more concise, and less error-prone than the original (more imperative) code. The reason Scala encourages a functional style is that it can help you write more understandable, less error-prone code.

But you can go even further. The refactored `printArgs` method is not *purely* functional because it has side effects—in this case, its side effect is printing to the standard output stream. The telltale sign of a function with side effects is that its result type is `Unit`. If a function isn't returning any interesting value, which is what a result type of `Unit` means, the only way that function can make a difference in the world is through some kind of side effect. A more functional approach would be to define a method that formats the passed `args` for printing, but just returns the formatted string, as shown in Listing 3.9:

```
def formatArgs(args: List[String]) = args.mkString("\n")
```

Listing 3.9 · A function without side effects or `var`s.

Now you're really functional: no side effects or `var`s in sight. The `mkString` method, which you can call on any iterable collection (including arrays, lists, sets, and maps), returns a string consisting of the result of calling `toString` on each element, separated by the passed string. Thus if `args` contains three elements `"zero"`, `"one"`, and `"two"`, `formatArgs` will return `"zero\none\ntwo"`. Of course, this function doesn't actually print anything out like the `printArgs` methods did, but you can easily pass its result to `println` to accomplish that:

```
println(formatArgs(args))
```

Every useful program is likely to have side effects of some form; otherwise, it wouldn't be able to provide value to the outside world. Preferring methods without side effects encourages you to design programs where side-effecting code is minimized. One benefit of this approach is that it can help make your programs easier to test.

For example, to test any of the three `printArgs` methods shown earlier in this section, you'd need to redefine `println`, capture the output passed to it, and make sure it is what you expect. By contrast, you could test the `formatArgs` function simply by checking its result:

```
val res = formatArgs(List("zero", "one", "two"))
assert(res == "zero\none\ntwo")
```

Scala's `assert` method checks the passed `Boolean` and if it is false, throws `AssertionError`. If the passed `Boolean` is true, `assert` just returns quietly. You'll learn more about assertions and tests in Chapter 25.

That said, bear in mind that neither vars nor side effects are inherently evil. Scala is not a pure functional language that forces you to program everything in the functional style. Scala is a hybrid imperative/functional language. You may find that in some situations an imperative style is a better fit for the problem at hand, and in such cases you should not hesitate to use it. To help you learn how to program without vars, however, we'll show you many specific examples of code with vars and how to transform those vars to vals in Chapter 7.

A balanced attitude for Scala programmers

Prefer vals, immutable objects, and methods without side effects. Reach for them first. Use vars, mutable objects, and methods with side effects when you have a specific need and justification for them.

Step 12. Transform with `map` and `for-yield`

When programming in an imperative style, you mutate data structures in place until you achieve the goal of the algorithm. In a functional style, you transform immutable data structures into new ones to achieve the goal.

An important method that facilitates functional transformations on immutable collections is `map`. Like `foreach`, `map` takes a function as a parameter. But unlike `foreach`, which uses the passed function to perform a side effect for each element, `map` uses the passed function to transform each element into a new value. The result of `map` is a new collection containing those new values. For example, given this list of strings:

```
val adjectives = List("One", "Two", "Red", "Blue")
```

You could transform it into a new list of new strings like this:

```
val nouns = adjectives.map(adj => adj + " Fish")
// List(One Fish, Two Fish, Red Fish, Blue Fish)
```

Another way to perform this transformation is to use a `for` expression in which you introduce the body with the keyword `yield` instead of do:

```
val nouns =
  for adj <- adjectives yield
    adj + " Fish"
// List(One Fish, Two Fish, Red Fish, Blue Fish)
```

The `for-yield` produces exactly the same result as map because the compiler transforms the `for-yield` expression into the map call.[11] Because the list returned by map contains the values produced by the passed function, the element type of the returned list will be the result type of the function. In the previous example the passed function returns a string, so map returns a `List[String]`. If the function passed to map results in a different type, then the `List` returned by map will have that type as its element type. For example, in the following map call, the passed function transforms a string to an integer, the length of each element string. Therefore, the result of map is a new `List[Int]` containing those lengths:

```
val lengths = nouns.map(noun => noun.length)
// List(8, 8, 8, 9)
```

As before, you could alternatively use a `for` expression with `yield` to achieve the same transformation:

```
val lengths =
  for noun <- nouns yield
    noun.length
// List(8, 8, 8, 9)
```

The map method appears on many types, not just `List`. This enables for expressions to be used with many types. One example is `Vector`, which is an immutable sequence that provides "effectively constant time" performance for all its operations. Because `Vector` offers a map method with an

---

[11] The details of how the compiler rewrites for expressions will be given in Section 7.3 and in *Advanced Programming in Scala*.

appropriate signature, you can perform the same kinds of functional transformations on Vectors as you can on Lists, either by calling map directly
or using for-yield. Here's an example:

```scala
val ques = Vector("Who", "What", "When", "Where", "Why")
val usingMap = ques.map(q => q.toLowerCase + "?")
// Vector(who?, what?, when?, where?, why?)
val usingForYield =
  for q <- ques yield
    q.toLowerCase + "?"
// Vector(who?, what?, when?, where?, why?)
```

Notice that when you map a List, you get a new List back. When you
map a Vector, you get a new Vector back. You'll find this pattern holds
true for most types that define a map method.

As a final example, consider Scala's Option type. Scala uses Option to
represent an optional value, eschewing Java's traditional technique of using
null for this purpose.[12] An Option is either a Some, which indicates that a
value exists, or None, which indicates that no value exists.

For an example showing Option in action, consider the find method.
All of Scala's collection types, including List and Vector, offer a find
method that looks for an element that matches a given *predicate*, a function
that accepts an argument of the element type and returns boolean. The result
type of find is Option[E], where E is the element type of the collection. The
find method iterates through the elements of the collection, passing each to
the predicate. If the predicate returns true, find stops iterating and returns
that element, wrapped in a Some. If find makes it all the way to the end of
the elements without any passing the predicate, it returns None. Here are a
few examples, in which the result type of find is always Option[String]:

```scala
val startsW = ques.find(q => q.startsWith("W")) // Some(Who)
val hasLen4 = ques.find(q => q.length == 4)      // Some(What)
val hasLen5 = ques.find(q => q.length == 5)      // Some(Where)
val startsH = ques.find(q => q.startsWith("H")) // None
```

---

[12]In Java 8, an Optional type was added to the standard library, but many pre-existing
Java libraries still use null to indicate a missing optional value.

Although `Option` is not a collection, it does offer a `map` method.[13] If the `Option` is a `Some`, which is called a "defined" option, `map` returns a new `Option` containing the result of passing the original `Some`'s element to the function passed to `map`. Here's an example that transforms `startsW`, a `Some` containing the string `"Who"`:

```
startsW.map(word => word.toUpperCase)      // Some(WHO)
```

As with `List` and `Vector`, you can achieve the same transformation on `Option` with a `for-yield`:

```
for word <- startsW yield word.toUpperCase // Some(WHO)
```

If you invoke `map` on a `None`, an option that is *not* defined, you will get `None` back. Here's an example showing `map` invoked on `startsH`, a `None`:

```
startsH.map(word => word.toUpperCase)      // None
```

And here is the same transformation with `for-yield`:

```
for word <- startsH yield word.toUpperCase // None
```

You can transform many other types with `map` and `for-yield`, but this is enough for now. This step has given you a glimpse of how much Scala code is written: as functional transformations of immutable data structures.

Conclusion

With the knowledge you've gained in this chapter, you should be able to start using Scala for small tasks, especially scripts. In later chapters, we will dive further into these topics and introduce other topics that weren't even hinted at here.

---

[13]One way to think of `Option`, however, is as a collection that contains either zero (the `None` case) or one (the `Some` case) elements.

Chapter 4

Classes and Objects

You've now seen the basics of classes and objects in Scala from the previous two chapters. In this chapter, we'll take you a bit deeper. You'll learn more about classes, fields, and methods, and get an overview of semicolon inference. We'll discuss singleton objects, including how to use them to write and run a Scala application. If you are familiar with Java, you'll find that the concepts in Scala are similar, but not exactly the same. So even if you're a Java guru, it will pay to read on.

4.1 Classes, fields, and methods

A class is a blueprint for objects. Once you define a class, you can create objects from the class blueprint with the keyword new. For example, given the class definition:

```scala
class ChecksumAccumulator:
  // class definition goes here, indented
```

You can create ChecksumAccumulator objects with:

```scala
new ChecksumAccumulator
```

Inside a class definition, you place fields and methods, which are collectively called *members*. Fields, which you define with either val or var, are variables that refer to objects. Methods, which you define with def, contain executable code. The fields hold the state, or data, of an object, whereas the methods can use that data to do the computational work of the object. When you instantiate a class, the runtime sets aside some memory to hold the image of that object's state (*i.e.*, the content of its fields). For example, if you defined a `ChecksumAccumulator` class and gave it a `var` field named `sum`:

```
class ChecksumAccumulator:
  var sum = 0
```

and you instantiated it twice with:

```
val acc = new ChecksumAccumulator
val csa = new ChecksumAccumulator
```

The image of the objects in memory might look like this:

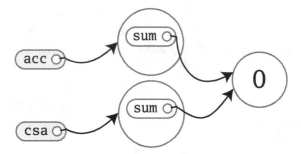

Since `sum`, a field declared inside class `ChecksumAccumulator`, is a `var`, not a `val`, you can later reassign to `sum` a different `Int` value, like this:

```
acc.sum = 3
```

Now the picture would look like this:

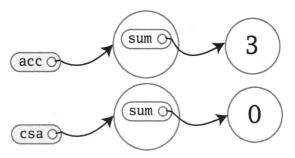

One thing to notice about this picture is that there are two `sum` variables, one in the object referenced by `acc` and the other in the object referenced by csa. Fields are also known as *instance variables*, because every instance gets its own set of the variables. Collectively, an object's instance variables make up the memory image of the object. You see this illustrated here not only in that you see two sum variables, but also that when you changed one, the other was unaffected.

Another thing to note in this example is that you were able to mutate the object acc referred to, even though acc is a val. What you can't do with acc (or csa), given that they are vals, not vars, is reassign a different object to them. For example, the following attempt would fail:

```
// Won't compile, because acc is a val
acc = new ChecksumAccumulator
```

What you can count on, therefore, is that acc will always refer to the same ChecksumAccumulator object with which you initialize it, but the fields contained inside that object might change over time.

One important way to pursue robustness of an object is to ensure that the object's state—the values of its instance variables—remains valid during its entire lifetime. The first step is to prevent outsiders from accessing the fields directly by making the fields *private*. Because private fields can only be accessed by methods defined in the same class, all the code that can update the state will be localized to the class. To declare a field private, you place a private access modifier in front of the field, like this:

```
class ChecksumAccumulator:
  private var sum = 0
```

Given this definition of ChecksumAccumulator, any attempt to access sum from the outside of the class would fail:

```
val acc = new ChecksumAccumulator
acc.sum = 5 // Won't compile, because sum is private
```

> **Note**
> The way you make members public in Scala is by not explicitly specifying any access modifier. Put another way, where you'd say "public" in Java, you simply say nothing in Scala. Public is Scala's default access level.

Now that sum is private, the only code that can access sum is code defined inside the body of the class itself. Thus, ChecksumAccumulator won't be of much use to anyone unless we define some methods in it:

59

```
class ChecksumAccumulator:

  private var sum = 0

  def add(b: Byte): Unit =
    sum += b

  def checksum(): Int =
    return ~(sum & 0xFF) + 1
```

The ChecksumAccumulator now has two methods, add and checksum, both of which exhibit the basic form of a function definition, shown in Figure 2.1 on page 26.[1]

Any parameters to a method can be used inside the method. One important characteristic of method parameters in Scala is that they are vals, not vars.[2] If you attempt to reassign a parameter inside a method in Scala, therefore, it won't compile:

```
def add(b: Byte): Unit =
  b = 1     // This won't compile, because b is a val
  sum += b
```

Although add and checksum in this version of ChecksumAccumulator correctly implement the desired functionality, you can express them using a more concise style. First, the return at the end of the checksum method is superfluous and can be dropped. In the absence of any explicit return statement, a Scala method returns the last value computed by the method.

The recommended style for methods is in fact to avoid having explicit, and especially multiple, return statements. Instead, think of each method as an expression that yields one value, which is returned. This philosophy will encourage you to make methods quite small, to factor larger methods into multiple smaller ones. On the other hand, design choices depend on the design context, and Scala makes it easy to write methods that have multiple, explicit returns if that's what you desire.

Because all checksum does is calculate a value, it does not need an explicit return. Another shorthand for methods is that if a method computes only a single result expression, and it is short, you can place it on

---

[1] The checksum method uses two operators: tilde (~), which is bitwise complement, and ampersand (&), which is bitwise and. Both operators are described in Section 5.7.

[2] The reason parameters are vals is that vals are easier to reason about. You needn't look further to determine if a val is reassigned, as you must do with a var.

the same line as the def itself. For the utmost in conciseness, you can leave off the result type and Scala will infer it. With these changes, class ChecksumAccumulator looks like this:

```
class ChecksumAccumulator:
  private var sum = 0
  def add(b: Byte) = sum += b
  def checksum() = ~(sum & 0xFF) + 1
```

Although the Scala compiler will correctly infer the result types of the add and checksum methods shown in the previous example, readers of the code will also need to *mentally infer* the result types by studying the bodies of the methods. As a result it is often better to explicitly provide the result types of public methods declared in a class even when the compiler would infer it for you. Listing 4.1 shows this style.

```
// In file ChecksumAccumulator.scala
class ChecksumAccumulator:
  private var sum = 0
  def add(b: Byte): Unit = sum += b
  def checksum(): Int = ~(sum & 0xFF) + 1
```

Listing 4.1 · Final version of class ChecksumAccumulator.

Methods with a result type of Unit, such as ChecksumAccumulator's add method, are executed for their side effects. A side effect is generally defined as mutating state somewhere external to the method or performing an I/O action. In add's case, the side effect is that sum is reassigned. A method that is executed only for its side effects is known as a *procedure*.

4.2 Semicolon inference

In a Scala program, a semicolon at the end of a statement is usually optional. You can type one if you want but you don't have to if the statement appears by itself on a single line. On the other hand, a semicolon is required if you write multiple statements on a single line:

```
val s = "hello"; println(s)
```

If you want to enter a statement that spans multiple lines, most of the time you can simply enter it and Scala will separate the statements in the correct place. For example, the following is treated as one four-line statement:

```
if x < 2 then
  "too small"
else
  "ok"
```

The rules of semicolon inference

The precise rules for statement separation are surprisingly simple for how well they work. In short, a line ending is treated as a semicolon unless one of the following conditions is true:

1. The line in question ends in a word that would not be legal as the end of a statement, such as a period or an infix operator.

2. The next line begins with a word that cannot start a statement.

3. The line ends while inside parentheses (...) or brackets [...], because these cannot contain multiple statements anyway.

4.3   Singleton objects

As mentioned in Chapter 1, one way in which Scala is more object-oriented than Java is that classes in Scala cannot have static members. Instead, Scala has *singleton objects*. A singleton object definition looks like a class definition, except instead of the keyword `class` you use the keyword `object`. Listing 4.2 shows an example.

The singleton object in this figure is named `ChecksumAccumulator`, the same name as the class in the previous example. When a singleton object shares the same name with a class, it is called that class's *companion object*. You must define both the class and its companion object in the same source file. The class is called the *companion class* of the singleton object. A class and its companion object can access each other's private members.

The `ChecksumAccumulator` singleton object has one method, named `calculate`, which takes a `String` and calculates a checksum for the char-

```
// In file ChecksumAccumulator.scala
import scala.collection.mutable

object ChecksumAccumulator:

  private val cache = mutable.Map.empty[String, Int]

  def calculate(s: String): Int =
    if cache.contains(s) then
      cache(s)
    else
      val acc = new ChecksumAccumulator
      for c <- s do
        acc.add((c >> 8).toByte)
        acc.add(c.toByte)
      val cs = acc.checksum()
      cache += (s -> cs)
      cs
```

Listing 4.2 · Companion object for class `ChecksumAccumulator`.

acters in the `String`. It also has one private field, `cache`, a mutable map in which previously calculated checksums are cached.[3] The first line of the method, "`if cache.contains(s) then`", checks the cache to see if the passed string is already contained as a key in the map. If so, it just returns the mapped value, `cache(s)`. Otherwise, it executes the else clause, which calculates the checksum. The first line of the else clause defines a `val` named `acc` and initializes it with a new `ChecksumAccumulator` instance.[4] The next line is a `for` expression, which cycles through each character in the passed string, converts the character into two `Bytes`, and passes each `Byte` to the `add` method of the `ChecksumAccumulator` instance to which `acc` refers.[5] After the `for` expression completes, the next line of the method invokes `checksum`

---

[3]We used a cache here to show a singleton object with a field. A cache such as this is a performance optimization that trades off memory for computation time. In general, you would likely use such a cache only if you encountered a performance problem that the cache solves, and might use a weak map, such as `WeakHashMap` in `scala.collection.mutable`, so that entries in the cache could be garbage collected if memory becomes scarce.

[4]Because the keyword new is only used to instantiate classes, the new object created here is an instance of the `ChecksumAccumulator` class, not the singleton object of the same name.

[5]The >> operator, which performs a bitwise shift right, is described in Section 5.7.

63

on acc, which gets the checksum for the passed String, and stores it into a val named cs. In the next line, cache += (s -> cs), the passed string key is mapped to the integer checksum value, and this key-value pair is added to the cache map. The last expression of the method, cs, ensures the checksum is the result of the method.

If you are a Java programmer, one way to think of singleton objects is as the home for any static methods you might have written in Java. You can invoke methods on singleton objects using a similar syntax: the name of the singleton object, a dot, and the name of the method. For example, you can invoke the calculate method of singleton object ChecksumAccumulator like this:

```
ChecksumAccumulator.calculate("Every value is an object.")
```

A singleton object is more than a holder of static methods, however. It is a first-class object. You can think of a singleton object's name, therefore, as a "name tag" attached to the object:

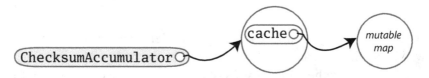

Defining a singleton object doesn't define a type (at the Scala level of abstraction). Given just a definition of object ChecksumAccumulator, you can't make a variable of type ChecksumAccumulator. Rather, the type named ChecksumAccumulator is defined by the singleton object's companion class. However, singleton objects extend a superclass and can mix in traits. Given each singleton object is an instance of its superclasses and mixed-in traits, you can invoke its methods via these types, refer to it from variables of these types, and pass it to methods expecting these types. We'll show some examples of singleton objects inheriting from classes and traits in Chapter 12.

One difference between classes and singleton objects is that singleton objects cannot take parameters, whereas classes can. Because you can't instantiate a singleton object with the new keyword, you have no way to pass parameters to it. Each singleton object is implemented as an instance of a *synthetic class* referenced from a static variable, so they have the same initialization semantics as Java statics.[6] In particular, a singleton object is initialized the first time some code accesses it.

A singleton object that does not share the same name with a companion class is called a *standalone object*. You can use standalone objects for many purposes, including collecting related utility methods together or defining an entry point to a Scala application. This use case is shown in the next section.

4.4 Case classes

Often when you write a class, you need implementations of methods such as equals, hashCode, toString, accessor methods, or factory methods. These can be time-consuming and error-prone to write. Scala offers "case classes," which can generate implementations of several methods based on the values passed to its primary constructor. You declare a case class by placing the case modifier in front of class, like this:

```
case class Person(name: String, age: Int)
```

With the addition of the case modifier, the compiler will generate several useful methods for you. First, the compiler will create a companion object and place a factory method in it named apply. You can therefore construct a new Person object like this:

```
val p = Person("Sally", 39)
```

The compiler will rewrite this line of code to an invocation of the generated factory method: Person.apply("Sally", 39).

Second, the compiler will store all class parameters in fields and generate accessor methods with the same name as the parameter.[7] For example, you can access the values given for a Person's name and age like this:

```
p.name // Sally
p.age  // 39
```

Third, the compiler will provide an implementation of toString for you:

```
p.toString   // Person(Sally,39)
```

---

[6]The name of the synthetic class is the object name plus a dollar sign. Thus the synthetic class for the singleton object named ChecksumAccumulator is ChecksumAccumulator$.

[7]These are called *parametric fields*, which will be described in Section 10.6.

Fourth, the compiler will generate an implementation of hashCode and equals for your class. These methods will base their result on the parameters passed to the constructor. For example, a Person object will consider both name and age when comparing for equality or computing a hash code:

```
p == Person("Sally", 21)                          // false
p.hashCode == Person("Sally", 21).hashCode   // false
p == Person("James", 39)                          // false
p.hashCode == Person("James", 39).hashCode   // false
p == Person("Sally", 39)                          // true
p.hashCode == Person("Sally", 39).hashCode   // true
```

The compiler will not generate any method that you implement yourself. It will use your implementation. You can also add other fields and methods to the class and its companion. Here's an example where you define an apply method in the Person companion object, so the compiler will not generate one, and you add another method, appendToName, to the class:

```
case class Person(name: String, age: Int):
  def appendToName(suffix: String): Person =
    Person(s"$name$suffix", age)

object Person:
  // Ensure non-empty name is capitalized
  def apply(name: String, age: Int): Person =
    val capitalizedName =
      if !name.isEmpty then
        val firstChar = name.charAt(0).toUpper
        val restOfName = name.substring(1)
        s"$firstChar$restOfName"
      else throw new IllegalArgumentException("Empty name")
    new Person(capitalizedName, age)
```

This apply method ensures the first character of the name is capitalized:

```
val q = Person("sally", 39)    // Person(Sally,39)
```

You can also call the appendToName method you defined in the class:

```
q.appendToName(" Smith")       // Person(Sally Smith,39)
```

Finally, the compiler adds a `copy` method to your class and an `unapply` method to the companion. The `copy` method will be described in Chapter 13. The `unapply` method will be covered in *Advanced Programming in Scala*.

All these conventions add a lot of convenience—at a small price. You have to write the case modifier, and your classes and objects become a bit larger. They are larger because additional methods are generated and an implicit field is added for each constructor parameter.

4.5 A Scala application

To run a Scala program, you must supply the name of a standalone singleton object with a `main` method that takes one parameter, an `Array[String]`, and has a result type of `Unit`. Any standalone object with a `main` method of the proper signature can be used as the entry point into an application.[8] An example is shown in Listing 4.3:

```
// In file Summer.scala
import ChecksumAccumulator.calculate

object Summer:
  def main(args: Array[String]): Unit =
    for arg <- args do
      println(arg + ": " + calculate(arg))
```

Listing 4.3 · The `Summer` application.

The name of the singleton object in Listing 4.3 is `Summer`. Its `main` method has the proper signature, so you can use it as an application. The first statement in the file is an import of the `calculate` method defined in the `ChecksumAccumulator` object in the previous example. This import statement allows you to use the method's simple name in the rest of the file.[9] The body of the `main` method simply prints out each argument and the checksum for the argument, separated by a colon.

---

[8]You can designate methods with other names as main functions with an `@main` annotation. This technique will be described in Section 23.3.

[9]If you're a Java programmer, you can think of this import as similar to the static import feature introduced in Java 5. One difference in Scala, however, is that you can import members from any object, not just singleton objects.

Note

Scala implicitly imports members of packages `java.lang` and `scala`, as well as the members of a singleton object named `Predef`, into every Scala source file. `Predef`, which resides in package `scala`, contains many useful methods. For example, when you say `println` in a Scala source file, you're actually invoking `println` on `Predef`. (`Predef.println` turns around and invokes `Console.println`, which does the real work.) When you say `assert`, you're invoking `Predef.assert`.

To run the Summer application, place the code from Listing 4.3 into a file named `Summer.scala`. Because Summer uses `ChecksumAccumulator`, place the code for `ChecksumAccumulator`, both the class shown in Listing 4.1 and its companion object shown in Listing 4.2, into a file named `ChecksumAccumulator.scala`.

One difference between Scala and Java is that whereas Java requires you to put a public class in a file named after the class—for example, you'd put class `SpeedRacer` in file `SpeedRacer.java`—in Scala, you can name `.scala` files anything you want, no matter what Scala classes or code you put in them. In general in the case of non-scripts, however, it is recommended style to name files after the classes they contain as is done in Java, so that programmers can more easily locate classes by looking at file names. This is the approach we've taken with the two files in this example, `Summer.scala` and `ChecksumAccumulator.scala`.

Neither `ChecksumAccumulator.scala` nor `Summer.scala` are scripts, because they end in a definition. A script, by contrast, must end in a result expression. Thus if you try to run `Summer.scala` as a script, the Scala interpreter will complain that `Summer.scala` does not end in a result expression (assuming of course you didn't add any expression of your own after the Summer object definition). Instead, you'll need to actually compile these files with the Scala compiler, then run the resulting class files. One way to do this is to use `scalac`, which is the basic Scala compiler, like this:

```
$ scalac ChecksumAccumulator.scala Summer.scala
```

This compiles your source files and produces Java class files that you can then run via the `scala` command, the same command you used to invoke the interpreter in previous examples. However, instead of giving it a filename with a `.scala` extension containing Scala code to interpret as you did in every previous example,[10] in this case you'll give it the name of a standalone object containing a `main` method of the proper signature. You can run the Summer application, therefore, by typing:

```
$ scala Summer of love
```

You will see checksums printed for the two command line arguments:

```
of: -213
love: -182
```

4.6 Conclusion

This chapter has given you the basics of classes and objects in Scala, and shown you how to compile and run applications. In the next chapter, you'll learn about Scala's basic types and how to use them.

---

[10]The actual mechanism that the `scala` program uses to "interpret" a Scala source file is that it compiles the Scala source code to Java bytecodes, loads them immediately via a class loader, and executes them.

Chapter 5

Basic Types and Operations

Now that you've seen classes and objects in action, it's a good time to look at Scala's basic types and operations in more depth. If you're familiar with Java, you'll be glad to find that Java's basic types and operators have the same meaning in Scala. However, there are some interesting differences that will make this chapter worth reading even if you're an experienced Java developer. Because some aspects of Scala covered in this chapter are essentially the same as in Java, we've inserted notes indicating what sections Java developers can safely skip.

In this chapter, you'll get an overview of Scala's basic types, including `Strings` and the value types `Int`, `Long`, `Short`, `Byte`, `Float`, `Double`, `Char`, and `Boolean`. You'll learn the operations you can perform on these types, including how operator precedence works in Scala expressions. You'll also learn how Scala "enriches" these basic types, giving you additional operations beyond those supported by Java.

5.1 Some basic types

Several fundamental types of Scala, along with the ranges of values that instances of these types may have, are shown in Table 5.1. Collectively, types `Byte`, `Short`, `Int`, `Long`, and `Char` are called *integral types*. The integral types plus `Float` and `Double` are called *numeric types*.

Other than `String`, which resides in package `java.lang`, all of the types shown in Table 5.1 are members of package `scala`.[1] For example, the full

---

[1]Packages, which were briefly described in Step 1 in Chapter 2, will be covered in depth in Chapter 12.

71

Table 5.1 · Some basic types

Basic type	Range
Byte	8-bit signed two's complement integer (-2^7 to 2^7 - 1, inclusive)
Short	16-bit signed two's complement integer (-2^{15} to 2^{15} - 1, inclusive)
Int	32-bit signed two's complement integer (-2^{31} to 2^{31} - 1, inclusive)
Long	64-bit signed two's complement integer (-2^{63} to 2^{63} - 1, inclusive)
Char	16-bit unsigned Unicode character (0 to 2^{16} - 1, inclusive)
String	a sequence of Chars
Float	32-bit IEEE 754 single-precision float
Double	64-bit IEEE 754 double-precision float
Boolean	true or false

name of Int is scala.Int. However, given that all the members of package scala and java.lang are automatically imported into every Scala source file, you can just use the simple names (*i.e.*, names like Boolean, Char, or String) everywhere.

Savvy Java developers will note that Scala's basic types have the exact same ranges as the corresponding types in Java. This enables the Scala compiler to transform instances of Scala *value types*, such as Int or Double, down to Java primitive types in the bytecodes it produces.

5.2 Literals

All of the basic types listed in Table 5.1 can be written with *literals*. A literal is a way to write a constant value directly in code.

Fast track for Java programmers
The syntax of most literals shown in this section are exactly the same as in Java, so if you're a Java master, you can safely skip much of this section. Some differences you should read about are Scala's literals for raw strings, described starting on page 75, and string interpolation, described starting on page 77. Also, Scala does not support octal literals; integer literals that start with a 0, such as 031, do not compile.

Integer literals

Integer literals for the types `Int`, `Long`, `Short`, and `Byte` come in two forms: decimal and hexadecimal. The way an integer literal begins indicates the base of the number. If the number begins with a 0x or 0X, it is hexadecimal (base 16), and may contain 0 through 9 as well as upper or lowercase digits A through F. You can include underscores (_) to help improve the readability of large values. Some examples are:

```
val hex = 0x5                     // 5: Int
val hex2 = 0x00FF                 // 255: Int
val magic = 0xcafebabe            // -889275714: Int
val billion = 1_000_000_000       // 1000000000: Int
```

Note that the Scala REPL always prints integer values in base 10, no matter what literal form you may have used to initialize it. Thus the REPL displays the value of the hex2 variable you initialized with literal 0x00FF as decimal 255. (Of course, you don't need to take our word for it. A good way to start getting a feel for the language is to try these statements out in the interpreter as you read this chapter.) If the number begins with a non-zero digit, and is otherwise undecorated, it is decimal (base 10). For example:

```
val dec1 = 31   // 31: Int
val dec2 = 255  // 255: Int
val dec3 = 20   // 20: Int
```

If an integer literal ends in an L or l, it is a `Long`; otherwise it is an `Int`. Some examples of `Long` integer literals are:

```
val prog = 0XCAFEBABEL  // 3405691582: Long
val tower = 35L         // 35: Long
val of = 31l            // 31: Long
```

If an `Int` literal is assigned to a variable of type `Short` or `Byte`, the literal is treated as if it were a `Short` or `Byte` type so long as the literal value is within the valid range for that type. For example:

```
val little: Short = 367 // 367: Short
val littler: Byte = 38  // 38: Byte
```

Floating point literals

Floating point literals are made up of decimal digits, optionally containing a decimal point, and optionally followed by an E or e and an exponent. Some examples of floating-point literals are:

```
val big = 1.2345              // 1.2345: Double
val bigger = 1.2345e1         // 12.345: Double
val biggerStill = 123E45      // 1.23E47: Double
val trillion = 1_000_000_000e3 // 1.0E12: Double
```

Note that the exponent portion means the power of 10 by which the other portion is multiplied. Thus, 1.2345e1 is 1.2345 *times* 10^1, which is 12.345. If a floating-point literal ends in an F or f, it is a Float; otherwise it is a Double. Optionally, a Double floating-point literal can end in D or d. Some examples of Float literals are:

```
val little = 1.2345F    // 1.2345: Float
val littleBigger = 3e5f // 300000.0: Float
```

That last value expressed as a Double could take these (and other) forms:

```
val anotherDouble = 3e5 // 300000.0: Double
val yetAnother = 3e5D   // 300000.0: Double
```

Larger numeric literals

In Scala 3 includes an experimental feature that eliminates size limits for numeric literals and allows them be used to initialize arbitrary types. You can enable the feature with this language import:

```
import scala.language.experimental.genericNumberLiterals
```

Here are two examples from the standard library:

```
val invoice: BigInt = 1_000_000_000_000_000_000_000
val pi: BigDecimal = 3.141592653589793238462643383
```

Character literals

Character literals are composed of any Unicode character between single quotes, such as:

```
scala> val a = 'A'
val a: Char = A
```

In addition to providing an explicit character between the single quotes, you can identify a character using its Unicode code point. To do so, write \u followed by four hex digits with the code point, like this:

```
scala> val d = '\u0041'
val d: Char = A
scala> val f = '\u0044'
val f: Char = D
```

In fact, such Unicode characters can appear anywhere in a Scala program. For instance you could also write an identifier like this:

```
scala> val B\u0041\u0044 = 1
val BAD: Int = 1
```

This identifier is treated as identical to BAD, the result of expanding the two Unicode characters in the code above. In general, it is a bad idea to name identifiers like this because it is hard to read. Rather, this syntax is intended to allow Scala source files that include non-ASCII Unicode characters to be represented in ASCII.

Finally, there are also a few character literals represented by special escape sequences, shown in Table 5.2. For example:

```
scala> val backslash = '\\'
val backslash: Char = \
```

String literals

A string literal is composed of characters surrounded by double quotes:

```
scala> val hello = "hello"
val hello: String = hello
```

75

Table 5.2 · Special character literal escape sequences

Literal	Meaning
\n	line feed (\u000A)
\b	backspace (\u0008)
\t	tab (\u0009)
\f	form feed (\u000C)
\r	carriage return (\u000D)
\"	double quote (\u0022)
\'	single quote (\u0027)
\\	backslash (\u005C)

The syntax of the characters within the quotes is the same as with character literals. For example:

```
scala> val escapes = "\\\"\'"
val escapes: String = \"'
```

Because this syntax is awkward for strings that contain a lot of escape sequences or strings that span multiple lines, Scala includes a special syntax for *raw strings*. You start and end a raw string with three double quotation marks in a row ("""). The interior of a raw string may contain any characters whatsoever, including newlines, quotation marks, and special characters, except of course three quotes in a row. For example, the following program prints out a message using a raw string:

```
println("""Welcome to Ultamix 3000.
          Type "HELP" for help.""")
```

However, running this code does not produce quite what is desired:

```
Welcome to Ultamix 3000.
          Type "HELP" for help.
```

The issue is that the leading spaces before the second line are included in the string! To help with this common situation, you can call stripMargin on strings. To use this method, put a pipe character (|) at the front of each line, and then call stripMargin on the whole string:

```
println(""""|Welcome to Ultamix 3000.
            |Type "HELP" for help.""".stripMargin)
```

Now the code behaves as desired:

```
Welcome to Ultamix 3000.
Type "HELP" for help.
```

Boolean literals

The Boolean type has two literals, true and false:

```
val bool = true  // true: Boolean
val fool = false // false: Boolean
```

That's all there is to it. You are now literally[2] an expert in Scala.

5.3 String interpolation

Scala includes a flexible mechanism for string interpolation, which allows you to embed expressions within string literals. Its most common use case is to provide a concise and readable alternative to string concatenation. Here's an example:

```
val name = "reader"
println(s"Hello, $name!")
```

The expression, s"Hello, $name!" is a *processed* string literal. Because the letter s immediately precedes the open quote, Scala will use the *s string interpolator* to process the literal. The s interpolator will evaluate each embedded expression, invoke toString on each result, and replace the embedded expressions in the literal with those results. Thus s"Hello, $name!" yields "Hello, reader!", the same result as "Hello, " + name + "!".

You can place any expression after a dollar sign ($) in a processed string literal. For single-variable expressions, you can often just place the variable name after the dollar sign. Scala will interpret all characters up to the first

---

[2]figuratively speaking

77

non-identifier character as the expression. If the expression includes non-identifier characters, you must place it in curly braces, with the open curly brace immediately following the dollar sign. Here's an example:

```
scala> s"The answer is ${6 * 7}."
val res0: String = The answer is 42.
```

Scala provides two other string interpolators by default: raw and f. The raw string interpolator behaves like s, except it does not recognize character literal escape sequences (such as those shown in Table 5.2). For example, the following statement prints four backslashes, not two:

```
println(raw"No\\\\escape!") // prints: No\\\\escape!
```

The f string interpolator allows you to attach printf-style formatting instructions to embedded expressions. You place the instructions after the expression, starting with a percent sign (%), using the syntax specified by java.util.Formatter. For example, here's how you might format pi:

```
scala> f"${math.Pi}%.5f"
val res1: String = 3.14159
```

If you provide no formatting instructions for an embedded expression, the f string interpolator will default to %s, which means the toString value will be substituted, just like the s string interpolator. For example:

```
scala> val pi = "Pi"
val pi: String = Pi

scala> f"$pi is approximately ${math.Pi}%.8f."
val res2: String = Pi is approximately 3.14159265.
```

In Scala, string interpolation is implemented by rewriting code at compile time. The compiler will treat any expression consisting of an identifier followed immediately by the open double quote of a string literal as a string interpolator expression. The s, f, and raw string interpolators are implemented via this general mechanism. Libraries and users can define other string interpolators for other purposes.

5.4 Operators are methods

Scala provides a rich set of operators for its basic types. As mentioned in previous chapters, these operators are actually just a nice syntax for ordinary method calls. For example, 1 + 2 really means the same thing as 1.+(2). In other words, class Int contains a method named + that takes an Int and returns an Int result. This + method is invoked when you add two Ints:

```
val sum = 1 + 2            // Scala invokes 1.+(2)
```

To prove this to yourself, you can write the expression explicitly as a method invocation:

```
scala> val sumMore = 1.+(2)
val sumMore: Int = 3
```

In fact, Int contains several *overloaded* + methods that take different parameter types.[3] For example, Int has another method, also named +, that takes and returns a Long. If you add a Long to an Int, this alternate + method will be invoked, as in:

```
scala> val longSum = 1 + 2L    // Scala invokes 1.+(2L)
val longSum: Long = 3
```

The + symbol is an operator—an infix operator to be specific. Operator notation is not limited to methods like + that look like operators in other languages. You can use *any* method in operator notation, so long as it takes just one parameter.[4] For example, class String has a method, indexOf, that takes one Char parameter. The indexOf method searches the string for the first occurrence of the specified character and returns its index or −1 if it doesn't find the character. You can use indexOf as an operator, like this:

```
scala> val s = "Hello, world!"
val s: String = Hello, world!

scala> s indexOf 'o'    // Scala invokes s.indexOf('o')
val res0: Int = 4
```

---

[3]*Overloaded* methods have the same name but different argument types. More on method overloading in Section 6.11.

[4]In future versions of Scala, methods with non-symbolic names will only be allowed as operators if they are declared with the infix modifier.

79

Any single-parameter method can be an operator

In Scala operators are not special language syntax; any method that accepts a single parameter can be an operator. What makes a single-parameter method an operator is how you *use* it. When you write "s.indexOf('o')", indexOf is not an operator. But when you write "s indexOf 'o'", indexOf *is* an operator, because you're using it in operator notation.

So far, you've seen examples of *infix* operator notation, which means the method to invoke sits between the object and the parameter (or parameters) you wish to pass to the method, as in "7 + 2". Scala also has two other operator notations: prefix and postfix. In prefix notation, you put the method name before the object on which you are invoking the method (for example, the '-' in -7). In postfix notation, you put the method after the object (for example, the "toLong" in "7 toLong").

In contrast to the infix operator notation—in which operators take two operands, one to the left and the other to the right—prefix and postfix operators are *unary*: they take just one operand. In prefix notation, the operand is to the right of the operator. Some examples of prefix operators are -2.0, !found, and ~0xFF. As with the infix operators, these prefix operators are a shorthand way of invoking methods. In this case, however, the name of the method has "unary_" prepended to the operator character. For instance, Scala will transform the expression -2.0 into the method invocation "(2.0).unary_-". You can demonstrate this to yourself by typing the method call both via operator notation and explicitly:

```
scala> -2.0    // Scala invokes (2.0).unary_-
val res2: Double = -2.0

scala> (2.0).unary_-
val res3: Double = -2.0
```

The only identifiers that can be used as prefix operators are +, -, !, and ~. Thus, if you define a method named unary_!, you could invoke that method on a value or variable of the appropriate type using prefix operator notation, such as !p. But if you define a method named unary_*, you wouldn't be able to use prefix operator notation because * isn't one of the four identifiers that can be used as prefix operators. You could invoke the method normally, as in `p.unary_*`, but if you attempted to invoke it via `*p`, Scala will parse it as if you'd written `*.p`, which is probably not what you had in mind![5]

Postfix operators are methods that take no arguments, when they are invoked without a dot or parentheses. In Scala, you can leave off empty parentheses on method calls. The convention is that you include parentheses if the method has side effects, such as `println()`, but you can leave them off if the method has no side effects, such as `toLowerCase` invoked on a `String`:

```
scala> val s = "Hello, world!"
val s: String = Hello, world!

scala> s.toLowerCase
val res4: String = hello, world!
```

In this latter case of a method that requires no arguments, you can alternatively leave off the dot and use postfix operator notation. However, the compiler will require that you import scala.language.postfixOps before you call a method in postfix notation:

```
scala> import scala.language.postfixOps

scala> s toLowerCase
val res5: String = hello, world!
```

In this case, `toLowerCase` is used as a postfix operator on the operand s.

Therefore, to see what operators you can use with Scala's basic types, all you really need to do is look at the methods declared in the type's classes in the Scala API documentation. Given that this is a Scala tutorial, however, we'll give you a quick tour of most of these methods in the next few sections.

Fast track for Java programmers
Many aspects of Scala described in the remainder of this chapter are the same as in Java. If you're a Java guru in a rush, you can safely skip to Section 5.8 on page 85, which describes how Scala differs from Java in the area of object equality.

---

[5]All is not necessarily lost, however. There is an extremely slight chance your program with the `*p` might compile as C++.

5.5 Arithmetic operations

You can invoke arithmetic methods via infix operator notation for addition (+), subtraction (−), multiplication (∗), division (/), and remainder (%) on any numeric type. Here are some examples:

```
1.2 + 2.3     // 3.5: Double
3 - 1         // 2: Int
'b' - 'a'     // 1: Int
2L * 3L       // 6: Long
11 / 4        // 2: Int
11 % 4        // 3: Int
11.0f / 4.0f  // 2.75: Float
11.0 % 4.0    // 3.0: Double
```

When both the left and right operands are integral types (Int, Long, Byte, Short, or Char), the / operator will tell you the whole number portion of the quotient, excluding any remainder. The % operator indicates the remainder of an implied integer division.

The floating-point remainder you get with % is not the one defined by the IEEE 754 standard. The IEEE 754 remainder uses rounding division, not truncating division, in calculating the remainder, so it is quite different from the integer remainder operation. If you really want an IEEE 754 remainder, you can call IEEEremainder on scala.math, as in:

```
math.IEEEremainder(11.0, 4.0) // -1.0: Double
```

The numeric types also offer unary prefix operators + (method unary_+) and − (method unary_−), which allow you to indicate whether a literal number is positive or negative, as in −3 or +4.0. If you don't specify a unary + or −, a literal number is interpreted as positive. Unary + exists solely for symmetry with unary −, but has no effect. The unary − can also be used to negate a variable. Here are some examples:

```
val neg = 1 + -3 // -2: Neg
val y = +3       // 3: Int
-neg             // 2: Int
```

82

5.6   Relational and logical operations

You can compare numeric types with relational methods greater than (>), less
than (<), greater than or equal to (>=), and less than or equal to (<=), which
yield a Boolean result. In addition, you can use the unary '!' operator (the
unary_! method) to invert a Boolean value. Here are a few examples:

```
1 > 2              // false: Boolean
1 < 2              // true: Boolean
1.0 <= 1.0         // true: Boolean
3.5f >= 3.6f       // false: Boolean
'a' >= 'A'         // true: Boolean
val untrue = !true // false: Boolean
```

Logical methods, logical-and (&& and &) and logical-or (|| and |), take
Boolean operands in infix notation and yield a Boolean result. For example:

```
val toBe = true               // true: Boolean
val question = toBe || !toBe  // true: Boolean
val paradox = toBe && !toBe   // false: Boolean
```

The && and || operations *short-circuit* as in Java: expressions built from
these operators are only evaluated as far as needed to determine the result.
In other words, the right-hand side of && and || expressions won't be evalu-
ated if the left-hand side determines the result. For example, if the left-hand
side of a && expression evaluates to false, the result of the expression will
definitely be false, so right-hand side is not evaluated. Likewise, if the
left-hand side of a || expression evaluates to true, the result of the expres-
sion will definitely be true, so the right-hand side is not evaluated.

```
scala> def salt() = { println("salt"); false }
def salt(): Boolean

scala> def pepper() = { println("pepper"); true }
def pepper(): Boolean

scala> pepper() && salt()
pepper
salt
val res21: Boolean = false
```

83

```
scala> salt() && pepper()
salt
val res22: Boolean = false
```

In the first expression, `pepper` and `salt` are invoked, but in the second, only `salt` is invoked. Given `salt` returns `false`, there's no need to call `pepper`.

If you want to evaluate the right hand side no matter what, use & and |instead. The & method performs a logical-and operation, and | a logical-or, but don't short-circuit like && and ||. Here's an example:

```
scala> salt() & pepper()
salt
pepper
val res23: Boolean = false
```

> **Note**
> You may be wondering how short-circuiting can work given operators are just methods. Normally, all arguments are evaluated before entering a method, so how can a method avoid evaluating its second argument? The answer is that all Scala methods have a facility for delaying the evaluation of their arguments, or even declining to evaluate them at all. The facility is called *by-name parameters* and is discussed in Section 9.5.

5.7 Bitwise operations

Scala enables you to perform operations on individual bits of integer types with several bitwise methods. The bitwise methods are: bitwise-and (&), bitwise-or (|), and bitwise-xor (^).[6] The unary bitwise complement operator (~, the method `unary_~`) inverts each bit in its operand. For example:

```
1 & 2 // 0: Int
1 | 2 // 3: Int
1 ^ 3 // 2: Int
~1    // -2: Int
```

---

[6]The bitwise-xor method performs an *exclusive or* on its operands. Identical bits yield a 0. Different bits yield a 1. Thus 0011 ^ 0101 yields 0110.

The first expression, 1 & 2, bitwise-ands each bit in 1 (0001) and 2 (0010), which yields 0 (0000). The second expression, 1 | 2, bitwise-ors each bit in the same operands, yielding 3 (0011). The third expression, 1 ^ 3, bitwise-xors each bit in 1 (0001) and 3 (0011), yielding 2 (0010). The final expression, ~1, inverts each bit in 1 (0001), yielding -2, which in binary looks like 11111111111111111111111111111110.

Scala integer types also offer three shift methods: shift left (<<), shift right (>>), and unsigned shift right (>>>). The shift methods, when used in infix operator notation, shift the integer value on the left of the operator by the amount specified by the integer value on the right. Shift left and unsigned shift right fill with zeroes as they shift. Shift right fills with the highest bit (the sign bit) of the left-hand value as it shifts. Here are some examples:

```
-1 >> 31  // -1: Int
-1 >>> 31 // 1: Int
1 << 2    // 4: Int
```

-1 in binary is 11111111111111111111111111111111. In the first example, -1 >> 31, -1 is shifted to the right 31 bit positions. Since an Int consists of 32 bits, this operation effectively moves the leftmost bit over until it becomes the rightmost bit.[7] Since the >> method fills with ones as it shifts right, because the leftmost bit of -1 is 1, the result is identical to the original left operand, 32 one bits, or -1. In the second example, -1 >>> 31, the leftmost bit is again shifted right until it is in the rightmost position, but this time filling with zeroes along the way. Thus the result this time is binary 00000000000000000000000000000001, or 1. In the final example, 1 << 2, the left operand, 1, is shifted left two positions (filling in with zeroes), resulting in binary 00000000000000000000000000000100, or 4.

5.8   Object equality

If you want to compare two objects for equality, you can use either == or its inverse !=. Here are a few simple examples:

---

[7]The leftmost bit in an integer type is the sign bit. If the leftmost bit is 1, the number is negative. If 0, the number is positive.

85

```
1 == 2 // false: Boolean
1 != 2 // true: Boolean
2 == 2 // true: Boolean
```

These operations actually apply to all objects, not just basic types. For example, you can use == to compare lists:

```
List(1, 2, 3) == List(1, 2, 3) // true: Boolean
List(1, 2, 3) == List(4, 5, 6) // false: Boolean
```

Going further, you can compare two objects that have different types:

```
1 == 1.0                  // true: Boolean
List(1, 2, 3) == "hello" // false: Boolean
```

You can even compare against null, or against things that might be null. No exception will be thrown:

```
List(1, 2, 3) == null // false: Boolean
null == List(1, 2, 3) // false: Boolean
```

As you see, == has been carefully crafted so that you get just the equality comparison you want in most cases. This is accomplished with a very simple rule: First check the left side for null. If it is not null, call the equals method. Since equals is a method, the precise comparison you get depends on the type of the left-hand argument. Since there is an automatic null check, you do not have to do the check yourself.[8]

This kind of comparison will yield true on different objects, so long as their contents are the same and their equals method is written to be based on contents. For example, here is a comparison between two strings that happen to have the same five letters in them:

```
("he" + "llo") == "hello" // true: Boolean
```

---

[8]The automatic check does not look at the right-hand side, but any reasonable equals method should return false if its argument is null.

86

> ## How Scala's == differs from Java's
>
> In Java, you can use == to compare both primitive and reference types.
> On primitive types, Java's == compares value equality, as in Scala. On
> reference types, however, Java's == compares *reference equality*, which
> means the two variables point to the same object on the JVM's heap.
> Scala provides a facility for comparing reference equality, as well,
> under the name eq. However, eq and its opposite, ne, only apply to
> objects that directly map to Java objects. The full details about eq and
> ne are given in Sections 17.1 and 17.2. Also, see Chapter 8 on how to
> write a good equals method.

5.9 Operator precedence and associativity

Operator precedence determines which parts of an expression are evaluated
before the other parts. For example, the expression 2 + 2 * 7 evaluates to 16,
not 28, because the * operator has a higher precedence than the + operator.
Thus the multiplication part of the expression is evaluated before the addition
part. You can of course use parentheses in expressions to clarify evaluation
order or to override precedence. For example, if you really wanted the result
of the expression above to be 28, you could write the expression like this:

```
(2 + 2) * 7
```

Given that Scala doesn't have operators, per se, just a way to use methods
in operator notation, you may be wondering how operator precedence works.
Scala decides precedence based on the first character of the methods used in
operator notation (there's one exception to this rule, which will be discussed
in the following pages). If the method name starts with a *, for example,
it will have a higher precedence than a method that starts with a +. Thus
2 + 2 * 7 will be evaluated as 2 + (2 * 7). Similarly, a +++ b *** c (in which
a, b, and c are variables, and +++ and *** are methods) will be evaluated
a +++ (b *** c), because the *** method has a higher precedence than the
+++ method.

Table 5.3 shows the precedence given to the first character of a method
in decreasing order of precedence, with characters on the same line having
the same precedence. The higher a character is in this table, the higher the

87

Table 5.3 · Operator precedence

(all other special characters)
* / %
+ −
:
< >
= !
&
^
|
(all letters)
(all assignment operators)

precedence of methods that start with that character. Here's an example that illustrates the influence of precedence:

```
2 << 2 + 2 // 32: Int
```

The << method starts with the character <, which appears lower in Table 5.3 than the character +, which is the first and only character of the + method. Thus << will have lower precedence than +, and the expression will be evaluated by first invoking the + method, then the << method, as in 2 << (2 + 2). 2 + 2 is 4, by our math, and 2 << 4 yields 32. If you swap the operators, you'll get a different result:

```
2 + 2 << 2 // 16: Int
```

Since the first characters are the same as in the previous example, the methods will be invoked in the same order. First the + method will be invoked, then the << method. So 2 + 2 will again yield 4, and 4 << 2 is 16.

The one exception to the precedence rule, alluded to earlier, concerns *assignment operators*, which end in an equals character. If an operator ends in an equals character (=), and the operator is not one of the comparison operators <=, >=, ==, or !=, then the precedence of the operator is the same as that of simple assignment (=). That is, it is lower than the precedence of any other operator. For instance:

```
x *= y + 1
```

means the same as:

```
x *= (y + 1)
```

because *= is classified as an assignment operator whose precedence is lower than +, even though the operator's first character is *, which would suggest a precedence higher than +.

When multiple operators of the same precedence appear side by side in an expression, the *associativity* of the operators determines the way operators are grouped. The associativity of an operator in Scala is determined by its *last* character. As mentioned on page 41 of Chapter 3, any method that ends in a ':' character is invoked on its right operand, passing in the left operand. Methods that end in any other character are the other way around: They are invoked on their left operand, passing in the right operand. So a * b yields a.*(b), but a ::: b yields b.:::(a).

No matter what associativity an operator has, however, its operands are always evaluated left to right. So if a is an expression that is not just a simple reference to an immutable value, then a ::: b is more precisely treated as the following block:

```
{ val x = a; b.:::(x) }
```

In this block a is still evaluated before b, and then the result of this evaluation is passed as an operand to b's ::: method.

This associativity rule also plays a role when multiple operators of the same precedence appear side by side. If the methods end in ':', they are grouped right to left; otherwise, they are grouped left to right. For example, a ::: b ::: c is treated as a ::: (b ::: c). But a * b * c, by contrast, is treated as (a * b) * c.

Operator precedence is part of the Scala language. You needn't be afraid to use it. Nevertheless, it is good style to use parentheses to clarify what operators are operating upon what expressions. Perhaps the only precedence you can truly count on other programmers knowing without looking up is that multiplicative operators, *, /, and %, have a higher precedence than the additive ones + and −. Thus even if a + b << c yields the result you want without parentheses, the extra clarity you get by writing (a + b) << c may reduce

Table 5.4 · Some rich operations

Code	Result
0.max(5)	5
0.min(5)	0
-2.7.abs	2.7
-2.7.round	-3L
1.5.isInfinity	false
(1.0 / 0).isInfinity	true
4 to 6	Range(4, 5, 6)
"bob".capitalize	"Bob"
"robert".drop(2)	"bert"

the frequency with which your peers utter your name in operator notation, for example, by shouting in disgust, "bills !*&^%~ code!".[9]

5.10   Rich operations

You can invoke many more methods on Scala's basic types than were described in the previous sections. A few examples are shown in Table 5.4. As of Scala 3, these methods are available via *implicit conversions*, a deprecated technique that will eventually be replaced with *extension methods*, a technique described in detail in Chapter 22. All you need to know for now is that for each basic type described in this chapter, there is also a "rich wrapper" that provides several additional methods. To see all the available methods on the basic types, therefore, you should look at the API documentation on the rich wrapper for each basic type. Those classes are listed in Table 5.5.

5.11   Conclusion

The main take-aways from this chapter are that operators in Scala are method calls, and that implicit conversions to rich variants exist for Scala's basic types that add even more useful methods. In the next chapter, we'll show

---

[9]By now you should be able to figure out that given this code, the Scala compiler would invoke (bills.!*&^%~(code)).!.

Table 5.5 · Rich wrapper classes

Basic type	Rich wrapper
Byte	scala.runtime.RichByte
Short	scala.runtime.RichShort
Int	scala.runtime.RichInt
Long	scala.runtime.RichLong
Char	scala.runtime.RichChar
Float	scala.runtime.RichFloat
Double	scala.runtime.RichDouble
Boolean	scala.runtime.RichBoolean
String	scala.collection.immutable.StringOps

you what it means to design objects in a functional style that gives new implementations of some of the operators that you have seen in this chapter.

Chapter 6

Functional Objects

With the understanding of Scala basics you've gained from previous chapters, you're ready to design more full-featured classes in Scala. In this chapter, the emphasis is on classes that define functional objects, or objects that do not have any mutable state. As a running example, we'll create several variants of a class that models rational numbers as immutable objects. Along the way, we'll show you more aspects of object-oriented programming in Scala: class parameters and constructors, methods and operators, private members, overriding, checking preconditions, overloading, and self references.

6.1 A specification for class `Rational`

A *rational number* is a number that can be expressed as a ratio $\frac{n}{d}$, where n and d are integers, except that d cannot be zero. n is called the *numerator* and d the *denominator*. Examples of rational numbers are $\frac{1}{2}$, $\frac{2}{3}$, $\frac{112}{239}$, and $\frac{2}{1}$. Compared to floating-point numbers, rational numbers have the advantage that fractions are represented exactly, without rounding or approximation.

The class we'll design in this chapter must model the arithmetic behavior of rational numbers, including allowing them to be added, subtracted, multiplied, and divided. To add two rationals, you must first obtain a common denominator, then add the two numerators. For example, to add $\frac{1}{2} + \frac{2}{3}$, you multiply both parts of the left operand by 3 and both parts of the right operand by 2, which gives you $\frac{3}{6} + \frac{4}{6}$. Adding the two numerators yields the result, $\frac{7}{6}$. To multiply two rational numbers, you can simply multiply their numerators and multiply their denominators. Thus, $\frac{1}{2} * \frac{2}{5}$ gives $\frac{2}{10}$, which can be represented more compactly in its "normalized" form as $\frac{1}{5}$. You divide by swapping the numerator and denominator of the right operand and then multiplying. For instance $\frac{1}{2} / \frac{3}{5}$ is the same as $\frac{1}{2} * \frac{5}{3}$, or $\frac{5}{6}$.

One, maybe rather trivial, observation is that in mathematics, rational numbers do not have mutable state. You can add one rational number to another, but the result will be a new rational number. The original numbers will not have "changed." The immutable `Rational` class we'll design in this chapter will have the same property. Each rational number will be represented by one `Rational` object. When you add two `Rational` objects, you'll create a new `Rational` object to hold the sum.

This chapter will give you a glimpse of some of the ways Scala enables you to write libraries that feel like native language support. For example, at the end of this chapter you'll be able to do this with class `Rational`:

```
scala> val oneHalf = Rational(1, 2)
val oneHalf: Rational = 1/2

scala> val twoThirds = Rational(2, 3)
val twoThirds: Rational = 2/3

scala> (oneHalf / 7) + (1 - twoThirds)
val res0: Rational = 17/42
```

6.2   Constructing a `Rational`

A good place to start designing class `Rational` is to consider how client programmers will create a new `Rational` object. Given we've decided to make `Rational` objects immutable, we'll require that clients provide all data needed by an instance (in this case, a numerator and a denominator) when they construct the instance. Thus, we will start the design with this:

```
class Rational(n: Int, d: Int)
```

One of the first things to note about this line of code is that if a class doesn't have a body, you don't need to specify empty curly braces and cannot terminate with a colon. The identifiers n and d in the parentheses after the class name, `Rational`, are called *class parameters*. The Scala compiler will gather up these two class parameters and create a *primary constructor* that takes the same two parameters.

Immutable object trade-offs

Immutable objects offer several advantages over mutable objects, and
one potential disadvantage. First, immutable objects are often easier to
reason about than mutable ones, because they do not have complex state
spaces that change over time. Second, you can pass immutable objects
around quite freely, whereas you may need to make defensive copies
of mutable objects before passing them to other code. Third, there is
no way for two threads concurrently accessing an immutable to corrupt
its state once it has been properly constructed, because no thread can
change the state of an immutable. Fourth, immutable objects make safe
hash table keys. If a mutable object is mutated after it is placed into a
HashSet, for example, that object may not be found the next time you
look into the HashSet.

The main disadvantage of immutable objects is that they sometimes
require that a large object graph be copied, whereas an update could
be done in its place. In some cases this can be awkward to express
and might also cause a performance bottleneck. As a result, it is not
uncommon for libraries to provide mutable alternatives to immutable
classes. For example, class StringBuilder is a mutable alternative to
the immutable String. We'll give you more information on designing
mutable objects in Scala in Chapter 16.

Note

This initial Rational example highlights a difference between Java and
Scala. In Java, classes have constructors, which can take parameters;
whereas in Scala, classes can take parameters directly. The Scala notation
is more concise—class parameters can be used directly in the body of the
class; there's no need to define fields and write assignments that copy
constructor parameters into fields. This can yield substantial savings in
boilerplate code, especially for small classes.

The Scala compiler will compile any code you place in the class body,
which isn't part of a field or a method definition, into the primary constructor.
For example, you could print a debug message like this:

```scala
class Rational(n: Int, d: Int):
  println("Created " + n + "/" + d)
```

Given this code, the Scala compiler would place the call to println into

Rational's primary constructor. The `println` call will, therefore, print its debug message whenever you create a new `Rational` instance:

```
scala> new Rational(1, 2)
Created 1/2
val res0: Rational = Rational@6121a7dd
```

When instantiating classes that take parameters, like `Rational`, you can optionally leave off the new keyword. Such an expression is using what is called a *universal apply method*. Here's an example:

```
scala> Rational(1, 2)
Created 1/2
val res1: Rational = Rational@5dc7841c
```

6.3   Reimplementing the `toString` method

When we created an instance of `Rational` in the previous example, the REPL printed "Rational@5dc7841c". The REPL obtained this somewhat funny looking string by calling `toString` on the `Rational` object. By default, class `Rational` inherits the implementation of `toString` defined in class `java.lang.Object`, which just prints the class name, an @ sign, and a hexadecimal number. The result of `toString` is primarily intended to help programmers by providing information that can be used in debug print statements, log messages, test failure reports, and REPL and debugger output. The result currently provided by `toString` is not especially helpful because it doesn't give any clue about the rational number's value. A more useful implementation of `toString` would print out the values of the `Rational`'s numerator and denominator. You can *override* the default implementation by adding a method `toString` to class `Rational`, like this:

```
class Rational(n: Int, d: Int):
  override def toString = s"$n/$d"
```

The `override` modifier in front of a method definition signals that a previous method definition is overridden (more on this in Chapter 10). Since `Rational` numbers will display nicely now, we removed the debug `println` statement we put into the body of previous version of class `Rational`. You can test the new behavior of `Rational` in the REPL:

```
scala> val x = Rational(1, 3)
x: Rational = 1/3

scala> val y = Rational(5, 7)
y: Rational = 5/7
```

6.4 Checking preconditions

As a next step, we will turn our attention to a problem with the current behavior of the primary constructor. As mentioned at the beginning of this chapter, rational numbers may not have a zero in the denominator. Currently, however, the primary constructor accepts a zero passed as d:

```
scala> Rational(5, 0) // 5/0
val res1: Rational = 5/0
```

One of the benefits of object-oriented programming is that it allows you to encapsulate data inside objects so that you can ensure the data is valid throughout its lifetime. In the case of an immutable object such as Rational, this means that you should ensure the data is valid when the object is constructed. Given that a zero denominator is an invalid state for a Rational number, you should not let a Rational be constructed if a zero is passed in the d parameter.

The best way to approach this problem is to define as a *precondition* of the primary constructor that d must be non-zero. A precondition is a constraint on values passed into a method or constructor, a requirement which callers must fulfill. One way to do that is to use require,[1] like this:

```
class Rational(n: Int, d: Int):
  require(d != 0)
  override def toString = s"$n/$d"
```

The require method takes one boolean parameter. If the passed value is true, require will return normally. Otherwise, require will prevent the object from being constructed by throwing an IllegalArgumentException.

---

[1] The require method is defined in standalone object, Predef. As mentioned in Section 4.5, Predef's members are imported automatically into every Scala source file.

6.5   Adding fields

Now that the primary constructor is properly enforcing its precondition, we
will turn our attention to supporting addition. To do so, we'll define a public
add method on class Rational that takes another Rational as a parameter. To keep Rational immutable, the add method must not add the passed
rational number to itself. Rather, it must create and return a new Rational
that holds the sum. You might think you could write add this way:

```
class Rational(n: Int, d: Int): // This won't compile
  require(d != 0)
  override def toString = s"$n/$d"
  def add(that: Rational): Rational =
    Rational(n * that.d + that.n * d, d * that.d)
```

However, given this code the compiler will complain:

```
5 |    Rational(n * that.d + that.n * d, d * that.d)
  |                          ^^^^^^
  |value n in class Rational cannot be accessed as a member
  |     of (that : Rational) from class Rational.
5 |    Rational(n * that.d + that.n * d, d * that.d)
  |                 ^^^^^^
  |value d in class Rational cannot be accessed as a member
  |     of (that : Rational) from class Rational.
5 |    Rational(n * that.d + that.n * d, d * that.d)
  |                                         ^^^^^^
  |value d in class Rational cannot be accessed as a member
  |     of (that : Rational) from class Rational.
```

Although class parameters n and d are in scope in the code of your add
method, you can only access their value on the object on which add was
invoked. Thus, when you say n or d in add's implementation, the compiler is
happy to provide you with the values for these class parameters. But it won't
let you say that.n or that.d because that does not refer to the Rational
object on which add was invoked.[2] To access the numerator and denominator

---

[2]Actually, you could add a Rational to itself, in which case that would refer to the
object on which add was invoked. But because you can pass any Rational object to add, the
compiler still won't let you say that.n.

on that, you'll need to make them into fields. Listing 6.1 shows how you could add these fields to class Rational.[3]

```scala
class Rational(n: Int, d: Int):
  require(d != 0)
  val numer: Int = n
  val denom: Int = d
  override def toString = s"$numer/$denom"
  def add(that: Rational): Rational =
    Rational(
      numer * that.denom + that.numer * denom,
      denom * that.denom
    )
```

Listing 6.1 · Rational with fields.

In the version of Rational shown in Listing 6.1, we added two fields named numer and denom, and initialized them with the values of class parameters n and d.[4] We also changed the implementation of toString and add so that they use the fields, not the class parameters. This version of class Rational compiles. You can test it by adding some rational numbers:

```scala
val oneHalf = Rational(1, 2)    // 1/2
val twoThirds = Rational(2, 3)  // 2/3
oneHalf.add(twoThirds)          // 7/6
```

One other thing you can do now that you couldn't do before is access the numerator and denominator values from outside the object. Simply access the public numer and denom fields, like this:

```scala
val r = Rational(1, 2) // 1/2
r.numer                // 1
r.denom                // 2
```

---

[3]In Section 10.6 you'll find out about *parametric fields*, which provide a shorthand for writing the same code.

[4]Even though n and d are used in the body of the class, given they are only used inside constructors, the Scala compiler will not emit fields for them. Thus, given this code the Scala compiler will generate a class with two Int fields, one for numer and one for denom.

6.6 Self references

The keyword `this` refers to the object instance on which the currently executing method was invoked, or if used in a constructor, the object instance being constructed. As an example, consider adding a method, `lessThan`, which tests whether the given `Rational` is smaller than a parameter:

```
def lessThan(that: Rational) =
  this.numer * that.denom < that.numer * this.denom
```

Here, `this.numer` refers to the numerator of the object on which `lessThan` was invoked. You can also leave off the `this` prefix and write just `numer`; the two notations are equivalent.

As an example of where you can't do without `this`, consider adding a `max` method to class `Rational` that returns the greater of the given rational number and an argument:

```
def max(that: Rational) =
  if this.lessThan(that) then that else this
```

Here, the first `this` is redundant. You could have left it off and written: `lessThan(that)`. But the second `this` represents the result of the method in the case where the test returns false; were you to omit it, there would be nothing left to return!

6.7 Auxiliary constructors

Sometimes you need multiple constructors in a class. In Scala, constructors other than the primary constructor are called *auxiliary constructors*. For example, a rational number with a denominator of 1 can be written more succinctly as simply the numerator. Instead of $\frac{5}{1}$, for example, you can just write 5. It might be nice, therefore, if instead of writing `Rational(5, 1)`, client programmers could simply write `Rational(5)`. This would require adding an auxiliary constructor to `Rational` that takes only one argument, the numerator, with the denominator predefined to be 1. Listing 6.2 shows what that would look like.

Auxiliary constructors in Scala start with `def this(...)`. The body of `Rational`'s auxiliary constructor merely invokes the primary constructor,

```scala
class Rational(n: Int, d: Int):

  require(d != 0)

  val numer: Int = n
  val denom: Int = d

  def this(n: Int) = this(n, 1) // auxiliary constructor

  override def toString = s"$numer/$denom"

  def add(that: Rational): Rational =
    Rational(
      numer * that.denom + that.numer * denom,
      denom * that.denom
    )
```

Listing 6.2 · `Rational` with an auxiliary constructor.

passing along its lone argument, n, as the numerator and 1 as the denominator. You can see the auxiliary constructor in action by typing the following into the REPL:

```scala
val y = Rational(3)    // 3/1
```

In Scala, every auxiliary constructor must invoke another constructor of the same class as its first action. In other words, the first statement in every auxiliary constructor in every Scala class will have the form "this(...)". The invoked constructor is either the primary constructor (as in the Rational example), or another auxiliary constructor that comes textually before the calling constructor. The net effect of this rule is that every constructor invocation in Scala will end up eventually calling the primary constructor of the class. The primary constructor is thus the single point of entry of a class.

Note

If you're familiar with Java, you may wonder why Scala's rules for constructors are a bit more restrictive than Java's. In Java, a constructor must either invoke another constructor of the same class, or directly invoke a constructor of the superclass, as its first action. In a Scala class, only the primary constructor can invoke a superclass constructor. The increased restriction in Scala is really a design trade-off that needed to be paid in exchange for the greater conciseness and simplicity of Scala's constructors compared to Java's. Superclasses and the details of how constructor invocation and inheritance interact will be explained in Chapter 10.

6.8   Private fields and methods

In the previous version of `Rational`, we simply initialized numer with n and denom with d. As a result, the numerator and denominator of a `Rational` can be larger than needed. For example, the fraction $\frac{66}{42}$ could be normalized to an equivalent reduced form, $\frac{11}{7}$, but `Rational`'s primary constructor doesn't currently do this:

```
Rational(66, 42)    // 66/42
```

To normalize in this way, you need to divide the numerator and denominator by their *greatest common divisor*. For example, the greatest common divisor of 66 and 42 is 6. (In other words, 6 is the largest integer that divides evenly into both 66 and 42.) Dividing both the numerator and denominator of $\frac{66}{42}$ by 6 yields its reduced form, $\frac{11}{7}$. Listing 6.3 shows one way to do this:

In this version of `Rational`, we added a private field, g, and modified the initializers for numer and denom. (An *initializer* is the code that initializes a variable; for example, the "n / g" that initializes numer.) Because g is private, it can be accessed inside the body of the class, but not outside. We also added a private method, gcd, which calculates the greatest common divisor of two passed Ints. For example, gcd(12, 8) is 4. As you saw in Section 4.1, to make a field or method private you simply place the `private` keyword in front of its definition. The purpose of the private "helper method" gcd is to factor out code needed by some other part of the class, in this case, the primary constructor. To ensure g is always positive, we pass the absolute value of n and d, which we obtain by invoking abs on them, a method you can invoke on any Int to get its absolute value.

```
class Rational(n: Int, d: Int):

  require(d != 0)

  private val g = gcd(n.abs, d.abs)
  val numer = n / g
  val denom = d / g

  def this(n: Int) = this(n, 1)

  def add(that: Rational): Rational =
    Rational(
      numer * that.denom + that.numer * denom,
      denom * that.denom
    )

  override def toString = s"$numer/$denom"

  private def gcd(a: Int, b: Int): Int =
    if b == 0 then a else gcd(b, a % b)
```

Listing 6.3 · `Rational` with a private field and method.

The Scala compiler will place the code for the initializers of `Rational`'s three fields into the primary constructor in the order in which they appear in the source code. Thus, g's initializer, gcd(n.abs, d.abs), will execute before the other two, because it appears first in the source. Field g will be initialized with the result, the greatest common divisor of the absolute value of the class parameters, n and d. Field g is then used in the initializers of numer and denom. By dividing n and d by their greatest common divisor, g, every `Rational` will be constructed in its normalized form:

```
Rational(66, 42)   // 11/7
```

6.9 Defining operators

The current implementation of `Rational` addition is OK, but could be made more convenient to use. You might ask yourself why you can write:

```
x + y
```

if x and y are integers or floating-point numbers, but you have to write:

103

```
x.add(y)
```

or at least:

```
x add y
```

if they are rational numbers. There's no convincing reason why this should be so. Rational numbers are numbers just like other numbers. In a mathematical sense they are even more natural than, say, floating-point numbers. Why should you not use the natural arithmetic operators on them? In Scala you can do this. In the rest of this chapter, we'll show you how.

The first step is to replace add by the usual mathematical symbol. This is straightforward, as + is a legal identifier in Scala. We can simply define a method with + as its name. While we're at it, we may as well implement a method named * that performs multiplication. The result is shown in Listing 6.4:

```
class Rational(n: Int, d: Int):
  require(d != 0)

  private val g = gcd(n.abs, d.abs)
  val numer = n / g
  val denom = d / g

  def this(n: Int) = this(n, 1)

  def + (that: Rational): Rational =
    Rational(
      numer * that.denom + that.numer * denom,
      denom * that.denom
    )

  def * (that: Rational): Rational =
    Rational(numer * that.numer, denom * that.denom)

  override def toString = s"$numer/$denom"

  private def gcd(a: Int, b: Int): Int =
    if b == 0 then a else gcd(b, a % b)
```

Listing 6.4 · Rational with operator methods.

With class Rational defined in this manner, you can now write:

```
val x = Rational(1, 2)    // 1/2
val y = Rational(2, 3)    // 2/3
x + y                     // 7/6
```

As always, the operator syntax on the last input line is equivalent to a method call. You could also write:

```
x.+(y)                    // 7/6
```

but this is not as readable.

Another thing to note is that given Scala's rules for operator precedence, which were described in Section 5.9, the * method will bind more tightly than the + method for `Rationals`. In other words, expressions involving + and * operations on `Rationals` will behave as expected. For example, x + x * y will execute as x + (x * y), not (x + x) * y:

```
x + x * y      // 5/6
(x + x) * y    // 2/3
x + (x * y)    // 5/6
```

6.10 Identifiers in Scala

You have now seen the two most important ways to form an identifier in Scala: alphanumeric and operator. Scala has very flexible rules for forming identifiers. Besides the two forms you have seen there are also two others. All four forms of identifier formation are described in this section.

An *alphanumeric identifier* starts with a letter or underscore, which can be followed by further letters, digits, or underscores. The '$' character also counts as a letter; however, it is reserved for identifiers generated by the Scala compiler. Identifiers in user programs should not contain '$' characters, even though it will compile; if they do, this might lead to name clashes with identifiers generated by the Scala compiler.

Scala follows Java's convention of using camel-case[5] identifiers, such as `toString` and `HashSet`. Although underscores are legal in identifiers, they are not used that often in Scala programs, in part to be consistent with Java, but also because underscores have many other non-identifier uses in Scala

---

[5]This style of naming identifiers is called *camel case* because the identifiersHaveHumps consisting of the embedded capital letters.

code. As a result, it is best to avoid identifiers like `to_string`, `__init__`, or `name_`. Camel-case names of fields, method parameters, local variables, and functions should start with a lower case letter, for example: `length`, `flatMap`, and `s`. Camel-case names of classes and traits should start with an upper case letter, for example: `BigInt`, `List`, and `UnbalancedTreeMap`.[6]

> **Note**
> One consequence of using a trailing underscore in an identifier is that if you attempt, for example, to write a declaration like this, "val name_: Int = 1", you'll get a compiler error. The compiler will think you are trying to declare a `val` named "name_:". To get this to compile, you would need to insert an extra space before the colon, as in: "val name_ : Int = 1".

One way in which Scala's conventions depart from Java's involves constant names. In Scala, the word *constant* does not just mean `val`. Even though a `val` does remain constant after it is initialized, it is still a variable. For example, method parameters are `val`s, but each time the method is called those `val`s can hold different values. A constant is more permanent. For example, `scala.math.Pi` is defined to be the double value closest to the real value of π, the ratio of a circle's circumference to its diameter. This value is unlikely to change ever; thus, `Pi` is clearly a constant. You can also use constants to give names to values that would otherwise be *magic numbers* in your code: literal values with no explanation, which in the worst case appear in multiple places. You may also want to define constants for use in pattern matching, a use case that will be described in Section 13.2. In Java, the convention is to give constants names that are all upper case, with underscores separating the words, such as `MAX_VALUE` or `PI`. In Scala, the convention is merely that the first character should be upper case. Thus, constants named in the Java style, such as `X_OFFSET`, will work as Scala constants, but the Scala convention is to use camel case for constants, such as `XOffset`.

An *operator identifier* consists of one or more operator characters. Operator characters are printable ASCII characters such as +, :, ?, ~ or #.[7] Here

---

[6]In Section 14.5, you'll see that sometimes you may want to give a special kind of class known as a *case class* a name consisting solely of operator characters. For example, the Scala API contains a class named `::`, which facilitates pattern matching on `List`s.

[7]More precisely, an operator character belongs to the Unicode set of mathematical symbols(Sm) or other symbols(So), or to the 7-bit ASCII characters that are not letters, digits, parentheses, square brackets, curly braces, single or double quote, or an underscore, period,

are some examples of operator identifiers:

+   ++   :::   <?>   :->

The Scala compiler will internally "mangle" operator identifiers to turn them into legal Java identifiers with embedded $ characters. For instance, the identifier :-> would be represented internally as $colon$minus$greater. If you ever wanted to access this identifier from Java code, you'd need to use this internal representation.

Because operator identifiers in Scala can become arbitrarily long, there is a small difference between Java and Scala. In Java, the input x<-y would be parsed as four lexical symbols, so it would be equivalent to x < - y. In Scala, <- would be parsed as a single identifier, giving x <- y. If you want the first interpretation, you need to separate the < and the - characters by a space. This is unlikely to be a problem in practice, as very few people would write x<-y in Java without inserting spaces or parentheses between the operators.

A *mixed identifier* consists of an alphanumeric identifier, which is followed by an underscore and an operator identifier. For example, unary_+ used as a method name defines a unary + operator. Or, myvar_= used as method name defines an assignment operator. In addition, the mixed identifier form myvar_= is generated by the Scala compiler to support *properties* (more on that in Chapter 16).

A *literal identifier* is an arbitrary string enclosed in back ticks (` ... `). Some examples of literal identifiers are:

`x`   `<clinit>`   `yield`

The idea is that you can put any string that's accepted by the runtime as an identifier between back ticks. The result is always a Scala identifier. This works even if the name contained in the back ticks would be a Scala reserved word. A typical use case is accessing the static yield method in Java's Thread class. You cannot write Thread.yield() because yield is a reserved word in Scala. However, you can still name the method in back ticks, *e.g.*, Thread.`yield`().

---

semi-colon, comma, or back tick character.

6.11 Method overloading

Back to class `Rational`. With the latest changes, you can now do addition and multiplication operations in a natural style on rational numbers. But one thing still missing is mixed arithmetic. For instance, you cannot multiply a rational number by an integer because the operands of ∗ always have to be `Rationals`. So for a rational number `r` you can't write `r ∗ 2`. You must write `r ∗ Rational(2)`, which is not as nice.

To make `Rational` even more convenient, we'll add new methods to the class that perform mixed addition and multiplication on rational numbers and integers. While we're at it, we'll add methods for subtraction and division too. The result is shown in Listing 6.5.

There are now two versions each of the arithmetic methods: one that takes a rational as its argument and another that takes an integer. In other words, each of these method names is *overloaded* because each name is now being used by multiple methods. For example, the name + is used by one method that takes a `Rational` and another that takes an `Int`. In a method call, the compiler picks the version of an overloaded method that correctly matches the types of the arguments. For instance, if the argument `y` in `x.+(y)` is a `Rational`, the compiler will pick the method + that takes a `Rational` parameter. But if the argument is an integer, the compiler will pick the method + that takes an `Int` parameter instead. If you try this:

```
val r = Rational(2, 3)    // 2/3
r ∗ r                     // 4/9
r ∗ 2                     // 4/3
```

You'll see that the ∗ method invoked is determined in each case by the type of the right operand.

> **Note**
> Scala's process of overloaded method resolution is very similar to Java's. In every case, the chosen overloaded version is the one that best matches the static types of the arguments. Sometimes there is no unique best matching version; in that case the compiler will give you an "ambiguous reference" error.

```
class Rational(n: Int, d: Int):
  require(d != 0)

  private val g = gcd(n.abs, d.abs)
  val numer = n / g
  val denom = d / g

  def this(n: Int) = this(n, 1)

  def + (that: Rational): Rational =
    Rational(
      numer * that.denom + that.numer * denom,
      denom * that.denom
    )

  def + (i: Int): Rational =
    Rational(numer + i * denom, denom)

  def - (that: Rational): Rational =
    Rational(
      numer * that.denom - that.numer * denom,
      denom * that.denom
    )

  def - (i: Int): Rational =
    Rational(numer - i * denom, denom)

  def * (that: Rational): Rational =
    Rational(numer * that.numer, denom * that.denom)

  def * (i: Int): Rational =
    Rational(numer * i, denom)

  def / (that: Rational): Rational =
    Rational(numer * that.denom, denom * that.numer)

  def / (i: Int): Rational =
    Rational(numer, denom * i)

  override def toString = s"$numer/$denom"

  private def gcd(a: Int, b: Int): Int =
    if b == 0 then a else gcd(b, a % b)
```

Listing 6.5 · Rational with overloaded methods.

6.12 Extension methods

Now that you can write r * 2, you might also want to swap the operands, as in 2 * r. Unfortunately this does not work yet:

```
scala> 2 * r
 1 |2 * r
   |^^^
   |None of the overloaded alternatives of method * in
   |  class Int with types
   | (x: Double): Double
   | (x: Float): Float
   | (x: Long): Long
   | (x: Int): Int
   | (x: Char): Int
   | (x: Short): Int
   | (x: Byte): Int
   |match arguments ((r : Rational))
```

The problem here is that 2 * r is equivalent to 2.*(r), so it is a method call on the number 2, which is an integer. But the Int class contains no multiplication method that takes a Rational argument—it couldn't because class Rational is not a standard class in the Scala library.

However, there is another way to solve this problem in Scala: You can create extension methods on Int that take rational numbers. Try adding these lines in the REPL:

```
extension (x: Int)
  def + (y: Rational) = Rational(x) + y
  def - (y: Rational) = Rational(x) - y
  def * (y: Rational) = Rational(x) * y
  def / (y: Rational) = Rational(x) / y
```

This defines four extension methods on Int, each of which take a Rational. The compiler can use these automatically in a number of situations. With the extension methods defined, you can now retry the example that failed before:

```
val r = Rational(2,3)    // 2/3
2 * r                    // 4/3
```

For extension methods to work, they need to be in scope. If you place the extension method definitions inside class `Rational`, it won't be in scope in the REPL. For now, you'll need to define it directly in the REPL.

As you can glimpse from this example, extension methods are a very powerful technique for making libraries more flexible and more convenient to use. Because they are so powerful, they can also be misused. You'll find out more on extension methods, including ways to bring them into scope where they are needed, in Chapter 22.

6.13 A word of caution

As this chapter has demonstrated, creating methods with operator names and defining extension methods can help you design libraries for which client code is concise and easy to understand. Scala gives you a great deal of power to design such easy-to-use libraries. But please bear in mind that with power comes responsibility.

If used unartfully, both operator methods and extension methods can give rise to client code that is hard to read and understand. Because extension methods are applied implicitly by the compiler, not explicitly written down in the source code, it can be non-obvious to client programmers what extension methods are being applied. And although operator methods will usually make client code more concise, they will only make it more readable to the extent client programmers will be able to recognize and remember the meaning of each operator.

The goal you should keep in mind as you design libraries is not merely enabling concise client code, but readable, understandable client code. Conciseness will often be a big part of that readability, but you can take conciseness too far. By designing libraries that enable tastefully concise and at the same time understandable client code, you can help those client programmers work productively.

6.14 Conclusion

In this chapter, you saw more aspects of classes in Scala. You saw how to add parameters to a class, define several constructors, define operators as methods, and customize classes so that they are natural to use. Maybe most importantly, you saw that defining and using immutable objects is a quite natural way to code in Scala.

Although the final version of `Rational` shown in this chapter fulfills the requirements set forth at the beginning of the chapter, it could still be improved. We will in fact return to this example later in the book. For example, in Chapter 8, you'll learn how to override `equals` and `hashcode` to allow `Rational`s to behave better when compared with == or placed into hash tables. In Chapter 22, you'll learn how to place extension method definitions in a companion object for `Rational`, so they can be more easily placed into scope when client programmers are working with `Rational`s.

Chapter 7

Built-in Control Structures

Scala has only a handful of built-in control structures. The only control structures are if, while, for, try, match, and function calls. The reason Scala has so few is that it has included function literals since its inception. Instead of accumulating one higher-level control structure after another in the base syntax, Scala accumulates them in libraries. (Chapter 9 will show precisely how that is done.) This chapter will show those few control structures that are built in.

One thing you will notice is that almost all of Scala's control structures result in some value. This is the approach taken by functional languages, where programs are viewed as computing a value, thus the components of a program should also compute values. You can also view this approach as the logical conclusion of a trend already present in imperative languages. In imperative languages, function calls can return a value, even though having the called function update an output variable passed as an argument would work just as well. In addition, imperative languages often have a ternary operator (such as the ?: operator of C, C++, and Java), which behaves exactly like if, but results in a value. Scala adopts this ternary operator model, but calls it if. In other words, Scala's if can result in a value. Scala then continues this trend by having for, try, and match also result in values.

Programmers can use these result values to simplify their code, just as they use return values of functions. Without this facility, the programmer must create temporary variables just to hold results that are calculated inside a control structure. Removing these temporary variables makes the code a little simpler, and it also prevents many bugs where you set the variable in one branch but forget to set it in another.

113

Overall, Scala's basic control structures, minimal as they are, provide all of the essentials from imperative languages. Further, they allow you to shorten your code by consistently having result values. To show you how this works, we'll take a closer look at each of Scala's basic control structures.

7.1 If expressions

Scala's `if` works just like in many other languages. It tests a condition and then executes one of two code branches depending on whether the condition holds true. Here is a common example, written in an imperative style:

```
var filename = "default.txt"
if !args.isEmpty then
  filename = args(0)
```

This code declares a variable, `filename`, and initializes it to a default value. It then uses an `if` expression to check whether any arguments were supplied to the program. If so, it changes the variable to hold the value specified in the argument list. If no arguments were supplied, it leaves the variable set to the default value.

This code can be written more nicely because, as mentioned in Step 3 in Chapter 2, Scala's `if` is an expression that results in a value. Listing 7.1 shows how you can accomplish the same effect as the previous example, without using any vars:

```
val filename =
  if !args.isEmpty then args(0)
  else "default.txt"
```

Listing 7.1 · Scala's idiom for conditional initialization.

This time, the `if` has two branches. If `args` is not empty, the initial element, `args(0)`, is chosen; otherwise, the default value is chosen. The `if` expression results in the chosen value, and the `filename` variable is initialized with that value. This code is slightly shorter, but its real advantage is that it uses a `val` instead of a `var`. Using a `val` is the functional style, and it helps you in much the same way as a `final` variable in Java. It tells readers of the code that the variable will never change, saving them from scanning all code in the variable's scope to see if it ever changes.

A second advantage to using a val instead of a var is that it better supports *equational reasoning*. The introduced variable is *equal* to the expression that computes it, assuming that expression has no side effects. Thus, any time you are about to write the variable name, you could instead write the expression. Instead of println(filename), for example, you could just write this:

```
println(if (!args.isEmpty) args(0) else "default.txt")
```

The choice is yours. You can write it either way. Using vals helps you safely make this kind of refactoring as your code evolves over time.

> Look for opportunities to use vals. They can make your code both easier to read and easier to refactor.

7.2   While loops

Scala's while loop behaves as in other languages. It has a condition and a body, and the body is executed over and over as long as the condition holds true. Listing 7.2 shows an example:

```
def gcdLoop(x: Long, y: Long): Long =
  var a = x
  var b = y
  while a != 0 do
    val temp = a
    a = b % a
    b = temp
  b
```

Listing 7.2 · Calculating greatest common divisor with a while loop.

The while construct is called a "loop," not an expression, because it doesn't result in an interesting value. The type of the result is Unit. It turns out that a value (and in fact, only one value) exists whose type is Unit. It is called the *unit value* and is written (). The existence of () is how Scala's Unit differs from Java's void. Try this in the REPL:

```
scala> def greet() = println("hi")
def greet(): Unit

scala> val iAmUnit = greet() == ()
hi
val iAmUnit: Boolean = true
```

Because the type of the `println("hi")` expression is Unit, greet is defined to be a procedure with a result type of Unit. Therefore, greet returns the unit value, (). This is confirmed in the next line: the iAmUnit variable is true because greet's result equals the unit value, ().

As of Scala 3, Scala no longer offers a do-while loop, a looping control structure that tested the condition after the loop body instead of before. Instead, you can place the statements of the loop body first after while, finish with the boolean condition, and follow that with a "do ()". Listing 7.3 shows a Scala script that uses this approach to echo lines read from the standard input, until an empty line is entered:

```
import scala.io.StdIn.readLine
while
  val line = readLine()
  println(s"Read: $line")
  line != ""
do ()
```

Listing 7.3 · Executing a loop body at least once without do-while.

One other construct that results in the unit value, which is relevant here, is reassignment to vars. For example, were you to attempt to read lines in Scala using the following while loop idiom from Java (and C and C++), you'll run into trouble:

```
var line = ""            // This doesn't compile!
while (line = scala.io.StdIn.readLine()) != "" do
  println(s"Read: $line")
```

116

If you attempt to compile this code, Scala will give you an error stating that you cannot compare values of type Unit and String using !=. Whereas in Java, assignment results in the value assigned (in this case a line from the standard input), in Scala assignment always results in the unit value, (). Thus, the value of the assignment "line = readLine()" will always be () and never be "". As a result, were it to compile, this while loop's condition would never be false, and the loop would, therefore, never terminate.

Because the while loop results in no value, it is often left out of pure functional languages. Such languages have expressions, not loops. Scala includes the while loop nonetheless because sometimes an imperative solution can be more readable, especially to programmers with a predominantly imperative background. For example, if you want to code an algorithm that repeats a process until some condition changes, a while loop can express it directly while the functional alternative, which likely uses recursion, may be less obvious to some readers of the code.

For example, Listing 7.4 shows an alternate way to determine the greatest common divisor of two numbers.[1] Given the same two values for x and y, the gcd function shown in Listing 7.4 will return the same result as the gcdLoop function, shown in Listing 7.2. The difference between these two approaches is that gcdLoop is written in an imperative style, using vars and and a while loop, whereas gcd is written in a more functional style that involves recursion (gcd calls itself) and requires no vars.

```
def gcd(x: Long, y: Long): Long =
  if y == 0 then x else gcd(y, x % y)
```

Listing 7.4 · Calculating greatest common divisor with recursion.

In general, we recommend you challenge while loops in your code in the same way you challenge vars. In fact, while loops and vars often go hand in hand. Because while loops don't result in a value, to make any kind of difference to your program, a while loop will usually either need to update vars or perform I/O. You can see this in action in the gcdLoop example shown previously. As that while loop does its business, it updates vars a and b. Thus, we suggest you be a bit suspicious of while loops in

---

[1]The gcd function shown in Listing 7.4 uses the same approach used by the like-named function, first shown in Listing 6.3, to calculate greatest common divisors for class Rational. The main difference is that instead of Ints the gcd of Listing 7.4 works with Longs.

your code. If there isn't a good justification for a particular `while`, try to find a way to do the same thing without it.

7.3 For expressions

Scala's `for` expression is a Swiss army knife of iteration. It lets you combine a few simple ingredients in different ways to express a wide variety of iterations. Simple uses enable common tasks such as iterating through a sequence of integers. More advanced expressions can iterate over multiple collections of different kinds, filter out elements based on arbitrary conditions, and produce new collections.

Iteration through collections

The simplest thing you can do with `for` is to iterate through all the elements of a collection. For example, Listing 7.5 shows some code that prints out all files in the current directory. The I/O is performed using the Java API. First, we create a `java.io.File` on the current directory, `"."`, and call its `listFiles` method. This method returns an array of `File` objects, one per directory and file contained in the current directory. We store the resulting array in the `filesHere` variable.

```
val filesHere = (new java.io.File(".")).listFiles

for file <- filesHere do
  println(file)
```

Listing 7.5 · Listing files in a directory with a `for` expression.

With the "`file <- filesHere`" syntax, which is called a *generator*, we iterate through the elements of `filesHere`. In each iteration, a new `val` named `file` is initialized with an element value. The compiler infers the type of `file` to be `File`, because `filesHere` is an `Array[File]`. For each iteration, the body of the `for` expression, `println(file)`, will be executed. Because `File`'s `toString` method yields the name of the file or directory, the names of all the files and directories in the current directory will be printed.

The `for` expression syntax works for any kind of collection, not just arrays.[2] One convenient special case is the `Range` type, which you briefly saw

---

[2]To be precise, the expression to the right of the <- symbol in a for expression can be

in Table 5.4 on page 90. You can create Ranges using syntax like "1 to 5" and can iterate through them with a for. Here is a simple example:

```
scala> for i <- 1 to 4 do
         println(s"Iteration $i")
Iteration 1
Iteration 2
Iteration 3
Iteration 4
```

If you don't want to include the upper bound of the range in the values that are iterated over, use until instead of to:

```
scala> for i <- 1 until 4 do
         println(s"Iteration $i")
Iteration 1
Iteration 2
Iteration 3
```

Iterating through integers like this is common in Scala, but not nearly as much as in other languages. In other languages, you might use this facility to iterate through an array, like this:

```
// Not common in Scala...
for i <- 0 to filesHere.length - 1 do
  println(filesHere(i))
```

This for expression introduces a variable i, sets it in turn to each integer between 0 and filesHere.length - 1, and executes the body of the for expression for each setting of i. For each setting of i, the i'th element of filesHere is extracted and processed.

The reason this kind of iteration is less common in Scala is that you can just iterate over the collection directly. When you do, your code becomes shorter and you sidestep many of the off-by-one errors that can arise when iterating through arrays. Should you start at 0 or 1? Should you add -1, +1, or nothing to the final index? Such questions are easily answered, but also easily answered wrongly. It is safer to avoid such questions entirely.

---

any type that has certain methods (in this case foreach) with appropriate signatures. Details on how the Scala compiler processes for expressions are described in Chapter 3.

Filtering

Sometimes you don't want to iterate through a collection in its entirety; you want to filter it down to some subset. You can do this with a for expression by adding a *filter*, an if clause inside the for's parentheses. For example, the code shown in Listing 7.6 lists only those files in the current directory whose names end with ".scala":

```
val filesHere = (new java.io.File(".")).listFiles

for file <- filesHere if file.getName.endsWith(".scala") do
  println(file)
```

Listing 7.6 · Finding .scala files using a for with a filter.

You could alternatively accomplish the same goal with this code:

```
for file <- filesHere do
  if file.getName.endsWith(".scala") then
    println(file)
```

This code yields the same output as the previous code, and likely looks more familiar to programmers with an imperative background. The imperative form, however, is only an option because this particular for expression is executed for its printing side-effects and results in the unit value (). As demonstrated later in this section, the for expression is called an "expression" because it can result in an interesting value, a collection whose type is determined by the for expression's <- clauses.

You can include more filters if you want. Just keep adding if clauses. For example, to be extra defensive, the code in Listing 7.7 prints only files and not directories. It does so by adding a filter that checks the file's isFile method.

```
for
  file <- filesHere
  if file.isFile
  if file.getName.endsWith(".scala")
do println(file)
```

Listing 7.7 · Using multiple filters in a for expression.

Nested iteration

If you add multiple <- clauses, you will get nested "loops." For example, the for expression shown in Listing 7.8 has two nested loops. The outer loop iterates through filesHere, and the inner loop iterates through fileLines(file) for any file that ends with .scala.

```
def fileLines(file: java.io.File) =
  scala.io.Source.fromFile(file).getLines().toArray

def grep(pattern: String) =
  for
    file <- filesHere
    if file.getName.endsWith(".scala")
    line <- fileLines(file)
    if line.trim.matches(pattern)
  do println(s"$file: ${line.trim}")

grep(".*gcd.*")
```

Listing 7.8 · Using multiple generators in a for expression.

Mid-stream variable bindings

Note that the previous code repeats the expression line.trim. This is a non-trivial computation, so you might want to only compute it once. You can do this by binding the result to a new variable using an equals sign (=). The bound variable is introduced and used just like a val, only with the val keyword left out. Listing 7.9 shows an example.

In Listing 7.9, a variable named trimmed is introduced halfway through the for expression. That variable is initialized to the result of line.trim. The rest of the for expression then uses the new variable in two places, once in an if and once in println.

Producing a new collection

While all of the examples so far in this section have operated on the iterated values and then forgotten them, you can also generate a value to remember for each iteration. As described in Step 12 in Chapter 3, you prefix the body

121

```
def grep(pattern: String) =
  for
    file <- filesHere
    if file.getName.endsWith(".scala")
    line <- fileLines(file)
    trimmed = line.trim
    if trimmed.matches(pattern)
  do println(s"$file: $trimmed")
grep(".*gcd.*")
```

Listing 7.9 · Mid-stream assignment in a `for` expression.

of the `for` expression by the keyword `yield` instead of do. For example, here is a function that identifies the `.scala` files and stores them in an array:

```
def scalaFiles =
  for
    file <- filesHere
    if file.getName.endsWith(".scala")
  yield file
```

Each time the body of the `for` expression executes, it produces one value, in this case simply `file`. When the `for` expression completes, the result will include all of the yielded values contained in a single collection. The type of the resulting collection is based on the kind of collections processed in the iteration clauses. In this case the result is an `Array[File]`, because `filesHere` is an array and the type of the yielded expression is `File`.

As another example, the `for` expression shown in Listing 7.10 first transforms the `Array[File]` named `filesHere`, which contains all files in the current directory, to one that contains only `.scala` files. For each of these it generates an `Array[String]`, the result of the `fileLines` method, whose definition is shown in Listing 7.8. Each element of this `Array[String]` contains one line from the current file being processed. This `Array[String]` containing lines is transformed into another `Array[String]` containing only trimmed lines that include the substring `"for"`. Finally, for each of these, an integer length is yielded. The result of this `for` expression is an `Array[Int]` containing those lengths.

122

```
val forLineLengths =
  for
    file <- filesHere
    if file.getName.endsWith(".scala")
    line <- fileLines(file)
    trimmed = line.trim
    if trimmed.matches(".*for.*")
  yield trimmed.length
```

Listing 7.10 · Transforming an `Array[File]` to `Array[Int]` with a `for`.

At this point, you have seen all the major features of Scala's `for` expression, but we went through them rather quickly. A more thorough coverage of `for` expressions is given in *Advanced Programming in Scala*.

7.4   Exception handling with `try` expressions

Scala's exceptions behave just like in many other languages. Instead of returning a value in the normal way, a method can terminate by throwing an exception. The method's caller can either catch and handle that exception, or it can itself simply terminate, in which case the exception propagates to the caller's caller. The exception propagates in this way, unwinding the call stack, until a method handles it or there are no more methods left.

Throwing exceptions

Throwing an exception in Scala looks the same as in Java. You create an exception object and then throw it with the `throw` keyword:

```
throw new IllegalArgumentException
```

Although it may seem somewhat paradoxical, in Scala, `throw` is an expression that has a result type. Here's an example where result type matters:

```
def half(n: Int) =
  if n % 2 == 0 then
    n / 2
  else
    throw new RuntimeException("n must be even")
```

123

What happens here is that if n is even, `half` will return half of n. If n is not even, an exception will be thrown before `half` can return anything at all. Because of this, it is safe to treat a thrown exception as any kind of value whatsoever. Any context that tries to use the return from a `throw` will never get to do so, and thus no harm will come.

Technically, an exception throw has type `Nothing`. You can use a `throw` as an expression even though it will never actually evaluate to anything. This little bit of technical gymnastics might sound weird, but is frequently useful in cases like the previous example. One branch of an `if` computes a value, while the other throws an exception and computes `Nothing`. The type of the whole `if` expression is then the type of that branch which does compute something. Type `Nothing` is discussed further in Section 17.3.

Catching exceptions

You catch exceptions using the syntax shown in Listing 7.11 The syntax for `catch` clauses was chosen for its consistency with an important part of Scala: *pattern matching*. Pattern matching, a powerful feature, is described briefly in this chapter and in more detail in Chapter 13.

```
import java.io.FileReader
import java.io.FileNotFoundException
import java.io.IOException

try
  val f = new FileReader("input.txt")
  // Use and close file
catch
  case ex: FileNotFoundException => // Handle missing file
  case ex: IOException => // Handle other I/O error
```

Listing 7.11 · A `try-catch` clause in Scala.

The behavior of this `try-catch` expression is the same as in other languages with exceptions. The body is executed, and if it throws an exception, each `catch` clause is tried in turn. In this example, if the exception is of type `FileNotFoundException`, the first clause will execute. If it is of type

IOException, the second clause will execute. If the exception is of neither type, the try-catch will terminate and the exception will propagate further.

> **Note**
>
> One difference you'll quickly notice in Scala is that, unlike Java, Scala does not require you to catch checked exceptions or declare them in a throws clause. You can declare a throws clause if you wish with the @throws annotation, but it is not required. See Section 9.2 for more information on @throws.

The finally clause

You can guard an expression with a finally clause if you want to cause some code to execute no matter how the expression completes. For example, you might want to be sure an open file gets closed even if a method exits by throwing an exception. Listing 7.12 shows an example.[3]

```
import java.io.FileReader

val file = new FileReader("input.txt")
try
  println(file.read()) // Use the file
finally
  file.close()  // Be sure to close the file
```

Listing 7.12 · A try-finally clause in Scala.

> **Note**
>
> Listing 7.12 shows the idiomatic way to ensure a non-memory resource, such as a file, socket, or database connection, is closed. First you acquire the resource. Then you start a try block in which you use the resource. Lastly, you close the resource in a finally block. Alternatively, in Scala you can employ a technique called the *loan pattern* to achieve the same goal more concisely. The loan pattern will be described in Section 9.4.

---

[3]Although you must always either surround the case statements of a catch clause in curly braces, or indent the case statements in a block, try and finally do not require curly braces or an indented block if they contain only one expression. For example, you could write: try t() catch { case e: Exception => ... } finally f().

125

Yielding a value

As with most other Scala control structures, try-catch-finally results in a value. For example, Listing 7.13 shows how you can try to parse a URL but use a default value if the URL is badly formed. The result is that of the try clause if no exception is thrown, or the relevant catch clause if an exception is thrown and caught. If an exception is thrown but not caught, the expression has no result at all. The value computed in the finally clause, if there is one, is dropped. Usually finally clauses do some kind of clean up, such as closing a file. Normally, they should not change the value computed in the main body or a catch clause of the try.

```
import java.net.URL
import java.net.MalformedURLException

def urlFor(path: String) =
  try new URL(path)
  catch case e: MalformedURLException =>
    new URL("https://www.scala-lang.org")
```

Listing 7.13 · A catch clause that yields a value.

If you're familiar with Java, it's worth noting that Scala's behavior differs from Java only because Java's try-finally does not result in a value. As in Java, if a finally clause includes an explicit return statement, or throws an exception, that return value or exception will "overrule" any previous one that originated in the try block or one of its catch clauses. For example, given this, rather contrived, function definition:

```
def f(): Int = try return 1 finally return 2
```

calling f() results in 2. By contrast, given:

```
def g(): Int = try 1 finally 2
```

calling g() results in 1. Both of these functions exhibit behavior that could surprise most programmers, so it's usually best to avoid returning values from finally clauses. The best way to think of finally clauses is as a way to ensure some side effect happens, such as closing an open file.

7.5 Match expressions

Scala's `match` expression lets you select from a number of *alternatives*, just like `switch` statements in other languages. In general a `match` expression lets you select using arbitrary *patterns*, which will be described in Chapter 13. The general form can wait. For now, just consider using `match` to select among a number of alternatives.

As an example, the script in Listing 7.14 reads a food name from the argument list and prints a companion to that food. This `match` expression examines `firstArg`, which has been set to the first argument out of the argument list. If it is the string `"salt"`, it prints `"pepper"`, while if it is the string `"chips"`, it prints `"salsa"`, and so on. The default case is specified with an underscore (_), a wildcard symbol frequently used in Scala as a placeholder for a completely unknown value.

```
val firstArg = if !args.isEmpty then args(0) else ""

firstArg match
  case "salt" => println("pepper")
  case "chips" => println("salsa")
  case "eggs" => println("bacon")
  case _ => println("huh?")
```

Listing 7.14 · A `match` expression with side effects.

There are a few important differences from Java's `switch` statement. One is that any kind of constant, as well as other things, can be used in cases in Scala, not just the integer-type, enum, and string constants of Java's case statements. In Listing 7.14, the alternatives are strings. Another difference is that there are no `break`s at the end of each alternative. Instead the `break` is implicit, and there is no fall through from one alternative to the next. The common case—not falling through—becomes shorter, and a source of errors is avoided because programmers can no longer fall through by accident.

The most significant difference from Java's `switch`, however, may be that `match` expressions result in a value. In the previous example, each alternative in the `match` expression prints out a value. It would work just as well to yield the value rather than print it, as shown in Listing 7.15. The value that results from this `match` expression is stored in the `friend` variable. Aside from the code getting shorter (in number of tokens anyway), the code now disentangles two separate concerns: first it chooses a food and then prints it.

```
val firstArg = if !args.isEmpty then args(0) else ""
val friend =
  firstArg match
    case "salt" => "pepper"
    case "chips" => "salsa"
    case "eggs" => "bacon"
    case _ => "huh?"
println(friend)
```

Listing 7.15 · A match expression that yields a value.

7.6   Living without break and continue

You may have noticed that there has been no mention of break or continue. Scala leaves out these commands because they do not mesh well with function literals, a feature described in the next chapter. It is clear what continue means inside a while loop, but what would it mean inside a function literal? While Scala supports both imperative and functional styles of programming, in this case it leans slightly towards functional programming in exchange for simplifying the language. Do not worry, though. There are many ways to program without break and continue, and if you take advantage of function literals, those alternatives can often be shorter than the original code.

The simplest approach is to replace every continue by an if and every break by a boolean variable. The boolean variable indicates whether the enclosing while loop should continue. For example, suppose you are searching through an argument list for a string that ends with ".scala" but does not start with a hyphen. In Java you could—if you were quite fond of while loops, break, and continue—write the following:

```
int i = 0;                    // This is Java
boolean foundIt = false;
while (i < args.length) {
  if (args[i].startsWith("-")) {
    i = i + 1;
```

```
      continue;
    }
    if (args[i].endsWith(".scala")) {
      foundIt = true;
      break;
    }
    i = i + 1;
  }
```

To transliterate this Java code directly to Scala, instead of doing an `if` and then a `continue`, you could write an `if` that surrounds the entire remainder of the `while` loop. To get rid of the `break`, you would normally add a boolean variable indicating whether to keep going, but in this case you can reuse `foundIt`. Using both of these tricks, the code ends up looking as shown in Listing 7.16.

```
var i = 0
var foundIt = false

while i < args.length && !foundIt do
  if !args(i).startsWith("-") then
    if args(i).endsWith(".scala") then
      foundIt = true
    else
      i = i + 1
  else
    i = i + 1
```

Listing 7.16 · Looping without break or continue.

This Scala code in Listing 7.16 is quite similar to the original Java code. All the basic pieces are still there and in the same order. There are two reassignable variables and a `while` loop. Inside the loop, there is a test that `i` is less than `args.length`, a check for `"-"`, and a check for `".scala"`.

If you wanted to get rid of the `vars` in Listing 7.16, one approach you could try is to rewrite the loop as a recursive function. You could, for example, define a `searchFrom` function that takes an integer as an input, searches forward from there, and then returns the index of the desired argument. Using this technique the code would look as shown in Listing 7.17:

```
def searchFrom(i: Int): Int =
  if i >= args.length then -1
  else if args(i).startsWith("-") then searchFrom(i + 1)
  else if args(i).endsWith(".scala") then i
  else searchFrom(i + 1)
val i = searchFrom(0)
```

Listing 7.17 · A recursive alternative to looping with vars.

The version in Listing 7.17 gives a human-meaningful name to what the function does, and it uses recursion to substitute for looping. Each `continue` is replaced by a recursive call with `i + 1` as the argument, effectively skipping to the next integer. Many people find this style of programming easier to understand, once they get used to the recursion.

Note

The Scala compiler will not actually emit a recursive function for the code shown in Listing 7.17. Because all of the recursive calls are in *tail-call* position, the compiler will generate code similar to a `while` loop. Each recursive call will be implemented as a jump back to the beginning of the function. Tail-call optimization is discussed in Section 8.10.

7.7   Variable scope

Now that you've seen Scala's built-in control structures, we'll use them in this section to explain how scoping works in Scala.

Fast track for Java programmers

If you're a Java programmer, you'll find that Scala's scoping rules are almost identical to Java's. One difference between Java and Scala is that Scala allows you to define variables of the same name in nested scopes. So if you're a Java programmer, you may wish to at least skim this section.

Variable declarations in Scala programs have a *scope* that defines where you can use the name. The most common example of scoping is that indentation generally introduces a new scope, so anything defined at a particular indentation level leaves scope after an outdent. As an illustration, consider the function shown in Listing 7.18.

```
def printMultiTable() =
  var i = 1
  // only i in scope here
  while i <= 10 do
    var j = 1
    // both i and j in scope here
    while j <= 10 do
      val prod = (i * j).toString
      // i, j, and prod in scope here
      var k = prod.length
      // i, j, prod, and k in scope here
      while k < 4 do
        print(" ")
        k += 1
      print(prod)
      j += 1
    // i and j still in scope; prod and k out of scope
    println()
    i += 1
  // i still in scope; j, prod, and k out of scope
```

Listing 7.18 · Variable scoping when printing a multiplication table.

The printMultiTable function shown in Listing 7.18 prints out a multiplication table.[4] The first statement of this function introduces a variable named i and initializes it to the integer 1. You can then use the name i for the remainder of the function.

The next statement in printMultiTable is a while loop:

---

[4]The printMultiTable function shown in Listing 7.18 is written in an imperative style. We'll refactor it into a functional style in the next section.

```
while i <= 10 do
  var j = 1
  ...
```

You can use i here because it is still in scope. In the first statement inside that while loop, you introduce another variable, this time named j, and again initialize it to 1. Because the variable j was defined inside the indented body of the while loop, it can be used only within that while loop. If you were to attempt to do something with j after the end of this while loop, after the comment that says j, prod, and k are out of scope, your program would not compile.

All variables defined in this example—i, j, prod, and k—are *local variables*. Such variables are "local" to the function in which they are defined. Each time a function is invoked, a new set of its local variables is used.

Once a variable is defined, you can't define a new variable with the same name in the same scope. For example, the following script with two variables named a in the same scope would not compile:

```
val a = 1
val a = 2 // Does not compile
println(a)
```

You can, on the other hand, define a variable in an inner scope that has the same name as a variable in an outer scope. The following script would compile and run:

```
val a = 1
if a == 1 then
  val a = 2 // Compiles just fine
  println(a)
println(a)
```

When executed, the script shown previously would print 2 then 1, because the a defined inside the if expression is a different variable, which is in scope only until the end of the if's indented block. One difference to note between Scala and Java is that Java will not let you create a variable in an inner scope that has the same name as a variable in an outer scope. In a Scala program, an inner variable is said to *shadow* a like-named outer variable, because the outer variable becomes invisible in the inner scope.

You might have already noticed something that looks like shadowing in the REPL:

```
scala> val a = 1
a: Int = 1

scala> val a = 2
a: Int = 2

scala> println(a)
2
```

In the REPL, you can reuse variable names to your heart's content. Among other things, this allows you to change your mind if you made a mistake when you defined a variable the first time in the REPL. You can do this because conceptually the REPL creates a new nested scope for each new statement you type in.

Keep in mind that shadowing can be very confusing to readers, because variable names adopt new meanings in nested scopes. It is usually better to choose a new, meaningful variable name rather than to shadow an outer variable.

7.8 Refactoring imperative-style code

To help you gain insight into the functional style, in this section we'll refactor the imperative approach to printing a multiplication table shown in Listing 7.18. Our functional alternative is shown in Listing 7.19.

The imperative style reveals itself in Listing 7.18 in two ways. First, invoking `printMultiTable` has a side effect: printing a multiplication table to the standard output. In Listing 7.19, we refactored the function so that it returns the multiplication table as a string. Since the function no longer prints, we renamed it `multiTable`. As mentioned previously, one advantage of side-effect-free functions is they are easier to unit test. To test `printMultiTable`, you would need to somehow redefine `print` and `println` so you could check the output for correctness. You could test `multiTable` more easily by checking its string result.

The other telltale sign of the imperative style in `printMultiTable` is its `while` loop and `vars`. By contrast, the `multiTable` function uses `vals`, for expressions, *helper functions*, and calls to `mkString`.

```
// Returns a row as a sequence
def makeRowSeq(row: Int) =
  for col <- 1 to 10 yield
    val prod = (row * col).toString
    val padding = " " * (4 - prod.length)
    padding + prod
// Returns a row as a string
def makeRow(row: Int) = makeRowSeq(row).mkString
// Returns table as a string with one row per line
def multiTable() =

  val tableSeq = // a sequence of row strings
    for row <- 1 to 10
    yield makeRow(row)

  tableSeq.mkString("\n")
```

Listing 7.19 · A functional way to create a multiplication table.

We factored out the two helper functions, makeRow and makeRowSeq, to make the code easier to read. Function makeRowSeq uses a for expression whose generator iterates through column numbers 1 through 10. The body of this for calculates the product of row and column, determines the padding needed for the product, and yields the result of concatenating the padding and product strings. The result of the for expression will be a sequence (some subclass of Seq) containing these yielded strings as elements. The other helper function, makeRow, simply invokes mkString on the result returned by makeRowSeq. mkString will concatenate the strings in the sequence and return them as one string.

The multiTable method first initializes tableSeq with the result of a for expression whose generator iterates through row numbers 1 to 10, and for each calls makeRow to get the string for that row. This string is yielded; thus the result of this for expression will be a sequence of row strings. The only remaining task is to convert the sequence of strings into a single string. The call to mkString accomplishes this, and because we pass "\n", we get an end of line character inserted between each string. If you pass the string returned by multiTable to println, you'll see the same output that's produced by calling printMultiTable.

134

1	2	3	4	5	6	7	8	9	10
2	4	6	8	10	12	14	16	18	20
3	6	9	12	15	18	21	24	27	30
4	8	12	16	20	24	28	32	36	40
5	10	15	20	25	30	35	40	45	50
6	12	18	24	30	36	42	48	54	60
7	14	21	28	35	42	49	56	63	70
8	16	24	32	40	48	56	64	72	80
9	18	27	36	45	54	63	72	81	90
10	20	30	40	50	60	70	80	90	100

7.9 Conclusion

Scala's built-in control structures are minimal, but they do the job. They act much like their imperative equivalents, but because they tend to result in a value, they support a functional style, too. Just as important, they are careful in what they omit, thus leaving room for one of Scala's most powerful features, the function literal, which will be described in the next chapter.

Chapter 8

Functions and Closures

When programs get larger, you need some way to divide them into smaller, more manageable pieces. For dividing up control flow, Scala offers an approach familiar to all experienced programmers: divide the code into functions. In fact, Scala offers several ways to define functions that are not present in Java. Besides methods, which are functions that are members of some object, there are also functions nested within functions, function literals, and function values. This chapter takes you on a tour through all of these flavors of functions in Scala.

8.1 Methods

The most common way to define a function is as a member of some object; such a function is called a *method*. As an example, Listing 8.1 shows two methods that together read a file with a given name and print out all lines whose length exceeds a given width. Every printed line is prefixed with the name of the file it appears in.

The `padLines` method takes `text` and `minWidth` as parameters. It calls `linesIterator` on `text`, which returns an iterator of the lines in the string, excluding any end-of-line characters. The `for` expression processes each of these lines by calling the helper method, `padLine`. The `padLine` method takes two parameters: a `minWidth` and a `line`. It tests whether the length of the line is less than the given width, and, if so, appends an appropriate number of spaces to the end of the line so that its length is `minWidth`.

So far, this is very similar to what you would do in any object-oriented language. However, the concept of a function in Scala is more general than

137

```
object Padding:

  def padLines(text: String, minWidth: Int): String =
    val paddedLines =
      for line <- text.linesIterator yield
        padLine(line, minWidth)
    paddedLines.mkString("\n")

  private def padLine(line: String, minWidth: Int): String =
    if line.length >= minWidth then line
    else line + " " * (minWidth - line.length)
```

Listing 8.1 · Padding with a private padLine method.

a method. Scala's other ways to express functions will be explained in the following sections.

8.2   Local functions

The construction of the padLines method in the previous section demon-strated an important design principle of the functional programming style: programs should be decomposed into many small functions that each do a well-defined task. Individual functions are often quite small. The advantage of this style is that it gives a programmer many building blocks that can be flexibly composed to do more difficult things. Each building block should be simple enough to be understood individually.

One problem with this approach is that all the helper function names can pollute the program namespace. In the REPL this is not so much of a problem, but once functions are packaged in reusable classes and objects, it's desirable to hide the helper functions from clients of a class. They often do not make sense individually, and you often want to keep enough flexibility to delete the helper functions if you later rewrite the class in a different way.

In Java, your main tool for this purpose is the private method. This private-method approach works in Scala as well, as demonstrated in List-ing 8.1, but Scala offers an additional approach: you can define functions inside other functions. Just like local variables, such local functions are vis-ible only in their enclosing block. Here's an example:

```
def padLines(text: String, minWidth: Int): String =
  def padLine(line: String, minWidth: Int): String =
    if line.length >= minWidth then line
    else line + " " * (minWidth - line.length)
  val paddedLines =
    for line <- text.linesIterator yield
      padLine(line, minWidth)
  paddedLines.mkString("\n")
```

In this example, we refactored the original Padding version, shown in Listing 8.1, by transforming private method, padLine, into a local function of padLines. To do so we removed the private modifier, which can only be applied (and is only needed) for members, and placed the definition of padLine inside the definition of padLines. As a local function, padLine is in scope inside padLines, but inaccessible outside.

Now that padLine is defined inside padLines, however, another improvement becomes possible. Notice how minWidth is passed unchanged into the helper function? This is not necessary because local functions can access the parameters of their enclosing function. You can just use the parameters of the outer padLines function, as shown in Listing 8.2.

```
object Padding:

  def padLines(text: String, minWidth: Int): String =

    def padLine(line: String): String =
      if line.length >= minWidth then line
      else line + " " * (minWidth - line.length)

    val paddedLines =
      for line <- text.linesIterator yield
        padLine(line)

    paddedLines.mkString("\n")
```

Listing 8.2 · LongLines with a local processLine function.

Simpler, isn't it? This use of an enclosing function's parameters is a common and useful example of the general nesting Scala provides. The nesting and scoping described in Section 7.7 applies to all Scala constructs, including functions. It's a simple principle, but very powerful.

8.3   First-class functions

Scala has *first-class functions*. Not only can you define functions and call them, but you can write down functions as unnamed *literals* and then pass them around as *values*. We introduced function literals in Chapter 2 and showed the basic syntax in Figure 2.2 on page 32.

A function literal is compiled into a Java method handle that, when instantiated at runtime, is a *function value*.[1] Thus the distinction between function literals and values is that function literals exist in the source code, whereas function values exist as objects at runtime. The distinction is much like that between classes (source code) and objects (runtime).

Here is a simple example of a function literal that adds one to a number:

```
(x: Int) => x + 1
```

The => designates that this function converts the parameter on the left (any integer x) to the result of evaluating the expression on the right (x + 1). So, this is a function mapping any integer x to x + 1.

Function values are objects, so you can store them in variables if you like. They are functions, too, so you can invoke them using the usual parentheses function-call notation. Here is an example of both activities:

```
val increase = (x: Int) => x + 1
increase(10)    // 11
```

If you want to have more than one statement in the function literal, you can place one statement per line after the => in an indented block. Just like a method, when the function value is invoked, all of the statements will be executed, and the value returned from the function is whatever results from evaluating the last expression.

```
val addTwo = (x: Int) =>
  val increment = 2
  x + increment
addTwo(10)    // 12
```

---

[1]Every function value is an instance of one of several FunctionN traits in package scala, such as Function0 for functions with no parameters, Function1 for functions with one parameter, and so on. Each FunctionN trait has an apply method used to invoke the function.

So now you have seen the nuts and bolts of function literals and function values. Many Scala libraries give you opportunities to use them. For example, a `foreach` method is available for all collections.[2] It takes a function as an argument and invokes that function on each of its elements. Here is how it can be used to print out all of the elements of a list:

```
scala> val someNumbers = List(-11, -10, -5, 0, 5, 10)
val someNumbers: List[Int] = List(-11, -10, -5, 0, 5, 10)

scala> someNumbers.foreach((x: Int) => println(x))
-11
-10
-5
0
5
10
```

As another example, collection types also have a `filter` method. This method selects those elements of a collection that pass a test the user supplies. That test is supplied using a function. For example, the function `(x: Int) => x > 0` could be used for filtering. This function maps positive integers to true and all others to false. Here is how to use it with `filter`:

```
scala> someNumbers.filter((x: Int) => x > 0)
val res4: List[Int] = List(5, 10)
```

Methods like `foreach` and `filter` are described further later in the book. Chapter 14 talks about their use in class `List`. Chapter 15 discusses their use with other collection types.

8.4   Short forms of function literals

Scala provides a number of ways to leave out redundant information and write function literals more briefly. Keep your eyes open for these opportunities, because they allow you to remove clutter from your code.

One way to make a function literal more brief is to leave off the parameter types. Thus, the previous example with filter could be written like this:

---

[2]A `foreach` method is defined in trait `Iterable`, a common supertrait of `List`, `Set`, `Array`, and `Map`. See Chapter 15 for the details.

```
scala> someNumbers.filter((x) => x > 0)
val res5: List[Int] = List(5, 10)
```

The Scala compiler knows that x must be an integer, because it sees that you are immediately using the function to filter a list of integers (referred to by someNumbers). This is called *target typing* because the targeted usage of an expression (in this case, an argument to someNumbers.filter()) is allowed to influence the typing of that expression (in this case to determine the type of the x parameter). The precise details of target typing are not important. You can simply start by writing a function literal without the argument type, and if the compiler gets confused, add in the type. Over time you'll get a feel for which situations the compiler can and cannot puzzle out.

A second way to remove useless characters is to leave out parentheses around a parameter whose type is inferred. In the previous example, the parentheses around x are unnecessary:

```
scala> someNumbers.filter(x => x > 0)
val res6: List[Int] = List(5, 10)
```

8.5   Placeholder syntax

To make a function literal even more concise, you can use underscores as placeholders for one or more parameters, so long as each parameter appears only one time within the function literal. For example, _ > 0 is very short notation for a function that checks whether a value is greater than zero:

```
scala> someNumbers.filter(_ > 0)
val res7: List[Int] = List(5, 10)
```

You can think of the underscore as a "blank" in the expression that needs to be "filled in." This blank will be filled in with an argument to the function each time the function is invoked. For example, given that someNumbers was initialized on page 141 to the value List(-11, -10, -5, 0, 5, 10), the filter method will replace the blank in _ > 0 first with -11, as in -11 > 0, then with -10, as in -10 > 0, then with -5, as in -5 > 0, and so on to the end of the List. The function literal _ > 0, therefore, is equivalent to the slightly more verbose x => x > 0, as demonstrated here:

```
scala> someNumbers.filter(x => x > 0)
val res8: List[Int] = List(5, 10)
```

Sometimes when you use underscores as placeholders for parameters, the compiler might not have enough information to infer missing parameter types. For example, suppose you write _ + _ by itself:

```
scala> val f = _ + _
              ^
```

```
      error: missing parameter type for expanded function
  ((x$1: <error>, x$2) => x$1.$plus(x$2))
```

In such cases, you can specify the types using a colon, like this:

```
scala> val f = (_: Int) + (_: Int)
val f: (Int, Int) => Int = $$Lambda$1075/1481958694@289fff3c
```

```
scala> f(5, 10)
val res9: Int = 15
```

Note that _ + _ expands into a literal for a function that takes two parameters. This is why you can use this short form only if each parameter appears in the function literal exactly once. Multiple underscores mean multiple parameters, not reuse of a single parameter repeatedly. The first underscore represents the first parameter, the second underscore the second parameter, the third underscore the third parameter, and so on.

8.6   Partially applied functions

In Scala, when you invoke a function, passing in any needed arguments, you *apply* that function *to* the arguments. For example, given the following function:

```
def sum(a: Int, b: Int, c: Int) = a + b + c
```

You could apply the function sum to the arguments 1, 2, and 3 like this:

```
sum(1, 2, 3)    // 6
```

When you use placeholder syntax where each underscore is used to forward a parameter to a method, you are writing a *partially applied function*. A partially applied function is an expression in which you don't supply all of the arguments needed by the function. Instead, you supply some, or none, of the needed arguments. For example, to create a partially applied function expression involving sum, in which you supply none of the three required arguments, you could use an underscore for each parameter. The resulting function can then be stored in a variable. Here's an example:

```
val a = sum(_, _, _) // a has type (Int, Int, Int) => Int
```

Given this code, the Scala compiler instantiates a function value that takes the three integer parameters missing from the partially applied function expression, sum(_, _, _), and assigns a reference to that new function value to the variable a. When you apply three arguments to this new function value, it will turn around and invoke sum, passing in those same three arguments:

```
a(1, 2, 3)    // 6
```

Here's what just happened: The variable named a refers to a function value object. This function value is an instance of a class generated automatically by the Scala compiler from sum(_, _, _), the partially applied function expression. The class generated by the compiler has an apply method that takes three arguments.[3] The generated class's apply method takes three arguments because three is the number of arguments missing in the sum(_, _, _) expression. The Scala compiler translates the expression a(1, 2, 3) into an invocation of the function value's apply method, passing in the three arguments 1, 2, and 3. Thus, a(1, 2, 3) is a short form for:

```
a.apply(1, 2, 3)    // 6
```

This apply method, defined in the class generated automatically by the Scala compiler from the expression sum(_, _, _), simply forwards those three missing parameters to sum, and returns the result. In this case apply invokes sum(1, 2, 3), and returns what sum returns, which is 6.

Another way to think about this kind of expression, in which an underscore is used to represent an entire parameter list, is as a way to transform a def into a function value. For example, if you have a local function, such as sum(a: Int, b: Int, c: Int): Int, you can "wrap" it in a function value whose apply method has the same parameter list and result types. When you apply this function value to some arguments, it in turn applies sum to

---

[3]The generated class extends trait Function3, which declares a three-arg apply method.

those same arguments and returns the result. Although you can't assign a method or nested function to a variable, or pass it as an argument to another function, you can do these things if you wrap the method or nested function in a function value.

Now, although sum(_, _, _) is indeed a partially applied function, it may not be obvious to you why it is called this. It has this name because you are not applying that function to all of its arguments. In the case of sum(_, _, _), you are applying it to *none* of its arguments. But you can also express a partially applied function by supplying only *some* of the required arguments. Here's an example:

```
val b = sum(1, _, 3) // b has type Int => Int
```

In this case, you've supplied the first and last argument to sum, but not the middle argument. Since only one argument is missing, the Scala compiler generates a new function class whose apply method takes one argument. When invoked with that one argument, this generated function's apply method invokes sum, passing in 1, the argument passed to the function, and 3. Here are some examples:

```
b(2)    // 6
b(5)    // 9
```

In the first case, b.apply invoked sum(1, 2, 3), and in the second case, b.apply invoked sum(1, 5, 3).

If you are writing a partially applied function expression in which you leave off all parameters, such as sum(_, _, _), you can express it more concisely by leaving off the entire parameter list. Here's an example:

```
val c = sum // c has type (Int, Int, Int) => Int
```

Because sum is the name of a method, not a variable that refers to a value, the compiler will create a function value with the same signature as the method that wraps the method call, a process that is called *eta expansion*. In other words, sum is a more concise way to write sum(_, _, _). Here's an example invocation of the function referenced by c:

```
c(10, 20, 30)    // 60
```

8.7 Closures

So far in this chapter, all the examples of function literals have referred only to passed parameters. For example, in (x: Int) => x > 0, the only variable used in the function body, x > 0, is x, which is defined as a parameter to the function. You can, however, refer to variables defined elsewhere:

```
(x: Int) => x + more   // how much more?
```

This function adds "more" to its argument, but what is more? From the point of view of this function, more is a *free variable* because the function literal does not itself give a meaning to it. The x variable, by contrast, is a *bound variable* because it does have a meaning in the context of the function: it is defined as the function's lone parameter, an Int. If you try using this function literal by itself, without any more defined in its scope, the compiler will complain:

```
scala> (x: Int) => x + more
1 |(x: Int) => x + more
  |                 ^^^^
  |                 Not found: more
```

On the other hand, the same function literal will work fine so long as there is something available named more:

```
var more = 1
val addMore = (x: Int) => x + more
addMore(10)    // 11
```

The function value (the object) that's created at runtime from this function literal is called a *closure*. The name arises from the act of "closing" the function literal by "capturing" the bindings of its free variables. A function literal with no free variables, such as (x: Int) => x + 1, is called a *closed term*, where a *term* is a bit of source code. Thus a function value created at runtime from this function literal is not a closure in the strictest sense, because (x: Int) => x + 1 is already closed as written. But any function literal with free variables, such as (x: Int) => x + more, is an *open term*. Therefore, any function value created at runtime from (x: Int) => x + more will, by definition, require that a binding for its free variable, more, be captured. The resulting function value, which will contain a reference to the captured more

146

variable, is called a closure because the function value is the end product of the act of closing the open term, (x: Int) => x + more.

This example brings up a question: What happens if more changes after the closure is created? In Scala, the answer is that the closure sees the change. For example:

```
more = 9999
addMore(10)     // 10009
```

Intuitively, Scala's closures capture variables themselves, not the value to which variables refer.[4] As the previous example shows, the closure created for (x: Int) => x + more sees the change to more made outside the closure. The same is true in the opposite direction. Changes made by a closure to a captured variable are visible outside the closure. Here's an example:

```
val someNumbers = List(-11, -10, -5, 0, 5, 10)
var sum = 0
someNumbers.foreach(sum +=  _)
sum     // -11
```

This example uses a roundabout way to sum the numbers in a List. Variable sum is in a surrounding scope from the function literal sum += _, which adds numbers to sum. Even though it is the closure modifying sum at runtime, the resulting total, −11, is still visible outside the closure.

What if a closure accesses some variable that has several different copies as the program runs? For example, what if a closure uses a local variable of some function, and the function is invoked many times? Which instance of that variable gets used at each access?

Only one answer is consistent with the rest of the language: the instance used is the one that was active at the time the closure was created. For example, here is a function that creates and returns "increase" closures:

```
def makeIncreaser(more: Int) = (x: Int) => x + more
```

Each time this function is called it will create a new closure. Each closure will access the more variable that was active when the closure was created.

---

[4]By contrast, Java's lambdas do not allow you to access local variables in surrounding scopes unless they are final or effectively final, so there is no difference between capturing a variable and capturing its currently held value.

```
val inc1 = makeIncreaser(1)
val inc9999 = makeIncreaser(9999)
```

When you call makeIncreaser(1), a closure is created and returned that captures the value 1 as the binding for more. Similarly, when you call makeIncreaser(9999), a closure that captures the value 9999 for more is returned. When you apply these closures to arguments (in this case, there's just one argument, x, which must be passed in), the result that comes back depends on how more was defined when the closure was created:

```
inc1(10)       // 11
inc9999(10)    // 10009
```

It makes no difference that the more in this case is a parameter to a method call that has already returned. The Scala compiler rearranges things in cases like these so that the captured parameter lives out on the heap, instead of the stack, and thus can outlive the method call that created it. This rearrangement is all taken care of automatically, so you don't have to worry about it. Capture any variable you like: val, var, or parameter.[5]

8.8 Special function call forms

Most functions and function calls you encounter will be as you have seen so far in this chapter. The function will have a fixed number of parameters, the call will have an equal number of arguments, and the arguments will be specified in the same order and number as the parameters.

Since function calls are so central to programming in Scala, however, a few special forms of function definitions and function calls have been added to the language to address some special needs. Scala supports repeated parameters, named arguments, and default arguments.

Repeated parameters

Scala allows you to indicate that the last parameter to a function may be repeated. This allows clients to pass variable length argument lists to the

---

[5]On the other hand, when programming in the functional style you'll only capture vals. Also, when programming in an imperative style in a concurrent setting, capturing vars can lead to concurrency bugs due to unsynchronized access to shared mutable state.

function. To denote a repeated parameter, place an asterisk after the type of the parameter. For example:

```
scala> def echo(args: String*) =
         for arg <- args do println(arg)
def echo(args: String*): Unit
```

Defined this way, echo can be called with zero to many String arguments:

```
scala> echo()

scala> echo("one")
one

scala> echo("hello", "world!")
hello
world!
```

Inside the function, the type of the repeated parameter is a Seq of the declared type of the parameter. Thus, the type of args inside the echo function, which is declared as type "String*" is actually Seq[String]. Nevertheless, if you have a sequence of the appropriate type, and you attempt to pass it as a repeated parameter, you'll get a compiler error:

```
scala> val seq = Seq("What's", "up", "doc?")
val seq: Seq[String] = List(What's, up, doc?)

scala> echo(seq)
1 |echo(seq)
  |      ^^^
  |      Found:    (seq : Seq[String])
  |      Required: String
```

To accomplish this, you'll need to append the sequence argument with a symbol, like this:

```
scala> echo(seq*)
What's
up
doc?
```

This notation tells the compiler to pass each element of seq as its own argument to echo, rather than all of it as a single argument.

Named arguments

In a normal function call, the arguments in the call are matched one by one in the order of the parameters of the called function:

```
def speed(distance: Float, time: Float) = distance / time
speed(100, 10)    // 10.0
```

In this call, the 100 is matched to distance and the 10 to time. The 100 and 10 are matched in the same order as the formal parameters are listed.

Named arguments allow you to pass arguments to a function in a different order. The syntax is simply that each argument is preceded by a parameter name and an equals sign. For example, the following call to speed is equivalent to speed(100,10):

```
speed(distance = 100, time = 10)    // 10.0
```

Called with named arguments, the arguments can be reversed without changing the meaning:

```
speed(time = 10, distance = 100)    // 10.0
```

It is also possible to mix positional and named arguments. In that case, the positional arguments come first. Named arguments are most frequently used in combination with default parameter values.

Default parameter values

Scala lets you specify default values for function parameters. The argument for such a parameter can optionally be omitted from a function call, in which case the corresponding argument will be filled in with the default.

For example, were you to create a companion object for the Rational class shown in Listing 6.5, you could define an apply factory method as shown in Listing 8.3. Function apply has two parameters, numer and denom, and it has a default value of 1 for denom.

If you call the function as Rational(42), thus specifying no argument to be used for denom, then denom will be set to its default value of 1. You could

```
// In same source file as class Rational
object Rational:
  def apply(numer: Int, denom: Int = 1) =
    new Rational(numer, denom)
```

Listing 8.3 · A parameter with a default value.

also call the function with an explicit denominator. For example, you could set the denominator to 83 by calling the function as `Rational(42, 83)`.[6]

Default parameters are especially helpful when used in combination with named parameters. In Listing 8.4, the `point` function has two optional parameters, x and y. Both parameters have a default value of 0.

```
def point(x: Int = 0, y: Int = 0) = (x, y)
```

Listing 8.4 · A function with two parameters that have defaults.

Function `point` can be called as `point()` to have both parameters filled in with their default values. Using named arguments, however, either of the parameters can be specified while leaving the other as the default. To specify x, leaving y at its default, call it like this:

```
point(x = 42)
```

To specify y, leaving x at its default, call it like this:

```
point(y = 1000)
```

8.9 "SAM" types

In Java, a lambda expression can be used anywhere an instance of a class or interface that contains just a *single abstract method* (SAM) is required. Java's `ActionListener` is such an interface, because it contains a single abstract method, `actionPerformed`. Thus a lambda expression can be used to register an action listener on a Swing button. Here's an example:

---

[6]A default parameter value of 1 could also have been used for class Rational's d parameter in Listing 6.5, as in class `Rational(n: Int, d: Int = 1)`, instead of using the auxiliary constructor that fills in 1 for d.

151

```
JButton button = new JButton(); // This is Java
button.addActionListener(
  event -> System.out.println("pressed!")
);
```

In Scala, you could also use an anonymous inner class instance in the same situation, but you might prefer to use a function literal, like this:

```
val button = new JButton
button.addActionListener(
  _ => println("pressed!")
)
```

Scala enables a function literal to be used in this case, because as in Java, Scala will allow a function type to be used where an instance of a class or trait declaring a single abstract method (SAM) is required. This will work with any SAM. For example, you might define a trait, Increaser, with a single abstract method, increase:

```
trait Increaser:
  def increase(i: Int): Int
```

You could then define a method that takes an Increaser:

```
def increaseOne(increaser: Increaser): Int =
  increaser.increase(1)
```

To invoke your new method, you could pass in an anonymous instance of trait Increaser, like this:

```
increaseOne(
  new Increaser:
    def increase(i: Int): Int = i + 7
)
```

In Scala versions 2.12 and greater, however, you could alternatively just use a function literal, because Increaser is a SAM type:

```
increaseOne(i => i + 7) // Scala
```

8.10 Tail recursion

In Section 7.2, we mentioned that to transform a `while` loop that updates vars into a more functional style that uses only `vals`, you will usually need to use recursion. Here's an example of a recursive function that approximates a value by repeatedly improving a guess until it is good enough:

```
def approximate(guess: Double): Double =
  if isGoodEnough(guess) then guess
  else approximate(improve(guess))
```

A function like this is often used in search problems, with appropriate implementations for `isGoodEnough` and `improve`. If you want the `approximate` function to run faster, you might be tempted to write it with a `while` loop to try and speed it up, like this:

```
def approximateLoop(initialGuess: Double): Double =
  var guess = initialGuess
  while !isGoodEnough(guess) do
    guess = improve(guess)
  guess
```

Which of the two versions of `approximate` is preferable? In terms of brevity and `var` avoidance, the first, functional one wins. But is the imperative approach perhaps more efficient? In fact, if we measure execution times, it turns out that they are almost exactly the same!

This might seem surprising because a recursive call looks much more "expansive" than a simple jump from the end of a loop to its beginning. However, in the case of `approximate` above, the Scala compiler is able to apply an important optimization. Note that the recursive call is the last thing that happens in the evaluation of function `approximate`'s body. Functions like `approximate`, which call themselves as their last action, are called *tail recursive*. The Scala compiler detects tail recursion and replaces it with a jump back to the beginning of the function, after updating the function parameters with the new values.

The moral is that you should not shy away from using recursive algorithms to solve your problem. Often, a recursive solution is more elegant and concise than a loop-based one. If the solution is tail recursive, there won't be any runtime overhead to be paid.

Tracing tail-recursive functions

A tail-recursive function will not build a new stack frame for each call; all calls will execute in a single frame. This may surprise a programmer inspecting a stack trace of a program that failed. For example, this function calls itself some number of times then throws an exception:

```
def boom(x: Int): Int =
  if x == 0 then throw new Exception("boom!")
  else boom(x - 1) + 1
```

This function is *not* tail recursive, because it performs an increment operation after the recursive call. You'll get what you expect when you run it:

```
scala>  boom(3)
java.lang.Exception: boom!
      at .boom(<console>:5)
      at .boom(<console>:6)
      at .boom(<console>:6)
      at .boom(<console>:6)
      at .<init>(<console>:6)
...
```

If you now modify boom so that it does become tail recursive:

```
def bang(x: Int): Int =
  if x == 0 then throw new Exception("bang!")
  else bang(x - 1)
```

You'll get:

```
scala> bang(5)
java.lang.Exception: bang!
      at .bang(<console>:5)
      at .<init>(<console>:6) ...
```

This time, you see only a single stack frame for bang. You might think that bang crashed before it called itself, but this is not the case.

You would typically add a `scala.annotation.tailrec` annotation to a method that needs to be tail recursive, for instance because you expect that it would recurse very deeply otherwise. To make sure that the Scala

Tail call optimization

The compiled code for `approximate` is essentially the same as the compiled code for `approximateLoop`. Both functions compile down to the same thirteen instructions of Java bytecodes. If you look through the bytecodes generated by the Scala compiler for the tail recursive method, `approximate`, you'll see that although both `isGoodEnough` and `improve` are invoked in the body of the method, `approximate` is not. The Scala compiler optimized away the recursive call:

```
public double approximate(double);
  Code:
    0:    aload_0
    1:    astore_3
    2:    aload_0
    3:    dload_1
    4:    invokevirtual    #24; //Method isGoodEnough:(D)Z
    7:    ifeq    12
    10:   dload_1
    11:   dreturn
    12:   aload_0
    13:   dload_1
    14:   invokevirtual    #27; //Method improve:(D)D
    17:   dstore_1
    18:   goto    2
```

compiler does perform tail-recursion optimization on a method, you can add `@tailrec` in front of the method definition. If the optimization cannot be performed, you will then get a compiler error that indicates why the method is not tail recursive.

Limits of tail recursion

The use of tail recursion in Scala is fairly limited because the JVM instruction set makes implementing more advanced forms of tail recursion very difficult. Scala only optimizes directly recursive calls back to the same function making the call. If the recursion is indirect, as in the following example of two mutually recursive functions, no optimization is possible:

```
def isEven(x: Int): Boolean =
  if x == 0 then true else isOdd(x - 1)
def isOdd(x: Int): Boolean =
  if x == 0 then false else isEven(x - 1)
```

You also won't get a tail-call optimization if the final call goes to a function value. Consider for instance the following recursive code:

```
val funValue = nestedFun
def nestedFun(x: Int): Unit =
  if x != 0 then
    println(x)
    funValue(x - 1)
```

The funValue variable refers to a function value that essentially wraps a call to nestedFun. When you apply the function value to an argument, it turns around and applies nestedFun to that same argument, and returns the result. Therefore, you might hope the Scala compiler would perform a tail-call optimization, but in this case it would not. Tail-call optimization is limited to situations where a method or nested function calls itself directly as its last operation, without going through a function value or some other intermediary. (If you don't fully understand tail recursion yet, see Section 8.10).

8.11 Conclusion

This chapter has given you a grand tour of functions in Scala. In addition to methods, Scala provides local functions, function literals, and function values. In addition to normal function calls, Scala provides partially applied functions and functions with repeated parameters. When possible, function calls are implemented as optimized tail calls, and thus many nice-looking recursive functions run just as quickly as hand-optimized versions that use while loops. The next chapter will build on these foundations and show how Scala's rich support for functions helps you abstract over control.

Chapter 9

Control Abstraction

In Chapter 7, we pointed out that Scala doesn't have many built-in control abstractions because it gives you the ability to create your own. In the previous chapter, you learned about function values. In this chapter, we'll show you how to apply function values to create new control abstractions. Along the way, you'll also learn about currying and by-name parameters.

9.1 Reducing code duplication

All functions are separated into common parts, which are the same in every invocation of the function, and non-common parts, which may vary from one function invocation to the next. The common parts are in the body of the function, while the non-common parts must be supplied via arguments. When you use a function value as an argument, the non-common part of the algorithm is itself some other algorithm! At each invocation of such a function, you can pass in a different function value as an argument, and the invoked function will, at times of its choosing, invoke the passed function value. These *higher-order functions*—functions that take functions as parameters—give you extra opportunities to condense and simplify code.

One benefit of higher-order functions is they enable you to create control abstractions that allow you to reduce code duplication. For example, suppose you are writing a file browser, and you want to provide an API that allows users to search for files matching some criterion. First, you add a facility to search for files whose names end in a particular string. This would enable your users to find, for example, all files with a ".scala" extension. You could provide such an API by defining a public filesEnding method inside

157

a singleton object like this:

```scala
object FileMatcher:
  private def filesHere = (new java.io.File(".")).listFiles

  def filesEnding(query: String) =
    for file <- filesHere if file.getName.endsWith(query)
    yield file
```

The `filesEnding` method obtains the list of all files in the current directory using the private helper method `filesHere`, then filters them based on whether each file name ends with the user-specified query. Given `filesHere` is private, the `filesEnding` method is the only accessible method defined in `FileMatcher`, the API you provide to your users.

So far so good, and there is no repeated code yet. Later on, though, you decide to let people search based on any part of the file name. This is good for when your users cannot remember if they named a file `phb-important.doc`, `joyful-phb-report.doc`, `may2020salesdoc.phb`, or something entirely different; they just know that "phb" appears in the name somewhere. You go back to work and add this function to your `FileMatcher` API:

```scala
def filesContaining(query: String) =
  for file <- filesHere if file.getName.contains(query)
  yield file
```

This function works just like `filesEnding`. It searches `filesHere`, checks the name, and returns the file if the name matches. The only difference is that this function uses `contains` instead of `endsWith`.

The months go by, and the program becomes more successful. Eventually, you give in to the requests of a few power users who want to search based on regular expressions. These sloppy users have immense directories with thousands of files, and they would like to do things like find all "pdf" files that have "oopsla" in their filename somewhere. To support them, you write this function:

```scala
def filesRegex(query: String) =
  for file <- filesHere if file.getName.matches(query)
  yield file
```

Experienced programmers will notice all of this repetition and wonder if it can be factored into a common helper function. Doing it the obvious way does not work, however. You would like to be able to do the following:

```
def filesMatching(query: String, method) =
  for file <- filesHere if file.getName.method(query)
  yield file
```

This approach would work in some dynamic languages, but Scala does not allow pasting together code at runtime like this. So what do you do?

Function values provide an answer. While you cannot pass around a method name as a value, you can get the same effect by passing around a function value that calls the method for you. In this case, you could add a matcher parameter to the method whose sole purpose is to check a file name against a query:

```
def filesMatching(query: String,
    matcher: (String, String) => Boolean) =

  for file <- filesHere if matcher(file.getName, query)
  yield file
```

In this version of the method, the if clause now uses matcher to check the file name against the query. Precisely what this check does depends on what is specified as the matcher. Take a look, now, at the type of matcher itself. It is a function, and thus has a => in the type. This function takes two string arguments—the file name and the query—and returns a boolean, so the type of this function is (String, String) => Boolean.

Given this new filesMatching helper method, you can simplify the three searching methods by having them call the helper method, passing in an appropriate function:

```
def filesEnding(query: String) =
  filesMatching(query, _.endsWith(_))

def filesContaining(query: String) =
  filesMatching(query, _.contains(_))

def filesRegex(query: String) =
  filesMatching(query, _.matches(_))
```

The function literals shown in this example use the placeholder syntax, introduced in the previous chapter, which may not as yet feel very natural to you. So here's a clarification of how placeholders are used: The function literal _.endsWith(_), used in the filesEnding method, means the same thing as:

```
(fileName: String, query: String) => fileName.endsWith(query)
```

Because filesMatching takes a function that requires two String arguments, you need not specify the types of the arguments; you could just write (fileName, query) => fileName.endsWith(query). Since the parameters are each used only once in the body of the function (*i.e.*, the first parameter, fileName, is used first in the body, and the second parameter, query, is used second), you can use the placeholder syntax: _.endsWith(_). The first underscore is a placeholder for the first parameter, the file name, and the second underscore a placeholder for the second parameter, the query string.

This code is already simplified, but it can actually be even shorter. Notice that the query gets passed to filesMatching, but filesMatching does nothing with the query except to pass it back to the passed matcher function. This passing back and forth is unnecessary because the caller already knew the query to begin with! You might as well remove the query parameter from filesMatching and matcher, thus simplifying the code as shown in Listing 9.1.

```
object FileMatcher:
  private def filesHere = (new java.io.File(".")).listFiles

  private def filesMatching(matcher: String => Boolean) =
    for file <- filesHere if matcher(file.getName)
    yield file

  def filesEnding(query: String) =
    filesMatching(_.endsWith(query))

  def filesContaining(query: String) =
    filesMatching(_.contains(query))

  def filesRegex(query: String) =
    filesMatching(_.matches(query))
```

Listing 9.1 · Using closures to reduce code duplication.

This example demonstrates the way in which first-class functions can help you eliminate code duplication where it would be very difficult to do so without them. Moreover, this example demonstrates how closures can help you reduce code duplication. The function literals used in the previous example, such as _.endsWith(_) and _.contains(_), are instantiated at runtime into function values that are *not* closures because they don't capture any free variables. Both variables used in the expression, _.endsWith(_), for example, are represented by underscores, which means they are taken from arguments to the function. Thus, _.endsWith(_) uses two bound variables, and no free variables. By contrast, the function literal _.endsWith(query), used in the most recent example, contains one bound variable, the argument represented by the underscore, and one free variable named query. It is only because Scala supports closures that you were able to remove the query parameter from filesMatching in the most recent example, thereby simplifying the code even further.

9.2   Simplifying client code

The previous example demonstrated that higher-order functions can help reduce code duplication as you implement an API. Another important use of higher-order functions is to put them in an API itself to make client code more concise. A good example is provided by the special-purpose looping methods of Scala's collection types.[1] Many of these are listed in Table 3.1 in Chapter 3, but take a look at just one example for now to see why these methods are so useful.

Consider exists, a method that determines whether a passed value is contained in a collection. You could, of course, search for an element by having a var initialized to false, looping through the collection checking each item, and setting the var to true if you find what you are looking for. Here's a method that uses this approach to determine whether a passed List contains a negative number:

---

[1] These special-purpose looping methods are defined in trait Iterable, which is extended by List, Set, and Map. See Chapter 15 for a discussion.

```
def containsNeg(nums: List[Int]): Boolean =
  var exists = false
  for num <- nums do
    if num < 0 then
      exists = true
  exists
```

If you define this method in the REPL, you can call it like this:

```
containsNeg(List(1, 2, 3, 4))    // false
containsNeg(List(1, 2, -3, 4))   // true
```

A more concise way to define the method, though, is by calling the higher-order function `exists` on the passed `List`, like this:

```
def containsNeg(nums: List[Int]) = nums.exists(_ < 0)
```

This version of `containsNeg` yields the same results as the previous:

```
containsNeg(Nil)                 // false
containsNeg(List(0, -1, -2))     // true
```

The `exists` method represents a control abstraction. It is a special-purpose looping construct provided by the Scala library, rather than built into the Scala language like `while` or `for`. In the previous section, the higher-order function, `filesMatching`, reduces code duplication in the implementation of the `object FileMatcher`. The `exists` method provides a similar benefit, but because `exists` is public in Scala's collections API, the code duplication it reduces is client code of that API. If `exists` didn't exist, and you wanted to write a `containsOdd` method to test whether a list contains odd numbers, you might write it like this:

```
def containsOdd(nums: List[Int]): Boolean =
  var exists = false
  for num <- nums do
    if num % 2 == 1 then
      exists = true
  exists
```

If you compare the body of `containsNeg` with that of `containsOdd`, you'll find that everything is repeated except the test condition of an `if` expression. Using `exists`, you could write this instead:

```
def containsOdd(nums: List[Int]) = nums.exists(_ % 2 == 1)
```

The body of the code in this version is again identical to the body of the corresponding `containsNeg` method (the version that uses `exists`), except the condition for which to search is different. Yet the amount of code duplication is much smaller because all of the looping infrastructure is factored out into the `exists` method itself.

There are many other looping methods in Scala's standard library. As with `exists`, they can often shorten your code if you recognize opportunities to use them.

9.3   Currying

In Chapter 1, we said that Scala allows you to create new control abstractions that "feel like native language support." Although the examples you've seen so far are indeed control abstractions, it is unlikely anyone would mistake them for native language support. To understand how to make control abstractions that feel more like language extensions, you first need to understand the functional programming technique called *currying*.

A curried function is applied to multiple argument lists, instead of just one. Listing 9.2 shows a regular, non-curried function, which adds two Int parameters, x and y.

```
def plainOldSum(x: Int, y: Int) = x + y
plainOldSum(1, 2)    // 3
```

Listing 9.2 · Defining and invoking a "plain old" function.

By contrast, Listing 9.3 shows a similar function that's curried. Instead of one list of two Int parameters, you apply this function to two lists of one Int parameter each.

```
def curriedSum(x: Int)(y: Int) = x + y
curriedSum(1)(2)    // 3
```

Listing 9.3 · Defining and invoking a curried function.

What's happening here is that when you invoke `curriedSum`, you actually get two traditional function invocations back to back. The first function invocation takes a single Int parameter named x, and returns a function value for the second function. This second function takes the Int parameter y. Here's a function named first that does in spirit what the first traditional function invocation of curriedSum would do:

```
def first(x: Int) = (y: Int) => x + y
```

Applying the first function to 1—in other words, invoking the first function and passing in 1—yields the second function:

```
val second = first(1) // second has type Int => Int
```

Applying the second function to 2 yields the result:

```
second(2)    // 3
```

These first and second functions are just an illustration of the currying process. They are not directly connected to the curriedSum function. Nevertheless, there is a way to get an actual reference to curriedSum's "second" function. You can use eta expansion to use curriedSum in a partially applied function expression, like this:

```
val onePlus = curriedSum(1) // onePlus has type Int => Int
```

The result is a reference to a function that, when invoked, adds one to its sole Int argument and returns the result:

```
onePlus(2)    // 3
```

And here's how you'd get a function that adds two to its sole Int argument:

```
val twoPlus = curriedSum(2)
twoPlus(2)    // 4
```

9.4 Writing new control structures

In languages with first-class functions, you can effectively make new control structures even though the syntax of the language is fixed. All you need to do is create methods that take functions as arguments.

For example, here is the "twice" control structure, which repeats an operation two times and returns the result:

```
def twice(op: Double => Double, x: Double) = op(op(x))
twice(_ + 1, 5)    // 7.0
```

The type of op in this example is Double => Double, which means it is a function that takes one Double as an argument and returns another Double.

Any time you find a control pattern repeated in multiple parts of your code, you should think about implementing it as a new control structure. Earlier in the chapter you saw filesMatching, a very specialized control pattern. Consider now a more widely used coding pattern: open a resource, operate on it, and then close the resource. You can capture this in a control abstraction using a method like the following:

```
def withPrintWriter(file: File, op: PrintWriter => Unit) =
  val writer = new PrintWriter(file)
  try op(writer)
  finally writer.close()
```

Given such a method, you can use it like this:

```
withPrintWriter(
  new File("date.txt"),
  writer => writer.println(new java.util.Date)
)
```

The advantage of using this method is that it's withPrintWriter, not user code, that assures the file is closed at the end. So it's impossible to forget to close the file. This technique is called the *loan pattern*, because a control-abstraction function, such as withPrintWriter, opens a resource and "loans" it to a function. For instance, withPrintWriter in the previous example loans a PrintWriter to the function, op. When the function completes, it signals that it no longer needs the "borrowed" resource. The resource is then closed in a finally block, to ensure it is indeed closed, regardless of whether the function completes by returning normally or throwing an exception.

One way in which you can make the client code look a bit more like a built-in control structure is to use curly braces instead of parentheses to surround the argument list. In any method invocation in Scala in which you're passing in exactly one argument, you can opt to use curly braces to surround the argument instead of parentheses.

For example, instead of:

```
val s = "Hello, world!"
s.charAt(1)      // 'e'
```

You could write:

```
s.charAt { 1 }   // 'e'
```

In the second example, you used curly braces instead of parentheses to surround the arguments to charAt. This curly braces technique will work, however, only if you're passing in one argument. Here's an attempt at violating that rule:

```
s.substring { 7, 9 }
1 |s.substring { 7, 9 }
  |                ^
  |                     end of statement expected but ',' found
1 |s.substring { 7, 9 }
  |                 ^
  |                     ';' expected, but integer literal found
```

Because you are attempting to pass in two arguments to substring, you get an error when you try to surround those arguments with curly braces. Instead, you'll need to use parentheses:

```
s.substring(7, 9)   // "wo"
```

The purpose of this ability to substitute curly braces for parentheses for passing in one argument is to enable client programmers to write function literals between curly braces. This can make a method call feel more like a control abstraction. Take the withPrintWriter method defined previously as an example. In its most recent form, withPrintWriter takes two arguments, so you can't use curly braces. Nevertheless, because the function passed to withPrintWriter is the last argument in the list, you can use currying to pull the first argument, the File, into a separate argument list. This will leave the function as the lone parameter of the second argument list. Listing 9.4 shows how you'd need to redefine withPrintWriter.

The new version differs from the old one only in that there are now two parameter lists with one parameter each instead of one parameter list with two parameters. Look between the two parameters. In the previous version of withPrintWriter, shown on page 165, you see ...File, op.... But in

```
def withPrintWriter(file: File)(op: PrintWriter => Unit) =
  val writer = new PrintWriter(file)
  try op(writer)
  finally writer.close()
```

Listing 9.4 · Using the loan pattern to write to a file.

this version, you see ...File)(op.... Given the above definition, you can call the method with a more pleasing syntax:

```
val file = new File("date.txt")

withPrintWriter(file) { writer =>
  writer.println(new java.util.Date)
}
```

In this example, the first argument list, which contains one File argument, is written surrounded by parentheses. The second argument list, which contains one function argument, is surrounded by curly braces.

9.5   By-name parameters

The withPrintWriter method shown in the previous section differs from built-in control structures of the language, such as if and while, in that the "body" of the control abstraction (the code between the curly braces) takes an argument. The function passed to withPrintWriter requires one argument of type PrintWriter. This argument shows up as the "writer =>" in:

```
withPrintWriter(file) { writer =>
  writer.println(new java.util.Date)
}
```

But what if you want to implement something more like if or while, where there is no value to pass into the body? To help with such situations, Scala provides by-name parameters.

As a concrete example, suppose you want to implement an assertion construct called myAssert.[2] The myAssert function will take a function value

---

[2]You'll call this myAssert, not assert, because Scala provides an assert of its own, which will be described in Section 25.1.

167

as input and consult a flag to decide what to do. If the flag is set, myAssert will invoke the passed function and verify that it returns true. If the flag is turned off, myAssert will quietly do nothing at all.

Without using by-name parameters, you could write myAssert like this:

```
var assertionsEnabled = true

def myAssert(predicate: () => Boolean) =
  if assertionsEnabled && !predicate() then
    throw new AssertionError
```

The definition is fine, but using it is a little bit awkward:

```
myAssert(() => 5 > 3)
```

You would really prefer to leave out the empty parameter list and => symbol in the function literal and write the code like this:

```
myAssert(5 > 3) // Won't work, because missing () =>
```

By-name parameters exist precisely so that you can do this. To make a by-name parameter, you give the parameter a type starting with => instead of () =>. For example, you could change myAssert's predicate parameter into a by-name parameter by changing its type, "() => Boolean", into "=> Boolean". Listing 9.5 shows how that would look:

```
def byNameAssert(predicate: => Boolean) =
  if assertionsEnabled && !predicate then
    throw new AssertionError
```

Listing 9.5 · Using a by-name parameter.

Now you can leave out the empty parameter in the property you want to assert. The result is that using byNameAssert looks exactly like using a built-in control structure:

```
byNameAssert(5 > 3)
```

A by-name type, in which the empty parameter list, (), is left out, is only allowed for parameters. There is no such thing as a by-name variable or a by-name field.

Now, you may be wondering why you couldn't simply write myAssert using a plain old Boolean for the type of its parameter, like this:

```
def boolAssert(predicate: Boolean) =
  if assertionsEnabled && !predicate then
    throw new AssertionError
```

This formulation is also legal, of course, and the code using this version of boolAssert would still look exactly as before:

```
boolAssert(5 > 3)
```

Nevertheless, one difference exists between these two approaches that is important to note. Because the type of boolAssert's parameter is Boolean, the expression inside the parentheses in boolAssert(5 > 3) is evaluated *before* the call to boolAssert. The expression 5 > 3 yields true, which is passed to boolAssert. By contrast, because the type of byNameAssert's predicate parameter is => Boolean, the expression inside the parentheses in byNameAssert(5 > 3) is *not* evaluated before the call to byNameAssert. Instead a function value will be created whose apply method will evaluate 5 > 3, and this function value will be passed to byNameAssert.

The difference between the two approaches, therefore, is that if assertions are disabled, you'll see any side effects that the expression inside the parentheses may have in boolAssert, but not in byNameAssert. For example, if assertions are disabled, attempting to assert on "x / 0 == 0" will yield an exception in boolAssert's case:

```
val x = 5
assertionsEnabled = false

boolAssert(x / 0 == 0)
java.lang.ArithmeticException: / by zero
  ... 27 elided
```

But attempting to assert on the same code in byNameAssert's case will *not* yield an exception:

```
byNameAssert(x / 0 == 0)   // Returns normally
```

9.6   Conclusion

This chapter has shown you how to build on Scala's rich function support to build control abstractions. You can use functions within your code to factor out common control patterns, and you can take advantage of higher-order functions in the Scala library to reuse control patterns that are common across all programmers' code. We also discussed how to use currying and by-name parameters so that your own higher-order functions can be used with a concise syntax.

In the previous chapter and this one, you have seen quite a lot of information about functions. The next few chapters will go back to discussing more object-oriented features of the language.

Chapter 10

Composition and Inheritance

Chapter 6 introduced some basic object-oriented aspects of Scala. This chapter picks up where Chapter 6 left off and dives into Scala's support for object-oriented programming in much greater detail.

We'll compare two fundamental relationships between classes: composition and inheritance. Composition means one class holds a reference to another, using the referenced class to help it fulfill its mission. Inheritance is the superclass/subclass relationship.

In addition to these topics, we'll discuss abstract classes, parameterless methods, extending classes, overriding methods and fields, parametric fields, invoking superclass constructors, polymorphism and dynamic binding, final members and classes, and factory objects and methods.

10.1 A two-dimensional layout library

As a running example in this chapter, we'll create a library for building and rendering two-dimensional layout elements. Each element will represent a rectangle filled with text. For convenience, the library will provide factory methods named "elem" that construct new elements from passed data. For example, you'll be able to create a layout element containing a string using a factory method with the following signature:

```
elem(s: String): Element
```

As you can see, elements will be modeled with a type named Element. You'll be able to call above or beside on an element, passing in a second element, to get a new element that combines the two. For example, the following expression would construct a larger element consisting of two columns, each with a height of two:

```
val column1 = elem("hello") above elem("***")
val column2 = elem("***") above elem("world")
column1 beside column2
```

Printing the result of this expression would give you:

```
hello ***
*** world
```

Layout elements are a good example of a system in which objects can be constructed from simple parts with the aid of composing operators. In this chapter, we'll define classes that enable element objects to be constructed from vectors, lines, and rectangles. These basic element objects will be the simple parts. We'll also define composing operators above and beside. Such composing operators are also often called *combinators* because they combine elements of some domain into new elements.

Thinking in terms of combinators is generally a good way to approach library design: it pays to think about the fundamental ways to construct objects in an application domain. What are the simple objects? In what ways can more interesting objects be constructed out of simpler ones? How do combinators hang together? What are the most general combinations? Do they satisfy any interesting laws? If you have good answers to these questions, your library design is on track.

10.2   Abstract classes

Our first task is to define type `Element`, which represents layout elements. Since elements are two dimensional rectangles of characters, it makes sense to include a member, `contents`, that refers to the contents of a layout element. The contents can be represented as a vector of strings, where each string represents a line. Hence, the type of the result returned by `contents` will be `Vector[String]`. Listing 10.1 shows what it will look like.

In this class, `contents` is declared as a method that has no implementation. In other words, the method is an *abstract* member of class `Element`. A class with abstract members must itself be declared abstract, which is done by writing an `abstract` modifier in front of the `class` keyword:

```
abstract class Element:
  def contents: Vector[String]
```

Listing 10.1 · Defining an abstract method and class.

```
abstract class Element ...
```

The `abstract` modifier signifies that the class may have abstract members that do not have an implementation. As a result, you cannot instantiate an abstract class. If you try to do so, you'll get a compiler error:

```
scala> new Element
1 |new Element
  |    ^^^^^^^
  |    Element is abstract; it cannot be instantiated
```

Later in this chapter, you'll see how to create subclasses of class `Element`, which you'll be able to instantiate because they fill in the missing definition for `contents`.

Note that the `contents` method in class `Element` does not carry an `abstract` modifier. A method is abstract if it does not have an implementation (*i.e.*, no equals sign or body). Unlike Java, no abstract modifier is necessary (or allowed) on method declarations. Methods that have an implementation are called *concrete*.

Another bit of terminology distinguishes between *declarations* and *definitions*. Class `Element` *declares* the abstract method `contents`, but currently *defines* no concrete methods. In the next section, however, we'll enhance `Element` by defining some concrete methods.

10.3 Defining parameterless methods

As a next step, we'll add methods to `Element` that reveal its width and height, as shown in Listing 10.2. The `height` method returns the number of lines in `contents`. The `width` method returns the length of the first line, or if there are no lines in the element, returns zero. (This means you cannot define an element with a height of zero and a non-zero width.)

Note that none of `Element`'s three methods has a parameter list, not even an empty one. For example, instead of:

173

```
abstract class Element:
  def contents: Vector[String]
  def height: Int = contents.length
  def width: Int = if height == 0 then 0 else contents(0).length
```

Listing 10.2 · Defining parameterless methods width and height.

```
def width(): Int
```

the method is defined without parentheses:

```
def width: Int
```

Such *parameterless methods* are quite common in Scala. By contrast, methods defined with empty parentheses, such as def height(): Int, are called *empty-paren methods*. The recommended convention is to use a parameterless method whenever there are no parameters *and* the method accesses state only by reading fields of the containing object (in particular, it does not change mutable state). This convention supports the *uniform access principle*,[1] which says that client code should not be affected by a decision to implement an attribute as a field or method.

For instance, we could implement width and height as fields, instead of methods, simply by changing the def in each definition to a val:

```
abstract class Element:
  def contents: Vector[String]
  val height = contents.length
  val width = if height == 0 then 0 else contents(0).length
```

The two pairs of definitions are completely equivalent from a client's point of view. The only difference is that field accesses might be slightly faster than method invocations because the field values are pre-computed when the class is initialized, instead of being computed on each method call. On the other hand, the fields require extra memory space in each Element object. So it depends on the usage profile of a class whether an attribute is better represented as a field or method, and that usage profile might change over

---

[1] Meyer, *Object-Oriented Software Construction* [Mey00]

time. The point is that clients of the Element class should not be affected when its internal implementation changes.

In particular, a client of class Element should not need to be rewritten if a field of that class gets changed into an access function, so long as the access function is *pure* (*i.e.*, it does not have any side effects and does not depend on mutable state). The client should not need to care either way.

So far so good. But there's still a slight complication with the way Java and Scala 2 handle things. The problem is that Java does not implement the uniform access principle, and Scala 2 does not fully enforce it. For example, it's string.length() in Java, not string.length, even though it's array.length, not array.length(). This can be confusing.

To bridge that gap, Scala 3 is very liberal when it comes to mixing parameterless and empty-paren methods defined in Java or Scala 2. In particular, you can override a parameterless method with an empty-paren method, and *vice versa*, so long as the parent class was written in Java or Scala 2. You can also leave off the empty parentheses on an invocation of any function defined in Java or Scala 2 that takes no arguments. For instance, the following two lines are both legal in Scala 3:

```
Array(1, 2, 3).toString
"abc".length
```

In principle it's possible to leave out all empty parentheses in calls to functions defined in Java or Scala 2. However, it's still recommended to write the empty parentheses when the invoked method represents more than a property of its receiver object. For instance, empty parentheses are appropriate if the method performs I/O, writes reassignable variables (vars), or reads vars other than the receiver's fields, either directly or indirectly by using mutable objects. That way, the parameter list acts as a visual clue that some interesting computation is triggered by the call. For instance:

```
"hello".length  // no () because no side-effect
println()       // better to not drop the ()
```

To summarize, it is encouraged in Scala to define methods that take no parameters and have no side effects as parameterless methods (*i.e.*, leaving off the empty parentheses). On the other hand, you should never define a method that has side-effects without parentheses, because invocations of that method

175

would then look like a field selection. So your clients might be surprised to see the side effects.

Similarly, whenever you invoke a function that has side effects, be sure to include the empty parentheses when you write the invocation, even if the compiler doesn't force you.[2] Another way to think about this is if the function you're calling performs an operation, use the parentheses. But if it merely provides access to a property, leave the parentheses off.

10.4   Extending classes

We still need to be able to create new element objects. You have already seen that "new Element" cannot be used for this because class Element is abstract. To instantiate an element, therefore, we will need to create a subclass that extends Element and implements the abstract contents method. Listing 10.3 shows one possible way to do that:

```
class VectorElement(conts: Vector[String]) extends Element:
  def contents: Vector[String] = conts
```

Listing 10.3 · Defining VectorElement as a subclass of Element.

Class VectorElement is defined to *extend* class Element. Just like in Java, you use an extends clause after the class name to express this:

```
... extends Element ...
```

Such an extends clause has two effects: It makes class VectorElement *inherit* all non-private members from class Element, and it makes the type VectorElement a *subtype* of the type Element. Given VectorElement extends Element, class VectorElement is called a *subclass* of class Element. Conversely, Element is a *superclass* of VectorElement. If you leave out an extends clause, the Scala compiler implicitly assumes your class extends from scala.AnyRef, which on the Java platform is the same as class java.lang.Object. Thus, class Element implicitly extends class AnyRef. You can see these inheritance relationships in Figure 10.1.

---

[2]The compiler requires that you invoke parameterless methods defined in Scala 3 without empty parentheses and empty-parens methods defined in Scala 3 with empty parentheses.

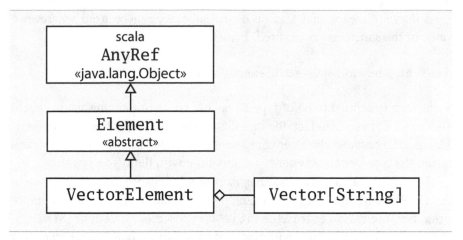

Figure 10.1 · Class diagram for VectorElement.

Inheritance means that all members of the superclass are also members of the subclass, with two exceptions. First, private members of the superclass are not inherited in a subclass. Second, a member of a superclass is not inherited if a member with the same name and parameters is already implemented in the subclass. In that case we say the member of the subclass *overrides* the member of the superclass. If the member in the subclass is concrete and the member of the superclass is abstract, we also say that the concrete member *implements* the abstract one.

For example, the contents method in VectorElement overrides (or alternatively: implements) abstract method contents in class Element.[3] By contrast, class VectorElement inherits the width and height methods from class Element. For example, given a VectorElement ve, you can query its width using ve.width, as if width were defined in class VectorElement:[4]

```
val ve = VectorElement(Vector("hello", "world"))
ve.width // 5
```

---

[3]One flaw with this design is that we aren't currently ensuring that every String element of the contents vector has the same length. This could be solved by checking the precondition in the primary constructor and throwing an exception if it is violated.

[4]As mentioned in Section 6.2, when instantiating classes that take parameters, like VectorElement, you can leave off the new keyword.

Subtyping means that a value of the subclass can be used wherever a value of the superclass is required. For example:

```
val e: Element = VectorElement(Vector("hello"))
```

Variable e is defined to be of type Element, so its initializing value should also be an Element. In fact, the initializing value's type is VectorElement. This is OK, because class VectorElement extends class Element, and as a result, the type VectorElement is compatible with the type Element.[5]

Figure 10.1 also shows the *composition* relationship that exists between VectorElement and Vector[String]. This relationship is called composition because class VectorElement is "composed of" a Vector[String], in that the Scala compiler will place into the binary class it generates for VectorElement a field that holds a reference to the passed conts vector. We'll discuss some design considerations concerning composition and inheritance later in this chapter, in Section 10.11.

10.5   Overriding methods and fields

The uniform access principle is just one aspect where Scala treats fields and methods more uniformly than Java. Another difference is that in Scala, fields and methods belong to the same namespace. This makes it possible for a field to override a parameterless method. For instance, you could change the implementation of contents in class VectorElement from a method to a field without having to modify the abstract method definition of contents in class Element, as shown in Listing 10.4:

```
class VectorElement(conts: Vector[String]) extends Element:
  val contents: Vector[String] = conts
```

Listing 10.4 · Overriding a parameterless method with a field.

Field contents (defined with a val) in this version of VectorElement is a perfectly good implementation of the parameterless method contents (declared with a def) in class Element. On the other hand, in Scala it is

---

[5]For more perspective on the difference between subclass and subtype, see the glossary entry for *subtype*.

forbidden to define a field and method with the same name in the same class, whereas this is allowed in Java.

For example, this Java class would compile just fine:

```
// This is Java
class CompilesFine {
  private int f = 0;
  public int f() {
    return 1;
  }
}
```

But the corresponding Scala class would not compile:

```
class WontCompile:
  private var f = 0 // Won't compile, because a field
  def f = 1          // and method have the same name
```

Generally, Scala has just two namespaces for definitions in place of Java's four. Java's four namespaces are fields, methods, types, and packages. By contrast, Scala's two namespaces are:

- values (fields, methods, packages, and singleton objects)

- types (class and trait names)

The reason Scala places fields and methods into the same namespace is precisely so you can override a parameterless method with a val, something you can't do with Java.[6]

10.6 Defining parametric fields

Consider again the definition of class VectorElement shown in the previous section. It has a parameter conts whose sole purpose is to be copied into the contents field. The name conts of the parameter was chosen just so that it would look similar to the field name contents without actually clashing

---

[6]The reason that packages share the same namespace as fields and methods in Scala is to enable you to import packages (in addition to just the names of types) and the fields and methods of singleton objects. This is also something you can't do in Java. It will be described in Section 12.3.

with it. This is a "code smell," a sign that there may be some unnecessary redundancy and repetition in your code.

You can avoid the code smell by combining the parameter and the field in a single *parametric field* definition, as shown in Listing 10.5:

```
// Extends Element shown in Listing 10.2
class VectorElement(
  val contents: Vector[String]
) extends Element
```

Listing 10.5 · Defining `contents` as a parametric field.

Note that now the `contents` parameter is prefixed by `val`. This is a shorthand that defines at the same time a parameter and field with the same name. Specifically, class `VectorElement` now has an (unreassignable) field `contents`, which can be accessed from outside the class. The field is initialized with the value of the parameter. It's as if the class had been written as follows, where x123 is an arbitrary fresh name for the parameter:

```
class VectorElement(x123: Vector[String]) extends Element:
  val contents: Vector[String] = x123
```

You can also prefix a class parameter with `var`, in which case the corresponding field would be reassignable. Finally, it is possible to add modifiers, such as `private`, `protected`,[7] or `override` to these parametric fields, just as you can for any other class member. Consider, for instance, the following class definitions:

```
class Cat:
  val dangerous = false
class Tiger(
  override val dangerous: Boolean,
  private var age: Int
) extends Cat
```

Tiger's definition is a shorthand for the following alternate class definition with an overriding member `dangerous` and a `private` member age:

---

[7]The `protected` modifier, which grants access to subclasses, will be covered in detail in Chapter 12.

```
class Tiger(param1: Boolean, param2: Int) extends Cat:
  override val dangerous = param1
  private var age = param2
```

Both members are initialized from the corresponding parameters. We chose the names of those parameters, param1 and param2, arbitrarily. The important thing was that they not clash with any other name in scope.

10.7 Invoking superclass constructors

You now have a complete system consisting of two classes: an abstract class Element, which is extended by a concrete class VectorElement. You might also envision other ways to express an element. For example, clients might want to create a layout element consisting of a single line given by a string. Object-oriented programming makes it easy to extend a system with new data-variants. You can simply add subclasses. For example, Listing 10.6 shows a LineElement class that extends VectorElement:

```
// Extends VectorElement shown in Listing 10.5
class LineElement(s: String) extends VectorElement(Vector(s)):
  override def width = s.length
  override def height = 1
```

Listing 10.6 · Invoking a superclass constructor.

Because LineElement extends VectorElement, and VectorElement's constructor takes a Vector[String] parameter, LineElement needs to pass an argument to the primary constructor of its superclass. To invoke a superclass constructor, you simply place the argument or arguments you want to pass in parentheses following the name of the superclass. For example, class LineElement passes Vector(s) to VectorElement's primary constructor by placing it in parentheses after the superclass VectorElement's name:

```
... extends VectorElement(Vector(s)) ...
```

With the new subclass, the inheritance hierarchy for layout elements now looks as shown in Figure 10.2.

181

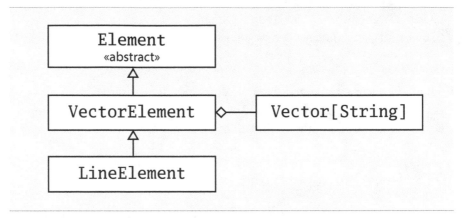

Figure 10.2 · Class diagram for LineElement.

10.8   Using override modifiers

Note that the definitions of width and height in LineElement carry an override modifier. In Section 6.3, you saw this modifier in the definition of a toString method. Scala requires such a modifier for all members that override a concrete member in a parent class. The modifier is optional if a member implements an abstract member with the same name. The modifier is forbidden if a member does not override or implement some other member in a base class. Since height and width in class LineElement override concrete definitions in class Element, override is required.

This rule provides useful information for the compiler that helps avoid some hard-to-catch errors and makes system evolution safer. For instance, if you happen to misspell the method or accidentally give it a different parameter list, the compiler will respond with an error message:

```
$ scalac LineElement.scala
-- [E037] Declaration Error: LineElement.scala:3:15 --
3 |   override def hight = 1
  |                  ^
  |                  method hight overrides nothing
```

The override convention is even more important when it comes to system evolution. Say you defined a library of 2D drawing methods. You made it publicly available, and it is widely used. In the next version of the library you want to add to your base class Shape a new method with this signature:

```
def hidden(): Boolean
```

Your new method will be used by various drawing methods to determine whether a shape needs to be drawn. This could lead to a significant speedup, but you cannot do this without the risk of breaking client code. After all, a client could have defined a subclass of Shape with a different implementation of hidden. Perhaps the client's method actually makes the receiver object disappear instead of testing whether the object is hidden. Because the two versions of hidden override each other, your drawing methods would end up making objects disappear, which is certainly not what you want!

These "accidental overrides" are the most common manifestation of what is called the "fragile base class" problem. The problem is that if you add new members to base classes (which we usually call superclasses) in a class hierarchy, you risk breaking client code. Scala cannot completely solve the fragile base class problem, but it improves on the situation compared to Java.[8] If the drawing library and its clients were written in Scala, then the client's original implementation of hidden could not have had an override modifier, because at the time there was no other method with that name.

Once you add the hidden method to the second version of your shape class, a recompile of the client would give an error like the following:

```
-- Error: Circle.scala:3:6 ---------------------------
3 |  def hidden(): Boolean =
  |      ^
  |
  |      error overriding method hidden in class Shape
  |        of type (): Boolean; method hidden of type
  |        (): Boolean needs `override` modifier
```

That is, instead of wrong behavior your client would get a compile-time error, which is usually much preferable.

---

[8]Java offers an @Override annotation that works similarly to Scala's override modifier, but unlike Scala's override, is not required.

10.9 Polymorphism and dynamic binding

You saw in Section 10.4 that a variable of type `Element` could refer to an object of type `VectorElement`. The name for this phenomenon is *polymorphism*, which means "many shapes" or "many forms." In this case, `Element` objects can have many forms.[9]

So far, you've seen two such forms: `VectorElement` and `LineElement`. You can create more forms of `Element` by defining new `Element` subclasses. For example, you could define a new form of `Element` that has a given width and height, and is filled everywhere with a given character:

```
// Extends Element shown in Listing 10.2
class UniformElement(
  ch: Char,
  override val width: Int,
  override val height: Int
) extends Element:
  private val line = ch.toString * width
  def contents = Vector.fill(height)(line)
```

The inheritance hierarchy for class `Element` now looks as shown in Figure 10.3. As a result, Scala will accept all of the following assignments, because the type of the assigning expression conforms to the type of the defined variable:

```
val e1: Element = VectorElement(Vector("hello", "world"))
val ve: VectorElement = LineElement("hello")
val e2: Element = ve
val e3: Element = UniformElement('x', 2, 3)
```

If you check the inheritance hierarchy, you'll find that in each of these four `val` definitions, the type of the expression to the right of the equals sign is below the type of the `val` being initialized to the left of the equals sign.

The other half of the story, however, is that method invocations on variables and expressions are *dynamically bound*. This means that the actual method implementation invoked is determined at run time based on the class

---

[9]This kind of polymorphism is called *subtyping polymorphism*. Other kinds of polymorphism in Scala are discussed in later chapters, *universal polymorphism* in Chapter 18 and *ad hoc polymorphism* in Chapters 21 and 23.

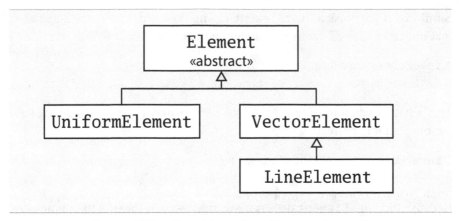

Figure 10.3 · Class hierarchy of layout elements.

of the object, not the type of the variable or expression. To demonstrate this behavior, we'll temporarily remove all existing members from our Element classes and add a method named demo to Element. We'll override demo in VectorElement and LineElement, but not in UniformElement:

```
abstract class Element:
  def demo = "Element's implementation invoked"

class VectorElement extends Element:
  override def demo = "VectorElement's implementation invoked"

class LineElement extends VectorElement:
  override def demo = "LineElement's implementation invoked"

// UniformElement inherits Element's demo
class UniformElement extends Element
```

If you enter this code into the REPL, you can then define this method that takes an Element and invokes demo on it:

```
def invokeDemo(e: Element) = e.demo
```

If you pass a VectorElement to invokeDemo, you'll see a message indicating VectorElement's implementation of demo was invoked, even though the type of the variable, e, on which demo was invoked is Element:

```
invokeDemo(new VectorElement)
// VectorElement's implementation invoked
```

Similarly, if you pass a LineElement to invokeDemo, you'll see a message that indicates LineElement's demo implementation was invoked:

```
invokeDemo(new LineElement)
// LineElement's implementation invoked
```

The behavior when passing a UniformElement may at first glance look suspicious, but it is correct:

```
invokeDemo(new UniformElement)
// Element's implementation invoked
```

Because UniformElement does not override demo, it inherits the implementation of demo from its superclass, Element. Thus, Element's implementation is the correct implementation of demo to invoke when the class of the object is UniformElement.

10.10   Declaring final members

Sometimes when designing an inheritance hierarchy, you want to ensure that a member cannot be overridden by subclasses. In Scala, as in Java, you do this by adding a final modifier to the member. As shown in Listing 10.7, you could place a final modifier on VectorElement's demo method.

```
class VectorElement extends Element:
  final override def demo =
    "VectorElement's implementation invoked"
```

Listing 10.7 · Declaring a final method.

Given this version of VectorElement, an attempt to override demo in its subclass, LineElement, would not compile:

```
-- Error: LineElement.scala:2:15 ---------------------
2 |   override def demo =
  |                ^
  |error overriding method demo in class VectorElement
  |  of type => String; method demo of type => String
  |  cannot override final member method demo in class
  |  VectorElement
```

186

You may also at times want to ensure that an entire class not be sub-classed. To do this you simply declare the entire class final by adding a final modifier to the class declaration. For example, Listing 10.8 shows how you would declare VectorElement final:

```
final class VectorElement extends Element:
  override def demo = "VectorElement's implementation invoked"
```

Listing 10.8 · Declaring a final class.

With this version of VectorElement, any attempt at defining a subclass would fail to compile:

```
-- [E093] Syntax Error: LineElement.scala:1:6 ---------
1 |class LineElement extends VectorElement:
  |          ^
  |       class LineElement cannot extend final class
  |          VectorElement
```

We'll now remove the final modifiers and demo methods, and go back to the earlier implementation of the Element family. We'll focus our attention in the remainder of this chapter to completing a working version of the layout library.

10.11   Using composition and inheritance

Composition and inheritance are two ways to define a new class in terms of another existing class. If what you're after is primarily code reuse, you should in general prefer composition to inheritance. Only inheritance suffers from the fragile base class problem, in which you can inadvertently break subclasses by changing a superclass.

One question you can ask yourself about an inheritance relationship is whether it models an *is-a* relationship.[10] For example, it would be reasonable to say that VectorElement *is-an* Element. Another question you can ask is whether clients will want to use the subclass type as a superclass type.[11] In

---

[10]Meyers, *Effective C++* [Mey91]
[11]Eckel, *Thinking in Java* [Eck98]

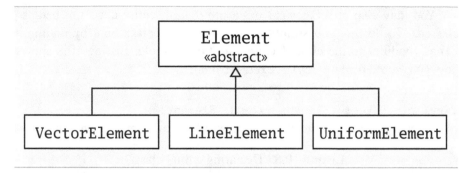

Figure 10.4 · Class hierarchy with revised LineElement.

the case of VectorElement, we do indeed expect clients will want to use a VectorElement as an Element.

If you ask these questions about the inheritance relationships shown in Figure 10.3, do any of the relationships seem suspicious? In particular, does it seem obvious to you that a LineElement *is-a* VectorElement? Do you think clients would ever need to use a LineElement as a VectorElement?

In fact, we defined LineElement as a subclass of VectorElement primarily to reuse VectorElement's definition of contents. Perhaps it would be better, therefore, to define LineElement as a direct subclass of Element, like this:

```
class LineElement(s: String) extends Element:
  val contents = Vector(s)
  override def width = s.length
  override def height = 1
```

In the previous version, LineElement had an inheritance relationship with VectorElement, from which it inherited contents. It now has a composition relationship with Vector: it holds a reference to a vector of strings from its own contents field.[12] Given this implementation of LineElement, the inheritance hierarchy for Element now looks as shown in Figure 10.4.

---

[12]Class VectorElement also has a composition relationship with Vector, because its parametric contents field holds a reference to a vector of strings. The code for VectorElement is shown in Listing 10.5 on page 180. Its composition relationship is represented in class diagrams by a diamond, as shown, for example, in Figure 10.1 on page 177.

10.12   Implementing above, beside, and toString

As a next step, we'll implement method above in class Element. Putting one element above another means concatenating the two contents values of the elements. So a first draft of method above could look like this:

```
def above(that: Element): Element =
  VectorElement(this.contents ++ that.contents)
```

The ++ operation concatenates two vectors. Some other vector methods will be explained in this chapter and a more comprehensive discussion will be given in Chapter 15.

The code shown previously is not quite sufficient because it does not let you put elements of different widths on top of each other. To keep things simple in this section, however, we'll leave this as is and only pass elements of the same length to above. In Section 10.14, we'll make an enhancement to above so that clients can use it to combine elements of different widths.

The next method to implement is beside. To put two elements beside each other, we'll create a new element in which every line results from concatenating corresponding lines of the two elements. As before, to keep things simple, we'll start by assuming the two elements have the same height. This leads to the following design of method beside:

```
def beside(that: Element): Element =
  val newContents = new Array[String](this.contents.length)
  for i <- 0 until this.contents.length do
    newContents(i) = this.contents(i) + that.contents(i)
  VectorElement(newContents.toVector)
```

The beside method first allocates an array, newContents, and fills it with the concatenation of the corresponding vector elements in this.contents and that.contents. It finally produces a new VectorElement containing the new contents by calling toVector on the array.

Although this implementation of beside works, it is in an imperative style, the telltale sign of which is the loop in which we index through vectors. Alternatively, the method could be abbreviated to one expression:

```
VectorElement(
  for (line1, line2) <- this.contents.zip(that.contents)
  yield line1 + line2)
```

189

The two vectors, this.contents and that.contents, are transformed into a vector of pairs (as Tuple2s are called) using the zip operator. The zip operator picks corresponding elements in its two operands and forms a vector of pairs. For instance, this expression:

```
Vector(1, 2, 3).zip(Vector("a", "b"))
```

will evaluate to:

```
Vector((1, "a"), (2, "b"))
```

If one of the two operand vectors is longer than the other, zip will drop the remaining elements. In the expression above, the third element of the left operand, 3, does not form part of the result, because it does not have a corresponding element in the right operand.

The zipped vector is then iterated over by a for expression. Here, the syntax "for ((line1, line2) <- ...)" allows you to name both elements of a pair in one *pattern* (*i.e.*, line1 stands now for the first element of the pair, and line2 stands for the second). Scala's pattern-matching system will be described in detail in Chapter 13. For now, you can just think of this as a way to define two vals, line1 and line2, for each step of the iteration.

The for expression has a yield part and therefore yields a result. The result is of the same kind as the expression iterated over (*i.e.*, it is a vector). Each element of the vector is the result of concatenating the corresponding lines, line1 and line2. So the end result of this code is the same as in the first version of beside, but because it avoids explicit vector indexing, the result is obtained in a less error-prone way.

You still need a way to display elements. As usual, this is done by defining a toString method that returns an element formatted as a string. Here is its definition:

```
override def toString = contents.mkString("\n")
```

The implementation of toString makes use of mkString, which is defined for all sequences, including vectors. As you saw in Section 7.8, an expression like "vec.mkString(sep)" returns a string consisting of all elements of the vector vec. Each element is mapped to a string by calling its toString method. A separator string sep is inserted between consecutive element strings. So the expression, "contents.mkString("\n")" formats

```
abstract class Element:
  def contents: Vector[String]

  def width: Int =
    if height == 0 then 0 else contents(0).length

  def height: Int = contents.length

  def above(that: Element): Element =
    VectorElement(this.contents ++ that.contents)

  def beside(that: Element): Element =
    VectorElement(
      for (line1, line2) <- this.contents.zip(that.contents)
      yield line1 + line2
    )

  override def toString = contents.mkString("\n")
end Element
```

Listing 10.9 · Class Element with above, beside, and toString.

the contents vector as a string, where each vector element appears on a line by itself.

Note that we did not declare toString with an empty parameter list. This follows the recommendations for the uniform access principle, because toString is a pure method that does not take any parameters. With the addition of these three methods, class Element now looks as shown in Listing 10.9.

10.13   Defining a factory object

You now have a hierarchy of classes for layout elements. This hierarchy could be presented to your clients "as is," but you might also choose to hide the hierarchy behind a factory object.

A factory object contains methods that construct other objects. Clients would then use these factory methods to construct objects, rather than constructing the objects directly via their constructors. An advantage of this approach is that object creation can be centralized and the details of how

191

objects are represented with classes can be hidden. This hiding will both make your library simpler for clients to understand, because less detail is exposed, and provide you with more opportunities to change your library's implementation later without breaking client code.

The first task in constructing a factory for layout elements is to choose where the factory methods should be located. Should they be members of a singleton object or of a class? What should the containing object or class be called? There are many possibilities. A straightforward solution is to create a companion object of class Element and make this the factory object for layout elements. That way, you need to expose only the class/object combo of Element to your clients, and you can hide the three implementation classes VectorElement, LineElement, and UniformElement.

Listing 10.10 is a design of the Element object that follows this scheme. The Element object contains three overloaded variants of an elem method and each constructs a different kind of layout object.

```
object Element:

  def elem(contents: Vector[String]): Element =
    VectorElement(contents)

  def elem(chr: Char, width: Int, height: Int): Element =
    UniformElement(chr, width, height)

  def elem(line: String): Element =
    LineElement(line)
```

Listing 10.10 · A factory object with factory methods.

With the advent of these factory methods, it makes sense to change the implementation of class Element so that it goes through the elem factory methods rather than creating new VectorElement instances explicitly. To call the factory methods without qualifying them with Element, the name of the singleton object, we will import Element.elem at the top of the source file. In other words, instead of invoking the factory methods with Element.elem inside class Element, we'll import Element.elem so we can just call the factory methods by their simple name, elem. Listing 10.11 shows what class Element will look like after these changes.

In addition, given the factory methods, the subclasses, VectorElement, LineElement, and UniformElement, could now be private because they

```
import Element.elem

abstract class Element:

  def contents: Vector[String]

  def width: Int =
    if height == 0 then 0 else contents(0).length

  def height: Int = contents.length

  def above(that: Element): Element =
    elem(this.contents ++ that.contents)

  def beside(that: Element): Element =
    elem(
      for (line1, line2) <- this.contents.zip(that.contents)
      yield line1 + line2
    )

  override def toString = contents.mkString("\n")
end Element
```

Listing 10.11 · Class `Element` refactored to use factory methods.

no longer need to be accessed directly by clients. In Scala, you can define classes and singleton objects inside other classes and singleton objects. One way to make the `Element` subclasses private is to place them inside the `Element` singleton object and declare them private there. The classes will still be accessible to the three `elem` factory methods, where they are needed. Listing 10.12 shows how that will look.

10.14 Heighten and widen

We need one last enhancement. The version of `Element` shown in Listing 10.11 is not quite sufficient because it does not allow clients to place elements of different widths on top of each other, or place elements of different heights beside each other.

For example, evaluating the following expression won't work correctly, because the second line in the combined element is longer than the first:

```
elem(Vector("hello")) above elem(Vector("world!"))
```

193

```
object Element:

  private class VectorElement(
    val contents: Vector[String]
  ) extends Element

  private class LineElement(s: String) extends Element:
    val contents = Vector(s)
    override def width = s.length
    override def height = 1

  private class UniformElement(
    ch: Char,
    override val width: Int,
    override val height: Int
  ) extends Element:
    private val line = ch.toString * width
    def contents = Vector.fill(height)(line)

  def elem(contents: Vector[String]): Element =
    VectorElement(contents)

  def elem(chr: Char, width: Int, height: Int): Element =
    UniformElement(chr, width, height)

  def elem(line: String): Element =
    LineElement(line)

end Element
```

Listing 10.12 · Hiding implementation with private classes.

Similarly, evaluating the following expression would not work properly, because the first VectorElement has a height of two and the second a height of only one:

```
elem(Vector("one", "two")) beside
elem(Vector("one"))
```

Listing 10.13 shows a private helper method, widen, which takes a width and returns an Element of that width. The result contains the contents of this Element, centered, padded to the left and right by any spaces needed to achieve the required width. Listing 10.13 also shows a similar method, heighten, which performs the same function in the vertical direction. The widen method is invoked by above to ensure that Elements placed above each other have the same width. Similarly, the heighten method is invoked by beside to ensure that elements placed beside each other have the same height. With these changes, the layout library is ready for use.

10.15   Putting it all together

A fun way to exercise almost all elements of the layout library is to write a program that draws a spiral with a given number of edges. This Spiral program, shown in Listing 10.14, will do just that.

Because Spiral is a standalone object with a main method with the proper signature, it is a Scala application. Spiral takes one command-line argument, an integer, and draws a spiral with the specified number of edges. For example, you could draw a six-edge spiral, as shown on the left, and larger spirals, as shown on the right.

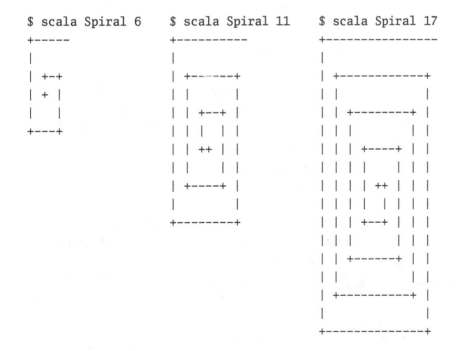

```
import Element.elem
abstract class Element:
  def contents:  Vector[String]

  def width: Int =
    if height == 0 then 0 else contents(0).length
  def height: Int = contents.length

  def above(that: Element): Element =
    val this1 = this.widen(that.width)
    val that1 = that.widen(this.width)
    elem(this1.contents ++ that1.contents)

  def beside(that: Element): Element =
    val this1 = this.heighten(that.height)
    val that1 = that.heighten(this.height)
    elem(
      for (line1, line2) <- this1.contents.zip(that1.contents)
      yield line1 + line2
    )

  def widen(w: Int): Element =
    if w <= width then this
    else
      val left = elem(' ', (w - width) / 2, height)
      val right = elem(' ', w - width - left.width, height)
      left beside this beside right

  def heighten(h: Int): Element =
    if h <= height then this
    else
      val top = elem(' ', width, (h - height) / 2)
      val bot = elem(' ', width, h - height - top.height)
      top above this above bot
  override def toString = contents.mkString("\n")
end Element
```

Listing 10.13 · Element with widen and heighten methods.

```scala
import Element.elem
object Spiral:
  val space = elem(" ")
  val corner = elem("+")
  def spiral(nEdges: Int, direction: Int): Element =
    if nEdges == 1 then
      elem("+")
    else
      val sp = spiral(nEdges - 1, (direction + 3) % 4)
      def verticalBar = elem('|', 1, sp.height)
      def horizontalBar = elem('-', sp.width, 1)
      if direction == 0 then
        (corner beside horizontalBar) above (sp beside space)
      else if direction == 1 then
        (sp above space) beside (corner above verticalBar)
      else if direction == 2 then
        (space beside sp) above (horizontalBar beside corner)
      else
        (verticalBar above corner) beside (space above sp)
  def main(args: Array[String]) =
    val nSides = args(0).toInt
    println(spiral(nSides, 0))
end Spiral
```

Listing 10.14 · The Spiral application.

10.16   Conclusion

In this section, you saw more concepts related to object-oriented programming in Scala. Among others, you encountered abstract classes, inheritance and subtyping, class hierarchies, parametric fields, and method overriding. You should have developed a feel for constructing a non-trivial class hierarchy in Scala. We'll work with the layout library again in Chapter 25.

Chapter 11

Traits

Traits are a fundamental unit of code reuse in Scala. A trait encapsulates method and field definitions, which can then be reused by mixing them into classes. Unlike class inheritance, in which each class must inherit from just one superclass, a class can mix in any number of traits. This chapter shows you how traits work and shows two of the most common ways they are useful: widening thin interfaces to rich ones, and defining stackable modifications. It also shows how to use the Ordered trait and compares traits to the multiple inheritance of other languages.

11.1 How traits work

A trait definition looks just like a class definition except that it uses the keyword trait. An example is shown in Listing 11.1:

```
trait Philosophical:
  def philosophize = "I consume memory, therefore I am!"
```

Listing 11.1 · The definition of trait Philosophical.

This trait is named Philosophical. It does not declare a superclass, so like a class, it has the default superclass of AnyRef. It defines one method, named philosophize, which is concrete. It's a simple trait, just enough to show how traits work.

Once a trait is defined, it can be *mixed in* to a class using either the extends or with keywords, or a comma. Scala programmers "mix in" traits

199

rather than inherit from them, because mixing in a trait has important differences from the multiple inheritance found in many other languages. This issue is discussed in Section 11.4. For example, Listing 11.2 shows a class that mixes in the `Philosophical` trait using `extends`:

```
class Frog extends Philosophical:
  override def toString = "green"
```

Listing 11.2 · Mixing in a trait using `extends`.

You can use the `extends` keyword to mix in a trait; in that case you implicitly inherit the trait's superclass. For instance, in Listing 11.2, class `Frog` subclasses `AnyRef` (the superclass of `Philosophical`) and mixes in `Philosophical`. Methods inherited from a trait can be used just like methods inherited from a superclass. Here's an example:

```
val frog = new Frog
frog.philosophize   // I consume memory, therefore I am!
```

A trait also defines a type. Here's an example in which `Philosophical` is used as a type:

```
val phil: Philosophical = frog
phil.philosophize   // I consume memory, therefore I am!
```

The type of `phil` is `Philosophical`, a trait. Thus, variable `phil` could have been initialized with any object whose class mixes in `Philosophical`.

If you wish to mix a trait into a class that explicitly extends a superclass, you use `extends` to indicate the superclass and a comma (or `with`) to mix in the trait. Listing 11.3 shows an example. If you want to mix in multiple traits, you add more `with` clauses. For example, given a trait `HasLegs`, you could mix both `Philosophical` and `HasLegs` into `Frog` as shown in Listing 11.4.

```
class Animal

class Frog extends Animal, Philosophical:
  override def toString = "green"
```

Listing 11.3 · Mixing in a trait using a comma.

```
class Animal
trait HasLegs

class Frog extends Animal, Philosophical, HasLegs:
  override def toString = "green"
```

Listing 11.4 · Mixing in multiple traits.

In the examples you've seen so far, class `Frog` has inherited an implementation of `philosophize` from trait `Philosophical`. Alternatively, `Frog` could override `philosophize`. The syntax looks the same as overriding a method declared in a superclass. Here's an example:

```
class Animal

class Frog extends Animal, Philosophical:
  override def toString = "green"
  override def philosophize = s"It ain't easy being $this!"
```

Because this new definition of `Frog` still mixes in trait `Philosophical`, you can still use it from a variable of that type. But because `Frog` overrides `Philosophical`'s implementation of `philosophize`, you'll get a new behavior when you call it:

```
val phrog: Philosophical = new Frog
phrog.philosophize   // It ain't easy being green!
```

At this point you might philosophize that traits are like Java interfaces with default methods, but they can actually do much more. Traits can, for example, declare fields and maintain state. In fact, you can do anything in a trait definition that you can do in a class definition, and the syntax looks exactly the same.

The key difference between classes and traits is that whereas in classes, super calls are statically bound, in traits, they are dynamically bound. If you write "`super.toString`" in a class, you know exactly which method implementation will be invoked. When you write the same thing in a trait, however, the method implementation to invoke for the super call is undefined when you define the trait. Rather, the implementation to invoke will be determined anew each time the trait is mixed into a concrete class. This

201

curious behavior of super is key to allowing traits to work as *stackable modifications*, which will be described in Section 11.3. The rules for resolving super calls will be given in Section 11.4.

11.2   Thin versus rich interfaces

One major use of traits is to automatically add methods to a class in terms of methods the class already has. That is, traits can enrich a *thin* interface, making it into a *rich* interface.

Thin versus rich interfaces represents a commonly faced trade-off in object-oriented design. The trade-off is between the implementers and the clients of an interface. A rich interface has many methods, which make it convenient for the caller. Clients can pick a method that exactly matches the functionality they need. A thin interface, on the other hand, has fewer methods, and thus is easier on the implementers. Clients calling into a thin interface, however, have to write more code. Given the smaller selection of methods to call, they may have to choose a less than perfect match for their needs and write extra code to use it.

Adding a concrete method to a trait tilts the thin-rich trade-off heavily towards rich interfaces, because it is is a one-time effort. You only need to implement the concrete method once, in the trait itself, instead of needing to reimplement it for every class that mixes in the trait. Thus, rich interfaces are less work to provide in Scala than in a language without traits.

To enrich an interface using traits, simply define a trait with a small number of abstract methods—the thin part of the trait's interface—and a potentially large number of concrete methods, all implemented in terms of the abstract methods. Then you can mix the enrichment trait into a class, implement the thin portion of the interface, and end up with a class that has all of the rich interface available.

A good example of a domain where a rich interface is convenient is comparison. Whenever you compare two objects that are ordered, it is convenient if you use a single method call to ask about the precise comparison you want. If you want "is less than," you would like to call <, and if you want "is less than or equal," you would like to call <=. With a thin comparison interface, you might just have the < method, and you would sometimes have to write things like "(x < y) || (x == y)". A rich interface would provide you with all of the usual comparison operators, thus allowing you to directly write things like "x <= y".

Suppose you took the `Rational` class from Chapter 6 and added comparison operations to it. You would end up with something like this:[1]

```scala
class Rational(n: Int, d: Int):
  // ...
  def < (that: Rational) =
    this.numer * that.denom < that.numer * this.denom
  def > (that: Rational) = that < this
  def <= (that: Rational) = (this < that) || (this == that)
  def >= (that: Rational) = (this > that) || (this == that)
```

This class defines four comparison operators (<, >, <=, and >=), and it's a classic demonstration of the costs of defining a rich interface. First, notice that three of the comparison operators are defined in terms of the first one. For example, > is defined as the reverse of <, and <= is defined as literally "less than or equal." Next, notice that all three of these methods would be the same for any other class that is comparable. There is nothing special about rational numbers regarding <=. In a comparison context, <= is *always* used to mean "less than or equals." Overall, there is quite a lot of boilerplate code in this class which would be the same in any other class that implements comparison operations.

This problem is so common that Scala provides a trait to help with it. The trait is called `Ordered`. To use it, you replace all of the individual comparison methods with a single `compare` method. The `Ordered` trait then defines <, >, <=, and >= for you in terms of this one method. Thus, trait `Ordered` allows you to enrich a class with comparison methods by implementing only one method, `compare`.

Here is how it looks if you define comparison operations on `Rational` by using the `Ordered` trait:

```scala
class Rational(n: Int, d: Int) extends Ordered[Rational]:
  // ...
  def compare(that: Rational) =
    (this.numer * that.denom) - (that.numer * this.denom)
```

---

[1]This example is based on the `Rational` class shown in Listing 6.5 on page 109, with equals, hashCode, and modifications to ensure a positive denom added.

There are just two things to do. First, this version of Rational mixes in the
Ordered trait. Unlike the traits you have seen so far, Ordered requires you
to specify a *type parameter* when you mix it in. Type parameters are not
discussed in detail until Chapter 18, but for now all you need to know is that
when you mix in Ordered, you must actually mix in Ordered[C], where C
is the class whose elements you compare. In this case, Rational mixes in
Ordered[Rational].

The second thing you need to do is define a compare method for comparing two objects. This method should compare the receiver, this, with
the object passed as an argument to the method. It should return an integer
that is zero if the objects are the same, negative if receiver is less than the
argument, and positive if the receiver is greater than the argument.

In this case, the comparison method of Rational uses a formula based
on converting the fractions to a common denominator and then subtracting
the resulting numerators. Given this mixin and the definition of compare,
class Rational now has all four comparison methods:

```
val half = new Rational(1, 2)
val third = new Rational(1, 3)
half < third    // false
half > third    // true
```

Any time you implement a class that is ordered by some comparison,
you should consider mixing in the Ordered trait. If you do, you will provide
the class's users with a rich set of comparison methods.

Beware that the Ordered trait does not define equals for you, because
it is unable to do so. The problem is that implementing equals in terms of
compare requires checking the type of the passed object, and because of type
erasure, Ordered itself cannot do this test. Thus, you need to define equals
yourself, even if you inherit Ordered. You can find out how to go about this
in *Advanced Programming in Scala*.

11.3   Traits as stackable modifications

You have now seen one major use of traits: turning a thin interface into a
rich one. Now we'll turn to a second major use: providing stackable modifications to classes. Traits let you *modify* the methods of a class, and they do
so in a way that allows you to *stack* those modifications with each other.

As an example, consider stacking modifications to a queue of integers. The queue will have two operations: put, which places integers in the queue, and get, which takes them back out. Queues are first-in, first-out, so get should return the integers in the same order they were put in the queue.

Given a class that implements such a queue, you could define traits to perform modifications such as these:

- Doubling: double all integers that are put in the queue

- Incrementing: increment all integers that are put in the queue

- Filtering: filter out negative integers from a queue

These three traits represent *modifications*, because they modify the behavior of an underlying queue class rather than defining a full queue class themselves. The three are also *stackable*. You can select any of the three you like, mix them into a class, and obtain a new class that has all of the modifications you chose.

An abstract IntQueue class is shown in Listing 11.5. IntQueue has a put method that adds new integers to the queue, and a get method that removes and returns them. A basic implementation of IntQueue that uses an ArrayBuffer is shown in Listing 11.6.

```scala
abstract class IntQueue:
  def get(): Int
  def put(x: Int): Unit
```

Listing 11.5 · Abstract class IntQueue.

```scala
import scala.collection.mutable.ArrayBuffer

class BasicIntQueue extends IntQueue:
  private val buf = ArrayBuffer.empty[Int]
  def get() = buf.remove(0)
  def put(x: Int) = buf += x
```

Listing 11.6 · A BasicIntQueue implemented with an ArrayBuffer.

Class BasicIntQueue has a private field holding an array buffer. The get method removes an entry from one end of the buffer, while the put method adds elements to the other end. Here's how this implementation looks when you use it:

```
val queue = new BasicIntQueue
queue.put(10)
queue.put(20)
queue.get()    // 10
queue.get()    // 20
```

So far so good. Now take a look at using traits to modify this behavior. Listing 11.7 shows a trait that doubles integers as they are put in the queue. The Doubling trait has two funny things going on. The first is that it declares a superclass, IntQueue. This declaration means that the trait can only be mixed into a class that also extends IntQueue. Thus, you can mix Doubling into BasicIntQueue, but not into Rational.

```
trait Doubling extends IntQueue:
  abstract override def put(x: Int) = super.put(2 * x)
```

Listing 11.7 · The Doubling stackable modification trait.

The second funny thing is that the trait has a super call on a method declared abstract. Such calls are illegal for normal classes because they will certainly fail at run time. For a trait, however, such a call can actually succeed. Since super calls in a trait are dynamically bound, the super call in trait Doubling will work so long as the trait is mixed in *after* another trait or class that gives a concrete definition to the method.

This arrangement is frequently needed with traits that implement stackable modifications. To tell the compiler you are doing this on purpose, you must mark such methods as abstract override. This combination of modifiers is only allowed for members of traits, not classes, and it means that the trait must be mixed into some class that has a concrete definition of the method in question.

Here's how it looks to use the trait:

```
class MyQueue extends BasicIntQueue, Doubling
val queue = new MyQueue
queue.put(10)
queue.get()    // 20
```

206

In the first line in this example, we define class MyQueue, which extends BasicIntQueue and mixes in Doubling. We then create a new MyQueue and put a 10 it, but because Doubling has been mixed in, the 10 is doubled. When we get an integer from the queue, it is a 20.

Note that MyQueue defines no new code. It simply identifies a class and mixes in a trait. In this situation, you could supply "BasicIntQueue with Doubling" directly to new instead of defining a named class. It would look as shown in Listing 11.8:[2]

```
val queue = new BasicIntQueue with Doubling
queue.put(10)
queue.get()    // 20
```

Listing 11.8 · Mixing in a trait when instantiating with new.

To see how to stack modifications, we need to define the other two modification traits, Incrementing and Filtering. Implementations of these traits are shown in Listing 11.9:

```
trait Incrementing extends IntQueue:
  abstract override def put(x: Int) = super.put(x + 1)

trait Filtering extends IntQueue:
  abstract override def put(x: Int) =
    if x >= 0 then super.put(x)
```

Listing 11.9 · Stackable modification traits Incrementing and Filtering.

Given these modifications, you can now pick and choose which ones you want for a particular queue. For example, here is a queue that both filters negative numbers and adds one to all numbers that it keeps:

```
val queue = new BasicIntQueue with Incrementing with Filtering
queue.put(-1)
queue.put(0)
queue.put(1)
queue.get()    // 1
queue.get()    // 2
```

---

[2]You must use with, not commas, to mix traits into an anonymous class.

The order of mixins is significant.[3] The precise rules are given in the following section, but, roughly speaking, traits further to the right take effect first. When you call a method on a class with mixins, the method in the trait furthest to the right is called first. If that method calls **super**, it invokes the method in the next trait to its left, and so on. In the previous example, `Filtering`'s `put` is invoked first, so it removes integers that were negative to begin with. `Incrementing`'s `put` is invoked second, so it adds one to those integers that remain.

If you reverse the order, first integers will be incremented, and *then* the integers that are still negative will be discarded:

```
val queue = new BasicIntQueue with
        Filtering with Incrementing
queue.put(-1)
queue.put(0)
queue.put(1)
queue.get()    // 0
queue.get()    // 1
queue.get()    // 2
```

Overall, code written in this style gives you a great deal of flexibility. You can define sixteen different classes by mixing in these three traits in different combinations and orders. That's a lot of flexibility for a small amount of code, so you should keep your eyes open for opportunities to arrange code as stackable modifications.

11.4 Why not multiple inheritance?

Traits are a way to inherit from multiple class-like constructs, but they differ in important ways from the multiple inheritance present in many languages. One difference is especially important: the interpretation of **super**. With multiple inheritance, the method called by a **super** call can be determined right where the call appears. With traits, the method called is determined by a *linearization* of the classes and traits that are mixed into a class. This is the difference that enables the stacking of modifications described in the previous section.

---

[3]Once a trait is mixed into a class, you can alternatively call it a *mixin*.

Before looking at linearization, take a moment to consider how to stack modifications in a language with traditional multiple inheritance. Imagine the following code, but this time interpreted as multiple inheritance instead of trait mixin:

```
// Multiple inheritance thought experiment
val q = new BasicIntQueue with Incrementing with Doubling
q.put(42)  // which put would be called?
```

The first question is: Which put method would get invoked by this call? Perhaps the rule would be that the last superclass wins, in which case Doubling would get called. Doubling would double its argument and call super.put, and that would be it. No incrementing would happen! Likewise, if the rule were that the first superclass wins, the resulting queue would increment integers but not double them. Thus neither ordering would work.

You might also entertain the possibility of allowing programmers to identify exactly which superclass method they want when they say super. You can in fact do that in Scala, by specifying the superclass in square brackets after super. Here's an example in which put implementations are explicitly invoked on both Incrementing and Doubling:

```
// Multiple inheritance thought experiment
trait MyQueue extends BasicIntQueue,
    Incrementing, Doubling:

  def put(x: Int) =
    super[Incrementing].put(x) // (this is rarely used,
    super[Doubling].put(x)     // but valid Scala)
```

If this were Scala's only approach, it would give us new problems (with the verbosity of this attempt being the least of its problems). What happens in this case is that the base class's put method gets called *twice*—once with an incremented value and once with a doubled value, but neither time with an incremented, doubled value.

There is simply no good solution to this problem using multiple inheritance. You would have to back up in your design and factor the code differently. By contrast, the traits solution in Scala is straightforward. You simply mix in Incrementing and Doubling, and Scala's special treatment of super in traits makes it all work out. Something is clearly different here from traditional multiple inheritance, but what?

As hinted previously, the answer is linearization. When you instantiate a class with new, Scala takes the class, and all of its inherited classes and traits, and puts them in a single, *linear* order. Then, whenever you call super inside one of those classes, the invoked method is the next one up the chain. If all of the methods but the last call super, the net result is stackable behavior.

Comparison with Java's default methods

Since Java 8, you can include default methods in interfaces. Although these resemble concrete methods in Scala traits, they are quite different because Java does not perform linearization. Because an interface cannot declare fields or extend a superclass other than Object, a default method can access object state only by invoking interface methods that are implemented by a subclass. By contrast, concrete methods in a Scala trait can access object state via fields declared in the trait or by invoking methods with super that access fields of supertraits or superclasses. In addition, if you are writing a Java class that inherits default methods with identical signatures from two different superinterfaces, Java will require that you implement that method yourself in the class. Your implementation can invoke either or both default methods by giving the name of the interface before super, as in "Doubling.super.put(x)". By contrast, Scala will ensure that your class inherits the nearest implementation in the linearization.

Rather than allowing you to implement stackable behavior, Java's default methods are aimed at allowing library designers to add methods to existing interfaces. Prior to Java 8, this was not practical because it would break binary compatibility of any class that implemented the interface. Java can now use a default implementation if a class doesn't provide an implementation, even if the class has not been recompiled since the addition of the new method to the interface.

The precise order of the linearization is described in the language specification. It is a little bit complicated, but the main thing you need to know is that, in any linearization, a class is always linearized in front of *all* its superclasses and mixed in traits. Thus, when you write a method that calls super, that method is definitely modifying the behavior of the superclasses and mixed in traits, not the other way around.

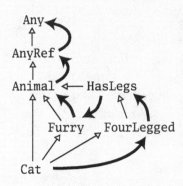

Figure 11.1 · Inheritance hierarchy and linearization of class `Cat`.

> **Note**
> The remainder of this section describes the details of linearization. You
> can safely skip the rest of this section if you are not interested in
> understanding those details right now.

The main properties of Scala's linearization are illustrated by the following example: Say you have a class `Cat`, which inherits from a superclass
`Animal` and two supertraits `Furry` and `FourLegged`. `FourLegged` extends
in turn another trait `HasLegs`:

```scala
class Animal
trait Furry extends Animal
trait HasLegs extends Animal
trait FourLegged extends HasLegs
class Cat extends Animal, Furry, FourLegged
```

Class `Cat`'s inheritance hierarchy and linearization are shown in Figure 11.1. Inheritance is indicated using traditional UML notation:[4] arrows
with white, triangular arrowheads indicate inheritance, with the arrowhead
pointing to the supertype. The arrows with darkened, non-triangular arrowheads depict linearization. The darkened arrowheads point in the direction
in which `super` calls will be resolved.

The linearization of `Cat` is computed from back to front as follows. The
last part of the linearization of `Cat` is the linearization of its superclass,

---

[4]Rumbaugh, *et al.*, *The Unified Modeling Language Reference Manual.* [Rum04]

Table 11.1 · Linearization of types in `Cat`'s hierarchy

Type	Linearization
`Animal`	Animal, AnyRef, Any
`Furry`	Furry, Animal, AnyRef, Any
`FourLegged`	FourLegged, HasLegs, Animal, AnyRef, Any
`HasLegs`	HasLegs, Animal, AnyRef, Any
`Cat`	Cat, FourLegged, HasLegs, Furry, Animal, AnyRef, Any

`Animal`. This linearization is copied over without any changes. (The linearization of each of these types is shown in Table 11.1 on page 212.) Because `Animal` doesn't explicitly extend a superclass or mix in any supertraits, it by default extends `AnyRef`, which extends `Any`. `Animal`'s linearization, therefore, looks like:

$$\text{Animal} \rightarrow \text{AnyRef} \rightarrow \text{Any}$$

The second to last part is the linearization of the first mixin, trait `Furry`, but all classes that are already in the linearization of `Animal` are left out now, so that each class appears only once in `Cat`'s linearization. The result is:

$$\text{Furry} \rightarrow \text{Animal} \rightarrow \text{AnyRef} \rightarrow \text{Any}$$

This is preceded by the linearization of `FourLegged`, where again any classes that have already been copied in the linearizations of the superclass or the first mixin are left out:

$$\text{FourLegged} \rightarrow \text{HasLegs} \rightarrow \text{Furry} \rightarrow \text{Animal} \rightarrow \text{AnyRef} \rightarrow \text{Any}$$

Finally, the first class in the linearization of `Cat` is `Cat` itself:

$$\text{Cat} \rightarrow \text{FourLegged} \rightarrow \text{HasLegs} \rightarrow \text{Furry} \rightarrow \text{Animal} \rightarrow \text{AnyRef} \rightarrow \text{Any}$$

When any of these classes and traits invokes a method via **super**, the implementation invoked will be the first implementation to its right in the linearization.

11.5   Trait parameters

As of Scala 3, traits can take value parameters. You define traits that take
parameters the same way you define classes that take parameters: by placing
a comma-separated list of them next to the trait name. For example, you can
pass a philosophical statement as a parameter to the `Philosophical` trait
shown in Listing 11.10:

```
trait Philosophical(message: String):
  def philosophize = message
```

Listing 11.10 · Defining a trait parameter.

Now that the `Philosophical` trait takes a parameter, each subclass must
pass it's own philosophical message as a parameter to the trait, like this:

```
class Frog extends Animal,
    Philosophical("I croak, therefore I am!")

class Duck extends Animal,
    Philosophical("I quack, therefore I am!")
```

In short, you must specify a trait's parameter value when defining a class
that mixes in the trait. Each `Philosophical` class's philosophy will now be
determined by the passed `message` parameter:

```
val frog = new Frog
frog.philosophize   // I croak, therefore I am!
val duck = new Duck
duck.philosophize   // I quack, therefore I am!
```

Trait parameters are evaluated immediately before the trait initializes.[5]
As with a class parameter, a trait parameter is by default[6] only available to
the trait body. To use the `message` parameter in a class that implements the
trait, therefore, you can capture the parameter by making it available from
a field. That field is then guaranteed to be initialized and available for the
implementing class during the class's initialization.

---

[5]Trait parameters in Scala 3 replaces *early initializers* in Scala 2.

[6]As with class parameters, you can use a parametric field to define a public field initialized with a passed trait parameter. This will be demonstrated in Section 20.5.

As you use parameterized traits, you may notice that the rules for trait parameters are slightly different than for class parameters. In both cases, you can only initialize once. However, although each class can only be extended by one subclass in a hierarchy, a trait can be mixed in by multiple subclasses. In that case, you must initialize the trait when defining the class that mixes in the trait highest up in the hierarchy. To illustrate, consider the superclass for any thoughtful animal shown in Listing 11.11:

```
class ProfoundAnimal extends Animal,
    Philosophical("In the beginning was the deed.")
```

Listing 11.11 · Supplying a trait parameter.

If a class's superclass does not itself extend the trait, you must specify the trait parameter when defining the class. ProfoundAnimal's superclass is Animal, and Animal does not extend Philosophical. Therefore, you must specify the trait parameter when defining ProfoundAnimal.

On the other hand, if the class's superclass also extends the trait, then you can no longer provide the trait parameter when defining the class. This is shown in Listing 11.12:

```
class Frog extends ProfoundAnimal, Philosophical
```

Listing 11.12 · *Not* supplying a trait parameter.

Frog's superclass ProfoundAnimal extends trait Philosophical and supplies its message parameter. When defining Frog, you can no longer specify the message as a parameter, since the parameter was already filled in by ProfoundAnimal. Thus, this frog will exhibit the behavior arising from ProfoundAnimal's initialization of Philosophical:

```
val frog = new Frog
frog.philosophize   // In the beginning was the deed.
```

Finally, a trait cannot pass parameters to its parent traits. For example, consider trait PhilosophicalAnimal that extends trait Philosophical:

```
trait PhilosophicalAnimal extends Animal with Philosophical
```

You might think that a thoughtful frog could be defined like this:

```
// Does not compile
class Frog extends PhilosophicalAnimal(
    "I croak, therefore I am!")
```

However, this does not work. Instead, you must explicitly specify the message to Philosophical when you define class Frog, like this:

```
class Frog extends
    Philosophical("I croak, therefore I am!"),
    PhilosophicalAnimal
```

Or like this:

```
class Frog extends PhilosophicalAnimal,
    Philosophical("I croak, therefore I am!")
```

11.6 Conclusion

This chapter has shown you how traits work and how to use them in several common idioms. You saw that traits are similar to multiple inheritance. But because traits interpret super using linearization, they both avoid some of the difficulties of traditional multiple inheritance and allow you to stack behaviors. You also saw the Ordered trait and learned how to write your own enrichment traits.

Now that you have seen all of these facets, it is worth stepping back and taking another look at traits as a whole. Traits do not merely support the idioms described in this chapter; they are a fundamental unit of code that is reusable through inheritance. As such, many experienced Scala programmers start with traits when they are at the early stages of implementation. Each trait can hold less than an entire concept, a mere fragment of a concept. As the design solidifies, the fragments can be combined into more complete concepts through trait mixin.

Chapter 12

Packages, Imports, and Exports

When working on a program, especially a large one, it is important to minimize *coupling*—the extent to which the various parts of the program rely on the other parts. Low coupling reduces the risk that a small, seemingly innocuous change in one part of the program will have devastating consequences in another part. One way to minimize coupling is to write in a modular style. You divide the program into a number of smaller modules, each of which has an inside and an outside. When working on the inside of a module—its *implementation*—you need only coordinate with other programmers working on that very same module. Only when you must change the outside of a module—its *interface*—is it necessary to coordinate with developers working on other modules.

This chapter shows several constructs that help you program in a modular style. It shows how to place things in packages, make names visible through imports, and control the visibility of definitions through access modifiers. The constructs are similar in spirit to constructs in Java, but there are some differences—usually ways that are more consistent—so it's worth reading this chapter even if you already know Java.

12.1 Putting code in packages

Scala code resides in the Java platform's global hierarchy of packages. The example code you've seen so far in this book has been in the *unnamed* package. You can place code into named packages in Scala in two ways. First, you can place the contents of an entire file into a package by putting a package clause at the top of the file, as shown in Listing 12.1.

```
package bobsrockets.navigation
class Navigator
```

Listing 12.1 · Placing the contents of an entire file into a package.

The `package` clause of Listing 12.1 places class `Navigator` into the package named `bobsrockets.navigation`. Presumably, this is the navigation software developed by Bob's Rockets, Inc.

Note

Because Scala code is part of the Java ecosystem, it is recommended to follow Java's reverse-domain-name convention for Scala packages that you release to the public. Thus, a better name for `Navigator`'s package might be `com.bobsrockets.navigation`. In this chapter, however, we'll leave off the "`com.`" to make the examples easier to understand.

The other way you can place code into packages in Scala is more like C# namespaces. You follow a package clause by a colon and an indented section of code containing the definitions that go into the package. This syntax is called a *packaging*. The packaging shown in Listing 12.2 has the same effect as the code in Listing 12.1:

```
package bobsrockets.navigation:
  class Navigator
```

Listing 12.2 · Long form of a simple package declaration.

For such simple examples, you might as well use the syntactic sugar shown in Listing 12.1. However, one use of the more general notation is to have different parts of a file in different packages. For example, if you want to email or post to a discussion forum a snippet of Scala code that involves several packages, you can use packaging, as shown in Listing 12.3.

12.2 Concise access to related code

When code is divided into a package hierarchy, it doesn't just help people browse through the code. It also tells the compiler that code in the same package is related in some way to each other. Scala takes advantage of this

```
package bobsrockets:
  package navigation:

    // In package bobsrockets.navigation
    class Navigator

    package launch:

      // In package bobsrockets.navigation.launch
      class Booster
```

Listing 12.3 · Multiple packages in the same file.

```
package bobsrockets:
  package navigation:

    class Navigator:
      // No need to say bobsrockets.navigation.StarMap
      val map = new StarMap

    class StarMap

    class Ship:
      // No need to say bobsrockets.navigation.Navigator
      val nav = new navigation.Navigator

    package fleets:

      class Fleet:
        // No need to say bobsrockets.Ship
        def addShip = new Ship
```

Listing 12.4 · Concise access to classes and packages.

```
package bobsrockets:
  class Ship

package bobsrockets.fleets:
  class Fleet:
    // Doesn't compile! Ship is not in scope.
    def addShip = new Ship
```

Listing 12.5 · Symbols in enclosing packages not automatically available.

```
// In file launch.scala
package launch:
  class Booster3

// In file bobsrockets.scala
package bobsrockets:

  package launch:
    class Booster2

  package navigation:
    package launch:
      class Booster1

    class MissionControl:
      val booster1 = new launch.Booster1
      val booster2 = new bobsrockets.launch.Booster2
      val booster3 = new _root_.launch.Booster3
```

Listing 12.6 · Accessing hidden package names.

relatedness by allowing short, unqualified names when accessing code that is in the same package.

Listing 12.4 gives three simple examples. First, as you would expect, a class can be accessed from within its own package without needing a prefix. That's why new StarMap compiles. Class StarMap is in the same package, bobsrockets.navigation, as the new expression that accesses it, so the package name doesn't need to be prefixed.

Second, a package itself can be accessed from its containing package without needing a prefix. In Listing 12.4, look at how class Navigator is instantiated. The new expression appears in package bobsrockets, which is the containing package of bobsrockets.navigation. Thus, it can access package bobsrockets.navigation as simply navigation.

Third, when using the nested packaging syntax, all names accessible in scopes outside the packaging are also available inside it. An example in Listing 12.4 is the way addShip() creates a new Ship. The method is defined within two packagings: an outer one for bobsrockets, and an inner one for bobsrockets.fleets. Since Ship is accessible in the outer packaging, it can be referenced from within addShip().

Note that this kind of access is only available if you explicitly nest the packagings. If you stick to one package per file, then—like in Java—the only names available will be the ones defined in the current package. In Listing 12.5, the packaging of `bobsrockets.fleets` has been moved to the top level. Since it is no longer enclosed in a packaging for `bobsrockets`, names from `bobsrockets` are not immediately in scope. As a result, `new Ship` gives a compile error. If nesting packages with indentation shifts your code uncomfortably to the right, you can also use multiple package clauses without the indentation.[1] For instance, the code below also defines class `Fleet` in two nested packages `bobsrockets` and `fleets`, just like you saw it in Listing 12.4:

```
package bobsrockets
package fleets
class Fleet:
  // No need to say bobsrockets.Ship
  def addShip = new Ship
```

One final trick is important to know. Sometimes, you end up coding in a heavily crowded scope where package names are hiding each other. In Listing 12.6, the scope of class `MissionControl` includes three separate packages named `launch`! There's one `launch` in `bobsrockets.navigation`, one in `bobsrockets`, and one at the top level. How would you reference each of `Booster1`, `Booster2`, and `Booster3`?

Accessing the first one is easiest. A reference to `launch` by itself will get you to package `bobsrockets.navigation.launch`, because that is the `launch` package defined in the closest enclosing scope. Thus, you can refer to the first booster class as simply `launch.Booster1`. Referring to the second one also is not tricky. You can write `bobsrockets.launch.Booster2` and be clear about which one you are referencing. That leaves the question of the third booster class: How can you access `Booster3`, considering that a nested `launch` package shadows the top-level one?

To help in this situation, Scala provides a package named `_root_` that is outside any package a user can write. Put another way, every top-level package you can write is treated as a member of package `_root_`. For example, both `launch` and `bobsrockets` of Listing 12.6 are members of package `_root_`. As a result, `_root_.launch` gives you the top-level `launch` package, and `_root_.launch.Booster3` designates the outermost booster class.

---

[1] This style of multiple package clauses without braces is called *chained package clauses*.

12.3 Imports

In Scala, packages and their members can be imported using `import` clauses. Imported items can then be accessed by a simple name like `File`, as opposed to requiring a qualified name like `java.io.File`. For example, consider the code shown in Listing 12.7.

```
package bobsdelights

abstract class Fruit(
  val name: String,
  val color: String
)

object Fruits:
  object Apple extends Fruit("apple", "red")
  object Orange extends Fruit("orange", "orange")
  object Pear extends Fruit("pear", "yellowish")
  val menu = List(Apple, Orange, Pear)
```

Listing 12.7 · Bob's delightful fruits, ready for import.

An `import` clause makes members of a package or object available by their names alone without needing to prefix them by the package or object name. Here are some simple examples:

```
// easy access to Fruit
import bobsdelights.Fruit

// easy access to all members of bobsdelights
import bobsdelights.*

// easy access to all members of Fruits
import bobsdelights.Fruits.*
```

The first of these corresponds to Java's single type import and the second to Java's *on-demand* import. Although on-demand imports were written with a trailing underscore (_) in Scala 2 instead of an asterisk (*), this was changed to asterisk in Scala 3 to be more consistent with other languages. The third import clause above corresponds to Java's import of static class fields.

These three imports give you a taste of what imports can do, but Scala imports are actually much more general. For one, imports in Scala can appear anywhere, not just at the beginning of a compilation unit. Also, they can refer to arbitrary values. For instance, the import shown in Listing 12.8 is possible:

```
def showFruit(fruit: Fruit) =
  import fruit.*
  s"${name}s are $color"
```

Listing 12.8 · Importing the members of a regular (not singleton) object.

Method `showFruit` imports all members of its parameter `fruit`, which is of type `Fruit`. The subsequent `println` statement can refer to `name` and `color` directly. These two references are equivalent to `fruit.name` and `fruit.color`. This syntax is particularly useful when you use objects as modules, which will be described in Chapter 7.

Scala's flexible imports

Scala's `import` clauses are quite a bit more flexible than Java's. There are three principal differences. In Scala, imports:

- may appear anywhere
- may refer to objects (singleton or regular) in addition to packages
- let you rename and hide some of the imported members

Another way Scala's imports are flexible is that they can import packages themselves, not just their non-package members. This is only natural if you think of nested packages being contained in their surrounding package. For example, in Listing 12.9, the package `java.util.regex` is imported. This makes `regex` usable as a simple name. To access the `Pattern` singleton object from the `java.util.regex` package, you can just say, `regex.Pattern`, as shown in Listing 12.9:

Imports in Scala can also rename or hide members. This is done with an *import selector clause* enclosed in braces, which follows the object from which members are imported. Here are some examples:

```
import Fruits.{Apple, Orange}
```

```
import java.util.regex
class AStarB:
  // Accesses java.util.regex.Pattern
  val pat = regex.Pattern.compile("a*b")
```

Listing 12.9 · Importing a package name.

This imports just members `Apple` and `Orange` from object `Fruits`.

```
import Fruits.{Apple as McIntosh, Orange}
```

This imports the two members `Apple` and `Orange` from object `Fruits`. However, the `Apple` object is renamed to `McIntosh`, so this object can be accessed with either `Fruits.Apple` or `McIntosh`. A renaming clause is always of the form "<original-name> as <new-name>". If you have only one name to import and rename, you can leave off the curly braces:

```
import java.sql.Date as SDate
```

This imports the SQL date class as `SDate`, so that you can simultaneously import the normal Java date class as simply `Date`.

```
import java.sql as S
```

This imports the `java.sql` package as `S`, so that you can write things like `S.Date`.

```
import Fruits.{*}
```

This imports all members from object `Fruits`. It means the same thing as `import Fruits.*`.

```
import Fruits.{Apple as McIntosh, *}
```

This imports all members from object `Fruits` but renames `Apple` to `McIntosh`.

```
import Fruits.{Pear as _, *}
```

This imports all members of `Fruits` *except* `Pear`. A clause of the form "<original-name> as _" excludes <original-name> from the names that are imported. In a sense, renaming something to '_' means hiding it altogether. This is useful to avoid ambiguities. Say you have two packages, Fruits and Laptops, which both define a class Apple. If you want to get just the laptop named Apple, and not the fruit, you could still use two imports on demand like this:

```
import Laptops.*
import Fruits.{Apple as _, *}
```

This would import all Laptops and all Fruits, except for Apple.

These examples demonstrate the great flexibility Scala offers when it comes to importing members selectively and possibly under different names. In summary, an import selector can consist of the following:

- A simple name x. This includes x in the set of imported names.

- A renaming clause x as y. This makes the member named x visible under the name y.

- A hiding clause x as _. This excludes x from the set of imported names.

- A *catch-all* '*'. This imports all members except those members mentioned in a preceding clause. If a catch-all is given, it must come last in the list of import selectors.

The simpler import clauses shown at the beginning of this section can be seen as special abbreviations of import clauses with a selector clause. For example, "import p.*" is equivalent to "import p.{*}" and "import p.n" is equivalent to "import p.{n}".

12.4 Implicit imports

Scala adds some imports implicitly to every program. In essence, it is as if the following three import clauses had been added to the top of every source file with extension ".scala":

```
import java.lang.* // everything in the java.lang package
import scala.*     // everything in the scala package
import Predef.*    // everything in the Predef object
```

225

The java.lang package contains standard Java classes. It is always implicitly imported in Scala source files.[2] Because java.lang is imported implicitly, you can write Thread instead of java.lang.Thread, for instance.

As you have no doubt realized by now, the scala package contains the standard Scala library, with many common classes and objects. Because the scala package is imported implicitly, you can write Int instead of scala.Int, for instance.

The Predef object contains many definitions of type aliases, methods, and conversions that are commonly used on Scala programs. For example, because Predef is imported implicitly, you can write assert instead of Predef.assert.

These three import clauses are treated a bit specially in that later imports overshadow earlier ones. For instance, the StringBuilder class is defined both in package scala and java.lang. Because the scala import overshadows the java.lang import, the simple name StringBuilder will refer to scala.StringBuilder, not java.lang.StringBuilder.

12.5 Access modifiers

Members of packages, classes, or objects can be labeled with the access modifiers private and protected. These modifiers restrict access to the members to certain regions of code. Scala's treatment of access modifiers roughly follows Java's but there are some important differences which are explained in this section.

Private members

Private members in Scala are treated similarly to Java. A member labeled private is visible only inside the class or object that contains the member definition. In Scala, this rule applies also for inner classes. This treatment is more consistent, but differs from Java. Consider the example shown in Listing 12.10.

In Scala, the access (new Inner).f is illegal because f is declared private in Inner and the access is not from within class Inner. By contrast, the first access to f in class InnerMost is OK, because that access

---

[2]Scala also originally had an implementation on .NET., where namespace System, the .NET analogue of package java.lang, was imported instead.

```
class Outer:
  class Inner:
    private def f = "f"
    class InnerMost:
      f // OK
  (new Inner).f // error: f is not accessible
```

Listing 12.10 · How private access differs in Scala and Java.

is contained in the body of class Inner. Java would permit both accesses because it lets an outer class access private members of its inner classes.

Protected members

Access to protected members in Scala is also a bit more restrictive than in Java. In Scala, a protected member is only accessible from subclasses of the class in which the member is defined. In Java such accesses are also possible from other classes in the same package. In Scala, there is another way to achieve this effect[3] so protected is free to be left as is. The example shown in Listing 12.11 illustrates protected accesses.

```
package p:
  class Super:
    protected def f = "f"
  class Sub extends Super:
    f
  class Other:
    (new Super).f  // error: f is not accessible
```

Listing 12.11 · How protected access differs in Scala and Java.

In Listing 12.11, the access to f in class Sub is OK because f is declared protected in Super and Sub is a subclass of Super. By contrast the access to f in Other is not permitted, because Other does not inherit from Super.

---

[3]Using *qualifiers*, described in "Scope of protection" on page 228.

In Java, the latter access would be still permitted because Other is in the same package as Super.

Public members

Scala has no explicit modifier for public members: Any member not labeled private or protected is public. Public members can be accessed from anywhere.

```
package bobsrockets

package navigation:
  private[bobsrockets] class Navigator:
    protected[navigation] def useStarChart() = {}
    class LegOfJourney:
      private[Navigator] val distance = 100

package launch:
  import navigation.*
  object Vehicle:
    private[launch] val guide = new Navigator
```

Listing 12.12 · Flexible scope of protection with access qualifiers.

Scope of protection

Access modifiers in Scala can be augmented with qualifiers. A modifier of the form private[X] or protected[X] means that access is private or protected "up to" X, where X designates some enclosing package, class or singleton object.

Qualified access modifiers give you very fine-grained control over visibility. In particular they enable you to express Java's accessibility notions, such as package private, package protected, or private up to outermost class, which are not directly expressible with simple modifiers in Scala. But they also let you express accessibility rules that cannot be expressed in Java.

Listing 12.12 presents an example with many access qualifiers being used. In this listing, class Navigator is labeled private[bobsrockets]. This means that this class is visible in all classes and objects that are contained in package bobsrockets. In particular, the access to Navigator in object Vehicle is permitted because Vehicle is contained in package launch, which is contained in bobsrockets. On the other hand, all code outside the package bobsrockets cannot access class Navigator.

This technique is quite useful in large projects that span several packages. It allows you to define things that are visible in several sub-packages of your project but that remain hidden from clients external to your project.[4]

Of course, the qualifier of a private may also be the directly enclosing package. An example is the access modifier of guide in object Vehicle in Listing 12.12. Such an access modifier is equivalent to Java's package-private access.

Table 12.1 · Effects of private qualifiers on LegOfJourney.distance

no access modifier	public access
private[bobsrockets]	access within outer package
private[navigation]	same as package visibility in Java
private[Navigator]	same as private in Java
private[LegOfJourney]	same as private in Scala

All qualifiers can also be applied to protected, with the same meaning as private. That is, a modifier protected[X] in a class C allows access to the labeled definition in all subclasses of C and also within the enclosing package, class, or object X. For instance, the useStarChart method in Listing 12.12 is accessible in all subclasses of Navigator and also in all code contained in the enclosing package navigation. It thus corresponds exactly to the meaning of protected in Java.

The qualifiers of private can also refer to an enclosing class or object. For instance the distance variable in class LegOfJourney in Listing 12.12 is labeled private[Navigator], so it is visible from everywhere in class Navigator. This gives the same access capabilities as for private members of inner classes in Java. A private[C] where C is the outermost enclosing class is the same as just private in Java.

To summarize, Table 12.1 on page 229 lists the effects of private qualifiers. Each line shows a qualified private modifier and what it would mean if such a modifier were attached to the distance variable declared in class LegOfJourney in Listing 12.12.

---

[4]This technique is possible in Java via the module system introduced in JDK 9.

Visibility and companion objects

In Java, static members and instance members belong to the same class, so access modifiers apply uniformly to them. You have already seen that in Scala there are no static members; instead you can have a companion object that contains members that exist only once. For instance, in Listing 12.13 object Rocket is a companion of class Rocket.

```scala
class Rocket:
  import Rocket.fuel
  private def canGoHomeAgain = fuel > 20

object Rocket:
  private def fuel = 10
  def chooseStrategy(rocket: Rocket) =
    if rocket.canGoHomeAgain then
      goHome()
    else
      pickAStar()

  def goHome() = {}
  def pickAStar() = {}
```

Listing 12.13: Accessing private members of companion classes and objects.

Scala's access rules privilege companion objects and classes when it comes to private or protected accesses. A class shares all its access rights with its companion object and *vice versa*. In particular, an object can access all private members of its companion class, just as a class can access all private members of its companion object.

For instance, the Rocket class in Listing 12.13 can access method fuel, which is declared private in object Rocket. Analogously, the Rocket object can access the private method canGoHomeAgain in class Rocket.

One exception where the similarity between Scala and Java breaks down concerns protected static members. A protected static member of a Java class C can be accessed in all subclasses of C. By contrast, a protected member in a companion object makes no sense, as singleton objects don't have any subclasses.

12.6 Top-level definitions

So far, the only code you have seen added to packages are classes, traits, and singleton objects. These are by far the most common definitions that are placed at the top level of a package. But Scala doesn't limit you to just those—Any kind of definition that you can put inside a class can also be at the top level of a package. If you have some helper method you'd like to be in scope for an entire package, go ahead and put it right at the top level of the package.

To do so, put the definitions in the package as you would a class, trait, or object. An example is shown in Listing 12.14. File ShowFruit.scala declares the showFruit utility method from Listing 12.8 as a member of package bobsdelights. Given that definition, any other code in any package can import the method just like it would import a class. For example, Listing 12.14 also shows the standalone object PrintMenu, which is located in a different package. PrintMenu can import the utility method showFruit in the same way it would import the class Fruit.

```scala
// In file ShowFruit.scala
package bobsdelights

def showFruit(fruit: Fruit) =
  import fruit.*
  s"${name}s are $color"

// In file PrintMenu.scala
package printmenu

import bobsdelights.Fruits
import bobsdelights.showFruit

object PrintMenu:
  def main(args: Array[String]) =
    println(
      for fruit <- Fruits.menu yield
        showFruit(fruit)
    )
```

Listing 12.14 · A package object.

Looking ahead, there are other uses of top-level definitions for kinds of

231

definitions you haven't seen yet. Top-level definitions are frequently used to hold package-wide type aliases (Chapter 20) and extension methods (Chapter 22). The scala package includes top-level definitions, which are available to all Scala code.

12.7 Exports

In Section 10.11 we recommended that you should prefer composition over inheritance, especially when your primary goal is code reuse. This is an application of the principle of least power: Composition treats components as blackboxes whereas inheritance can affect the internal workings of components through overriding. Sometimes the tight coupling implied by inheritance is the best solution for a problem, but where this is not necessary the looser coupling of composition is better.

In most popular object-oriented programming languages it is easier to use inheritance than composition. In Scala 2, for example, inheritance only required an extends clause whereas composition required a verbose elaboration of a sequence of forwarders. Most object-oriented languages have, therefore, been pushing programmers to a solution that is often too powerful.

Exports, a new feature introduced in Scala 3, aim to redress this imbalance. Exports make composition relationships as concise and easy to express as inheritance relationships. Exports also offer more flexibility than extends clauses, since members can be renamed or omitted.

As an example, imagine you wanted to make a type to represent positive integers. You could define it like this:[5]

```
case class PosInt(value: Int):
  require(value > 0)
```

This class enables you to state in a type that an integer is positive. However, as written you would need to access value to perform any arithmetic on its underlying Int:

```
val x = PosInt(88)
x.value + 1 // 89
```

---

[5]Two alternate ways to create this type that avoid boxing are AnyVals and opaque types. AnyVals will be covered in Section 17.4, opaque types in *Advanced Programming in Scala*.

You could make this more convenient by implementing a + method on PosInt that delegates to the underlying value's + method, like this:

```
case class PosInt(value: Int):
  require(value > 0)
  def +(x: Int): Int = value + x
```

With the addition of this forwarding method, you can now perform integer addition on PosInts without needing to access value:

```
val x = PosInt(77)
x + 1 // 78
```

You could make PosInt even more convenient by implementing all of Int's methods, but there are over one hundred of them. If you could define PosInt as a subclass of Int, you would inherit all of those methods and not need to reimplement them. But because Int is final, you cannot do this. This is why the PosInt class must use composition and delegation instead of inheritance.

In Scala 3, you can use the export keyword to indicate the forwarding methods you want, and the compiler will generate them for you. Here's how you would create a PosInt class that declares forwarding methods to correspondingly named methods on the underlying value:

```
case class PosInt(value: Int):
  require(value > 0)
  export value.*
```

With this design, you can call any methods on a PosInt that are declared directly on Int:

```
val x = PosInt(99)
x + 1 // 100
x - 1 // 98
x / 3 // 33
```

An export clause creates final methods called *export aliases* for each overloaded form of each exported method name. For example, the + method that takes an Int would have this signature on PosInt:

```
final def +(x: Int): Int = value + x
```

You can use all the various forms of syntax available for imports with exports. For example, you may decide that you would rather not offer symbolic shift operators, <<, >>, and >>>, on `PosInt`:

```
val x = PosInt(24)
x << 1  // 48 (shift left)
x >> 1  // 12 (shift right)
x >>> 1 // 12 (unsigned shift right)
```

You can rename those operators with **as** when you export them, similar to how you can rename identifers with **as** when you import them. Here's an example:

```
case class PosInt(value: Int):
  require(value > 0)
  export value.{<< as shl, >> as shr, >>> as ushr, *}
```

Given this export clause, the shift operators on `PosInt` will no longer have symbolic names:

```
val x = PosInt(24)
x shl 1  // 48
x shr 1  // 12
x ushr 1 // 12
```

You can also exclude methods from a wildcard export with "**as** _", similar to how you exclude an identifier from a wildcard import. For example, because the shift right (>>) and unsigned shift right (>>>) will always produce the same result on a positive integer, you may decide to offer only one right shift operator, shr. You could achieve this by excluding the >>> operator from the export with ">>> **as** _", like this:

```
case class PosInt(value: Int):
  require(value > 0)
  export value.{<< as shl, >> as shr, >>> as _, *}
```

Now, no alias of any name is created for the >>> method:

```
scala> val x = PosInt(39)
val x: PosInt = PosInt(39)

scala> x shr 1
```

```
val res0: Int = 19
scala> x >>> 1
1 |x >>> 1
  |^^^^^
  |value >>> is not a member of PosInt
```

12.8   Conclusion

In this chapter, you saw the basic constructs for dividing a program into packages. This gives you a simple and useful kind of modularity, so that you can work with very large bodies of code without different parts of the code trampling on each other. Scala's system is the same in spirit as Java's packages, but there are some differences where Scala chooses to be more consistent or more general. You also saw a new feature, exports, which aims to make composition as convenient as inheritance for code reuse.

Looking ahead, *Advanced Programming in Scala* describes a more flexible module system than division into packages. In addition to letting you separate code into several namespaces, that approach allows modules to be parameterized and inherit from each other. In the next chapter, we'll turn our attention to pattern matching.

Chapter 13

Pattern Matching

This chapter describes *case classes* and *pattern matching*, constructs that support you when writing regular, non-encapsulated data structures. These two constructs are particularly helpful for tree-like recursive data.

If you have programmed in a functional language before, then you will probably recognize pattern matching. But case classes will be new to you. Case classes are Scala's way to allow pattern matching on objects without requiring a large amount of boilerplate. Generally, all you need to do is add a single `case` keyword to each class that you want to be pattern matchable.

This chapter starts with an example of case classes and pattern matching. It then goes through all of the kinds of patterns that are supported, talks about the role of *sealed* classes, discusses enums, `Options`, and shows some non-obvious places in the language where pattern matching is used. Finally, a larger, more realistic example of pattern matching is shown.

13.1 A simple example

Before delving into all the rules and nuances of pattern matching, it is worth looking at a simple example to get the general idea. Let's say you need to write a library that manipulates arithmetic expressions, perhaps as part of a domain-specific language you are designing.

A first step to tackling this problem is the definition of the input data. To keep things simple, we'll concentrate on arithmetic expressions consisting of variables, numbers, and unary and binary operations. This is expressed by the hierarchy of Scala classes shown in Listing 13.1.

```
trait Expr
case class Var(name: String) extends Expr
case class Num(number: Double) extends Expr
case class UnOp(operator: String, arg: Expr) extends Expr
case class BinOp(operator: String,
    left: Expr, right: Expr) extends Expr
```

Listing 13.1 · Defining case classes.

The hierarchy includes a trait `Expr` with four subclasses, one for each kind of expression being considered. The bodies of all five classes are empty.

Case classes

The other noteworthy thing about the declarations of Listing 13.1 is that each subclass has a `case` modifier. Classes with such a modifier are called *case classes*. As mentioned in Section 4.4, using the `case` modifier makes the Scala compiler add some syntactic conveniences to your class.

First, it adds a factory method with the name of the class. This means that, for instance, you can write `Var("x")` to construct a `Var` object.

```
val v = Var("x")
```

The factory methods are particularly nice when you nest them. Because there are no noisy `new` keywords sprinkled throughout the code, you can take in the expression's structure at a glance:

```
val op = BinOp("+", Num(1), v)
```

The second syntactic convenience is that all arguments in the parameter list of a case class implicitly get a `val` prefix, so they are maintained as fields:

```
v.name    // x
op.left   // Num(1.0)
```

Third, the compiler adds "natural" implementations of methods `toString`, `hashCode`, and `equals` to your class. They will print, hash, and compare a whole tree consisting of the class and (recursively) all its arguments. Since `==` in Scala always delegates to `equals`, this means that elements of case classes are always compared structurally:

```
op.toString              // BinOp(+,Num(1.0),Var(x))
op.right == Var("x")     // true
```

Finally, the compiler adds a `copy` method to your class for making modified copies. This method is useful for making a new instance of the class that is the same as another one except that one or two attributes are different. The method works by using named and default parameters (see Section 8.8). You specify the changes you'd like to make by using named parameters. For any parameter you don't specify, the value from the old object is used. As an example, here is how you can make an operation just like op except that the operator has changed:

```
op.copy(operator = "-")   // BinOp(-,Num(1.0),Var(x))
```

All these conventions add a lot of convenience—at a small price. You have to write the case modifier, and your classes and objects become a bit larger. They are larger because additional methods are generated and an implicit field is added for each constructor parameter. However, the biggest advantage of case classes is that they support pattern matching.[1]

Pattern matching

Say you want to simplify arithmetic expressions of the kinds just presented. There is a multitude of possible simplification rules. The following three rules just serve as an illustration:

```
UnOp("-", UnOp("-", e))  => e   // Double negation
BinOp("+", e, Num(0)) => e      // Adding zero
BinOp("*", e, Num(1)) => e      // Multiplying by one
```

Using pattern matching, these rules can be taken almost as they are to form the core of a simplification function in Scala, as shown in Listing 13.2. The function, `simplifyTop`, can be used like this:

```
simplifyTop(UnOp("-", UnOp("-", Var("x"))))   // Var(x)
```

The right-hand side of `simplifyTop` consists of a `match` expression. `match` corresponds to `switch` in Java, but it's written after the selector expression. In other words, it's:

---

[1]Case classes support pattern matching by generating an *extractor* method, `unapply`, in the companion object. This will be described in *Advanced Programming in Scala*.

239

```
def simplifyTop(expr: Expr): Expr =
  expr match
    case UnOp("-", UnOp("-", e))  => e // Double negation
    case BinOp("+", e, Num(0)) => e // Adding zero
    case BinOp("*", e, Num(1)) => e // Multiplying by one
    case _ => expr
```

Listing 13.2 · The `simplifyTop` function, which does a pattern match.

selector `match` { *alternatives* }

instead of:

`switch` (*selector*) { *alternatives* }

A pattern match includes a sequence of *alternatives*, each starting with the keyword `case`. Each alternative includes a *pattern* and one or more expressions, which will be evaluated if the pattern matches. An arrow symbol `=>` separates the pattern from the expressions.

A `match` expression is evaluated by trying each of the patterns in the order they are written. The first pattern that matches is selected, and the part following the arrow is selected and executed.

A *constant pattern* like "+" or 1 matches values that are equal to the constant with respect to `==`. A *variable pattern* like e matches every value. The variable then refers to that value in the right hand side of the case clause. In this example, note that the first three alternatives evaluate to e, a variable that is bound within the associated pattern. The *wildcard pattern* (_) also matches every value, but it does not introduce a variable name to refer to that value. In Listing 13.2, notice how the `match` ends with a default case that does nothing to the expression. Instead, it just results in `expr`, the expression matched upon.

A *constructor pattern* looks like `UnOp("-", e)`. This pattern matches all values of type UnOp whose first argument matches "-". Its second argument will be bound to the name e. Note that the arguments to the constructor are themselves patterns. This allows you to write deep patterns using a concise notation. Here's an example:

```
UnOp("-", UnOp("-", e))
```

240

Imagine trying to implement this same functionality using the visitor design pattern![2] Almost as awkward, imagine implementing it as a long sequence of `if` statements, type tests, and type casts.

match compared to switch

Match expressions can be seen as a generalization of Java-style `switch`es. A Java-style `switch` can be naturally expressed as a `match` expression, where each pattern is a constant and the last pattern may be a wildcard (which represents the default case of the `switch`).

However, there are three differences to keep in mind: First, `match` is an *expression* in Scala (*i.e.*, it always results in a value). Second, Scala's alternative expressions never "fall through" into the next case. Third, if none of the patterns match, an exception named `MatchError` is thrown. This means you always have to make sure that all cases are covered, even if it means adding a default case where there's nothing to do.

```
expr match
  case BinOp(op, left, right) =>
    println(s"$expr is a binary operation")
  case _ =>
```

Listing 13.3 · A pattern match with an empty "default" case.

Listing 13.3 shows an example. The second case is necessary because without it, the `match` expression would throw a `MatchError` for every `expr` argument that is not a `BinOp`. In this example, no code is specified for that second case, so if that case runs it does nothing. The result of either case is the unit value '`()`', which is also the result of the entire `match` expression.

13.2 Kinds of patterns

The previous example showed several kinds of patterns in quick succession. Now take a minute to look at each pattern in detail.

The syntax of patterns is easy, so do not worry about that too much. All patterns look exactly like the corresponding expression. For instance,

---

[2]Gamma, *et al.*, *Design Patterns* [Gam95]

given the hierarchy of Listing 13.1, the pattern Var(x) matches any variable expression, binding x to the name of the variable. Used as an expression, Var(x)—exactly the same syntax—recreates an equivalent object, assuming x is already bound to the variable's name. Since the syntax of patterns is so transparent, the main thing to pay attention to is just what kinds of patterns are possible.

Wildcard patterns

The wildcard pattern (_) matches any object whatsoever. You have already seen it used as a default, catch-all alternative, like this:

```
expr match
  case BinOp(op, left, right) =>
    s"$expr is a binary operation"
  case _ => // handle the default case
    s"It's something else"
```

Wildcards can also be used to ignore parts of an object that you do not care about. For example, the previous example does not actually care what the elements of a binary operation are; it just checks whether or not it is a binary operation. Thus, the code can just as well use the wildcard pattern for the elements of the BinOp, as shown in Listing 13.4.

```
expr match
  case BinOp(_, _, _) => s"$expr is a binary operation"
  case _ => "It's something else"
```

Listing 13.4 · A pattern match with wildcard patterns.

Constant patterns

A constant pattern matches only itself. Any literal may be used as a constant. For example, 5, true, and "hello" are all constant patterns. Also, any val or singleton object can be used as a constant. For example, Nil, a singleton object, is a pattern that matches only the empty list. Listing 13.5 shows some examples of constant patterns:

Here is how the pattern match shown in Listing 13.5 looks in action:

```
def describe(x: Any) =
  x match
    case 5 => "five"
    case true => "truth"
    case "hello" => "hi!"
    case Nil => "the empty list"
    case _ => "something else"
```

Listing 13.5 · A pattern match with constant patterns.

```
describe(5)              // five
describe(true)          // truth
describe("hello")       // hi!
describe(Nil)           // the empty list
describe(List(1,2,3))   // something else
```

Variable patterns

A variable pattern matches any object, just like a wildcard. But unlike a wildcard, Scala binds the variable to whatever the object is. You can then use this variable to act on the object further. For example, Listing 13.6 shows a pattern match that has a special case for zero, and a default case for all other values. The default case uses a variable pattern so that it has a name for the value, no matter what it is.

```
expr match
  case 0 => "zero"
  case somethingElse => s"not zero $somethingElse"
```

Listing 13.6 · A pattern match with a variable pattern.

Variable or constant?

Constant patterns can have symbolic names. You saw this already when we used Nil as a pattern. Here is a related example, where a pattern match involves the constants E (2.71828...) and Pi (3.14159...):

```
scala> import math.{E, Pi}
import math.{E, Pi}

scala> E match
          case Pi => s"strange math? Pi = $Pi"
          case _ => "OK"


val res0: String = OK
```

As expected, E does not match Pi, so the "strange math" case is not used.

How does the Scala compiler know that Pi is a constant imported from `scala.math`, and not a variable that stands for the selector value itself? Scala uses a simple lexical rule for disambiguation: a simple name starting with a lowercase letter is taken to be a pattern variable; all other references are taken to be constants. To see the difference, create a lowercase alias for `pi` and try with that:

```
scala> val pi = math.Pi
pi: Double = 3.141592653589793

scala> E match
          case pi => s"strange math? Pi = $pi"


val res1: String = strange math? Pi = 2.718281828459045
```

Here the compiler will not even let you add a default case at all. Since `pi` is a variable pattern, it will match all inputs, and so no cases following it can be reached:

```
scala> E match
          case pi => s"strange math? Pi = $pi"
          case _ => "OK"


val res2: String = strange math? Pi = 2.718281828459045
3 |                   case _ => "OK"
  |
  |                            Unreachable case
```

You can still use a lowercase name for a pattern constant, if you need to, by using one of two tricks. First, if the constant is a field of some object, you can prefix it with a qualifier. For instance, `pi` is a variable pattern, but `this.pi` or `obj.pi` are constants even though they start with lowercase letters. If that does not work (because `pi` is a local variable, say), you can alternatively enclose the variable name in back ticks. For instance, `` `pi` `` would again be interpreted as a constant, not as a variable:

```
scala> E match
         case `pi` => s"strange math? Pi = $pi"
         case _ => "OK"

res4: String = OK
```

As you can see, the back-tick syntax for identifiers is used for two different purposes in Scala to help you code your way out of unusual circumstances. Here you see that it can be used to treat a lowercase identifier as a constant in a pattern match. Earlier on, in Section 6.10, you saw that it can also be used to treat a keyword as an ordinary identifier, *e.g.*, writing `Thread.`yield`()` treats `yield` as an identifier rather than a keyword.

Constructor patterns

Constructors are where pattern matching becomes really powerful. A constructor pattern looks like "`BinOp("+", e, Num(0))`". It consists of a name (`BinOp`) and then a number of patterns within parentheses: `"+"`, `e`, and `Num(0)`. Assuming the name designates a case class, such a pattern means to first check that the object is an instance of the named case class, and then to check that the constructor parameters of the object match the extra patterns supplied.

These extra patterns mean that Scala patterns support *deep matches*. Such patterns not only check the top-level object supplied, but also the contents of the object against further patterns. Since the extra patterns can themselves be constructor patterns, you can use them to check arbitrarily deep into an object. For example, the pattern shown in Listing 13.7 checks that the top-level object is a `BinOp`, that its third constructor parameter is a `Num`, and that the value field of that number is 0. This pattern is one line long yet checks three levels deep.

245

```
expr match
  case BinOp("+", e, Num(0)) => "a deep match"
  case _ => ""
```

Listing 13.7 · A pattern match with a constructor pattern.

Sequence patterns

You can match against sequence types, like List or Array, just like you match against case classes. You use the same syntax, but now you can specify any number of elements within the pattern. Listing 13.8 shows a pattern that checks for a three-element list starting with zero.

```
xs match
  case List(0, _, _) => "found it"
  case _ => ""
```

Listing 13.8 · A sequence pattern with a fixed length.

If you want to match against a sequence without specifying how long it can be, you can specify _* as the last element of the pattern. This funny-looking pattern matches any number of elements within a sequence, including zero elements. Listing 13.9 shows an example that matches any list that starts with zero, regardless of how long the list is.

```
xs match
  case List(0, _*) => "found it"
  case _ => ""
```

Listing 13.9 · A sequence pattern with an arbitrary length.

Tuple patterns

You can match against tuples too. A pattern like (a, b, c) matches an arbitrary 3-tuple. An example is shown in Listing 13.10.

If you load the tupleDemo method shown in Listing 13.10 into the interpreter, and pass to it a tuple with three elements, you'll see:

```
def tupleDemo(obj: Any) =
  obj match
    case (a, b, c) => s"matched $a$b$c"
    case _ => ""
```

Listing 13.10 · A pattern match with a tuple pattern.

```
tupleDemo(("a ", 3, "-tuple"))    // matched a 3-tuple
```

Typed patterns

You can use a *typed pattern* as a convenient replacement for type tests and type casts. Listing 13.11 shows an example.

```
def generalSize(x: Any) =
  x match
    case s: String => s.length
    case m: Map[_, _] => m.size
    case _ => -1
```

Listing 13.11 · A pattern match with typed patterns.

Here are a few examples of using generalSize in the Scala interpreter:

```
generalSize("abc")                    // 3
generalSize(Map(1 -> 'a', 2 -> 'b'))  // 2
generalSize(math.Pi)                  // -1
```

The generalSize method returns the size or length of objects of various types. Its argument is of type Any, so it could be any value. If the argument is a String, the method returns the string's length. The pattern "s: String" is a typed pattern; it matches every (non-null) instance of String. The pattern variable s then refers to that string.

Note that even though s and x refer to the same value, the type of x is Any, while the type of s is String. So you can write s.length in the alternative expression that corresponds to the pattern, but you could not write x.length, because the type Any does not have a length member.

An equivalent but more long-winded way that achieves the effect of a match against a typed pattern employs a type test followed by a type cast. Scala uses a different syntax than Java for these. To test whether an expression expr has type String, say, you write:

```
expr.isInstanceOf[String]
```

To cast the same expression to type String, you use:

```
expr.asInstanceOf[String]
```

Using a type test and cast, you could rewrite the first case of the previous match expression as shown in Listing 13.12.

```
if x.isInstanceOf[String] then
  val s = x.asInstanceOf[String]
  s.length
else ...
```

Listing 13.12 · Using isInstanceOf and asInstanceOf (poor style).

The operators isInstanceOf and asInstanceOf are treated as predefined methods of class Any that take a type parameter in square brackets. In fact, x.asInstanceOf[String] is a special case of a method invocation with an explicit type parameter String.

As you will have noted by now, writing type tests and casts is rather verbose in Scala. That's intentional because it is not encouraged practice. You are usually better off using a pattern match with a typed pattern. That's particularly true if you need to do both a type test and a type cast, because both operations are then rolled into a single pattern match.

The second case of the match expression in Listing 13.11 contains the typed pattern "m: Map[_, _]". This pattern matches any value that is a Map of some arbitrary key and value types, and lets m refer to that value. Therefore, m.size is well typed and returns the size of the map. The underscores in the type pattern[3] are like wildcards in other patterns. You could have also used (lowercase) type variables instead.

---

[3] In the typed pattern, m: Map[_, _], the "Map[_, _]" portion is called a *type pattern*.

Type ascription

Casts are inherently unsafe. For example, even though the compiler has enough information to determine that a cast from Int to String would fail at runtime, it still compiles (and fails at runtime):

```
3.asInstanceOf[String]
// java.lang.ClassCastException: java.lang.Integer
//     cannot be cast to java.lang.String
```

An alternative to casts that is always safe is *type ascription*: placing a colon and type after a variable or expression. Type ascriptions are safe because any invalid ascription, such as ascribing an Int to type String, will give you a compiler error, not a run-time exception:

```
scala> 3: String // ': String' is the type ascription
1 |3: String
  |^
  |Found:    (3 : Int)
  |Required: String
```

A type ascription will compile in only two cases. First, you can use a type ascription to widen a type to one of its supertypes. For example:

```
scala> Var("x"): Expr // Expr is a supertype of Var
val res0: Expr = Var(x)
```

Second, you can use a type ascription to implicitly convert one type to another, such as implicitly converting an Int to Long:

```
scala> 3: Long
val res1: Long = 3
```

Type erasure

Can you also test for a map with specific element types? This would be handy, say, for testing whether a given value is a map from type Int to type Int. Let's try:

```
scala> def isIntIntMap(x: Any) =
         x match
           case m: Map[Int, Int] => true
           case _ => false

def isIntIntMap(x: Any): Boolean
3 |    case m: Map[Int, Int] => true
  |         ^^^^^^^^^^^^^^^^^
  |
  |             the type test for Map[Int, Int] cannot be
  |             checked at runtime
```

Scala uses the *erasure* model of generics, just like Java does. This means that no information about type arguments is maintained at runtime. Consequently, there is no way to determine at runtime whether a given Map object has been created with two Int arguments, rather than with arguments of different types. All the system can do is determine that a value is a Map of some arbitrary type parameters. You can verify this behavior by applying isIntIntMap to arguments of different instances of class Map:

```
isIntIntMap(Map(1 -> 1))           // true
isIntIntMap(Map("abc" -> "abc"))   // true
```

The first application returns true, which looks correct, but the second application also returns true, which might be a surprise. To alert you to the possibly non-intuitive runtime behavior, the compiler emits unchecked warnings like the one shown previously.

The only exception to the erasure rule is arrays, because they are handled specially in Java as well as in Scala. The element type of an array is stored with the array value, so you can pattern match on it. Here's an example:

```
def isStringArray(x: Any) =
  x match
    case a: Array[String] => "yes"
    case _ => "no"
isStringArray(Array("abc"))     // yes
isStringArray(Array(1, 2, 3))   // no
```

250

Variable binding

In addition to the standalone variable patterns, you can also add a variable to any other pattern. You write the variable name, an at sign (@), and then the pattern. This gives you a variable-binding pattern, which means the pattern is to perform the pattern match as normal, and if the pattern succeeds, set the variable to the matched object just as with a simple variable pattern.

As an example, Listing 13.13 shows a pattern match that looks for the absolute value operation being applied twice in a row. Such an expression can be simplified to only take the absolute value one time.

```
expr match
  case UnOp("abs", e @ UnOp("abs", _)) => e
  case _ =>
```

Listing 13.13 · A pattern with a variable binding (via the @ sign).

The example shown in Listing 13.13 includes a variable-binding pattern with e as the variable and UnOp("abs", _) as the pattern. If the entire pattern match succeeds, then the portion that matched the UnOp("abs", _) part is made available as variable e. The result of the case is just e, because e has an equal value to expr but with one less absolute value operation.

13.3   Pattern guards

Sometimes, syntactic pattern matching is not precise enough. For instance, say you are given the task of formulating a simplification rule that replaces sum expressions with two identical operands, such as e + e, by multiplications of two (*e.g.*, e * 2). In the language of Expr trees, an expression like:

```
BinOp("+", Var("x"), Var("x"))
```

would be transformed by this rule to:

```
BinOp("*", Var("x"), Num(2))
```

You might try to define this rule as follows:

251

```
scala> def simplifyAdd(e: Expr) =
         e match
           case BinOp("+", x, x) => BinOp("*", x, Num(2))
           case _ => e

3 |     case BinOp("+", x, x) => BinOp("*", x, Num(2))
  |                         ^
  |                           duplicate pattern variable: x
```

This fails because Scala restricts patterns to be *linear*: a pattern variable may only appear once in a pattern. However, you can re-formulate the match with a *pattern guard*, as shown in Listing 13.14:

```
def simplifyAdd(e: Expr) =
  e match
    case BinOp("+", x, y) if x == y =>
      BinOp("*", x, Num(2))
    case _ => e
```

Listing 13.14 · A `match` expression with a pattern guard.

A pattern guard comes after a pattern and starts with an `if`. The guard can be an arbitrary boolean expression, which typically refers to variables in the pattern. If a pattern guard is present, the match succeeds only if the guard evaluates to `true`. Hence, the first case above would only match binary operations with two equal operands.

Some other examples of guarded patterns are:

```
// match only positive integers
case n: Int if 0 < n => ...
```

```
// match only strings starting with the letter 'a'
case s: String if s(0) == 'a' => ...
```

13.4 Pattern overlaps

Patterns are tried in the order in which they are written. The version of `simplify` shown in Listing 13.15 presents an example where the order of the cases matters.

```
def simplifyAll(expr: Expr): Expr =
  expr match
    case UnOp("-", UnOp("-", e)) =>
      simplifyAll(e)   // '-' is its own inverse
    case BinOp("+", e, Num(0)) =>
      simplifyAll(e)   // '0' is a neutral element for '+'
    case BinOp("*", e, Num(1)) =>
      simplifyAll(e)   // '1' is a neutral element for '*'
    case UnOp(op, e) =>
      UnOp(op, simplifyAll(e))
    case BinOp(op, l, r) =>
      BinOp(op, simplifyAll(l), simplifyAll(r))
    case _ => expr
```

Listing 13.15 · Match expression in which case order matters.

The version of simplify shown in Listing 13.15 will apply simplification rules everywhere in an expression, not just at the top, as simplifyTop did. It can be derived from simplifyTop by adding two more cases for general unary and binary expressions (cases four and five in Listing 13.15).

The fourth case has the pattern UnOp(op, e); *i.e.*, it matches every unary operation. The operator and operand of the unary operation can be arbitrary. They are bound to the pattern variables op and e, respectively. The alternative in this case applies simplifyAll recursively to the operand e and then rebuilds the same unary operation with the (possibly) simplified operand. The fifth case for BinOp is analogous: it is a "catch-all" case for arbitrary binary operations, which recursively applies the simplification method to its two operands.

In this example, it is important that the catch-all cases come *after* the more specific simplification rules. If you wrote them in the other order, then the catch-all case would be run in favor of the more specific rules. In many cases, the compiler will even complain if you try. For example, here's a match expression that won't compile because the first case will match anything that would be matched by the second case:

```
scala> def simplifyBad(expr: Expr): Expr =
         expr match
           case UnOp(op, e) => UnOp(op, simplifyBad(e))
           case UnOp("-", UnOp("-", e)) => e
           case _ => expr

def simplifyBad(expr: Expr): Expr
4 |      case UnOp("-", UnOp("-", e)) => e
  |           ^^^^^^^^^^^^^^^^^^^^^^^
  |           Unreachable case
```

13.5   Sealed classes

Whenever you write a pattern match, you need to make sure you have covered all of the possible cases. Sometimes you can do this by adding a default case at the end of the match, but that only applies if there is a sensible default behavior. What do you do if there is no default? How can you ever feel safe that you covered all the cases?

You can enlist the help of the Scala compiler in detecting missing combinations of patterns in a match expression. To do this, the compiler needs to be able to tell which are the possible cases. In general, this is impossible in Scala because new case classes can be defined at any time and in arbitrary compilation units. For instance, nothing would prevent you from adding a fifth case class to the Expr class hierarchy in a different compilation unit from the one where the other four cases are defined.

The alternative is to make the superclass of your case classes *sealed*. A sealed class cannot have any new subclasses added except the ones in the same file. This is very useful for pattern matching because it means you only need to worry about the subclasses you already know about. What's more, you get better compiler support as well. If you match against case classes that inherit from a sealed class, the compiler will flag missing combinations of patterns with a warning message.

If you write a hierarchy of classes intended to be pattern matched, you should consider sealing them. Simply put the sealed keyword in front of the class at the top of the hierarchy. Programmers using your class hierarchy will then feel confident in pattern matching against it. The sealed keyword, therefore, is often a license to pattern match. Listing 13.16 shows an example in which Expr is turned into a sealed class.

```
sealed trait Expr
case class Var(name: String) extends Expr
case class Num(number: Double) extends Expr
case class UnOp(operator: String, arg: Expr) extends Expr
case class BinOp(operator: String,
    left: Expr, right: Expr) extends Expr
```

Listing 13.16 · A sealed hierarchy of case classes.

Now define a pattern match where some of the possible cases are left out:

```
def describe(e: Expr): String =
  e match
    case Num(_) => "a number"
    case Var(_) => "a variable"
```

You will get a compiler error like the following:

```
def describe(e: Expr): String
2 |   e match
  |   ^
  |   match may not be exhaustive.
  |
  |   It would fail on pattern case: UnOp(_, _),
  |   BinOp(_, _, _)
```

Such a compiler error tells you that there's a risk your code might produce a MatchError exception because some possible patterns (UnOp, BinOp) are not handled. The error points to a potential source of runtime faults, so it is usually a welcome help in getting your program right.

However, at times you might encounter a situation where the compiler is too picky in emitting the error. For instance, you might know from the context that you will only ever apply the describe method above to expressions that are either Nums or Vars, so you know that no MatchError will be produced. To make the error go away, you could add a third catch-all case to the method, like this:

```
def describe(e: Expr): String =
  e match
    case Num(_) => "a number"
    case Var(_) => "a variable"
    case _ => throw new RuntimeException // Should not happen
```

That works, but it is not ideal. You will probably not be very happy that you were forced to add code that will never be executed (or so you think), just to make the compiler shut up.

A more lightweight alternative is to add an @unchecked annotation to the selector expression of the match. This is done as follows:

```
def describe(e: Expr): String =
  (e: @unchecked) match
    case Num(_) => "a number"
    case Var(_)    => "a variable"
```

Annotations are described in greater detail in *Advanced Programming in Scala*. In general, you can add an annotation to an expression in the same way you add a type: follow the expression with a colon and the name of the annotation (preceded by an at sign). For example, in this case you add an @unchecked annotation to the variable e, with "e: @unchecked". The @unchecked annotation has a special meaning for pattern matching. If a match's selector expression carries this annotation, exhaustivity checking for the patterns that follow will be suppressed.

13.6 Pattern matching Options

You can use pattern matching to process Scala's standard Option type. As mentioned in Step 12 in Chapter 3, an Option can be of two forms: Some(x), where x is the actual value, or the None singleton object, which represents a missing value.

Optional values are produced by some of the standard operations on Scala's collections. For instance, the get method of Scala's Map produces Some(value) if a value corresponding to a given key has been found, or None if the given key is not defined in the Map. Here's an example:

```
val capitals = Map("France" -> "Paris", "Japan" -> "Tokyo")
capitals.get("France")        // Some(Paris)
capitals.get("North Pole")    // None
```

The most common way to take optional values apart is through a pattern match. For instance:

```
def show(x: Option[String]) =
  x match
    case Some(s) => s
    case None => "?"
show(capitals.get("Japan"))        // Tokyo
show(capitals.get("France"))       // Paris
show(capitals.get("North Pole"))   // ?
```

The Option type is used frequently in Scala programs. Compare this to the dominant idiom in Java of using null to indicate no value. For example, the get method of java.util.HashMap returns either a value stored in the HashMap or null if no value was found. This approach works for Java but is error prone because it is difficult in practice to keep track of which variables in a program are allowed to be null.

If a variable is allowed to be null, then you must remember to check it for null every time you use it. When you forget to check, you open the possibility that a NullPointerException may result at runtime. Because such exceptions may not happen very often, it can be difficult to discover the bug during testing. For Scala, the approach would not work at all because it is possible to store value types in hash maps, and null is not a legal element for a value type. For instance, a HashMap[Int, Int] cannot return null to signify "no element."

By contrast, Scala encourages the use of Option to indicate an optional value. This approach to optional values has several advantages over the null approach. First, it is far more obvious to readers of code that a variable whose type is Option[String] is an optional String than a variable of type String, which may sometimes be null. But most importantly, that programming error described earlier of using a variable that may be null without first checking it for null becomes a type error in Scala. If a variable is of type Option[String] and you try to use it as a String, your Scala program will not compile.

13.7   Patterns everywhere

Patterns are allowed in many parts of Scala, not just in standalone `match` expressions. Take a look at some other places you can use patterns.

Patterns in variable definitions

Anytime you define a `val` or a `var`, you can use a pattern instead of a simple identifier. For example, you can take apart a tuple and assign each of its parts to its own variable, as shown in Listing 13.17:

```
scala> val myTuple = (123, "abc")
val myTuple: (Int, String) = (123,abc)

scala> val (number, string) = myTuple
val number: Int = 123
val string: String = abc
```

Listing 13.17 · Defining multiple variables with one assignment.

This construct is quite useful when working with case classes. If you know the precise case class you are working with, then you can deconstruct it with a pattern. Here's an example:

```
scala> val exp = new BinOp("*", Num(5), Num(1))
val exp: BinOp = BinOp(*,Num(5.0),Num(1.0))

scala> val BinOp(op, left, right) = exp
val op: String = *
val left: Expr = Num(5.0)
val right: Expr = Num(1.0)
```

Case sequences as partial functions

A sequence of cases (*i.e.*, alternatives) in curly braces can be used anywhere a function literal can be used. Essentially, a case sequence *is* a function literal, only more general. Instead of having a single entry point and list of parameters, a case sequence has multiple entry points, each with their own list of parameters. Each case is an entry point to the function, and the parameters are specified with the pattern. The body of each entry point is the right-hand side of the case.

Here is a simple example:

```
val withDefault: Option[Int] => Int =
  case Some(x) => x
  case None => 0
```

The body of this function has two cases. The first case matches a Some, and returns the number inside the Some. The second case matches a None, and returns a default value of zero. Here is this function in use:

```
withDefault(Some(10))   // 10
withDefault(None)       // 0
```

This facility is quite useful for the Akka actors library, because it allows its `receive` method to be defined as a series of cases:

```
var sum = 0

def receive =
  case Data(byte) =>
    sum += byte
  case GetChecksum(requester) =>
    val checksum = ~(sum & 0xFF) + 1
    requester ! checksum
```

One other generalization is worth noting: a sequence of cases gives you a *partial* function. If you apply such a function on a value it does not support, it will generate a run-time exception. For example, here is a partial function that returns the second element of a list of integers:

```
val second: List[Int] => Int =
  case x :: y :: _ => y
```

When you compile this, the compiler will correctly warn that the match is not exhaustive:

```
2 |     case x :: y :: _ => y
  |          ^
  |     match may not be exhaustive.
  |
  |     It would fail on pattern case: List(_), Nil
```

This function will succeed if you pass it a three-element list, but not if you pass it an empty list:

```
scala> second(List(5, 6, 7))
val res24: Int = 6

scala> second(List())
scala.MatchError: List() (of class Nil$)
    at rs$line$10$.$init$$$anonfun$1(rs$line$10:2)
    at rs$line$12$.<init>(rs$line$12:1)
```

If you want to check whether a partial function is defined, you must first tell the compiler that you know you are working with partial functions. The type List[Int] => Int includes all functions from lists of integers to integers, whether or not the functions are partial. The type that only includes *partial* functions from lists of integers to integers is written PartialFunction[List[Int],Int]. Here is the second function again, this time written with a partial function type:

```
val second: PartialFunction[List[Int],Int] =
  case x :: y :: _ => y
```

Partial functions have a method isDefinedAt, which can be used to test whether the function is defined at a particular value. In this case, the function is defined for any list that has at least two elements:

```
second.isDefinedAt(List(5,6,7))    // true
second.isDefinedAt(List())         // false
```

The typical example of a partial function is a pattern matching function literal like the one in the previous example. In fact, such an expression gets translated by the Scala compiler to a partial function by translating the patterns twice—once for the implementation of the real function, and once to test whether the function is defined or not.

For instance, the function literal { case x :: y :: _ => y } gets translated to the following partial function value:

```
new PartialFunction[List[Int], Int]:
  def apply(xs: List[Int]) =
    xs match
      case x :: y :: _ => y
  def isDefinedAt(xs: List[Int]) =
    xs match
      case x :: y :: _ => true
      case _ => false
```

This translation takes effect whenever the declared type of a function literal is `PartialFunction`. If the declared type is just `Function1`, or is missing, the function literal is instead translated to a *complete function*.

In general, you should try to work with complete functions whenever possible, because using partial functions allows for runtime errors that the compiler cannot help you with. Sometimes partial functions are really helpful though. You might be sure that an unhandled value will never be supplied. Alternatively, you might be using a framework that expects partial functions and so will always check `isDefinedAt` before calling the function. An example of the latter is the `receive` method given previously, where the result is a partially defined function, defined precisely for those messages that the caller wants to handle.

Patterns in for expressions

You can also use a pattern in a `for` expression, as shown in Listing 13.18. This `for` expression retrieves all key/value pairs from the `capitals` map. Each pair is matched against the pattern `(country, city)`, which defines the two variables `country` and `city`.

```
for (country, city) <- capitals yield
  s"The capital of $country is $city"
//
// List(The capital of France is Paris,
//   The capital of Japan is Tokyo)
```

Listing 13.18 · A for expression with a tuple pattern.

The pair pattern shown in Listing 13.18 was special because the match against it can never fail. Indeed, `capitals` yields a sequence of pairs, so you can be sure that every generated pair can be matched against a pair pattern. But it is equally possible that a pattern might not match a generated value. Listing 13.19 shows an example where that is the case.

```
val results = List(Some("apple"), None, Some("orange"))

for Some(fruit) <- results yield fruit
// List(apple, orange)
```

Listing 13.19 · Picking elements of a list that match a pattern.

As you can see from this example, generated values that do not match the pattern are discarded. For instance, the second element None in the `results` list does not match the pattern `Some(fruit)`; therefore it does not show up in the result.

13.8   A larger example

After having learned the different forms of patterns, you might be interested in seeing them applied in a larger example. The proposed task is to write an expression formatter class that displays an arithmetic expression in a two-dimensional layout. Divisions such as "x / (x + 1)" should be printed vertically, by placing the numerator on top of the denominator, like this:

```
  x
-----
x + 1
```

As another example, here's the expression ((a / (b * c) + 1 / n) / 3) in two dimensional layout:

```
  a       1
----- + -
b * c    n
---------
    3
```

From these examples it looks like the class (we'll call it `ExprFormatter`) will have to do a fair bit of layout juggling, so it makes sense to use the layout library developed in Chapter 10. We'll also use the `Expr` family of case classes you saw previously in this chapter, and place both Chapter 10's layout library and this chapter's expression formatter into named packages. The full code for the example will be shown in Listings 13.20 and 13.21.

A useful first step is to concentrate on horizontal layout. A structured expression like:

```
BinOp("+",
    BinOp("*",
        BinOp("+", Var("x"), Var("y")),
        Var("z")),
    Num(1))
```

should print (x + y) * z + 1. Note that parentheses are mandatory around x + y, but would be optional around (x + y) * z. To keep the layout as legible as possible, your goal should be to omit parentheses wherever they are redundant, while ensuring that all necessary parentheses are present.

To know where to put parentheses, the code needs to know about the relative precedence of each operator, so it's a good idea to tackle this first. You could express the relative precedence directly as a map literal of the following form:

```
Map(
  "|" -> 0, "||" -> 0,
  "&" -> 1, "&&" -> 1, ...
)
```

However, this would involve some amount of pre-computation of precedences on your part. A more convenient approach is to just define groups of operators of increasing precedence and then calculate the precedence of each operator from that. Listing 13.20 shows the code.

The `precedence` variable is a map from operators to their precedences, which are integers starting with 0. It is calculated using a `for` expression with two generators. The first generator produces every index `i` of the `opGroups` vector. The second generator produces every operator `op` in `opGroups(i)`. For each such operator the `for` expression yields an association from the operator `op` to its index `i`. Hence, the relative position of an operator in the vector is taken to be its precedence.

```
package org.stairwaybook.expr
import org.stairwaybook.layout.Element.elem

sealed abstract class Expr
case class Var(name: String) extends Expr
case class Num(number: Double) extends Expr
case class UnOp(operator: String, arg: Expr) extends Expr
case class BinOp(operator: String,
    left: Expr, right: Expr) extends Expr

class ExprFormatter:
  // Contains operators in groups of increasing precedence
  private val opGroups =
    Vector(
      Set("|", "||"),
      Set("&", "&&"),
      Set("^"),
      Set("==", "!="),
      Set("<", "<=", ">", ">="),
      Set("+", "-"),
      Set("*", "%")
    )

  // A mapping from operators to their precedence
  private val precedence = {
    val assocs =
      for
        i <- 0 until opGroups.length
        op <- opGroups(i)
      yield op -> i
    assocs.toMap
  }

  private val unaryPrecedence = opGroups.length
  private val fractionPrecedence = -1

  // continued in Listing 13.21...
```

Listing 13.20 · The top half of the expression formatter.

```
// ...continued from Listing 13.20
import org.stairwaybook.layout.Element
private def format(e: Expr, enclPrec: Int): Element =
  e match
    case Var(name) =>
      elem(name)
    case Num(number) =>
      def stripDot(s: String) =
        if s endsWith ".0" then s.substring(0, s.length - 2)
        else s
      elem(stripDot(number.toString))
    case UnOp(op, arg) =>
      elem(op) beside format(arg, unaryPrecedence)
    case BinOp("/", left, right) =>
      val top = format(left, fractionPrecedence)
      val bot = format(right, fractionPrecedence)
      val line = elem('-', top.width.max(bot.width), 1)
      val frac = top above line above bot
      if enclPrec != fractionPrecedence then frac
      else elem(" ") beside frac beside elem(" ")
    case BinOp(op, left, right) =>
      val opPrec = precedence(op)
      val l = format(left, opPrec)
      val r = format(right, opPrec + 1)
      val oper = l beside elem(" " + op + " ") beside r
      if enclPrec <= opPrec then oper
      else elem("(") beside oper beside elem(")")
  end match
def format(e: Expr): Element = format(e, 0)
end ExprFormatter
```

Listing 13.21 · The bottom half of the expression formatter.

Associations are written with an infix arrow, *e.g.*, op -> i. So far you have seen associations only as part of map constructions, but they are also values in their own right. In fact, the association op -> i is nothing else but the pair (op, i).

Now that you have fixed the precedence of all binary operators except /, it makes sense to generalize this concept to also cover unary operators. The precedence of a unary operator is higher than the precedence of every binary operator. Thus we can set unaryPrecedence (shown in Listing 13.20) to the length of the opGroups vector, which is one more than the precedence of the * and % operators. The precedence of a fraction is treated differently from the other operators because fractions use vertical layout. However, it will prove convenient to assign to the division operator the special precedence value -1, so we'll initialize fractionPrecedence to -1 (shown in Listing 13.20).

After these preparations, you are ready to write the main format method. This method takes two arguments: an expression e, of type Expr, and the precedence enclPrec of the operator directly enclosing the expression e. (If there's no enclosing operator, enclPrec should be zero.) The method yields a layout element that represents a two-dimensional array of characters.

Listing 13.21 shows the remainder of class ExprFormatter, which includes two methods. The first method, the private format method, does most of the work to format expressions. The last method, also named format, is the lone public method in the library, which takes an expression to format. The private format method does its work by performing a pattern match on the kind of expression. The match expression has five cases. We'll discuss each case individually.

The first case is:

```
case Var(name) =>
  elem(name)
```

If the expression is a variable, the result is an element formed from the variable's name.

The second case is:

```
case Num(number) =>
  def stripDot(s: String) =
    if s endsWith ".0" then s.substring(0, s.length - 2)
    else s
  elem(stripDot(number.toString))
```

If the expression is a number, the result is an element formed from the number's value. The stripDot function cleans up the display of a floating-point number by stripping any ".0" suffix from a string.

The third case is:

```
case UnOp(op, arg) =>
  elem(op) beside format(arg, unaryPrecedence)
```

If the expression is a unary operation UnOp(op, arg) the result is formed from the operation op and the result of formatting the argument arg with the highest-possible environment precedence.[4] This means that if arg is a binary operation (but not a fraction) it will always be displayed in parentheses.

The fourth case is:

```
case BinOp("/", left, right) =>
  val top = format(left, fractionPrecedence)
  val bot = format(right, fractionPrecedence)
  val line = elem('-', top.width.max(bot.width), 1)
  val frac = top above line above bot
  if enclPrec != fractionPrecedence then frac
  else elem(" ") beside frac beside elem(" ")
```

If the expression is a fraction, an intermediate result frac is formed by placing the formatted operands left and right on top of each other, separated by a horizontal line element. The width of the horizontal line is the maximum of the widths of the formatted operands. This intermediate result is also the final result unless the fraction appears itself as an argument of another fraction. In the latter case, a space is added on each side of frac. To see the reason why, consider the expression "(a / b) / c".

Without the widening correction, formatting this expression would give:

```
                          a
                          -
                          b
                          -
                          c
```

---

[4]The value of unaryPrecedence is the highest possible precedence, because it was initialized to one more than the precedence of the * and % operators.

The problem with this layout is evident—it's not clear where the top-level fractional bar is. The expression above could mean either "(a / b) / c" or "a / (b / c)". To disambiguate, a space should be added on each side to the layout of the nested fraction "a / b".

Then the layout becomes unambiguous:

```
                    a
                    -
                    b
                   ---
                    c
```

The fifth and last case is:

```
case BinOp(op, left, right) =>
  val opPrec = precedence(op)
  val l = format(left, opPrec)
  val r = format(right, opPrec + 1)
  val oper = l beside elem(" " + op + " ") beside r
  if enclPrec <= opPrec then oper
  else elem("(") beside oper beside elem(")")
```

This case applies for all other binary operations. Since it comes after the case starting with:

```
case BinOp("/", left, right) => ...
```

you know that the operator op in the pattern BinOp(op, left, right) cannot be a division. To format such a binary operation, you need to format first its operands left and right. The precedence parameter for formatting the left operand is the precedence opPrec of the operator op, while for the right operand it is one more than that. This scheme ensures that parentheses also reflect the correct associativity.

For instance, the operation:

```
BinOp("-", Var("a"), BinOp("-", Var("b"), Var("c")))
```

would be correctly parenthesized as "a - (b - c)". The intermediate result oper is then formed by placing the formatted left and right operands side-by-side, separated by the operator. If the precedence of the current operator

```
import org.stairwaybook.expr.*

object Express:
  def main(args: Array[String]): Unit =
    val f = new ExprFormatter
    val e1 = BinOp("*", BinOp("/", Num(1), Num(2)),
                        BinOp("+", Var("x"), Num(1)))
    val e2 = BinOp("+", BinOp("/", Var("x"), Num(2)),
                        BinOp("/", Num(1.5), Var("x")))
    val e3 = BinOp("/", e1, e2)
    def show(e: Expr) = println(s"${f.format(e)}\n\n")
    for e <- Vector(e1, e2, e3) do show(e)
```

Listing 13.22 · An application that prints formatted expressions.

is smaller than the precedence of the enclosing operator, oper is placed between parentheses; otherwise, it is returned as is.

This finishes the design of the private format function. The only remaining method is the public format method, which allows client programmers to format a top-level expression without passing a precedence argument. Listing 13.22 shows a demo program that exercises ExprFormatter.

Because this object defines a main method, it is a runnable application. You can run the Express program with the command:

```
scala Express
```

This will give the following output:

```
 1
 - * (x + 1)
 2


 x   1.5
 - + ---
 2    x
```

```
1
- * (x + 1)
2
-----------
  x    1.5
  - + ---
  2    x
```

13.9   Conclusion

In this chapter, you learned about Scala's case classes and pattern matching in detail. By using them, you can take advantage of several concise idioms not normally available in object-oriented languages. However, Scala's pattern matching goes further than this chapter describes. If you want to use pattern matching on one of your classes, but you do not want to open access to your classes the way case classes do, you can use the *extractors* described in *Advanced Programming in Scala*. In the next chapter, we'll look at lists.

Chapter 14

Working with Lists

Lists are probably the most commonly used data structure in Scala programs. This chapter explains lists in detail. We will present many common operations that can be performed on lists. We'll also cover some important design principles for programs working on lists.

14.1 List literals

You saw lists already in the preceding chapters, so you know that a list containing the elements `'a'`, `'b'`, and `'c'` is written `List('a', 'b', 'c')`. Here are some other examples:

```scala
val fruit = List("apples", "oranges", "pears")
val nums = List(1, 2, 3, 4)
val diag3 =
  List(
    List(1, 0, 0),
    List(0, 1, 0),
    List(0, 0, 1)
  )
val empty = List()
```

Lists are quite similar to arrays, but there are two important differences. First, lists are immutable. That is, elements of a list cannot be changed by assignment. Second, lists have a recursive structure (*i.e.*, a *linked list*), whereas arrays are flat.

271

14.2 The List type

Like arrays, lists are *homogeneous*: the elements of a list all have the same type. The type of a list that has elements of type T is written List[T]. For instance, here are the same four lists with explicit types added:

```
val fruit: List[String] = List("apples", "oranges", "pears")
val nums: List[Int] = List(1, 2, 3, 4)
val diag3: List[List[Int]] =
  List(
    List(1, 0, 0),
    List(0, 1, 0),
    List(0, 0, 1)
  )
val empty: List[Nothing] = List()
```

The list type in Scala is *covariant*. This means that for each pair of types S and T, if S is a subtype of T, then List[S] is a subtype of List[T]. For instance, List[String] is a subtype of List[Object]. This is natural because every list of strings can also be seen as a list of objects.[1]

Note that the empty list has type List[Nothing]. Nothing is considered the "bottom type" of Scala's class hierarchy. It is a special type that is a subtype of every other Scala type. Because lists are covariant, it follows that List[Nothing] is a subtype of List[T] for any type T. So the empty list object, which has type List[Nothing], can also be seen as an object of every other list type of the form List[T]. That's why it is permissible to write code like:

```
// List[Nothing] is also of type List[String]!
val xs: List[String] = List()
```

14.3 Constructing lists

All lists are built from two fundamental building blocks, Nil and :: (pronounced "cons"). Nil represents the empty list. The infix operator, ::, expresses list extension at the front. That is, x :: xs represents a list whose

---

[1]Chapter 18 gives more details on covariance and other kinds of variance.

first element is x, followed by (the elements of) list xs. Hence, the previous
list values could also have been defined as follows:

```
val fruit = "apples" :: ("oranges" :: ("pears" :: Nil))
val nums  = 1 :: (2 :: (3 :: (4 :: Nil)))
val diag3 = (1 :: (0 :: (0 :: Nil))) ::
            (0 :: (1 :: (0 :: Nil))) ::
            (0 :: (0 :: (1 :: Nil))) :: Nil
val empty = Nil
```

In fact the previous definitions of fruit, nums, diag3, and empty in terms of
List(...) are just wrappers that expand to these definitions. For instance,
List(1, 2, 3) creates the list 1 :: (2 :: (3 :: Nil)).

Because it ends in a colon, the :: operation associates to the right:
A :: B :: C is interpreted as A :: (B :: C). Therefore, you can drop the
parentheses in the previous definitions. For instance:

```
val nums = 1 :: 2 :: 3 :: 4 :: Nil
```

is equivalent to the previous definition of nums.

14.4 Basic operations on lists

All operations on lists can be expressed in terms of the following three:

head	returns the first element of a list
tail	returns a list consisting of all elements except the first
isEmpty	returns true if the list is empty

These operations are defined as methods of class List. Some examples are
shown in Table 14.1. The head and tail methods are defined only for non-
empty lists. When selected from an empty list, they throw an exception:

```
scala> Nil.head
java.util.NoSuchElementException: head of empty list
```

As an example of how lists can be processed, consider sorting the elements of
a list of numbers into ascending order. One simple way to do so is *insertion
sort*, which works as follows: To sort a non-empty list x :: xs, sort the
remainder xs and insert the first element x at the right position in the result.

Table 14.1 · Basic list operations

What it is	What it does
empty.isEmpty	returns true
fruit.isEmpty	returns false
fruit.head	returns "apples"
fruit.tail.head	returns "oranges"
diag3.head	returns List(1, 0, 0)

Sorting an empty list yields the empty list. Expressed as Scala code, the insertion sort algorithm looks as shown in Listing 14.1.

```
def isort(xs: List[Int]): List[Int] =
  if xs.isEmpty then Nil
  else insert(xs.head, isort(xs.tail))

def insert(x: Int, xs: List[Int]): List[Int] =
  if xs.isEmpty || x <= xs.head then x :: xs
  else xs.head :: insert(x, xs.tail)
```

Listing 14.1 · Sorting a List[Int] via the insertion sort algorithm.

14.5   List patterns

Lists can also be taken apart using pattern matching. List patterns correspond one-by-one to list expressions. You can either match on all elements of a list using a pattern of the form List(...), or you take lists apart bit by bit using patterns composed from the :: operator and the Nil constant.

Here's an example of the first kind of pattern:

```
scala> val List(a, b, c) = fruit
val a: String = apples
val b: String = oranges
val c: String = pears
```

The pattern List(a, b, c) matches lists of length 3, and binds the three elements to the pattern variables a, b, and c. If you don't know the number of list elements beforehand, it's better to match with : : instead. For instance, the pattern a : : b : : rest matches lists of length 2 or greater:

> About pattern matching on Lists
>
> If you review the possible forms of patterns explained in Chapter 13, you might find that neither List(...) nor : : look like it fits the kinds of patterns defined there. In fact, List(...) is an instance of a library-defined *extractor* pattern. Such patterns will be discussed in *Advanced Programming in Scala*. The "cons" pattern x : : xs is a special case of an infix operation pattern. As an expression, an infix operation is equivalent to a method call. For patterns, the rules are different: As a pattern, an infix operation such as p op q is equivalent to op(p, q). That is, the infix operator op is treated as a constructor pattern. In particular, a cons pattern such as x : : xs is treated as : :(x, xs).
>
> This hints that there should be a class named : : that corresponds to the pattern constructor. Indeed, there is such a class—it is named : : and is exactly the class that builds non-empty lists. So : : exists twice in Scala, once as a name of a class and again as a method in class List. The effect of the method : : is to produce an instance of the class scala.::. You can find out more details about how the List class is implemented in *Advanced Programming in Scala*.

```
scala> val a :: b :: rest = fruit
val a: String = apples
val b: String = oranges
val rest: List[String] = List(pears)
```

Taking lists apart with patterns is an alternative to taking them apart with the basic methods head, tail, and isEmpty. For instance, here's insertion sort again, this time written with pattern matching:

```
def isort(xs: List[Int]): List[Int] =
  xs match
    case List()   => List()
    case x :: xs1 => insert(x, isort(xs1))
```

```
def insert(x: Int, xs: List[Int]): List[Int] =
  xs match
    case List()  => List(x)
    case y :: ys => if x <= y then x :: xs
                    else y :: insert(x, ys)
```

Often, pattern matching over lists is clearer than decomposing them with methods, so pattern matching should be a part of your list processing toolbox.

This is all you need to know about lists in Scala to use them correctly. However, there are also a large number of methods that capture common patterns of operations over lists. These methods make list processing programs more concise and often clearer. The next two sections present the most important methods defined in the List class.

14.6   First-order methods on class List

This section explains most first-order methods defined in the List class. A method is *first-order* if it does not take any functions as arguments. We will also introduce some recommended techniques to structure programs that operate on lists by using two examples.

Concatenating two lists

An operation similar to :: is list concatenation, written ':::'. Unlike ::, ::: takes two lists as operands. The result of xs ::: ys is a new list that contains all the elements of xs, followed by all the elements of ys.

Here are some examples:

```
List(1, 2) ::: List(3, 4, 5)  // List(1, 2, 3, 4, 5)
List() ::: List(1, 2, 3)      // List(1, 2, 3)
List(1, 2, 3) ::: List(4)     // List(1, 2, 3, 4)
```

Like cons, list concatenation associates to the right. An expression like this:

```
xs ::: ys ::: zs
```

is interpreted like this:

```
xs ::: (ys ::: zs)
```

276

The Divide and Conquer principle

Concatenation (:::) is implemented as a method in class List. It would also be possible to implement concatenation "by hand," using pattern matching on lists. It's instructive to try to do that yourself, because it shows a common way to implement algorithms using lists. First, we'll settle on a signature for the concatenation method, which we'll call append. In order not to mix things up too much, assume that append is defined outside the List class, so it will take the two lists to be concatenated as parameters. These two lists must agree on their element type, but that element type can be arbitrary. This can be expressed by giving append a type parameter[2] that represents the element type of the two input lists:

```
def append[T](xs: List[T], ys: List[T]): List[T]
```

To design the implementation of append, it pays to remember the "divide and conquer" design principle for programs over recursive data structures such as lists. Many algorithms over lists first split an input list into simpler cases using a pattern match. That's the *divide* part of the principle. They then construct a result for each case. If the result is a non-empty list, some of its parts may be constructed by recursive invocations of the same algorithm. That's the *conquer* part of the principle.

To apply this principle to the implementation of the append method, the first question to ask is on which list to match. This is less trivial in the case of append than for many other methods because there are two choices. However, the subsequent "conquer" phase tells you that you need to construct a list consisting of all elements of both input lists. Since lists are constructed from the back towards the front, ys can remain intact, whereas xs will need to be taken apart and prepended to ys. Thus, it makes sense to concentrate on xs as a source for a pattern match. The most common pattern match over lists simply distinguishes an empty from a non-empty list. So this gives the following outline of an append method:

```
def append[T](xs: List[T], ys: List[T]): List[T] =
  xs match
    case List() => ???
    case x :: xs1 => ???
```

---

[2]Type parameters will be explained in more detail in Chapter 18.

All that remains is to fill in the two places marked with ???.[3] The first such place is the alternative where the input list xs is empty. In this case concatenation yields the second list:

```
case List() => ys
```

The second place left open is the alternative where the input list xs consists of some head x followed by a tail xs1. In this case the result is also a non-empty list. To construct a non-empty list you need to know what the head and the tail of that list should be. You know that the first element of the result list is x. As for the remaining elements, these can be computed by appending the second list, ys, to the rest of the first list, xs1.

This completes the design and gives:

```
def append[T](xs: List[T], ys: List[T]): List[T] =
  xs match
    case List() => ys
    case x :: xs1 => x :: append(xs1, ys)
```

The computation of the second alternative illustrated the "conquer" part of the divide and conquer principle: Think first what the shape of the desired output should be, then compute the individual parts of that shape, using recursive invocations of the algorithm where appropriate. Finally, construct the output from these parts.

Taking the length of a list: length

The length method computes the length of a list.

```
List(1, 2, 3).length  // 3
```

On lists, unlike arrays, length is a relatively expensive operation. It needs to traverse the whole list to find its end, and therefore takes time proportional to the number of elements in the list. That's why it's not a good idea to replace a test such as xs.isEmpty by xs.length == 0. The result of the two tests is equivalent, but the second one is slower, in particular if the list xs is long.

---

[3]The ??? method, which throws scala.NotImplementedError and has result type Nothing, can be used as a temporary implementation during development.

Accessing the end of a list: init and last

You know already the basic operations head and tail, which respectively take the first element of a list, and the rest of the list except the first element. They each have a dual operation: last returns the last element of a (non-empty) list, whereas init returns a list consisting of all elements except the last one:

```
val abcde = List('a', 'b', 'c', 'd', 'e')
abcde.last  // e
abcde.init  // List(a, b, c, d)
```

Like head and tail, these methods throw an exception when applied to an empty list:

```
scala> List().init
java.lang.UnsupportedOperationException: init of empty list
    at ...

scala> List().last
java.util.NoSuchElementException: last of empty list
    at ...
```

Unlike head and tail, which both run in constant time, init and last need to traverse the whole list to compute their result. As a result, they take time proportional to the length of the list.

> It's a good idea to organize your data so that most accesses are at the head of a list, rather than the last element.

Reversing lists: reverse

If at some point in the computation an algorithm demands frequent accesses to the end of a list, it's sometimes better to reverse the list first and work with the result instead. Here's how to do the reversal:

```
abcde.reverse  // List(e, d, c, b, a)
```

279

Like all other list operations, `reverse` creates a new list rather than changing the one it operates on. Since lists are immutable, such a change would not be possible anyway. To verify this, check that the original value of `abcde` is unchanged after the `reverse` operation:

```
abcde  // List(a, b, c, d, e)
```

The `reverse`, `init`, and `last` operations satisfy some laws that can be used for reasoning about computations and for simplifying programs.

1. `reverse` is its own inverse:

   `xs.reverse.reverse` *equals* `xs`

2. `reverse` turns `init` to `tail` and `last` to `head`, except that the elements are reversed:

   `xs.reverse.init` *equals* `xs.tail.reverse`
   `xs.reverse.tail` *equals* `xs.init.reverse`
   `xs.reverse.head` *equals* `xs.last`
   `xs.reverse.last` *equals* `xs.head`

Reverse could be implemented using concatenation (`:::`), like in the following method, `rev`:

```
def rev[T](xs: List[T]): List[T] =
  xs match
    case List() => xs
    case x :: xs1 => rev(xs1) ::: List(x)
```

However, this method is less efficient than one would hope for. To study the complexity of `rev`, assume that the list xs has length n. Notice that there are n recursive calls to `rev`. Each call except the last involves a list concatenation. List concatenation xs `:::` ys takes time proportional to the length of its first argument xs. Hence, the total complexity of `rev` is:

$$n + (n - 1) + \ldots + 1 = (1 + n) * n/2$$

In other words, rev's complexity is quadratic in the length of its input argument. This is disappointing when compared to the standard reversal of a mutable, linked list, which has linear complexity. However, the current implementation of rev is not the best implementation possible. In the example starting on page 293, you will see how to speed it up.

Prefixes and suffixes: drop, take, and splitAt

The drop and take operations generalize tail and init in that they return arbitrary prefixes or suffixes of a list. The expression "xs.take(n)" returns the first n elements of the list xs. If n is greater than xs.length, the whole list xs is returned. The operation "xs.drop(n)" returns all elements of the list xs, except for the first n ones. If n is greater than xs.length, the empty list is returned.

The splitAt operation splits the list at a given index, returning a pair of two lists.[4] It is defined by the equality:

$$xs.splitAt(n) \quad equals \quad (xs.take(n), xs.drop(n))$$

However, splitAt avoids traversing the list xs twice. Here are some examples of these three methods:

```
abcde.take(2)      // List(a, b)
abcde.drop(2)      // List(c, d, e)
abcde.splitAt(2)   // (List(a, b),List(c, d, e))
```

Element selection: apply and indices

Random element selection is supported through the apply method; however it is a less common operation for lists than it is for arrays.

```
abcde.apply(2)  // c  (rare in Scala)
```

As for all other types, apply is implicitly inserted when an object appears in the function position in a method call. So the line above can be shortened to:

```
abcde(2)          // c  (rare in Scala)
```

---

[4]As mentioned in Section 10.12, the term *pair* is an informal name for Tuple2.

One reason why random element selection is less popular for lists than for arrays is that xs(n) takes time proportional to the index n. In fact, apply is simply defined by a combination of drop and head:

$$\text{xs.apply(n)} \quad \textit{equals} \quad \text{(xs.drop(n)).head}$$

This definition also makes clear that list indices range from 0 up to the length of the list minus one, the same as for arrays. The indices method returns a list consisting of all valid indices of a given list:

```
abcde.indices  // Range 0 until 5
```

Flattening a list of lists: flatten

The flatten method takes a list of lists and flattens it out to a single list:

```
List(List(1, 2), List(3), List(), List(4, 5)).flatten
// List(1, 2, 3, 4, 5)

fruit.map(_.toList).flatten
// List(a, p, p, l, e, s, o, r, a, n, g, e,
//      s, p, e, a, r, s)
```

It can only be applied to lists whose elements are all lists. Trying to flatten any other list will give a compilation error:

```
scala> List(1, 2, 3).flatten
1 |List(1, 2, 3).flatten
  |                  ^
  |
  |                          No implicit view available from
  |                          Int => IterableOnce[B]
  |                          where, B is a type variable.
```

Zipping lists: zip and unzip

The zip operation takes two lists and forms a list of pairs:

```
abcde.indices.zip(abcde)
// Vector((0,a), (1,b), (2,c), (3,d), (4,e))
```

282

If the two lists are of different length, any unmatched elements are dropped:

```
val zipped = abcde.zip(List(1, 2, 3))
// List((a,1), (b,2), (c,3))
```

A useful special case is to zip a list with its index. This is done most efficiently with the `zipWithIndex` method, which pairs every element of a list with the position where it appears in the list.

```
abcde.zipWithIndex
// List((a,0), (b,1), (c,2), (d,3), (e,4))
```

Any list of tuples can also be changed back to a tuple of lists by using the unzip method:

```
zipped.unzip  // (List(a, b, c),List(1, 2, 3))
```

The zip and unzip methods provide one way to operate on multiple lists together. See Section 14.9 for a more efficient way to do this.

Displaying lists: `toString` and `mkString`

The `toString` operation returns the canonical string representation of a list:

```
abcde.toString  // List(a, b, c, d, e)
```

If you want a different representation you can use the `mkString` method. The operation `xs mkString (pre, sep, post)` involves four operands: the list `xs` to be displayed, a prefix string `pre` to be displayed in front of all elements, a separator string `sep` to be displayed between successive elements, and a postfix string `post` to be displayed at the end.

The result of the operation is the string:

$$\text{pre} + \text{xs}(0) + \text{sep} + \ldots + \text{sep} + \text{xs}(\text{xs.length} - 1) + \text{post}$$

The `mkString` method has two overloaded variants that let you drop some or all of its arguments. The first variant only takes a separator string:

```
xs.mkString(sep)   equals  xs.mkString("", sep, "")
```

The second variant lets you omit all arguments:

```
xs.mkString   equals  xs.mkString("")
```

Here are some examples:

```
abcde.mkString("[", ",", "]")      // [a,b,c,d,e]
abcde.mkString("")                 // abcde
abcde.mkString                     // abcde
abcde.mkString("List(", ", ", ")") // List(a, b, c, d, e)
```

There are also variants of the mkString methods called addString which append the constructed string to a StringBuilder object,[5] rather than returning them as a result:

```
val buf = new StringBuilder
abcde.addString(buf, "(", ";", ")")   // (a;b;c;d;e)
```

The mkString and addString methods are inherited from List's super trait Iterable, so they are applicable to all other collections as well.

Converting lists: iterator, toArray, copyToArray

To convert data between the flat world of arrays and the recursive world of lists, you can use method toArray in class List and toList in class Array:

```
val arr = abcde.toArray  // Array(a, b, c, d, e)
arr.toList               // List(a, b, c, d, e)
```

There's also a method copyToArray, which copies list elements to successive array positions within some destination array. The operation:

```
xs.copyToArray(arr, start)
```

copies all elements of the list xs to the array arr, beginning with position start. You must ensure that the destination array arr is large enough to hold the list in full. Here's an example:

```
val arr2 = new Array[Int](10)
      // Array(0, 0, 0, 0, 0, 0, 0, 0, 0, 0)
List(1, 2, 3).copyToArray(arr2, 3)
arr2  // Array(0, 0, 0, 1, 2, 3, 0, 0, 0, 0)
```

---

[5]This is class scala.StringBuilder, not java.lang.StringBuilder.

Finally, if you need to access list elements via an iterator, you can use the `iterator` method:

```
val it = abcde.iterator
it.next()   // a
it.next()   // b
```

Example: Merge sort

The insertion sort presented earlier is concise to write, but it is not very efficient. Its average complexity is proportional to the square of the length of the input list. A more efficient algorithm is *merge sort*.

> **The fast track**
>
> This example provides another illustration of the divide and conquer principle and currying, as well as a useful discussion of algorithmic complexity. If you prefer to move a bit faster on your first pass through this book, however, you can safely skip to Section 14.7.

Merge sort works as follows: First, if the list has zero or one elements, it is already sorted, so the list can be returned unchanged. Longer lists are split into two sub-lists, each containing about half the elements of the original list. Each sub-list is sorted by a recursive call to the sort function, and the resulting two sorted lists are then combined in a merge operation.

For a general implementation of merge sort, you want to leave open the type of list elements to be sorted and the function to be used for the comparison of elements. You obtain a function of maximal generality by passing these two items as parameters. This leads to the implementation shown in Listing 14.2.

The complexity of `msort` is order $(n \, log(n))$, where n is the length of the input list. To see why, note that splitting a list in two and merging two sorted lists each take time proportional to the length of the argument list(s). Each recursive call of `msort` halves the number of elements in its input, so there are about $log(n)$ consecutive recursive calls until the base case of lists of length 1 is reached. However, for longer lists each call spawns off two further calls. Adding everything up, we obtain at each of the $log(n)$ call levels, every element of the original lists takes part in one split operation and one merge operation.

285

```
def msort[T](less: (T, T) => Boolean)
    (xs: List[T]): List[T] =

  def merge(xs: List[T], ys: List[T]): List[T] =
    (xs, ys) match
      case (Nil, _) => ys
      case (_, Nil) => xs
      case (x :: xs1, y :: ys1) =>
        if less(x, y) then x :: merge(xs1, ys)
        else y :: merge(xs, ys1)
  val n = xs.length / 2
  if n == 0 then xs
  else
    val (ys, zs) = xs.splitAt(n)
    merge(msort(less)(ys), msort(less)(zs))
```

Listing 14.2 · A merge sort function for Lists.

Hence, every call level has a total cost proportional to n. Since there are $log(n)$ call levels, we obtain an overall cost proportional to $n\ log(n)$. That cost does not depend on the initial distribution of elements in the list, so the worst case cost is the same as the average case cost. This property makes merge sort an attractive algorithm for sorting lists.

Here is an example of how msort is used:

```
msort((x: Int, y: Int) => x < y)(List(5, 7, 1, 3))
    // List(1, 3, 5, 7)
```

The msort function is a classical example of the currying concept discussed in Section 9.3. Currying makes it easy to specialize the function for particular comparison functions. Here's an example:

```
val intSort = msort((x: Int, y: Int) => x < y)
      // intSort has type List[Int] => List[Int]
```

The intSort variable refers to a function that takes a list of integers and sorts them in numerical order. In this example, msort is partially applied, as described in Section 8.6, because it is missing an argument list. In this case, the missing argument is the list that should be sorted. As another example, here's how you could define a function that sorts a list of integers in reverse numerical order:

```
val reverseIntSort = msort((x: Int, y: Int) => x > y)
```

Because you provided the comparison function already via currying, you now need only provide the list to sort when you invoke the intSort or reverseIntSort functions. Here are some examples:

```
val mixedInts = List(4, 1, 9, 0, 5, 8, 3, 6, 2, 7)
intSort(mixedInts)
      // List(0, 1, 2, 3, 4, 5, 6, 7, 8, 9)
reverseIntSort(mixedInts)
      // List(9, 8, 7, 6, 5, 4, 3, 2, 1, 0)
```

14.7 Higher-order methods on class List

Many operations over lists have a similar structure. Several patterns appear time and time again. Some examples are: transforming every element of a list in some way, verifying whether a property holds for all elements of a list, extracting from a list elements satisfying a certain criterion, or combining the elements of a list using some operator. In imperative languages, such patterns would traditionally be expressed by idiomatic combinations of for or while loops. In Scala, they can be expressed more concisely and directly using higher-order operators,[6] which are implemented as methods in class List. These higher-order operators are discussed in this section.

Mapping over lists: map, flatMap and foreach

The operation xs map f takes as operands a list xs of type List[T] and a function f of type T => U. It returns the list that results from applying the function f to each list element in xs. For instance:

---

[6]By *higher-order operators*, we mean higher-order functions used in operator notation. As mentioned in Section 9.1, a function is "higher-order" if it takes one or more other functions as parameters.

```
List(1, 2, 3).map(_ + 1)   // List(2, 3, 4)
val words = List("the", "quick", "brown", "fox")
words.map(_.length)        // List(3, 5, 5, 3)
words.map(_.toList.reverse.mkString)
       // List(eht, kciuq, nworb, xof)
```

The `flatMap` operator is similar to `map`, but it takes a function returning a list of elements as its right operand. It applies the function to each list element and returns the concatenation of all function results. The difference between `map` and `flatMap` is illustrated in the following example:

```
words.map(_.toList)
       // List(List(t, h, e), List(q, u, i, c, k),
       //    List(b, r, o, w, n), List(f, o, x))
words.flatMap(_.toList)
       // List(t, h, e, q, u, i, c, k, b, r, o, w, n, f, o, x)
```

You see that where `map` returns a list of lists, `flatMap` returns a single list in which all element lists are concatenated.

The differences and interplay between `map` and `flatMap` are also demonstrated by the following expression, which constructs a list of all pairs (i, j) such that $1 \leq j < i < 5$:

```
List.range(1, 5).flatMap(
  i => List.range(1, i).map(j => (i, j))
)
       // List((2,1), (3,1), (3,2), (4,1),
       //      (4,2), (4,3))
```

`List.range` is a utility method that creates a list of all integers in some range. It is used twice in this example: once to generate a list of integers from 1 (including) until 5 (excluding), and a second time to generate a list of integers from 1 until i, for each value of i taken from the first list. The `map` in this expression generates a list of tuples (i, j) where $j < i$. The outer `flatMap` in this example generates this list for each `i` between 1 and 5, and then concatenates all the results. Alternatively, the same list can be constructed with a `for` expression:

```
for i <- List.range(1, 5); j <- List.range(1, i) yield (i, j)
```

You can learn more about the interplay of for expressions and list operations in *Advanced Programming in Scala.*

The third map-like operation is foreach. Unlike map and flatMap, however, foreach takes a procedure (a function with result type Unit) as right operand. It simply applies the procedure to each list element. The result of the operation itself is again Unit; no list of results is assembled. As an example, here is a concise way of summing up all numbers in a list:

```scala
scala> var sum = 0
var sum: Int = 0

scala> List(1, 2, 3, 4, 5).foreach(sum += _)

scala> sum
val res39: Int = 15
```

Filtering lists: filter, partition, find, takeWhile, dropWhile, and span

The operation "xs.filter(p)" takes as operands a list xs of type List[T] and a predicate function p of type T => Boolean. It yields the list of all elements x in xs for which p(x) is true. For instance:

```scala
List(1, 2, 3, 4, 5).filter(_ % 2 == 0)   // List(2, 4)
words.filter(_.length == 3)              // List(the, fox)
```

The partition method is like filter but returns a pair of lists. One list contains all elements for which the predicate is true, while the other contains all elements for which the predicate is false. It is defined by the equality:

```scala
xs.partition(p)    equals   (xs.filter(p), xs.filter(!p(_)))
```

Here's an example:

```scala
List(1, 2, 3, 4, 5).partition(_ % 2 == 0)
     // (List(2, 4),List(1, 3, 5))
```

The find method is also similar to filter, but it returns the first element satisfying a given predicate, rather than all such elements. The operation xs.find(p) takes a list xs and a predicate p as operands. It returns an optional value. If there is an element x in xs for which p(x) is true, Some(x)

289

is returned. Otherwise, p is false for all elements, and None is returned. Here are some examples:

```
List(1, 2, 3, 4, 5).find(_ % 2 == 0)  // Some(2)
List(1, 2, 3, 4, 5).find(_ <= 0)      // None
```

The takeWhile and dropWhile operators also take a predicate as their right operand. The operation xs.takeWhile(p) takes the longest prefix of list xs such that every element in the prefix satisfies p. Analogously, the operation xs.dropWhile(p) removes the longest prefix from list xs such that every element in the prefix satisfies p. Here are some examples:

```
List(1, 2, 3, -4, 5).takeWhile(_ > 0) // List(1, 2, 3)
words.dropWhile(_.startsWith("t")) // List(quick, brown, fox)
```

The span method combines takeWhile and dropWhile in one operation, just like splitAt combines take and drop. It returns a pair of two lists, defined by the equality:

$$\text{xs span p} \quad equals \quad (\text{xs takeWhile p, xs dropWhile p})$$

Like splitAt, span avoids traversing the list xs twice:

```
List(1, 2, 3, -4, 5).span(_ > 0)
      // (List(1, 2, 3),List(-4, 5))
```

Predicates over lists: forall and exists

The operation xs.forall(p) takes as arguments a list xs and a predicate p. Its result is true if all elements in the list satisfy p. Conversely, the operation xs exists p returns true if there is an element in xs that satisfies the predicate p. For instance, to find out whether a matrix represented as a list of lists has a row with only zeroes as elements:

```
def hasZeroRow(m: List[List[Int]]) =
  m.exists(row => row.forall(_ == 0))
hasZeroRow(diag3)  // false
```

Folding lists: `foldLeft` and `foldRight`

Another common kind of operation combines the elements of a list with some operator. For instance:

$$\text{sum(List(a, b, c))} \quad equals \quad 0 + a + b + c$$

This is a special instance of a fold operation:

```
def sum(xs: List[Int]): Int = xs.foldLeft(0)(_ + _)
```

Similarly:

$$\text{product(List(a, b, c))} \quad equals \quad 1 * a * b * c$$

is a special instance of this fold operation:

```
def product(xs: List[Int]): Int = xs.foldLeft(1)(_ * _)
```

The `xs.foldLeft(z)(op)` operation involves three objects: a start value `z`, a list `xs`, and a binary operation `op`. The result of the fold is `op` applied between successive elements of the list prefixed by `z`. For instance:

$$\text{List(a, b, c).foldLeft(z)(op)} \quad equals \quad \text{op(op(op(z, a), b), c)}$$

Or, graphically:

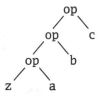

Here's another example that illustrates how `foldLeft` is used. To concatenate all words in a list of strings with spaces between them and in front, you can write this:

```
words.foldLeft("")(_ + " " + _)  // " the quick brown fox"
```

This gives an extra space at the beginning. To remove the space, you can use this slight variation:

```
words.tail.foldLeft(words.head)(_ + " " + _)
    // "the quick brown fox"
```

The `foldLeft` operation produces left-leaning operation trees. There is an analog, `foldRight`, that produces right-leaning trees. For instance:

List(a, b, c).foldRight(z)(op) *equals* op(a, op(b, op(c, z)))

Or, graphically:

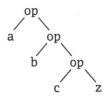

For associative operations, fold left and fold right are equivalent, but there might be a difference in efficiency. Consider for instance an operation corresponding to the `flatten` method, which concatenates all elements in a list of lists. This could be implemented with either fold left or fold right:

```
def flattenLeft[T](xss: List[List[T]]) =
    xss.foldLeft(List[T]())(_ ::: _)

def flattenRight[T](xss: List[List[T]]) =
    xss.foldRight(List[T]())(_ ::: _)
```

Because list concatenation, `xs ::: ys`, takes time proportional to its first argument `xs`, the implementation in terms of fold right in `flattenRight` is more efficient than the fold left implementation in `flattenLeft`. The problem is that `flattenLeft(xss)` copies the first element list `xss.head` $n - 1$ times, where n is the length of the list `xss`.

Note that both versions of `flatten` require a type annotation on the empty list that is the start value of the fold. This is due to a limitation in Scala's type inferencer, which fails to infer the correct type of the list automatically. If you try to leave out the annotation, you get the following:

```
scala> def flattenRight[T](xss: List[List[T]]) =
           xss.foldRight(List())(_ ::: _)
  2 |   xss.foldRight(List())(_ ::: _)
    |                            ^
    |                           Found:    (_$1 : List[T])
    |                           Required: List[Nothing]
```

292

To find out why the type inferencer goes wrong, you'll need to know about the types of the fold methods and how they are implemented. More on this in Section 14.10.

Example: List reversal using fold

Earlier in the chapter you saw an implementation of method `reverse`, named `rev`, whose running time was quadratic in the length of the list to be reversed. Here is a different implementation of `reverse` that has linear cost. The idea is to use a fold left operation based on the following scheme:

```
def reverseLeft[T](xs: List[T]) =
  xs.foldLeft(startvalue)(operation)
```

What remains is to fill in the *startvalue* and *operation* parts. In fact, you can try to deduce these parts from some simple examples. To deduce the correct value of *startvalue*, you can start with the smallest possible list, `List()`, and calculate as follows:

```
List()
```
   equals (by the properties of `reverseLeft`)
```
reverseLeft(List())
```
   equals (by the template for `reverseLeft`)
```
List().foldLeft(startvalue)(operation)
```
   equals (by the definition of `foldLeft`)

startvalue

Hence, *startvalue* must be `List()`. To deduce the second operand, you can pick the next smallest list as an example case. You know already that *startvalue* is `List()`, so you can calculate as follows:

```
List(x)
```
   equals (by the properties of `reverseLeft`)
```
reverseLeft(List(x))
```
   equals (by the template for `reverseLeft`, with *startvalue* = `List()`)
```
List(x).foldLeft(List())(operation)
```
   equals (by the definition of `foldLeft`)

operation`(List(), x)`

293

Hence, *operation*(List(), x) equals List(x), which can also be written as x :: List(). This suggests taking as *operation* the :: operator with its operands exchanged. (This operation is sometimes called "snoc," in reference to ::, which is called cons.) We arrive then at the following implementation for reverseLeft:

```
def reverseLeft[T](xs: List[T]) =
  xs.foldLeft(List[T]()) { (ys, y) => y :: ys }
```

Again, the type annotation in List[T]() is needed to make the type inferencer work. If you analyze the complexity of reverseLeft, you'll find that it applies a constant-time operation ("snoc") *n* times, where *n* is the length of the argument list. Thus, the complexity of reverseLeft is linear.

Sorting lists: sortWith

The operation xs.sortWith(before), where "xs" is a list and "before" is a function that can be used to compare two elements, sorts the elements of list xs. The expression before(x, y) should return true if x should come before y in the intended ordering for the sort. For instance:

```
List(1, -3, 4, 2, 6).sortWith(_ < _)  // List(-3, 1, 2, 4, 6)
words.sortWith(_.length > _.length)
      // List(quick, brown, the, fox)
```

Note that sortWith performs a merge sort similar to the msort algorithm shown in the last section. But sortWith is a method of class List, whereas msort is defined outside lists.

14.8 Methods of the List object

So far, all operations you have seen in this chapter are implemented as methods of class List, so you invoke them on individual list objects. There are also a number of methods in the globally accessible object scala.List, which is the companion object of class List. Some of these operations are factory methods that create lists. Others are operations that work on lists of some specific shape. Both kinds of methods will be presented in this section.

Creating lists from their elements: `List.apply`

You've already seen on several occasions list literals such as `List(1, 2, 3)`. There's nothing special about their syntax. A literal like `List(1, 2, 3)` is simply the application of the object `List` to the elements 1, 2, 3. That is, it is equivalent to `List.apply(1, 2, 3)`:

```
List.apply(1, 2, 3)  // List(1, 2, 3)
```

Creating a range of numbers: `List.range`

The `range` method, which you saw briefly earlier in the discussion of `map` and `flatmap`, creates a list consisting of a range of numbers. Its simplest form is `List.range(from, until)`, which creates a list of all numbers starting at `from` and going up to `until` minus one. So the end value, `until`, does not form part of the range.

There's also a version of `range` that takes a `step` value as third parameter. This operation will yield list elements that are `step` values apart, starting at `from`. The `step` can be positive or negative:

```
List.range(1, 5)      // List(1, 2, 3, 4)
List.range(1, 9, 2)   // List(1, 3, 5, 7)
List.range(9, 1, -3)  // List(9, 6, 3)
```

Creating uniform lists: `List.fill`

The `fill` method creates a list consisting of zero or more copies of the same element. It takes two parameters: the length of the list to be created, and the element to be repeated. Each parameter is given in a separate list:

```
List.fill(5)('a')       // List(a, a, a, a, a)
List.fill(3)("hello")   // List(hello, hello, hello)
```

If `fill` is given more than two arguments, then it will make multi-dimensional lists. That is, it will make lists of lists, lists of lists of lists, *etc.* The additional arguments go in the first argument list.

```
List.fill(2, 3)('b')  // List(List(b, b, b), List(b, b, b))
```

Tabulating a function: `List.tabulate`

The `tabulate` method creates a list whose elements are computed according to a supplied function. Its arguments are just like those of `List.fill`: the first argument list gives the dimensions of the list to create, and the second describes the elements of the list. The only difference is that instead of the elements being fixed, they are computed from a function:

```
val squares = List.tabulate(5)(n => n * n)
    // List(0, 1, 4, 9, 16)
val multiplication = List.tabulate(5,5)(_ * _)
    // List(List(0, 0, 0, 0, 0),
    // List(0, 1, 2, 3, 4), List(0, 2, 4, 6, 8),
    // List(0, 3, 6, 9, 12), List(0, 4, 8, 12, 16))
```

Concatenating multiple lists: `List.concat`

The `concat` method concatenates a number of element lists. The lists to be concatenated are supplied as direct arguments to `concat`:

```
List.concat(List('a', 'b'), List('c'))  // List(a, b, c)
List.concat(List(), List('b'), List('c'))  // List(b, c)
List.concat()  // List()
```

14.9   Processing multiple lists together

You already know the `zip` method on lists, which creates a list of pairs from two lists, and allows you to operate on the two lists at once:

```
(List(10, 20).zip(List(3, 4, 5))).map { (x, y) => x * y }
    // List(30, 80)
```

> **Note**
> The final map takes advantage of a Scala 3 feature called *parameter untupling*, in which a function literal with two or more parameters will be untupled automatically if the expected type is a function that accepts one parameter of a tuple type. For example, the map call in the previous expression means the same as: map { case (x, y) => x * y }.

The map method for two zipped lists maps pairs of elements rather than individual elements. One pair is for the first element of each list, another pair is for the second element of each list, and so on—as many pairs as the lists are long. Notice that the third element of the second list is discarded. The zip method zips up only as many elements as appear in all the lists together. Any extra elements on the end are discarded.

One drawback of operating on multiple lists via the zip method is that it creates an intermediate list (after the zip method is called) that is eventually discarded (when the map method is called). Creating this intermediate list can have an important cost if the lists have a lot of elements. The lazyZip method solves this issue. Its syntax is similar to the zip method:

```
(List(10, 20).lazyZip(List(3, 4, 5))).map(_ * _)
    // List(30, 80)
```

The difference between lazyZip and zip is that lazyZip does not immediately return a collection (hence the "lazy" prefix). Instead, it returns a value that provides methods (including map) operating on the two lazily zipped lists. In the above example, you can see that the map method takes as parameter a function that takes two parameters (as opposed to one pair), allowing the usage of the placeholder syntax.

There are also lazy zip analogs to exists and forall. They are just like the single-list versions of those methods except they operate on elements from multiple lists instead of just one:

```
(List("abc", "de").lazyZip(List(3, 2))).forall(_.length == _)
    // true
(List("abc", "de").lazyZip(List(3, 2))).exists(_.length != _)
    // false
```

The fast track
In the next (and final) section of this chapter, we provide insight into Scala's type inference algorithm. If you're not interested in such details right now, you can skip the entire section and go straight to the conclusion on page 301.

14.10 Understanding Scala's type inference algorithm

One difference between the previous uses of `sortWith` and `msort` concerns the admissible syntactic forms of the comparison function.

Compare:

```
msort((x: Char, y: Char) => x > y)(abcde)
      // List(e, d, c, b, a)
```

with:

```
abcde.sortWith(_ > _)  // List(e, d, c, b, a)
```

The two expressions are equivalent, but the first uses a longer form of comparison function with named parameters and explicit types. The second uses the concise form, `(_ > _)`, where named parameters are replaced by underscores. Of course, you could also use the first, longer form of comparison with `sortWith`.

However, the short form cannot be used with `msort`.

```
scala> msort(_ > _)(abcde)
1 |msort(_ > _)(abcde)
  |          ^^^
  |value > is not a member of Any, but could be made
  | available as an extension method.
```

To understand why, you need to know some details of Scala's type inference algorithm. Type inference in Scala is flow based. In a method application `m(args)`, the inferencer first checks whether the method m has a known type. If it does, that type is used to infer the expected type of the arguments. For instance, in `abcde.sortWith(_ > _)`, the type of abcde is `List[Char]`. Hence, `sortWith` is known to be a method that takes an argument of type `(Char, Char) => Boolean` and produces a result of type `List[Char]`. Since the parameter types of the function arguments are known, they need not be written explicitly. With what it knows about `sortWith`, the inferencer can deduce that `(_ > _)` should expand to `((x: Char, y: Char) => x > y)` where x and y are some arbitrary fresh names.

Now consider the second case, `msort(_ > _)(abcde)`. The type of `msort` is a curried, polymorphic method type that takes an argument of type `(T, T) => Boolean` to a function from `List[T]` to `List[T]` *where T is some as-yet unknown type.* The msort method needs to be instantiated with a type parameter before it can be applied to its arguments.

Because the precise instance type of msort in the application is not yet known, it cannot be used to infer the type of its first argument. The type inferencer changes its strategy in this case; it first type checks method arguments to determine the proper instance type of the method. However, when tasked to type check the short-hand function literal, (_ > _), it fails because it has no information about the types of the implicit function parameters that are indicated by underscores.

One way to resolve the problem is to pass an explicit type parameter to msort, as in:

```
msort[Char](_ > _)(abcde)   // List(e, d, c, b, a)
```

Because the correct instance type of msort is now known, it can be used to infer the type of the arguments. Another possible solution is to rewrite the msort method so that its parameters are swapped:

```
def msortSwapped[T](xs: List[T])(less:
    (T, T) => Boolean): List[T] = ...

  // same implementation as msort,
  // but with arguments swapped
```

Now type inference would succeed:

```
msortSwapped(abcde)(_ > _)  // List(e, d, c, b, a)
```

What has happened is that the inferencer used the known type of the first parameter abcde to determine the type parameter of msortSwapped. Once the precise type of msortSwapped was known, it could be used in turn to infer the type of the second parameter, (_ > _).

Generally, when tasked to infer the type parameters of a polymorphic method, the type inferencer consults the types of all value arguments in the first parameter list but no arguments beyond that. Since msortSwapped is a curried method with two parameter lists, the second argument (*i.e.*, the function value) did not need to be consulted to determine the type parameter of the method.

This inference scheme suggests the following library design principle: When designing a polymorphic method that takes some non-function arguments and a function argument, place the function argument last in a curried parameter list on its own. That way, the method's correct instance type can be inferred from the non-function arguments, and that type can in turn be used to type check the function argument. The net effect is that users of the method will be able to give less type information and write function literals in more compact ways.

Now to the more complicated case of a *fold* operation. Why is there the need for an explicit type parameter in an expression like the body of the flattenRight method shown on page 292?

```
xss.foldRight(List[T]())(_ ::: _)
```

The type of the foldRight method is polymorphic in two type variables. Given an expression:

```
xs.foldRight(z)(op)
```

The type of xs must be a list of some arbitrary type A, say xs: List[A]. The start value z can be of some other type B. The operation op must then take two arguments of type A and B, and return a result of type B, *i.e.*, op: (A, B) => B. Because the type of z is not related to the type of the list xs, type inference has no context information for z.

Now consider the expression in the erroneous version of flattenRight, also shown on page 292:

```
xss.foldRight(List())(_ ::: _)  // this won't compile
```

The start value z in this fold is an empty list, List(), so without additional type information its type is inferred to be a List[Nothing]. Hence, the inferencer will infer that the B type of the fold is List[Nothing]. Therefore, the operation (_ ::: _) of the fold is expected to be of the following type:

```
(List[T], List[Nothing]) => List[Nothing]
```

This is indeed a possible type for the operation in that fold but it is not a very useful one! It says that the operation always takes an empty list as second argument and always produces an empty list as result.

In other words, the type inference settled too early on a type for List(); it should have waited until it had seen the type of the operation op. So the (otherwise very useful) rule to only consider the first argument section in a curried method application for determining the method's type is at the root of the problem here. On the other hand, even if that rule were relaxed, the inferencer still could not come up with a type for op because its parameter types are not given. Hence, there is a Catch-22 situation that can only be resolved by an explicit type annotation from the programmer.

This example highlights some limitations of the local, flow-based type inference scheme of Scala. It is not present in the more global Hindley-Milner style of type inference used in functional languages, such as ML or Haskell. However, Scala's local type inference deals much more gracefully with object-oriented subtyping than the Hindley-Milner style does. Fortunately, the limitations show up only in some corner cases, and are usually easily fixed by adding an explicit type annotation.

Adding type annotations is also a useful debugging technique when you get confused by type error messages related to polymorphic methods. If you are unsure what caused a particular type error, just add some type arguments or other type annotations, which you think are correct. Then you should be able to quickly see where the real problem is.

14.11   Conclusion

Now you have seen many ways to work with lists. You have seen the basic operations like `head` and `tail`, the first-order operations like `reverse`, the higher-order operations like `map`, and the utility methods in the `List` object. Along the way, you learned a bit about how Scala's type inference works.

Lists are a real work horse in Scala, so you will benefit from knowing how to use them. For that reason, this chapter has delved deeply into how to use lists. Lists are just one kind of collection that Scala supports, however. The next chapter is broad, rather than deep, and shows you how to use a variety of Scala's collection types.

Chapter 15

Working with Other Collections

Scala has a rich collection library. This chapter gives you a tour of the most commonly used collection types and operations, showing just the parts you will use most frequently. *Advanced Programming in Scala* will provide a more comprehensive tour of what's available and show how Scala's composition constructs are used to provide such a rich API.

15.1   Sequences

Sequence types let you work with groups of data lined up in order. Because the elements are ordered, you can ask for the first element, second element, 103rd element, and so on. In this section, we'll give you a quick tour of the most important sequences.

Lists

Perhaps the most important sequence type to know about is class `List`, the immutable linked-list described in detail in the previous chapter. Lists support fast addition and removal of items to the beginning of the list, but they do not provide fast access to arbitrary indexes because the implementation must iterate through the list linearly.

This combination of features might sound odd, but they hit a sweet spot that works well for many algorithms. The fast addition and removal of initial elements means that pattern matching works well, as described in Chapter 13. The immutability of lists helps you develop correct, efficient algorithms because you never need to make copies of a list.

Here's a short example showing how to initialize a list, and access its head and tail:

```
val colors = List("red", "blue", "green")
colors.head  // red
colors.tail  // List(blue, green)
```

For a refresher on lists, see Step 8 in Chapter 3. You can find details on using lists in Chapter 14. Lists will also be discussed in *Advanced Programming in Scala*, which provides insight into how lists are implemented in Scala.

Arrays

Arrays allow you to hold a sequence of elements and efficiently access an element at an arbitrary position, either to get or update the element, with a zero-based index. Here's how you create an array whose size you know, but for which you don't yet know the element values:

```
val fiveInts = new Array[Int](5)  // Array(0, 0, 0, 0, 0)
```

Here's how you initialize an array when you do know the element values:

```
val fiveToOne = Array(5, 4, 3, 2, 1)  // Array(5, 4, 3, 2, 1)
```

As mentioned previously, arrays are accessed in Scala by placing an index in parentheses, not square brackets as in Java. Here's an example of both accessing and updating an array element:

```
fiveInts(0) = fiveToOne(4)
fiveInts  // Array(1, 0, 0, 0, 0)
```

Scala arrays are represented in the same way as Java arrays. So, you can seamlessly use existing Java methods that return arrays.[1]

You have seen arrays in action many times in previous chapters. The basics are in Step 7 in Chapter 3. Several examples of iterating through the elements of an array with a for expression are shown in Section 7.3.

---

[1] The difference in variance of Scala's and Java's arrays—*i.e.*, whether `Array[String]` is a subtype of `Array[AnyRef]`—will be discussed in Section 18.3.

List buffers

Class `List` provides fast access to the head of the list, but not the end. Thus, when you need to build a list by appending to the end, consider building the list backwards by prepending elements to the front. Then when you're done, call `reverse` to get the elements in the order you need.

Another alternative, which avoids the `reverse` operation, is to use a `ListBuffer`. A `ListBuffer` is a mutable object (contained in package `scala.collection.mutable`), which can help you build lists more efficiently when you need to append. `ListBuffer` provides constant time append and prepend operations. You append elements with the += operator, and prepend them with the +=: operator.[2] When you're done building, you can obtain a `List` by invoking `toList` on the `ListBuffer`. Here's an example:

```
import scala.collection.mutable.ListBuffer

val buf = new ListBuffer[Int]
buf += 1    // ListBuffer(1)
buf += 2    // ListBuffer(1, 2)
3 +=: buf   // ListBuffer(3, 1, 2)
buf.toList  // List(3, 1, 2)
```

Another reason to use `ListBuffer` instead of `List` is to prevent the potential for stack overflow. If you can build a list in the desired order by prepending, but the recursive algorithm that would be required is not tail recursive, you can use a `for` expression or `while` loop and a `ListBuffer` instead. You can see `ListBuffer` being used in this way in *Advanced Programming in Scala*.

Array buffers

An `ArrayBuffer` is like an array, except that you can additionally add and remove elements from the beginning and end of the sequence. All `Array` operations are available, though they are a little slower due to a layer of wrapping in the implementation. The new addition and removal operations are constant time on average, but occasionally require linear time due to the implementation needing to allocate a new array to hold the buffer's contents.

To use an `ArrayBuffer`, you must first import it from the mutable collections package:

---

[2]The += and +=: operators are aliases for `append` and `prepend`, respectively.

305

```
import scala.collection.mutable.ArrayBuffer
```

When you create an `ArrayBuffer`, you must specify a type parameter, but you don't need to specify a length. The `ArrayBuffer` will adjust the allocated space automatically as needed:

```
val buf = new ArrayBuffer[Int]()
```

You can append to an `ArrayBuffer` using the += method:

```
buf += 12  // ArrayBuffer(12)
buf += 15  // ArrayBuffer(12, 15)
```

All the normal array methods are available. For example, you can ask an `ArrayBuffer` its length or you can retrieve an element by its index:

```
buf.length  // 2
buf(0)      // 12
```

Strings (via `StringOps`)

One other sequence to be aware of is `StringOps`, which implements many sequence methods. Because `Predef` has an implicit conversion from `String` to `StringOps`, you can treat any string like a sequence. Here's an example:

```
def hasUpperCase(s: String) = s.exists(_.isUpper)
hasUpperCase("Robert Frost")   // true
hasUpperCase("e e cummings")   // false
```

In this example, the `exists` method is invoked on the string named s in the `hasUpperCase` method body. Because no method named "exists" is declared in class `String` itself, the Scala compiler will implicitly convert s to `StringOps`, which has the method. The `exists` method treats the string as a sequence of characters, and will return true if any of the characters are upper case.[3]

---

[3]The code given on page 13 of Chapter 1 presents a similar example.

15.2   Sets and maps

You have already seen the basics of sets and maps in previous chapters, starting with Step 10 in Chapter 3. In this section, we'll offer more insight into their use and show you a few more examples.

As mentioned previously, the Scala collections library offers both mutable and immutable versions of sets and maps. The hierarchy for sets is shown in Figure 3.2 on page 46, and the hierarchy for maps is shown in Figure 3.3 on page 48. As these diagrams show, the simple names Set and Map are used by three traits each, residing in different packages.

By default when you write "Set" or "Map" you get an immutable object. If you want the mutable variant, you need to do an explicit import. Scala gives you easier access to the immutable variants, as a gentle encouragement to prefer them over their mutable counterparts. The easy access is provided via the Predef object, which is implicitly imported into every Scala source file. Listing 15.1 shows the relevant definitions:

```scala
object Predef:
  type Map[A, +B] = collection.immutable.Map[A, B]
  type Set[A] = collection.immutable.Set[A]
  val Map = collection.immutable.Map
  val Set = collection.immutable.Set
  // ...
end Predef
```

Listing 15.1 · Default map and set definitions in Predef.

The "type" keyword is used in Predef to define Set and Map as aliases for the longer fully qualified names of the immutable set and map traits.[4] The vals named Set and Map are initialized to refer to the singleton objects for the immutable Set and Map. So Map is the same as Predef.Map, which is defined to be the same as scala.collection.immutable.Map. This holds both for the Map type and Map object.

If you want to use both mutable and immutable sets or maps in the same source file, the recommended approach is to import the name of the package that contains the mutable variants:

---

[4]The type keyword will be explained in more detail in Section 20.6.

307

```
import scala.collection.mutable
```

You can continue to refer to the immutable set as `Set`, as before, but can now refer to the mutable set as `mutable.Set`. Here's an example:

```
val mutaSet = mutable.Set(1, 2, 3)
```

Using sets

The key characteristic of sets is that they will ensure that at most one of each object, as determined by ==, will be contained in the set at any one time. As an example, we'll use a set to count the number of different words in a string.

The `split` method on `String` can separate a string into words, if you specify spaces and punctuation as word separators. The regular expression "[!,.]+" will suffice: It indicates the string should be split at each place that one or more space and/or punctuation characters exist.

```
val text = "See Spot run. Run, Spot. Run!"
val wordsArray = text.split("[ !,.]+")
        // Array(See, Spot, run, Run, Spot, Run)
```

To count the distinct words, you can convert them to the same case and then add them to a set. Because sets exclude duplicates, each distinct word will appear exactly one time in the set.

First, you can create an empty set using the `empty` method provided on the `Set` companion objects:

```
val words = mutable.Set.empty[String]
```

Then, just iterate through the words with a `for` expression, convert each word to lower case, and add it to the mutable set with the += operator:

```
for word <- wordsArray do
  words += word.toLowerCase
words  // Set(see, run, spot)
```

Thus, the text contained exactly three distinct words: spot, run, and see. The most commonly used methods on both mutable and immutable sets are shown in Table 15.1.

Table 15.1 · Common operations for sets

What it is	What it does
val nums = Set(1, 2, 3)	Creates an immutable set (nums.toString returns Set(1, 2, 3))
nums + 5	Adds an element to an immutable set (returns Set(1, 2, 3, 5))
nums - 3	Removes an element from an immutable set (returns Set(1, 2))
nums ++ List(5, 6)	Adds multiple elements (returns Set(1, 2, 3, 5, 6))
nums -- List(1, 2)	Removes multiple elements from an immutable set (returns Set(3))
nums & Set(1, 3, 5, 7)	Takes the intersection of two sets (returns Set(1, 3))
nums.size	Returns the size of the set (returns 3)
nums.contains(3)	Checks for inclusion (returns true)
import scala.collection.mutable	Makes the mutable collections easy to access
val words = mutable.Set.empty[String]	Creates an empty, mutable set (words.toString returns Set())
words += "the"	Adds an element (words.toString returns Set(the))
words -= "the"	Removes an element, if it exists (words.toString returns Set())
words ++= List("do", "re", "mi")	Adds multiple elements (words.toString returns Set(do, re, mi))
words --= List("do", "re")	Removes multiple elements (words.toString returns Set(mi))
words.clear	Removes all elements (words.toString returns Set())

Using maps

Maps let you associate a value with each element of a set. Using a map looks similar to using an array, except instead of indexing with integers counting from 0, you can use any kind of key. If you import the `mutable` package name, you can create an empty mutable map like this:

```
val map = mutable.Map.empty[String, Int]
```

Note that when you create a map, you must specify two types. The first type is for the *keys* of the map, the second for the *values*. In this case, the keys are strings and the values are integers. Setting entries in a map looks similar to setting entries in an array:

```
map("hello") = 1
map("there") = 2
map  // Map(hello -> 1, there -> 2)
```

Likewise, reading a map is similar to reading an array:

```
map("hello")  // 1
```

Putting it all together, here is a method that counts the number of times each word occurs in a string:

```
def countWords(text: String) =
  val counts = mutable.Map.empty[String, Int]
  for rawWord <- text.split("[ ,!.]+") do
    val word = rawWord.toLowerCase
    val oldCount =
      if counts.contains(word) then counts(word)
      else 0
    counts += (word -> (oldCount + 1))
  counts

countWords("See Spot run! Run, Spot. Run!")
      // Map(spot -> 2, see -> 1, run -> 3)
```

The way this code works is that a mutable map, named `counts`, maps each word to the number of times it occurs in the text. For each word in the text, the word's old count is looked up, that count is incremented by one, and the new count is saved back into `counts`. Note the use of `contains` to check whether a word has been seen yet or not. If `counts.contains(word)` is not true, then the word has not yet been seen and zero is used for the count.

Many of the most commonly used methods on both mutable and immutable maps are shown in Table 15.2.

Table 15.2 · Common operations for maps

What it is	What it does
`val nums = Map("i" -> 1, "ii" -> 2)`	Creates an immutable map (`nums.toString` returns `Map(i -> 1, ii -> 2)`)
`nums + ("vi" -> 6)`	Adds an entry to an immutable map (returns `Map(i -> 1, ii -> 2, vi -> 6)`)
`nums - "ii"`	Removes an entry from an immutable map (returns `Map(i -> 1)`)
`nums ++ List("iii" -> 3, "v" -> 5)`	Adds multiple entries (returns `Map(i -> 1, ii -> 2, iii -> 3, v -> 5)`)
`nums -- List("i", "ii")`	Removes multiple entries from an immutable map (returns `Map()`)
`nums.size`	Returns the size of the map (returns 2)
`nums.contains("ii")`	Checks for inclusion (returns `true`)
`nums("ii")`	Retrieves the value at a specified key (returns 2)
`nums.keys`	Returns the keys (returns an `Iterable` over the strings `"i"` and `"ii"`)
`nums.keySet`	Returns the keys as a set (returns `Set(i, ii)`)
`nums.values`	Returns the values (returns an `Iterable` over the integers 1 and 2)
`nums.isEmpty`	Indicates whether the map is empty (returns false)
`import scala.collection.mutable`	Makes the mutable collections easy to access

311

Table 15.2 · continued

`val words =` `mutable.Map.empty[String, Int]`	Creates an empty, mutable map
`words += ("one" -> 1)`	Adds a map entry from "one" to 1 (`words.toString` returns `Map(one -> 1)`)
`words -= "one"`	Removes a map entry, if it exists (`words.toString` returns `Map()`)
`words ++= List("one" -> 1,` `"two" -> 2, "three" -> 3)`	Adds multiple map entries (`words.toString` returns `Map(one -> 1, two -> 2, three -> 3)`)
`words --= List("one", "two")`	Removes multiple objects (`words.toString` returns `Map(three -> 3)`)

Default sets and maps

For most uses, the implementations of mutable and immutable sets and maps provided by the `Set()`, `scala.collection.mutable.Map()`, *etc.*, factories will likely be sufficient. The implementations provided by these factories use a fast lookup algorithm, usually involving a hash table, so they can quickly decide whether or not an object is in the collection.

The `scala.collection.mutable.Set()` factory method, for example, returns a `scala.collection.mutable.HashSet`, which uses a hash table internally. Similarly, the `scala.collection.mutable.Map()` factory returns a `scala.collection.mutable.HashMap`.

The story for immutable sets and maps is a bit more involved. The class returned by the `scala.collection.immutable.Set()` factory method, for example, depends on how many elements you pass to it, as shown in Table 15.3. For sets with fewer than five elements, a special class devoted exclusively to sets of each particular size is used to maximize performance. Once you request a set that has five or more elements in it, however, the factory method will return an implementation that uses hash tries.

Similarly, the `scala.collection.immutable.Map()` factory method will return a different class depending on how many key-value pairs you pass to it, as shown in Table 15.4. As with sets, for immutable maps with

Table 15.3 · Default immutable set implementations

Number of elements	Implementation
0	scala.collection.immutable.EmptySet
1	scala.collection.immutable.Set1
2	scala.collection.immutable.Set2
3	scala.collection.immutable.Set3
4	scala.collection.immutable.Set4
5 or more	scala.collection.immutable.HashSet

fewer than five elements, a special class devoted exclusively to maps of each particular size is used to maximize performance. Once a map has five or more key-value pairs in it, however, an immutable HashMap is used.

The default immutable implementation classes shown in Tables 15.3 and 15.4 work together to give you maximum performance. For example, if you add an element to an EmptySet, it will return a Set1. If you add an element to that Set1, it will return a Set2. If you then remove an element from the Set2, you'll get another Set1.

Table 15.4 · Default immutable map implementations

Number of elements	Implementation
0	scala.collection.immutable.EmptyMap
1	scala.collection.immutable.Map1
2	scala.collection.immutable.Map2
3	scala.collection.immutable.Map3
4	scala.collection.immutable.Map4
5 or more	scala.collection.immutable.HashMap

Sorted sets and maps

On occasion you may need a set or map whose iterator returns elements in a particular order. For this purpose, the Scala collections library provides traits SortedSet and SortedMap. These traits are implemented by classes TreeSet and TreeMap, which use a red-black tree to keep elements (in the case of TreeSet) or keys (in the case of TreeMap) in order. The order is determined by the Ordering trait, an implicit instance of which must be defined for the element type of the set, or key type of the map. These classes come both in immutable and mutable variants. Here are some `TreeSet` examples:

```
import scala.collection.immutable.TreeSet
val ts = TreeSet(9, 3, 1, 8, 0, 2, 7, 4, 6, 5)
            // TreeSet(0, 1, 2, 3, 4, 5, 6, 7, 8, 9)
val cs = TreeSet('f', 'u', 'n')  // TreeSet(f, n, u)
```

And here are a few `TreeMap` examples:

```
import scala.collection.immutable.TreeMap
var tm = TreeMap(3 -> 'x', 1 -> 'x', 4 -> 'x')
            // TreeMap(1 -> x, 3 -> x, 4 -> x)
tm += (2 -> 'x')
tm  // TreeMap(1 -> x, 2 -> x, 3 -> x, 4 -> x)
```

15.3 Selecting mutable versus immutable collections

For some problems, mutable collections work better, while for others, immutable collections work better. When in doubt, it is better to start with an immutable collection and change it later, if you need to, because immutable collections can be easier to reason about than mutable ones.

Also, it can be worthwhile to go the opposite way sometimes. If you find some code that uses mutable collections becoming complicated and hard to reason about, consider whether it would help to change some of the collections to immutable alternatives. In particular, if you find yourself worrying about making copies of mutable collections in just the right places, or thinking a lot about who "owns" or "contains" a mutable collection, consider switching some of the collections to their immutable counterparts.

Besides being potentially easier to reason about, immutable collections can usually be stored more compactly than mutable ones if the number of elements stored in the collection is small. For instance an empty mutable map in its default representation of `HashMap` takes up about 80 bytes, and about 16 more are added for each entry that's added to it. An empty immutable `Map` is a single object that's shared between all references, so referring to it essentially costs just a single pointer field.

What's more, the Scala collections library currently stores immutable maps and sets with up to four entries in a single object, which typically takes up between 16 and 40 bytes, depending on the number of entries stored in the collection.[5] So for small maps and sets, the immutable versions are much more compact than the mutable ones. Given that many collections are small, switching them to be immutable can bring important space savings and performance advantages.

To make it easier to switch from immutable to mutable collections, and vice versa, Scala provides some syntactic sugar. Even though immutable sets and maps do not support a true += method, Scala gives a useful alternate interpretation to +=. Whenever you write a += b, and a does not support a method named +=, Scala will try interpreting it as a = a + b.

For example, immutable sets do not support a += operator:

```
scala> val people = Set("Nancy", "Jane")
val people: Set[String] = Set(Nancy, Jane)

scala> people += "Bob"
1 |people += "Bob"
  |^^^^^^^^^^
  |value += is not a member of Set[String]
```

However, if you declare people as a var, instead of a val, then the collection can be "updated" with a += operation, even though it is immutable. First, a new collection will be created, and then people will be reassigned to refer to the new collection:

```
var people = Set("Nancy", "Jane")
people += "Bob"
people  // Set(Nancy, Jane, Bob)
```

After this series of statements, the people variable refers to a new immutable set, which contains the added string, "Bob". The same idea applies to any method ending in =, not just the += method. Here's the same syntax used with the -= operator, which removes an element from a set, and the ++= operator, which adds a collection of elements to a set:

---

[5]The "single object" is an instance of Set1 through Set4, or Map1 through Map4, as shown in Tables 15.3 and 15.4.

```
people -= "Jane"
people ++= List("Tom", "Harry")
people  // Set(Nancy, Bob, Tom, Harry)
```

To see how this is useful, consider again the following Map example from Section 1.1:

```
var capital = Map("US" -> "Washington", "France" -> "Paris")
capital += ("Japan" -> "Tokyo")
println(capital("France"))
```

This code uses immutable collections. If you want to try using mutable collections instead, all that is necessary is to import the mutable version of Map, thus overriding the default import of the immutable Map:

```
import scala.collection.mutable.Map  // only change needed!
var capital = Map("US" -> "Washington", "France" -> "Paris")
capital += ("Japan" -> "Tokyo")
println(capital("France"))
```

Not all examples are quite that easy to convert, but the special treatment of methods ending in an equals sign will often reduce the amount of code that needs changing.

By the way, this syntactic treatment works on any kind of value, not just collections. For example, here it is being used on floating-point numbers:

```
var roughlyPi = 3.0
roughlyPi += 0.1
roughlyPi += 0.04
roughlyPi  // 3.14
```

The effect of this expansion is similar to Java's assignment operators (+=, -=, *=, *etc.*), but it is more general because every operator ending in = can be converted.

15.4   Initializing collections

As you've seen previously, the most common way to create and initialize a collection is to pass the initial elements to a factory method on the companion object of your chosen collection. You just place the elements in parentheses after the companion object name, and the Scala compiler will transform that to an invocation of an `apply` method on that companion object:

```
List(1, 2, 3)
Set('a', 'b', 'c')
import scala.collection.mutable
mutable.Map("hi" -> 2, "there" -> 5)
Array(1.0, 2.0, 3.0)
```

Although most often you can let the Scala compiler infer the element type of a collection from the elements passed to its factory method, sometimes you may want to create a collection but specify a different type from the one the compiler would choose. This is especially an issue with mutable collections. Here's an example:

```
scala> import scala.collection.mutable

scala> val stuff = mutable.Set(42)
val stuff: scala.collection.mutable.Set[Int] = HashSet(42)

scala> stuff += "abracadabra"
1 |stuff += "abracadabra"
  |          ^^^^^^^^^^^^^
  |          Found:    ("abracadabra" : String)
  |          Required: Int
```

The problem here is that `stuff` was given an element type of `Int`. If you want it to have an element type of `Any`, you need to say so explicitly by putting the element type in square brackets, like this:

```
scala> val stuff = mutable.Set[Any](42)
val stuff: scala.collection.mutable.Set[Any] = HashSet(42)
```

Another special situation is if you want to initialize a collection with another collection. For example, imagine you have a list, but you want a `TreeSet` containing the elements in the list. Here's the list:

```
val colors = List("blue", "yellow", "red", "green")
```

You cannot pass the `colors` list to the factory method for `TreeSet`:

```
scala> import scala.collection.immutable.TreeSet
scala> val treeSet = TreeSet(colors)
1 |val treeSet = TreeSet(colors)
  |                              ^
  |No implicit Ordering defined for List[String]..
```

Instead, you'll need to convert the list to a `TreeSet` with the `to` method:

```
val treeSet = colors to TreeSet
      // TreeSet(blue, green, red, yellow)
```

The `to` method takes as parameter a companion object of a collection. You can use it to convert any collection to another.

Converting to array or list

In addition to the generic `to` method for converting a collection to another arbitary collection, you can also use more specific methods to convert to the most common Scala collection types. As you've seen previously, to initialize a new list with another collection, simply invoke `toList` on that collection:

```
treeSet.toList   // List(blue, green, red, yellow)
```

Or, if you need an array, invoke `toArray`:

```
treeSet.toArray   // Array(blue, green, red, yellow)
```

Note that although the original `colors` list was not sorted, the elements in the list produced by invoking `toList` on the `TreeSet` are in alphabetical order. When you invoke `toList` or `toArray` on a collection, the order of the elements in the resulting list or array will be the same as the order of elements produced by an iterator on that collection. Because a `TreeSet[String]`'s iterator will produce strings in alphabetical order, those strings will appear in alphabetical order in the list resulting from invoking `toList` on that `TreeSet`.

The difference between "xs to List" and "xs.toList" is that the implementation of `toList` may be overridden by the concrete collection type of xs to provide a more efficient way to convert its elements to a list than the default implementation, which copies all the elements of the collection. For instance, the `ListBuffer` collection does override its `toList` method with an implementation that runs in constant time and space.

Keep in mind, however, that conversion to lists or arrays usually requires copying all of the elements of the collection, and thus may be slow for large collections. Sometimes you need to do it, though, due to an existing API. Further, many collections only have a few elements anyway, in which case there is only a small speed penalty.

Converting between mutable and immutable sets and maps

Another situation that arises occasionally is the need to convert a mutable set or map to an immutable one, or *vice versa*. To accomplish this, you can use the `to` method shown on the previous page. Here's how you'd convert the immutable `TreeSet` from the previous example to a mutable set, and back again to an immutable one:

```
import scala.collection.mutable
treeSet  // TreeSet(blue, green, red, yellow)
val mutaSet = treeSet to mutable.Set
      // mutable.HashSet(red, blue, green, yellow)
val immutaSet = mutaSet to Set  //
      // Set(red, blue, green, yellow)
```

You can use the same technique to convert between mutable and immutable maps:

```
val muta = mutable.Map("i" -> 1, "ii" -> 2)
muta  // mutable.HashMap(i -> 1, ii -> 2)
val immu = muta to Map  // Map(ii -> 2, i -> 1)
```

15.5 Tuples

As described in Step 9 in Chapter 3, a tuple combines a fixed number of items together so that they can be passed around as a whole. Unlike an array or list, a tuple can hold objects with different types. Here is an example of a tuple holding an integer, a string, and the console:

```
(1, "hello", Console)
```

319

Tuples save you the tedium of defining simplistic data-heavy classes. Even though defining a class is already easy, it does require a certain minimum effort, which sometimes serves no purpose. Tuples save you the effort of choosing a name for the class, choosing a scope to define the class in, and choosing names for the members of the class. If your class simply holds an integer and a string, there is no clarity added by defining a class named AnIntegerAndAString.

Because tuples can combine objects of different types, tuples do not inherit from Iterable. If you find yourself wanting to group exactly one integer and exactly one string, then you want a tuple, not a List or Array.

A common application of tuples is returning multiple values from a method. For example, here is a method that finds the longest word in a collection and also returns its index:

```scala
def longestWord(words: Array[String]): (String, Int) =
  var word = words(0)
  var idx = 0
  for i <- 1 until words.length do
    if words(i).length > word.length then
      word = words(i)
      idx = i
  (word, idx)
```

Here is an example use of the method:

```scala
val longest = longestWord("The quick brown fox".split(" "))
// (quick,1)
```

The longestWord function here computes two items: word, the longest word in the array, and idx, the index of that word. To keep things simple, the function assumes there is at least one word in the list, and it breaks ties by choosing the word that comes earlier in the list. Once the function has chosen which word and index to return, it returns both of them together using the tuple syntax (word, idx).

To access elements of a tuple, you can use parentheses and a zero based index. The result will have the appropriate type. For example:

```scala
scala> longest(0)
val res0: String = quick
```

320

```
scala> longest(1)
val res1: Int = 1
```

Additionally, you can assign each element of the tuple to its own variable,[6] like this:

```
scala> val (word, idx) = longest
val word: String = quick
val idx: Int = 1

scala> word
val res55: String = quick
```

By the way, if you leave off the parentheses you get a different result:

```
scala> val word, idx = longest
val word: (String, Int) = (quick,1)
val idx: (String, Int) = (quick,1)
```

This syntax gives *multiple definitions* of the same expression. Each variable is initialized with its own evaluation of the expression on the right-hand side. That the expression evaluates to a tuple in this case does not matter. Both variables are initialized to the tuple in its entirety. See Chapter 16 for some examples where multiple definitions are convenient.

As a note of warning, tuples are almost too easy to use. Tuples are great when you combine data that has no meaning beyond "an A and a B." However, whenever the combination has some meaning, or you want to add some methods to the combination, it is better to go ahead and create a class. For example, do not use a 3-tuple for the combination of a month, a day, and a year. Make a Date class. It makes your intentions explicit, which both clears up the code for human readers and gives the compiler and language opportunities to help you catch mistakes.

15.6 Conclusion

This chapter has given an overview of the Scala collections library and the most important classes and traits in it. With this foundation you should be

---

[6]This syntax is actually a special case of *pattern matching*, as described in detail in Section 13.7.

321

able to work effectively with Scala collections, and know where to look in Scaladoc when you need more information. For more detailed information about Scala collections, look ahead to Chapter 24 and Chapter 4. For now, in the next chapter, we'll turn our attention from the Scala library back to the language and discuss Scala's support for mutable objects.

Chapter 16

Mutable Objects

In previous chapters, we put the spotlight on functional (immutable) objects. We did so because the idea of objects without any mutable state deserves to be better known. However, it is also perfectly possible to define objects with mutable state in Scala. Such mutable objects often come up naturally when you want to model objects in the real world that change over time.

This chapter explains what mutable objects are and what Scala provides in terms of syntax to express them. We will also introduce a larger case study on discrete event simulation, which involves mutable objects, as well as building an internal DSL for defining digital circuits to simulate.

16.1   What makes an object mutable?

You can observe the principal difference between a purely functional object and a mutable one even without looking at the object's implementation. When you invoke a method or dereference a field on some purely functional object, you will always get the same result.

For instance, given a list of characters:

```
val cs = List('a', 'b', 'c')
```

an application of cs.head will always return 'a'. This is the case even if there is an arbitrary number of operations on the list cs between the point where it is defined and the point where the access cs.head is made.

For a mutable object, on the other hand, the result of a method call or field access may depend on what operations were previously performed on the object. A good example of a mutable object is a bank account. Listing 16.1 shows a simplified implementation of bank accounts:

```scala
class BankAccount:
  private var bal: Int = 0
  def balance: Int = bal
  def deposit(amount: Int): Unit =
    require(amount > 0)
    bal += amount
  def withdraw(amount: Int): Boolean =
    if amount > bal then false
    else
      bal -= amount
      true
```

Listing 16.1 · A mutable bank account class.

The BankAccount class defines a private variable, bal, and three public methods: balance returns the current balance; deposit adds a given amount to bal; and withdraw tries to subtract a given amount from bal while assuring that the remaining balance won't be negative. The return value of withdraw is a Boolean indicating whether the requested funds were successfully withdrawn.

Even if you know nothing about the inner workings of the BankAccount class, you can still tell that BankAccounts are mutable objects:

```scala
val account = new BankAccount
account.deposit(100)
account.withdraw(80)  // true
account.withdraw(80)  // false
```

Note that the two final withdrawals in the previous interaction returned different results. The first withdraw operation returned true because the bank account contained sufficient funds to allow the withdrawal. The second operation, although the same as the first one, returned false because the balance of the account had been reduced so that it no longer covered the requested funds. So, clearly, bank accounts have mutable state, because the same operation can return different results at different times.

324

You might think that the mutability of `BankAccount` is immediately apparent because it contains a `var` definition. Mutation and `vars` usually go hand in hand, but things are not always so clear cut. For instance, a class might be mutable without defining or inheriting any `vars` because it forwards method calls to other objects that have mutable state. The reverse is also possible: A class might contain `vars` and still be purely functional. An example would be a class that caches the result of an expensive operation in a field for optimization purposes. To pick an example, assume the following unoptimized class `Keyed` with an expensive operation `computeKey`:

```
class Keyed:
  def computeKey: Int = ... // this will take some time
  ...
```

Provided that `computeKey` neither reads nor writes any `vars`, you can make `Keyed` more efficient by adding a cache:

```
class MemoKeyed extends Keyed:
  private var keyCache: Option[Int] = None
  override def computeKey: Int =
    if !keyCache.isDefined then
      keyCache = Some(super.computeKey)
    keyCache.get
```

Using `MemoKeyed` instead of `Keyed` can speed things up because the second time the result of the `computeKey` operation is requested, the value stored in the `keyCache` field can be returned instead of running `computeKey` once again. But except for this speed gain, the behavior of class `Keyed` and `MemoKeyed` is exactly the same. Consequently, if `Keyed` is purely functional, then so is `MemoKeyed`, even though it contains a reassignable variable.

16.2 Reassignable variables and properties

You can perform two fundamental operations on a reassignable variable: get its value or set it to a new value. In libraries such as JavaBeans, these operations are often encapsulated in separate getter and setter methods, which need to be defined explicitly.

In Scala, every `var` that is a non-private member of some object implicitly defines a getter and a setter method with it. These getters and setters are named differently from the Java convention, however. The getter of a var x is just named "x", while its setter is named "x_=".

For example, if it appears in a class, the var definition:

```
var hour = 12
```

generates a getter, "hour", and setter, "hour_=", in addition to a reassignable field. The field is always marked "object private," an internal designation that means it can be accessed only from the object that contains it. The getter and setter, on the other hand, get the same visibility as the original var. If the var definition is public, so are its getter and setter. If it is protected, they are also protected, and so on.

For instance, consider the class Time shown in Listing 16.2, which defines two public vars named hour and minute:

```
class Time:
  var hour = 12
  var minute = 0
```

Listing 16.2 · A class with public vars.

This implementation is equivalent to the class definition shown in Listing 16.3. In the definitions shown in Listing 16.3, the names of the local fields h and m are arbitrarily chosen so as not to clash with any names already in use.

```
class Time:
  private var h = 12
  private var m = 0

  def hour: Int = h
  def hour_=(x: Int) =
    h = x

  def minute: Int = m
  def minute_=(x: Int) =
    m = x
```

Listing 16.3 · How public vars are expanded into getter and setter methods.

326

An interesting aspect about this expansion of vars into getters and setters is that you can also choose to define a getter and a setter directly, instead of defining a var. By defining these access methods directly you can interpret the operations of variable access and variable assignment as you like. For instance, the variant of class Time shown in Listing 16.4 contains requirements that catch all assignments to hour and minute with illegal values.

```
class Time:
  private var h = 12
  private var m = 0

  def hour: Int = h
  def hour_=(x: Int) =
    require(0 <= x && x < 24)
    h = x

  def minute = m
  def minute_=(x: Int) =
    require(0 <= x && x < 60)
    m = x
```

Listing 16.4 · Defining getter and setter methods directly.

Some languages have a special syntactic construct for these variable-like quantities that are not plain variables in that their getter or setter can be redefined. For instance, C# has properties, which fulfill this role. In effect, Scala's convention of always interpreting a variable as a pair of setter and getter methods gives you the same capabilities as C# properties without requiring special syntax.

Properties can serve many different purposes. In the example shown in Listing 16.4, the setters enforced an invariant, thus protecting the variable from being assigned illegal values. You could also use a property to log all accesses to getters or setters of a variable. Or you could integrate variables with events, for instance by notifying some subscriber methods each time a variable is modified.

It's also possible, and sometimes useful, to define a getter and a setter without an associated field. For example, Listing 16.5 shows a Thermometer class, which encapsulates a temperature variable that can be read and updated. Temperatures can be expressed in Celsius or Fahrenheit degrees. This class allows you to get and set the temperature in either measure.

```scala
import scala.compiletime.uninitialized

class Thermometer:

  var celsius: Float = uninitialized

  def fahrenheit = celsius * 9 / 5 + 32
  def fahrenheit_=(f: Float) =
    celsius = (f - 32) * 5 / 9

  override def toString = s"${fahrenheit}F/${celsius}C"
```

Listing 16.5 · Defining a getter and setter without an associated field.

The first line in the body of this class defines a var, celsius, which will contain the temperature in degrees Celsius. The celsius variable is initially set to a default value by specifying 'uninitialized' as the "initializing value" of the variable. More precisely, an initializer "= uninitialized" of a field assigns a zero value to that field. The zero value depends on the field's type. It is 0 for numeric types, false for booleans, and null for reference types. This is the same as if the same variable was defined in Java without an initializer.

Note that you cannot simply leave off the "= uninitialized" initializer in Scala. If you had written:

```scala
var celsius: Float
```

this would declare an abstract variable, not an uninitialized one.[1]

The celsius variable definition is followed by a getter, "fahrenheit", and a setter, "fahrenheit_=", which access the same temperature, but in degrees Fahrenheit. There is no separate field that contains the current temperature value in Fahrenheit. Instead the getter and setter methods for Fahrenheit values automatically convert from and to degrees Celsius, respectively. Here's an example of interacting with a Thermometer object:

---

[1] Abstract variables will be explained in Chapter 20.

```
val t = new Thermometer
t  // 32.0F/0.0C

t.celsius = 100
t  // 212.0F/100.0C

t.fahrenheit = -40
t  // -40.0F/-40.0C
```

16.3 Case study: Discrete event simulation

The rest of this chapter shows by way of an extended example how mutable objects can be combined with first-class function values in interesting ways. You'll see the design and implementation of a simulator for digital circuits. This task is broken down into several subproblems, each of which is interesting individually.

First, you'll see a little language for digital circuits. The definition of this language will highlight a general method for embedding domain-specific languages (DSL) in a host language like Scala. Second, we'll present a simple but general framework for discrete event simulation. Its main task will be to keep track of actions that are performed in simulated time. Finally, we'll show how discrete simulation programs can be structured and built. The idea of such simulations is to model physical objects by simulated objects, and use the simulation framework to model physical time.

The example is taken from the classic textbook *Structure and Interpretation of Computer Programs* by Abelson and Sussman [Abe96]. What's different here is that the implementation language is Scala instead of Scheme, and that the various aspects of the example are structured into four software layers: one for the simulation framework, another for the basic circuit simulation package, a third for a library of user-defined circuits, and the last layer for each simulated circuit itself. Each layer is expressed as a class, and more specific layers inherit from more general ones.

The fast track
Understanding the discrete event simulation example presented in this chapter will take some time. If you feel you want to get on with learning more Scala instead, it's safe to skip ahead to the next chapter.

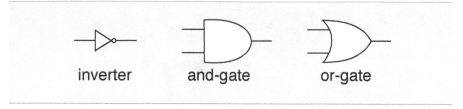

Figure 16.1 · Basic gates.

16.4 A language for digital circuits

We'll start with a "little language" to describe digital circuits. A digital circuit is built from *wires* and *function boxes*. Wires carry *signals*, which are transformed by function boxes. Signals are represented by booleans: `true` for signal-on and `false` for signal-off.

Figure 16.1 shows three basic function boxes (or *gates*):

- An *inverter*, which negates its signal.

- An *and-gate*, which sets its output to the conjunction of its inputs.

- An *or-gate*, which sets its output to the disjunction of its inputs.

These gates are sufficient to build all other function boxes. Gates have *delays*, so an output of a gate will change only some time after its inputs change.

We'll describe the elements of a digital circuit by the following set of Scala classes and functions. First, there is a class `Wire` for wires. We can construct wires like this:

```
val a = new Wire
val b = new Wire
val c = new Wire
```

or, equivalent but shorter, like this:

```
val a, b, c = new Wire
```

Second, there are three procedures which "make" the basic gates we need:

```
def inverter(input: Wire, output: Wire): Unit
def andGate(a1: Wire, a2: Wire, output: Wire): Unit
def orGate(o1: Wire, o2: Wire, output: Wire): Unit
```

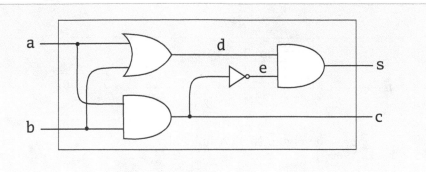

Figure 16.2 · A half-adder circuit.

What's unusual, given the functional emphasis of Scala, is that these procedures construct the gates as a side effect, instead of returning the constructed gates as a result. For instance, an invocation of inverter(a, b) places an inverter between the wires a and b. It turns out that this side-effecting construction makes it easier to construct complicated circuits gradually. Also, although methods most often have verb names, these have noun names that indicate which gate they are making. This reflects the declarative nature of the DSL: it should describe a circuit, not the actions of making one.

More complicated function boxes can be built from the basic gates. For instance, the method shown in Listing 16.6 constructs a half-adder. The halfAdder method takes two inputs, a and b, and produces a sum, s, defined by "s = (a + b) % 2" and a carry, c, defined by "c = (a + b) / 2". A diagram of the half-adder is shown in Figure 16.2.

```
def halfAdder(a: Wire, b: Wire, s: Wire, c: Wire) =
  val d, e = new Wire
  orGate(a, b, d)
  andGate(a, b, c)
  inverter(c, e)
  andGate(d, e, s)
```

Listing 16.6 · The halfAdder method.

Note that halfAdder is a parameterized function box just like the three methods that construct the primitive gates. You can use the halfAdder

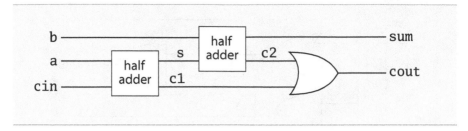

Figure 16.3 · A full-adder circuit.

method to construct more complicated circuits. For instance, Listing 16.7 defines a full, one-bit adder, shown in Figure 16.3, which takes two inputs, a and b, as well as a carry-in, cin, and which produces a sum output defined by "sum = (a + b + cin) % 2" and a carry-out output defined by "cout = (a + b + cin) / 2".

```
def fullAdder(a: Wire, b: Wire, cin: Wire,
    sum: Wire, cout: Wire) =
  val s, c1, c2 = new Wire
  halfAdder(a, cin, s, c1)
  halfAdder(b, s, sum, c2)
  orGate(c1, c2, cout)
```

Listing 16.7 · The fullAdder method.

Class Wire and functions inverter, andGate, and orGate represent a little language with which users can define digital circuits. It's a good example of an *internal* DSL, a domain-specific language defined as a library in a host language instead of being implemented on its own.

The implementation of the circuit DSL still needs to be worked out. Since the purpose of defining a circuit in the DSL is simulating the circuit, it makes sense to base the DSL implementation on a general API for discrete event simulation. The next two sections will present first the simulation API and then the implementation of the circuit DSL on top of it.

16.5   The Simulation API

The simulation API is shown in Listing 16.8. It consists of class `Simulation` in package `org.stairwaybook.simulation`. Concrete simulation libraries inherit this class and augment it with domain-specific functionality. The elements of the `Simulation` class are presented in this section.

```
abstract class Simulation:

  type Action = () => Unit

  case class WorkItem(time: Int, action: Action)

  private var curtime = 0
  def currentTime: Int = curtime

  private var agenda: List[WorkItem] = List()

  private def insert(ag: List[WorkItem],
      item: WorkItem): List[WorkItem] =

    if ag.isEmpty || item.time < ag.head.time then item :: ag
    else ag.head :: insert(ag.tail, item)

  def afterDelay(delay: Int)(block: => Unit) =

    val item = WorkItem(currentTime + delay, () => block)
    agenda = insert(agenda, item)

  private def next() =

    (agenda: @unchecked) match
      case item :: rest =>
        agenda = rest
        curtime = item.time
        item.action()

  def run() =

    afterDelay(0) {
      println("*** simulation started, time = " +
          currentTime + " ***")
    }
    while !agenda.isEmpty do next()
```

Listing 16.8 · The `Simulation` class.

A discrete event simulation performs user-defined *actions* at specified *times*. The actions, which are defined by concrete simulation subclasses, all share a common type:

```
type Action = () => Unit
```

This statement defines `Action` to be an alias of the type of procedure that takes an empty parameter list and returns `Unit`. `Action` is a *type member* of class `Simulation`. You can think of it as a more readable name for type `() => Unit`. Type members will be described in detail in Section 20.6.

The time at which an action is performed is simulated time; it has nothing to do with the actual "wall clock" time. Simulated times are represented simply as integers. The current simulated time is kept in a private variable:

```
private var curtime: Int = 0
```

The variable has a public accessor method, which retrieves the current time:

```
def currentTime: Int = curtime
```

This combination of private variable with public accessor is used to make sure that the current time cannot be modified outside the `Simulation` class. After all, you don't usually want your simulation objects to manipulate the current time, except possibly if your simulation models time travel.

An action that needs to be executed at a specified time is called a *work item*. Work items are implemented by the following class:

```
case class WorkItem(time: Int, action: Action)
```

We made the `WorkItem` class a case class because of the syntactic conveniences this entails: You can use the factory method, `WorkItem`, to create instances of the class, and you get accessors for the constructor parameters `time` and `action` for free. Note also that class `WorkItem` is nested inside class `Simulation`. Nested classes in Scala are treated similarly to Java. Section 20.7 will give more details.

The `Simulation` class keeps an *agenda* of all remaining work items that have not yet been executed. The work items are sorted by the simulated time at which they have to be run:

```
private var agenda: List[WorkItem] = List()
```

The agenda list will be kept in the proper sorted order by the insert method, which updates it. You can see insert being called from afterDelay, which is the only way to add a work item to the agenda:

```
def afterDelay(delay: Int)(block: => Unit) =
  val item = WorkItem(currentTime + delay, () => block)
  agenda = insert(agenda, item)
```

As the name implies, this method inserts an action (given by block) into the agenda so that it is scheduled for execution delay time units after the current simulation time. For instance, the following invocation would create a new work item to be executed at the simulated time, currentTime + delay:

```
afterDelay(delay) { count += 1 }
```

The code to be executed is contained in the method's second argument. The formal parameter for this argument has type "=> Unit" (*i.e.*, it is a computation of type Unit that is passed by name). Recall that by-name parameters are not evaluated when passed to a method. So in the call above, count would be incremented only when the simulation framework calls the action stored in the work item. Note that afterDelay is a curried function. It's a good example of the principle set forward in Section 9.5 that currying can be used to make method calls look more like built-in syntax.

The created work item still needs to be inserted into the agenda. This is done by the insert method, which maintains the invariant that the agenda is time-sorted:

```
private def insert(ag: List[WorkItem],
    item: WorkItem): List[WorkItem] =
  if ag.isEmpty || item.time < ag.head.time then item :: ag
  else ag.head :: insert(ag.tail, item)
```

The core of the Simulation class is defined by the run method:

```
def run() =
  afterDelay(0) {
    println("*** simulation started, time = " +
        currentTime + " ***")
  }
  while !agenda.isEmpty do next()
```

335

This method repeatedly takes the first item in the agenda, removes it from the agenda and executes it. It does this until there are no more items left in the agenda to execute. Each step is performed by calling the next method, which is defined as follows:

```
private def next() =
  (agenda: @unchecked) match
    case item :: rest =>
      agenda = rest
      curtime = item.time
      item.action()
```

The next method decomposes the current agenda with a pattern match into a front item, item, and a remaining list of work items, rest. It removes the front item from the current agenda, sets the simulated time curtime to the work item's time, and executes the work item's action.

Note that next can be called only if the agenda is non-empty. There's no case for an empty list, so you would get a MatchError exception if you tried to run next on an empty agenda.

In fact, the Scala compiler would normally warn you that you missed one of the possible patterns for a list:

```
27 |    agenda match
   |    ^^^^^^
   |    match may not be exhaustive.
   |
   |    It would fail on pattern case: Nil
```

In this case, the missing case is not a problem because you know that next is called only on a non-empty agenda. Therefore, you might want to disable the warning. You saw in Section 13.5 that this can be done by adding an @unchecked annotation to the selector expression of the pattern match. That's why the Simulation code uses "(agenda: @unchecked) match", not "agenda match".

That's it. This might look like surprisingly little code for a simulation framework. You might wonder how this framework could possibly support interesting simulations, if all it does is execute a list of work items? In fact the power of the simulation framework comes from the fact that actions stored in work items can themselves install further work items into the agenda when they are executed. That makes it possible to have long-running simulations evolve from simple beginnings.

16.6 Circuit Simulation

The next step is to use the simulation framework to implement the domain-specific language for circuits shown in Section 16.4. Recall that the circuit DSL consists of a class for wires and methods that create and-gates, or-gates, and inverters. These are all contained in a `BasicCircuitSimulation` class, which extends the simulation framework. This class is shown in Listings 16.9 and 16.10.

Class `BasicCircuitSimulation` declares three abstract methods that represent the delays of the basic gates: `InverterDelay`, `AndGateDelay`, and `OrGateDelay`. The actual delays are not known at the level of this class because they depend on the technology of circuits that are simulated. That's why the delays are left abstract in class `BasicCircuitSimulation`, so that their concrete definition is delegated to a subclass.[2] The implementation of class `BasicCircuitSimulation`'s other members is described next.

The `Wire` class

A wire needs to support three basic actions:

> `getSignal: Boolean`: returns the current signal on the wire.

> `setSignal(sig: Boolean)`: sets the wire's signal to `sig`.

> `addAction(p: Action)`: attaches the specified procedure p to the *actions* of the wire. The idea is that all action procedures attached to some wire will be executed every time the signal of the wire changes. Typically actions are added to a wire by components connected to the wire. An attached action is executed once at the time it is added to a wire, and after that, every time the signal of the wire changes.

Here is the implementation of the `Wire` class:

---

[2]The names of these "delay" methods start with a capital letter because they represent constants. They are methods so they can be overridden in subclasses. You'll find out how to do the same thing with `val`s in Section 20.3.

```
package org.stairwaybook.simulation

abstract class BasicCircuitSimulation extends Simulation:

  def InverterDelay: Int
  def AndGateDelay: Int
  def OrGateDelay: Int

  class Wire:

    private var sigVal = false
    private var actions: List[Action] = List.empty

    def getSignal = sigVal

    def setSignal(s: Boolean) =
      if s != sigVal then
        sigVal = s
        actions.foreach(_())

    def addAction(a: Action) =
      actions = a :: actions
      a()

  def inverter(input: Wire, output: Wire) =
    def invertAction() =
      val inputSig = input.getSignal
      afterDelay(InverterDelay) {
        output setSignal !inputSig
      }
    input addAction invertAction

  // continued in Listing 18.10...
```

Listing 16.9 · The first half of the BasicCircuitSimulation class.

```
// ...continued from Listing 18.9
def andGate(a1: Wire, a2: Wire, output: Wire) =
  def andAction() =
    val a1Sig = a1.getSignal
    val a2Sig = a2.getSignal
    afterDelay(AndGateDelay) {
      output setSignal (a1Sig & a2Sig)
    }
  a1 addAction andAction
  a2 addAction andAction

def orGate(o1: Wire, o2: Wire, output: Wire) =
  def orAction() =
    val o1Sig = o1.getSignal
    val o2Sig = o2.getSignal
    afterDelay(OrGateDelay) {
      output setSignal (o1Sig | o2Sig)
    }
  o1 addAction orAction
  o2 addAction orAction

def probe(name: String, wire: Wire) =
  def probeAction() =
    println(name + " " + currentTime +
        " new-value = " + wire.getSignal)
  wire addAction probeAction
```

Listing 16.10 · The second half of the BasicCircuitSimulation class.

```
class Wire:

  private var sigVal = false
  private var actions: List[Action] = List.empty

  def getSignal = sigVal

  def setSignal(s: Boolean) =
    if s != sigVal then
      sigVal = s
      actions.foreach(_())

  def addAction(a: Action) =
    actions = a :: actions
    a()
```

Two private variables make up the state of a wire. The variable `sigVal` represents the current signal, and the variable `actions` represents the action procedures currently attached to the wire. The only interesting method implementation is the one for `setSignal`: When the signal of a wire changes, the new value is stored in the variable `sigVal`. Furthermore, all actions attached to a wire are executed. Note the shorthand syntax for doing this: "`actions.foreach(_())`" applies the function, "`_()`", to each element in the `actions` list. As described in Section 8.5, the function "`_()`" is a shorthand for "`f => f()`"—*i.e.*, it takes a function (we'll call it `f`) and applies it to the empty parameter list.

The `inverter` method

The only effect of creating an inverter is that an action is installed on its input wire. This action is invoked once at the time the action is installed, and thereafter every time the signal on the input changes. The effect of the action is that the value of the inverter's output value is set (via `setSignal`) to the inverse of its input value. Since inverter gates have delays, this change should take effect only `InverterDelay` units of simulated time after the input value has changed and the action was executed. This suggests the following implementation:

```
def inverter(input: Wire, output: Wire) =
  def invertAction() =
    val inputSig = input.getSignal
    afterDelay(InverterDelay) {
      output setSignal !inputSig
    }

  input addAction invertAction
```

The effect of the `inverter` method is to add `invertAction` to the `input` wire. This action, when invoked, gets the input signal and installs another action that inverts the `output` signal into the simulation agenda. This other action is to be executed after `InverterDelay` units of simulated time. Note how the method uses the `afterDelay` method of the simulation framework to create a new work item that's going to be executed in the future.

The andGate and orGate methods

The implementation of and-gates is analogous to the implementation of inverters. The purpose of an and-gate is to output the conjunction of its input signals. This should happen at `AndGateDelay` simulated time units after any one of its two inputs changes. Hence, the following implementation:

```
def andGate(a1: Wire, a2: Wire, output: Wire) =
  def andAction() =
    val a1Sig = a1.getSignal
    val a2Sig = a2.getSignal
    afterDelay(AndGateDelay) {
      output setSignal (a1Sig & a2Sig)
    }

  a1 addAction andAction
  a2 addAction andAction
```

The effect of the `andGate` method is to add `andAction` to both of its input wires `a1` and `a2`. This action, when invoked, gets both input signals and installs another action that sets the `output` signal to the conjunction of both input signals. This other action is to be executed after `AndGateDelay` units of simulated time. Note that the output has to be recomputed if either of the input wires changes. That's why the same `andAction` is installed on each of

341

the two input wires a1 and a2. The orGate method is implemented similarly, except it performs a logical-or instead of a logical-and.

Simulation output

To run the simulator, you need a way to inspect changes of signals on wires. To accomplish this, you can simulate the action of putting a probe on a wire:

```
def probe(name: String, wire: Wire) =
  def probeAction() =
    println(name + " " + currentTime +
        " new-value = " + wire.getSignal)

  wire addAction probeAction
```

The effect of the probe procedure is to install a probeAction on a given wire. As usual, the installed action is executed every time the wire's signal changes. In this case it simply prints the name of the wire (which is passed as first parameter to probe), as well as the current simulated time and the wire's new value.

Running the simulator

After all these preparations, it's time to see the simulator in action. To define a concrete simulation, you need to inherit from a simulation framework class. To see something interesting, we'll create an abstract simulation class that extends BasicCircuitSimulation and contains method definitions for half-adders and full-adders as they were presented earlier in this chapter in Listings 16.6 and 16.7, respectively. This class, which we'll call CircuitSimulation, is shown in Listing 16.11.

A concrete circuit simulation will be an object that inherits from class CircuitSimulation. The object still needs to fix the gate delays according to the circuit implementation technology that's simulated. Finally, you will also need to define the concrete circuit that's going to be simulated.

You can do these steps interactively in the Scala interpreter:

```
scala> import org.stairwaybook.simulation.*
```

First, the gate delays. Define an object (call it MySimulation) that provides some numbers:

342

```
package org.stairwaybook.simulation

abstract class CircuitSimulation
  extends BasicCircuitSimulation:

  def halfAdder(a: Wire, b: Wire, s: Wire, c: Wire) =
    val d, e = new Wire
    orGate(a, b, d)
    andGate(a, b, c)
    inverter(c, e)
    andGate(d, e, s)

  def fullAdder(a: Wire, b: Wire, cin: Wire,
      sum: Wire, cout: Wire) =

    val s, c1, c2 = new Wire
    halfAdder(a, cin, s, c1)
    halfAdder(b, s, sum, c2)
    orGate(c1, c2, cout)
```

Listing 16.11 · The CircuitSimulation class.

```
scala> object MySimulation extends CircuitSimulation:
         def InverterDelay = 1
         def AndGateDelay = 3
         def OrGateDelay = 5
// defined object MySimulation
```

Because you are going to access the members of the MySimulation object repeatedly, an import of the object keeps the subsequent code shorter:

```
scala> import MySimulation.*
```

Next, the circuit. Define four wires, and place probes on two of them:

```
scala> val input1, input2, sum, carry = new Wire
val input1: MySimulation.Wire = ...
val input2: MySimulation.Wire = ...
val sum: MySimulation.Wire = ...
val carry: MySimulation.Wire = ...
```

343

```
scala> probe("sum", sum)
sum 0 new-value = false

scala> probe("carry", carry)
carry 0 new-value = false
```

Note that the probes immediately print an output. This is because every action installed on a wire is executed a first time when the action is installed.

Now define a half-adder connecting the wires:

```
scala> halfAdder(input1, input2, sum, carry)
```

Finally, set the signals, one after another, on the two input wires to true and run the simulation:

```
scala> input1 setSignal true

scala> run()
*** simulation started, time = 0 ***
sum 8 new-value = true

scala> input2 setSignal true

scala> run()
*** simulation started, time = 8 ***
carry 11 new-value = true
sum 15 new-value = false
```

16.7 Conclusion

This chapter brought together two techniques that seem disparate at first: mutable state and higher-order functions. Mutable state was used to simulate physical entities whose state changes over time. Higher-order functions were used in the simulation framework to execute actions at specified points in simulated time. They were also used in the circuit simulations as *triggers* that associate actions with state changes. Along the way, you saw a simple way to define a domain-specific language as a library. That's probably enough for one chapter!

If you feel like staying a bit longer, you might want to try more simulation examples. You can combine half-adders and full-adders to create larger circuits, or design new circuits from the basic gates defined so far and simulate them. In the next chapter, you'll learn about type parameterization in Scala, and see another example in which a combination of functional and imperative approaches yields a good solution.

Chapter 17

Scala's Hierarchy

This chapter will look at Scala's class hierarchy as a whole. In Scala, every class inherits from a common superclass named Any. Because every class is a subclass of Any, the methods defined in Any are "universal" methods: they may be invoked on any object. Scala also defines some interesting classes at the bottom of the hierarchy, Null and Nothing, which essentially act as common *sub*classes. For example, just as Any is a superclass of every other class, Nothing is a subclass of every other class. In this chapter, we'll give you a tour of Scala's class hierarchy.

17.1 Scala's class hierarchy

Figure 17.1 shows an outline of Scala's class hierarchy. At the top of the hierarchy is class Any, which defines methods that include the following:

```
final def ==(that: Any): Boolean
final def !=(that: Any): Boolean
def equals(that: Any): Boolean
def ##: Int
def hashCode: Int
def toString: String
```

Because every class inherits from Any, every object in a Scala program can be compared using ==, !=, or equals; hashed using ## or hashCode; and formatted using toString. The equality and inequality methods, == and !=, are declared final in class Any, so they cannot be overridden in subclasses.

The == method is essentially the same as equals and != is always the negation of equals.[1] So individual classes can tailor what == or != means by overriding the equals method.

> ## Multiversal equality
>
> Scala 3 introduced "multiversal equality," which can give you a compiler error for uses of == and = that represent likely bugs, such as comparing a String and an Int for equality. This mechanism will be described in Chapter 23.

The root class Any has two subclasses: AnyVal and AnyRef. AnyVal is the parent class of *value classes* in Scala. While you can define your own value classes (see Section 17.4), there are nine value classes built into Scala: Byte, Short, Char, Int, Long, Float, Double, Boolean, and Unit. The first eight of these correspond to Java's primitive types, and their values are represented at run time as Java's primitive values. The instances of these classes are all written as literals in Scala. For example, 42 is an instance of Int, 'x' is an instance of Char, and false an instance of Boolean. You cannot create instances of these classes using new. This is enforced by the "trick" that value classes are all defined to be both abstract and final.

So if you were to write:

```
scala> new Int
```

you would get:

```
1 |new Int
  |    ^^^
  |    Int is abstract; it cannot be instantiated
```

---

[1]The only case where == does not directly call equals is for Java's boxed numeric classes, such as Integer or Long. In Java, a new Integer(1) does not equal a new Long(1) even though for primitive values 1 == 1L. Since Scala is a more regular language than Java, it was necessary to correct this discrepancy by special-casing the == method for these classes. Likewise, the ## method provides a Scala version of hashing that is the same as Java's hashCode, except for boxed numeric types, where it works consistently with ==. For instance new Integer(1) and new Long(1) hash the same with ## even though their Java hashCodes are different.

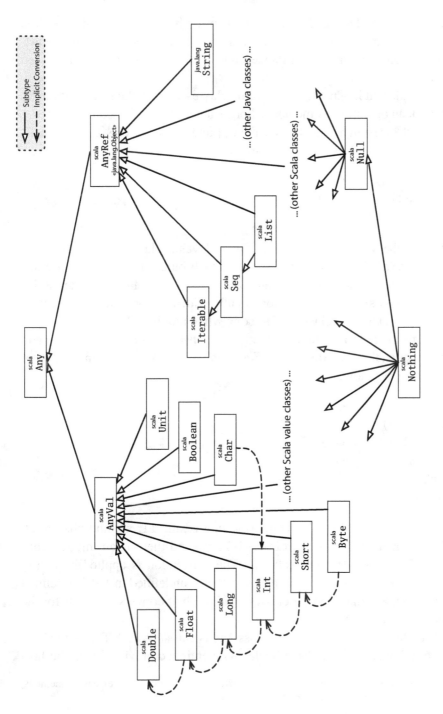

Figure 17.1 · Class hierarchy of Scala.

349

The other value class, Unit, corresponds roughly to Java's void type; it is used as the result type of a method that does not otherwise return an interesting result. Unit has a single instance value, which is written (), as discussed in Section 7.2.

As explained in Chapter 5, the value classes support the usual arithmetic and boolean operators as methods. For instance, Int has methods named + and *, and Boolean has methods named || and &&. Value classes also inherit all methods from class Any. For example:

```
42.toString    // 42
42.hashCode    // 42
42.equals(42)  // true
```

Note that the value class space is flat; all value classes are subtypes of scala.AnyVal, but they do not subclass each other. Instead there are implicit conversions between different value class types. For example, an instance of class scala.Int is automatically widened (by an implicit conversion) to an instance of class scala.Long when required.

As mentioned in Section 5.10, implicit conversions are also used to add more functionality to value types. For instance, the type Int supports all of the operations below:

```
42.max(43)  // 43
42.min(43)  // 42
1 until 5   // Range 1 until 5
1 to 5      // Range 1 to 5
3.abs       // 3
-3.abs      // 3
```

Here's how this works: The methods min, max, until, to, and abs are all defined in a class scala.runtime.RichInt, and there is an implicit conversion from class Int to RichInt. The conversion is applied implicitly whenever a method is invoked on an Int that is undefined in Int but defined in RichInt. Similar "booster classes" and implicit conversions exist for the other value classes.[2]

The other subclass of the root class Any is class AnyRef. This is the base class of all *reference classes* in Scala. As mentioned previously, on the Java

---

[2]This use case of implicit conversions will over time be replaced by extension methods, which will be described in Chapter 22.

platform AnyRef is in fact just an alias for class java.lang.Object. So classes written in Java, as well as classes written in Scala, all inherit from AnyRef.[3] One way to think of java.lang.Object, therefore, is as the way AnyRef is implemented on the Java platform. Thus, although you can use Object and AnyRef interchangeably in Scala programs on the Java platform, the recommended style is to use AnyRef everywhere.

17.2 How primitives are implemented

How is all this implemented? In fact, Scala stores integers in the same way as Java—as 32-bit words. This is important for efficiency on the JVM and also for interoperability with Java libraries. Standard operations like addition or multiplication are implemented as primitive operations. However, Scala uses the "backup" class java.lang.Integer whenever an integer needs to be seen as a (Java) object. This happens for instance when invoking the toString method on an integer number or when assigning an integer to a variable of type Any. Integers of type Int are converted transparently to "boxed integers" of type java.lang.Integer whenever necessary.

All this sounds a lot like auto-boxing in Java and it is indeed quite similar. There's one crucial difference though: Boxing in Scala is much less visible than boxing in Java. Try the following in Java:

```
// This is Java
boolean isEqual(int x, int y) {
  return x == y;
}
System.out.println(isEqual(421, 421));
```

You will surely get true. Now, change the argument types of isEqual to java.lang.Integer (or Object, the result will be the same):

```
// This is Java
boolean isEqual(Integer x, Integer y) {
  return x == y;
}
System.out.println(isEqual(421, 421));
```

---

[3]One reason the AnyRef alias exists, instead of just using the name java.lang.Object, is because Scala was originally designed to work on both the Java and .NET platforms. On .NET, AnyRef was an alias for System.Object.

You will find that you get `false`! What happens is that the number 421 gets boxed twice, so that the arguments for x and y are two different objects. Because == means reference equality on reference types, and `Integer` is a reference type, the result is `false`. This is one aspect where it shows that Java is not a pure object-oriented language. There is a difference between primitive types and reference types that can be clearly observed.

Now try the same experiment in Scala:

```
def isEqual(x: Int, y: Int) = x == y
isEqual(421, 421)  // true
def isEqual(x: Any, y: Any) = x == y
isEqual(421, 421)  // true
```

The equality operation == in Scala is designed to be transparent with respect to the type's representation. For value types, it is the natural (numeric or boolean) equality. For reference types other than Java's boxed numeric types, == is treated as an alias of the `equals` method inherited from `Object`. That method is originally defined as reference equality, but is overridden by many subclasses to implement their natural notion of equality. This also means that in Scala you never fall into Java's well-known trap concerning string comparisons. In Scala, string comparison works as it should:

```
val x = "abcd".substring(2)  // cd
val y = "abcd".substring(2)  // cd
x == y  // true
```

In Java, the result of comparing x with y would be false. The programmer should have used `equals` in this case, but it is easy to forget.

However, there are situations where you need reference equality instead of user-defined equality. For example, in some situations where efficiency is paramount, you would like to *hash cons* with some classes and compare their instances with reference equality.[4] For these cases, class `AnyRef` defines an additional `eq` method, which cannot be overridden and is implemented as reference equality (*i.e.*, it behaves like == in Java for reference types). There's also the negation of `eq`, which is called `ne`. For example:

---

[4]You hash cons instances of a class by caching all instances you have created in a weak collection. Then, any time you want a new instance of the class, you first check the cache. If the cache already has an element equal to the one you are about to create, you can reuse the existing instance. As a result of this arrangement, any two instances that are equal with `equals()` are also equal with reference equality.

```
val x = new String("abc")   // abc
val y = new String("abc")   // abc
x == y  // true
x eq y  // false
x ne y  // true
```

Equality in Scala is discussed further in Chapter 8.

17.3   Bottom types

At the bottom of the type hierarchy in Figure 17.1 you see the two classes `scala.Null` and `scala.Nothing`. These are special types that handle some "corner cases" of Scala's type system in a uniform way.

Class `Null` is the type of the `null` reference; it is a subclass of every reference class (*i.e.*, every class that itself inherits from AnyRef).[5] Null is not compatible with value types. You cannot, for example, assign a `null` value to an integer variable:

```
scala> val i: Int = null
1 |val i: Int = null
  |              ^^^^
  |            Found:    Null
  |            Required: Int
```

Type `Nothing` is at the very bottom of Scala's class hierarchy; it is a subtype of every other type. However, there exist no values of this type whatsoever. Why does it make sense to have a type without values? As discussed in Section 7.4, one use of `Nothing` is that it signals abnormal termination.

For instance there's the `error` method in the `sys` object of Scala's standard library, which is defined like this:

```
def error(message: String): Nothing =
  throw new RuntimeException(message)
```

The return type of `error` is `Nothing`, which tells users that the method will not return normally (it throws an exception instead). Because `Nothing` is a

---

[5]Scala 3 includes an option, `-Yexplicit-nulls`, which enables an experimental alternate treatment of `null` that aims to track which variables can and cannot be `null`. This option be described in *Advanced Programming in Scala*.

subtype of every other type, you can use methods like `error` in very flexible ways. For instance:

```scala
def divide(x: Int, y: Int): Int =
  if y != 0 then x / y
  else sys.error("can't divide by zero")
```

The "then" branch of the conditional, x / y, has type Int, whereas the else branch, the call to error, has type Nothing. Because Nothing is a subtype of Int, the type of the whole conditional is Int, as required.

17.4 Defining your own value classes

As mentioned in Section 17.1, you can define your own value classes to augment the ones that are built in. Like the built-in value classes, an instance of your value class will usually compile to Java bytecode that does not use the wrapper class. In contexts where a wrapper is needed, such as with generic code, the value will get boxed and unboxed automatically.[6]

Only certain classes can be made into value classes. For a class to be a value class, it must have exactly one parameter and it must have nothing inside it except defs. Furthermore, no other class can extend a value class, and a value class cannot redefine equals or hashCode.

To define a value class, make it a subclass of AnyVal, and put val before the one parameter. Here is an example value class:

```scala
class Dollars(val amount: Int) extends AnyVal:
  override def toString = "$" + amount
```

As described in Section 10.6, the val prefix allows the amount parameter to be accessed as a field. For example, the following code creates an instance of the value class, then retrieves the amount from it:

```scala
val money = new Dollars(1_000_000)
money.amount  // 1000000
```

In this example, money refers to an instance of the value class. It is of type Dollars in Scala source code, but the compiled Java bytecode will use type Int directly.

---

[6]Scala 3 also offers *opaque types*, which is more restrictive but guarantees the value will never be boxed. Opaque types will be described in *Advanced Programming in Scala*.

This example defines a `toString` method, and the compiler figures out when to use it. That's why printing money gives $1000000, with a dollar sign, but printing money.amount gives 1000000. You can even define multiple value types that are all backed by the same Int value. For example:

```
class SwissFrancs(val amount: Int) extends AnyVal:
  override def toString = s"$amount CHF"
```

Even though both `Dollars` and `SwissFrancs` are represented as integers at run time, they are distinct types at compile time:

```
scala> val dollars: Dollars = new SwissFrancs(1000)
1 |val dollars: Dollars = new SwissFrancs(1000)
  |                       ^^^^^^^^^^^^^^^^^^^^^^
  |
  |                       Found:    SwissFrancs
  |                       Required: Dollars
  |
```

Avoiding a types monoculture

To get the most benefit from the Scala class hierarchy, try to define a new class for each domain concept, even when it would be possible to reuse the same class for different purposes. Even if such a class is a so-called *tiny type* with no methods or fields, defining the additional class is a way to help the compiler be helpful to you.

For example, suppose you are writing some code to generate HTML. In HTML, a style name is represented as a string. So are anchor identifiers. HTML itself is also a string, so if you wanted, you could define helper code using strings to represent all of these things, like this:

```
def title(text: String, anchor: String, style: String): String =
  s"<a id='$anchor'><h1 class='$style'>$text</h1></a>"
```

That signature has four strings in it! Such *stringly typed* code is technically strongly typed, but since everything in sight is of type `String`, the compiler cannot help you detect the use of one when you meant to write the other. For example, it won't stop you from this travesty:

```
scala> title("chap:vcls", "bold", "Value Classes")
val res17: String = <a id='bold'><h1 class='Value
    Classes'>chap:vcls</h1></a>
```

355

This HTML is mangled. The intended display text "Value Classes" is being used as a style class, and the text being displayed is "chap.vcls," which was supposed to be an anchor. To top it off, the actual anchor identifier is "bold," which is supposed to be a style class. Despite this comedy of errors, the compiler utters not a peep.

The compiler can be more helpful if you define a tiny type for each domain concept. For example, you could define a small class for styles, anchor identifiers, display text, and HTML. Since these classes have one parameter and no members, they can be defined as value classes:

```scala
class Anchor(val value: String) extends AnyVal
class Style(val value: String) extends AnyVal
class Text(val value: String) extends AnyVal
class Html(val value: String) extends AnyVal
```

Given these classes, it is possible to write a version of `title` that has a less trivial type signature:

```scala
def title(text: Text, anchor: Anchor, style: Style): Html =
  Html(
    s"<a id='${anchor.value}'>" +
      s"<h1 class='${style.value}'>" +
      text.value +
      "</h1></a>"
  )
```

If you try to use this version with the arguments in the wrong order, the compiler can now detect the error. For example:

```scala
scala> title(Anchor("chap:vcls"), Style("bold"),
          Text("Value Classes"))
1 |title(new Anchor("chap:vcls"), new Style("bold"),
  |      ^^^^^^^^^^^^^^^^^^^^^^^^^
  |      Found:     Anchor
  |      Required: Text
1 |title(Anchor("chap:vcls"), Style("bold"),
  |                           ^^^^^^^^^^^^^^
  |                               Found:     Style
  |                               Required: Anchor
```

```
2 |         Text("Value Classes"))
  |         ^^^^^^^^^^^^^^^^^^^^^^^
  |
  |         Found:    Text
  |         Required: Style
```

17.5 Intersection types

You can join two or more types with ampersand (&) characters to form an *intersection type*, such as Incrementing & Filtering.[7] Here's an example using the classes and traits shown in Listings 11.5, 11.6, and 11.9:

```
scala> val q = new BasicIntQueue with
         Incrementing with Filtering
val q: BasicIntQueue & Incrementing & Filtering = anon$...
```

Here, q is initialized with an instance of an anonymous class that extends BasicIntQueue and mixes in Incrementing followed by Filtering. Its inferred type, BasicIntQueue & Incrementing & Filtering, is an intersection type that indicates the object to which q refers is an instance of all three mentioned types: BasicIntQueue, Incrementing, and Filtering.

An intersection type is a subtype of all combinations of its constituent types. For example, type B & I & F is a subtype of B, I, F, B & I, B & F, I & F, and reflexively, of B & I & F itself. What's more, because intersection types are commutative, the order of appearance of types in an intersection type does not matter: type I & F, for example, is equivalent to type F & I. Therefore, B & I & F is also a subtype of I & B, F & B, F & I, B & F & I, F & B & I, and so on. Here's an example that illustrates these relationships between intersection types:

```
// Compiles because B & I & F <: I & F
val q2: Incrementing & Filtering = q

// Compiles because I & F is equivalent to F & I
val q3: Filtering & Incrementing = q2
```

---

[7] You can pronounce Incrementing & Filtering as "Incrementing *and* Filtering."

17.6   Union types

Scala offers a dual to intersection types called *union types*, which consist of two or more types joined by pipe (|) characters, such as Plum | Apricot.[8] A union type indicates that an object is an instance of at least one mentioned type. For example, an object of type Plum | Apricot is either an instance of Plum, an instance of Apricot, or both.[9]

Like intersection types, union types are commutative: Plum | Apricot is equivalent to Apricot | Plum. Dually to intersection types, a union type is a *supertype* of all combinations of its constituent types. For example, Plum | Apricot is a supertype of both Plum and Apricot. Importantly, Plum | Apricot is not just *a* supertype of both Plum and Apricot, but their nearest common supertype, or *least upper bound*.

The addition of union and intersection types to Scala 3 ensures that Scala's type system forms a mathematical *lattice*. A lattice is a partial order in which any two types have both a unique least upper bound, or *LUB*, and a unique *greatest lower bound*. In Scala 3, the least upper bound of any two types is their union; the greatest lower bound is their intersection. For example, the least upper bound of Plum and Apricot is Plum | Apricot. Their greatest lower bound is Plum & Apricot.

Union types have important implications for the specification and implementation of type inference and type checking in Scala. Whereas in Scala 2, the type inference algorithm had to settle on an approximation of the least upper bound of some pairs of types, whose actual least upper bound was the limit of an infinite series, Scala 3 can simply form a union of those types.

To visualize this, consider the following hierarchy:

```
trait Fruit
trait Plum extends Fruit
trait Apricot extends Fruit
trait Pluot extends Plum, Apricot
```

These four types yield the hierarchy shown in Figure 17.2. Fruit is a supertype to both Plum and Apricot, but it is not the *nearest* common supertype. Rather, the union type Plum | Apricot is the nearest common

---

[8] You can pronounce Plum | Apricot as "Plum *or* Apricot."

[9] Several hybrid fruits resulting from crossing plums with apricots exist. Some examples are apriplums, apriums, plumcots, and pluots.

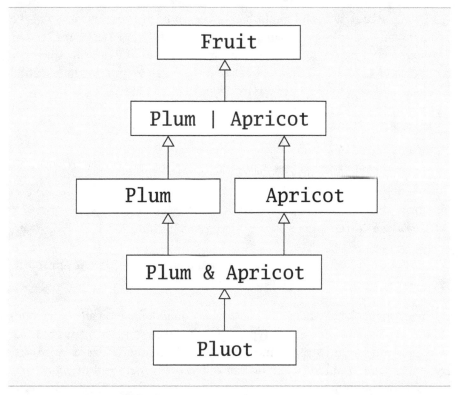

Figure 17.2 · Least upper and greatest lower bounds.

supertype, or least upper bound, of `Plum` and `Apricot`. As shown in Figure 17.2, this implies that the `Plum | Apricot` union type is a *subtype* of `Fruit`. And this is indeed the case, as illustrated here:

```
val plumOrApricot: Plum | Apricot = new Plum {}

// This compiles fine, because Plum | Apricot <: Fruit
val fruit: Fruit = plumOrApricot

// But you cannot use a Fruit where Plum | Apricot is needed
scala> val doesNotCompile: Plum | Apricot = fruit
1 |val doesNotCompile: Plum | Apricot = fruit
  |                                     ^^^^^
  |                              Found:    (fruit : Fruit)
  |                              Required: Plum | Apricot
```

359

Dually `Pluot` is a subtype to both `Plum` and `Apricot`, but it is not the *nearest* common subtype. Rather, the intersection type `Plum & Apricot` is the nearest common subtype, or greatest lower bound, of `Plum` and `Apricot`. As shown in Figure 17.2, this implies that the `Plum & Apricot` intersection type is a *supertype* of `Pluot`. And this is indeed the case:

```scala
val pluot: Pluot = new Pluot {}

// This compiles fine, because Pluot <: Plum & Apricot
val plumAndApricot: Plum & Apricot = pluot

// But you cannot use a Plum & Apricot where Pluot is needed
scala> val doesNotCompile: Pluot = plumAndApricot
1 |val doesNotCompile: Pluot = plumAndApricot
  |                            ^^^^^^^^^^^^^^
  |                 Found:    (plumAndApricot : Plum & Apricot)
  |                 Required: Pluot
```

You can invoke any method or access any field defined on any of the constituent types of an intersection type. On an instance of `Plum & Apricot`, for example, you can invoke any methods defined in either `Plum` or `Apricot`. By contrast, on a union type, you can only access members of *supertypes* that are common to the constituent types. On an instance of `Plum | Apricot`, therefore, you can access the members of `Fruit` (including members it inherits from `AnyRef` and `Any`), but you cannot access any members added in either `Plum` or `Apricot`. To access such members, you must perform a pattern match to determine the actual class of the value at runtime. Here's an example of such a pattern match:

```scala
def errorMessage(msg: Int | String): String =
  msg match
    case n: Int => s"Error number: ${n.abs}"
    case s: String => s + "!"
```

The `errorMessage` method's `msg` parameter has type `Int | String`. You could, therefore, directly invoke on `msg` only methods declared on `Any`, the sole common supertype of `Int` and `String`. You could not directly invoke any other methods defined on either `Int` or `String`. To access, for example, the `abs` method of `Int`, or the string concatenation operator (+) of `String`, you must perform a pattern match on `msg`, as shown in the errorMessage method body. Here are some examples of using the errorMessage method:

```
errorMessage("Oops")  // "Oops!"
errorMessage(-42)      // "Error number: 42"
```

17.7 Transparent traits

Traits have two main uses: They allow you to define classes through mixin composition, and they define types. Sometimes you may intend a trait to be used primarily as a mixin, and not as a type. For instance, you could decide that although traits Incrementing and Filtering from Section 11.3 are useful as mixins, they have limited value as types. By default, the types defined by these traits can be inferred. For example, the Scala compiler will infer the type of q in the following statement to be an intersection type that mentions both Incrementing and Filtering:

```
scala> val q = new BasicIntQueue with
            Incrementing with Filtering
val q: BasicIntQueue & Incrementing & Filtering = anon$...
```

You can indicate that you don't want the name of a trait to appear in inferred types by declaring it with the transparent modifier. For example, you could declare Incrementing and Filtering as transparent like this:

```
transparent trait Incrementing extends IntQueue:
  abstract override def put(x: Int) = super.put(x + 1)

transparent trait Filtering extends IntQueue:
  abstract override def put(x: Int) =
    if x >= 0 then super.put(x)
```

Now that traits Incrementing and Filtering are defined as transparent, their names will no longer appear in inferred types. For example, the type inferred from the same instance creation expression shown previously will no longer mention Incrementing or Filtering:

```
scala> val q = new BasicIntQueue with
            Incrementing with Filtering
val q: BasicIntQueue = anon$...
```

361

The `transparent` modifier only affects type *inference*. You can still use transparent traits as types if you write them out explicitly. Here's an example in which transparent traits `Incrementing` and `Filtering` appear in an explicit type annotation for variable q:

```
scala> val q: BasicIntQueue & Incrementing & Filtering =
           new BasicIntQueue with Incrementing with Filtering

val q: BasicIntQueue & Incrementing & Filtering = anon$...
```

In addition to traits marked explicitly as transparent, Scala 3 will treat `scala.Product`, `java.lang.Serializable`, and `java.lang.Comparable` as transparent as well. Because these types will never be inferred in Scala 3, if you really want to use them as types, you will need to do so through explicit type annotations or ascriptions.

17.8   Conclusion

In this chapter we showed you the classes at the top and bottom of Scala's class hierarchy. You also saw how to create your own value classes, including how to use them for "tiny types." You learned about intersection and union types, and saw how they turn Scala's type hierarchy into a lattice. Lastly, you learned how to use the `transparent` modifier to prevent Scala's type inference algorithm from using traits designed primarily as mixins as types. In the next chapter, you'll learn about type parameterization.

Chapter 18

Type Parameterization

In this chapter, we'll explain the details of type parameterization in Scala. Along the way we'll demonstrate some of the techniques for information hiding introduced in Chapter 12 by using a concrete example: the design of a class for purely functional queues.

Type parameterization allows you to write generic classes and traits. For example, sets are generic and take a type parameter: they are defined as Set[T]. As a result, any particular set instance might be a Set[String], a Set[Int], *etc.*, but it must be a set of *something*. Unlike Java, which allows raw types, Scala requires that you specify type parameters. Variance defines inheritance relationships of parameterized types, such as whether a Set[String], for example, is a subtype of Set[AnyRef].

The chapter contains three parts. The first part develops a data structure for purely functional queues. The second part develops techniques to hide internal representation details of this structure. The final part explains variance of type parameters and how it interacts with information hiding.

18.1   Functional queues

A functional queue is a data structure with three operations:

head	returns the first element of the queue
tail	returns a queue without its first element
enqueue	returns a new queue with a given element appended at the end

Unlike a mutable queue, a functional queue does not change its contents when an element is appended. Instead, a new queue is returned that contains the element. The goal of this chapter will be to create a class, which we'll name Queue, that works like this:

```
val q = Queue(1, 2, 3)  // Queue(1, 2, 3)
val q1 = q.enqueue(4)   // Queue(1, 2, 3, 4)
q                       // Queue(1, 2, 3)
```

If Queue were a mutable implementation, the enqueue operation in the second input line above would affect the contents of q; in fact both the result, q1, and the original queue, q, would contain the sequence 1, 2, 3, 4 after the operation. But for a functional queue, the appended value shows up only in the result, q1, not in the queue, q, being operated on.

Purely functional queues also have some similarity with lists. Both are so called *fully persistent* data structures, where old versions remain available even after extensions or modifications. Both support head and tail operations. But where a list is usually extended at the front, using a : : operation, a queue is extended at the end, using enqueue.

How can this be implemented efficiently? Ideally, a functional (immutable) queue should not have a fundamentally higher overhead than an imperative (mutable) one. That is, all three operations, head, tail, and enqueue, should operate in constant time.

One simple approach to implement a functional queue would be to use a list as representation type. Then head and tail would just translate into the same operations on the list, whereas enqueue would be concatenation.

This would give the following implementation:

```
class SlowAppendQueue[T](elems: List[T]): // Not efficient
  def head = elems.head
  def tail = new SlowAppendQueue(elems.tail)
  def enqueue(x: T) = SlowAppendQueue(elems ::: List(x))
```

The problem with this implementation is in the enqueue operation. It takes time proportional to the number of elements stored in the queue. If you want constant time append, you could also try to reverse the order of the elements in the representation list, so that the last element that's appended comes first in the list. This would lead to the following implementation:

```
class SlowHeadQueue[T](smele: List[T]): // Not efficient
  // smele is elems reversed
  def head = smele.last
  def tail = new SlowHeadQueue(smele.init)
  def enqueue(x: T) = SlowHeadQueue(x :: smele)
```

Now enqueue is constant time, but head and tail are not. They now take time proportional to the number of elements stored in the queue.

Looking at these two examples, it does not seem easy to come up with an implementation that's constant time for all three operations. In fact, it looks doubtful that this is even possible! However, by combining the two operations you can get very close. The idea is to represent a queue by two lists, called leading and trailing. The leading list contains elements towards the front, whereas the trailing list contains elements towards the back of the queue in reversed order. The contents of the whole queue are at each instant equal to "leading ::: trailing.reverse".

Now, to append an element, you just cons it to the trailing list using the :: operator, so enqueue is constant time. This means that, when an initially empty queue is constructed from successive enqueue operations, the trailing list will grow whereas the leading list will stay empty. Then, before the first head or tail operation is performed on an empty leading list, the whole trailing list is copied to leading, reversing the order of the elements. This is done in an operation called mirror. Listing 18.1 shows an implementation of queues that uses this approach.

What is the complexity of this implementation of queues? The mirror operation might take time proportional to the number of queue elements, but only if list leading is empty. It returns directly if leading is non-empty. Because head and tail call mirror, their complexity might be linear in the size of the queue, too. However, the longer the queue gets, the less often mirror is called.

Indeed, assume a queue of length n with an empty leading list. Then mirror has to reverse-copy a list of length n. However, the next time mirror will have to do any work is once the leading list is empty again, which will be the case after n tail operations. This means you can "charge" each of these n tail operations with one n'th of the complexity of mirror, which means a constant amount of work. Assuming that head, tail, and enqueue operations appear with about the same frequency, the *amortized* complexity

```
class Queue[T](
  private val leading: List[T],
  private val trailing: List[T]
):
  private def mirror =
    if leading.isEmpty then
      new Queue(trailing.reverse, Nil)
    else
      this

  def head = mirror.leading.head

  def tail =
    val q = mirror
    new Queue(q.leading.tail, q.trailing)

  def enqueue(x: T) =
    new Queue(leading, x :: trailing)
```

Listing 18.1 · A basic functional queue.

is hence constant for each operation. So functional queues are asymptotically just as efficient as mutable ones.

Now, there are some caveats that need to be attached to this argument. First, the discussion was only about asymptotic behavior; the constant factors might well be somewhat different. Second, the argument rested on the fact that head, tail and enqueue are called with about the same frequency. If head is called much more often than the other two operations, the argument is not valid, as each call to head might involve a costly re-organization of the list with mirror. The second caveat can be avoided; it is possible to design functional queues so that in a sequence of successive head operations only the first one might require a re-organization. You will find out at the end of this chapter how this is done.

18.2 Information hiding

The implementation of Queue shown in Listing 18.1 is now quite good with regards to efficiency. You might object, though, that this efficiency is paid for by exposing a needlessly detailed implementation. The Queue constructor, which is globally accessible, takes two lists as parameters, where one is reversed—hardly an intuitive representation of a queue. What's needed is a way to hide this constructor from client code. In this section, we'll show you some ways to accomplish this in Scala.

Private constructors and factory methods

In Java, you can hide a constructor by making it `private`. In Scala, the primary constructor does not have an explicit definition; it is defined implicitly by the class parameters and body. Nevertheless, it is still possible to hide the primary constructor by adding a `private` modifier in front of the class parameter list, as shown in Listing 18.2:

```
class Queue[T] private (
    private val leading: List[T],
    private val trailing: List[T]
):
```

Listing 18.2 · Hiding a primary constructor by making it private.

The `private` modifier between the class name and its parameters indicates that the constructor of Queue is private: it can be accessed only from within the class itself and its companion object. The class name Queue is still public, so you can use it as a type, but you cannot call its constructor:

```
scala> Queue(List(1, 2), List(3))
1 |Queue(List(1, 2), List(3))
  |^^^^^
  |constructor Queue cannot be accessed as a member of
  |Queue from module class rs$line$4$.
```

Now that the primary constructor of class Queue can no longer be called from client code, there needs to be some other way to create new queues. One possibility is to add an auxiliary constructor, like this:

```
def this() = this(Nil, Nil)
```

The auxiliary constructor shown in the previous example builds an empty queue. As a refinement, the auxiliary constructor could take a list of initial queue elements:

```
def this(elems: T*) = this(elems.toList, Nil)
```

Recall that T* is the notation for repeated parameters, as described in Section 8.8.

Another possibility is to add a factory method that builds a queue from such a sequence of initial elements. A neat way to do this is to define an object Queue that has the same name as the class being defined and contains an apply method, as shown in Listing 18.3:

```
object Queue:
  // constructs a queue with initial elements 'xs'
  def apply[T](xs: T*) = new Queue[T](xs.toList, Nil)
```

Listing 18.3 · An apply factory method in a companion object.

By placing this object in the same source file as class Queue, you make the object a companion object of the class. You saw in Section 12.5 that a companion object has the same access rights as its class. Because of this, the apply method in object Queue can create a new Queue object, even though the constructor of class Queue is private.

Note that, because the factory method is called apply, clients can create queues with an expression such as Queue(1, 2, 3). This expression expands to Queue.apply(1, 2, 3) since Queue is an object instead of a function. As a result, Queue looks to clients as if it were a globally defined factory method. In reality, Scala has no globally visible methods; every method must be contained in an object, class, or package. However, using methods named apply inside global objects, you can support usage patterns that look like invocations of global methods.

An alternative: private classes

Private constructors and private members are one way to hide the initialization and representation of a class. Another more radical way is to hide the class itself and only export a trait that reveals the public interface of the class. The code in Listing 18.4 implements this design. There's a trait Queue, which declares the methods head, tail, and enqueue. All three methods are implemented in a subclass QueueImpl, which is itself a private inner class of object Queue. This exposes to clients the same information as before, but

```scala
trait Queue[T]:
  def head: T
  def tail: Queue[T]
  def enqueue(x: T): Queue[T]

object Queue:

  def apply[T](xs: T*): Queue[T] =
    QueueImpl[T](xs.toList, Nil)

  private class QueueImpl[T](
    private val leading: List[T],
    private val trailing: List[T]
  ) extends Queue[T]:

    def mirror =
      if leading.isEmpty then
        QueueImpl(trailing.reverse, Nil)
      else
        this

    def head: T = mirror.leading.head

    def tail: QueueImpl[T] =
      val q = mirror
      QueueImpl(q.leading.tail, q.trailing)

    def enqueue(x: T) =
      QueueImpl(leading, x :: trailing)
```

Listing 18.4 · Type abstraction for functional queues.

using a different technique. Instead of hiding individual constructors and methods, this version hides the whole implementation class.

18.3 Variance annotations

Queue, as defined in Listing 18.4, is a trait, but not a type. Queue is not a type because it takes a type parameter.[1]

---

[1] Queue can be considered a *higher kinded* type. These will be discussed in *Advanced Programming in Scala.*

As a result, you cannot create variables of type Queue:

```
scala> def doesNotCompile(q: Queue) = {}
1 |def doesNotCompile(q: Queue) = {}
  |                      ^^^^^
  |                                   Missing type parameter for Queue
```

Instead, trait Queue enables you to specify *parameterized* types, such as Queue[String], Queue[Int], or Queue[AnyRef]:

```
scala> def doesCompile(q: Queue[AnyRef]) = {}
def doesCompile: (q: Queue[AnyRef]): Unit
```

Thus, Queue is a trait and Queue[String] is a type. Queue is also called a *type constructor* because you can construct a type with it by specifying a type parameter. (This is analogous to constructing an object instance with a plain-old constructor by specifying a value parameter.) The type constructor Queue "generates" a family of types, which includes Queue[Int], Queue[String], and Queue[AnyRef].

You can also say that Queue is a *generic* trait. (Classes and traits that take type parameters are "generic," but the types they generate are "parameterized," not generic.) The term "generic" means that you are defining many specific types with one generically written class or trait. For example, trait Queue in Listing 18.4 defines a generic queue. Queue[Int] and Queue[String], *etc.*, would be the specific queues.

The combination of type parameters and subtyping poses some interesting questions. For example, are there any special subtyping relationships between members of the family of types generated by Queue[T]? More specifically, should a Queue[String] be considered a subtype of Queue[AnyRef]? Or more generally, if S is a subtype of type T, then should Queue[S] be considered a subtype of Queue[T]? If so, you could say that trait Queue is *covariant* (or "flexible") in its type parameter T. Or, since it just has one type parameter, you could say simply that Queues are covariant. Covariant Queues would mean, for example, that you could pass a Queue[String] to the doesCompile method shown previously, which takes a value parameter of type Queue[AnyRef].

Intuitively, all this seems OK, since a queue of Strings looks like a special case of a queue of AnyRefs. In Scala, however, generic types have by default *nonvariant* (or "rigid") subtyping. That is, with Queue defined as in

Listing 18.4, queues with different element types would never be in a subtype relationship. A Queue[String] would not be usable as a Queue[AnyRef]. However, you can demand covariant (flexible) subtyping of queues by changing the first line of the definition of trait Queue like this:

```
trait Queue[+T] { ... }
```

Prefixing a formal type parameter with a + indicates that subtyping is covariant (flexible) in that parameter. By adding this single character, you are telling Scala that you want Queue[String], for example, to be considered a subtype of Queue[AnyRef]. The compiler will check that Queue is defined in a way that this subtyping is sound.

Besides +, there is also a prefix -, which indicates *contravariant* subtyping. If Queue were defined like this:

```
trait Queue[-T] { ... }
```

then if T is a subtype of type S, this would imply that Queue[S] is a subtype of Queue[T] (which in the case of queues would be rather surprising!). Whether a type parameter is covariant, contravariant, or nonvariant is called the parameter's *variance* . The + and – symbols you can place next to type parameters are called *variance annotations*.

In a purely functional world, many types are naturally covariant (flexible). However, the situation changes once you introduce mutable data. To find out why, consider the simple type of one-element cells that can be read or written, shown in Listing 18.5.

```
class Cell[T](init: T):
  private var current = init
  def get = current
  def set(x: T) =
    current = x
```

Listing 18.5 · A nonvariant (rigid) Cell class.

The Cell type of Listing 18.5 is declared nonvariant (rigid). For the sake of argument, assume for a moment that Cell was declared covariant instead—*i.e.*, it was declared class Cell[+T]—and that this passed the Scala compiler. (It doesn't, and we'll explain why shortly.) Then you could construct the following problematic statement sequence:

371

```
val c1 = new Cell[String]("abc")
val c2: Cell[Any] = c1
c2.set(1)
val s: String = c1.get
```

Seen by itself, each of these four lines looks OK. The first line creates a cell of strings and stores it in a val named c1. The second line defines a new val, c2, of type Cell[Any], which is initialized with c1. This is OK since Cells are assumed to be covariant. The third line sets the value of cell c2 to 1. This is also OK because the assigned value 1 is an instance of c2's element type Any. Finally, the last line assigns the element value of c1 into a string. Nothing strange here, as both sides are of the same type. But taken together, these four lines end up assigning the integer 1 to the string s. This is clearly a violation of type soundness.

Which operation is to blame for the runtime fault? It must be the second one, which uses covariant subtyping. The other statements are too simple and fundamental. Thus, a Cell of String is *not* also a Cell of Any, because there are things you can do with a Cell of Any that you cannot do with a Cell of String. You cannot use set with an Int argument on a Cell of String, for example.

In fact, were you to pass the covariant version of Cell to the Scala compiler, you would get a compile-time error:

```
4 |     def set(x: T) =
  |             ^^^^
  |     covariant type T occurs in contravariant position
  |     in type T of value x
```

Variance and arrays

It's interesting to compare this behavior with arrays in Java. In principle, arrays are just like cells except that they can have more than one element. Nevertheless, arrays are treated as covariant in Java.

You can try an example analogous to the cell interaction described here with Java arrays:

```
// this is Java
String[] a1 = { "abc" };
```

372

```
Object[] a2 = a1;
a2[0] = new Integer(17);
String s = a1[0];
```

If you try out this example, you will find that it compiles. But executing the program will cause an `ArrayStore` exception to be thrown when a2[0] is assigned to an `Integer`:

```
Exception in thread "main" java.lang.ArrayStoreException:
java.lang.Integer
        at JavaArrays.main(JavaArrays.java:8)
```

What happens here is that Java stores the element type of the array at runtime. Then, every time an array element is updated, the new element value is checked against the stored type. If it is not an instance of that type, an `ArrayStore` exception is thrown.

You might ask why Java adopted this design, which seems both unsafe and expensive. When asked this question, James Gosling, the principal inventor of the Java language, answered that they wanted to have a simple means to treat arrays generically. For instance, they wanted to be able to write a method to sort all elements of an array, using a signature like the following that takes an array of `Object`:

```
void sort(Object[] a, Comparator cmp) { ... }
```

Covariance of arrays was needed so that arrays of arbitrary reference types could be passed to this `sort` method. Of course, with the arrival of Java generics, such a `sort` method can now be written with a type parameter, so the covariance of arrays is no longer necessary. For compatibility reasons, though, it has persisted in Java to this day.

Scala tries to be purer than Java in not treating arrays as covariant. Here's what you get if you translate the first two lines of the array example to Scala:

```
scala> val a1 = Array("abc")
val a1: Array[String] = Array(abc)

scala> val a2: Array[Any] = a1
1 |val a2: Array[Any] = a1
  |                      ^^
  |                     Found:    (a1 : Array[String])
  |                     Required: Array[Any]
```

373

What happened here is that Scala treats arrays as nonvariant (rigid), so an Array[String] is not considered to conform to an Array[Any]. However, sometimes it is necessary to interact with legacy methods in Java that use an Object array as a means to emulate a generic array. For instance, you might want to call a sort method like the one described previously with an array of Strings as argument. To make this possible, Scala lets you cast an array of Ts to an array of any supertype of T:

```
val a2: Array[Object] = a1.asInstanceOf[Array[Object]]
```

The cast is always legal at compile-time, and it will always succeed at run-time because the JVM's underlying run-time model treats arrays as covariant, just as Java the language does. But you might get ArrayStore exceptions afterwards, again just as you would in Java.

18.4 Checking variance annotations

Now that you have seen some examples where variance is unsound, you may be wondering which kind of class definitions need to be rejected and which can be accepted. So far, all violations of type soundness involved some re-assignable field or array element. The purely functional implementation of queues, on the other hand, looks like a good candidate for covariance. However, the following example shows that you can "engineer" an unsound situation even if there is no reassignable field.

To set up the example, assume that queues as defined in Listing 18.4 are covariant. Then, create a subclass of queues that specializes the element type to Int and overrides the enqueue method:

```
class StrangeIntQueue extends Queue[Int]:
  override def enqueue(x: Int) =
    println(math.sqrt(x))
    super.enqueue(x)
```

The enqueue method in StrangeIntQueue prints out the square root of its (integer) argument before doing the append proper.

Now, you can write a counterexample in two lines:

```
val x: Queue[Any] = new StrangeIntQueue
x.enqueue("abc")
```

The first of these two lines is valid because `StrangeIntQueue` is a subclass of `Queue[Int]` and, assuming covariance of queues, `Queue[Int]` is a subtype of `Queue[Any]`. The second line is valid because you can append a `String` to a `Queue[Any]`. However, taken together, these two lines have the effect of applying a square root method to a string, which makes no sense.

Clearly it's not just mutable fields that make covariant types unsound. The problem is more general. It turns out that as soon as a generic parameter type appears as the type of a method parameter, the containing class or trait may not be covariant in that type parameter.

For queues, the enqueue method violates this condition:

```
class Queue[+T]:
  def enqueue(x: T) =
    ...
```

Running a modified queue class like the one above through a Scala compiler would yield:

```
17 |  def enqueue(x: T) =
   |                ^^^^
   |  covariant type T occurs in contravariant position
   |  in type T of value x
```

Reassignable fields are a special case of the rule that disallows type parameters annotated with + from being used as method parameter types. As mentioned in Section 16.2, a reassignable field, "var x: T", is treated in Scala as a getter method, "def x: T", and a setter method, "def x_=(y: T)". As you can see, the setter method has a parameter of the field's type T. So that type may not be covariant.

The fast track

In the rest of this section, we'll describe the mechanism by which the Scala compiler checks variance annotations. If you're not interested in such detail right now, you can safely skip to Section 18.5. The most important thing to understand is that the Scala compiler will check any variance annotations you place on type parameters. For example, if you try to declare a type parameter to be covariant (by adding a +), but that could lead to potential runtime errors, your program won't compile.

To verify correctness of variance annotations, the Scala compiler classifies all positions in a class or trait body as *positive*, *negative*, or *neutral*.

375

A "position" is any location in the class or trait (but from now on we'll just write "class") body where a type parameter may be used. For example, every method value parameter is a position because a method value parameter has a type. Therefore a type parameter could appear in that position.

The compiler checks each use of each of the class's type parameters. Type parameters annotated with + may only be used in positive positions, while type parameters annotated with – may only be used in negative positions. A type parameter with no variance annotation may be used in any position, and is, therefore, the only kind of type parameter that can be used in neutral positions of the class body.

To classify the positions, the compiler starts from the declaration of a type parameter and then moves inward through deeper nesting levels. Positions at the top level of the declaring class are classified as positive. By default, positions at deeper nesting levels are classified the same as that at enclosing levels, but there are a handful of exceptions where the classification changes. Method value parameter positions are classified to the *flipped* classification relative to positions outside the method, where the flip of a positive classification is negative, the flip of a negative classification is positive, and the flip of a neutral classification is still neutral.

Besides method value parameter positions, the current classification is also flipped at the type parameters of methods. A classification is sometimes flipped at the type argument position of a type, such as the Arg in C[Arg], depending on the variance of the corresponding type parameter. If C's type parameter is annotated with a + then the classification stays the same. If C's type parameter is annotated with a –, then the current classification is flipped. If C's type parameter has no variance annotation then the current classification is changed to neutral.

As a somewhat contrived example, consider the following class definition, where several positions are annotated with their classifications, $^+$ (for positive) or $^-$ (for negative):

```
abstract class Cat[-T, +U]:
  def meow[W⁻](volume: T⁻, listener: Cat[U⁺, T⁻]⁻)
    : Cat[Cat[U⁺, T⁻]⁻, U⁺]⁺
```

The positions of the type parameter, W, and the two value parameters, volume and listener, are all negative. Looking at the result type of meow, the position of the first Cat[U, T] argument is negative because Cat's first type parameter, T, is annotated with a –. The type U inside this argument is again in positive position (two flips), whereas the type T inside that argument is still in negative position.

You see from this discussion that it's quite hard to keep track of variance positions. That's why it's a welcome relief that the Scala compiler does this job for you.

Once the classifications are computed, the compiler checks that each type parameter is only used in positions that are classified appropriately. In this case, T is only used in negative positions, and U is only used in positive positions. So class Cat is type correct.

18.5 Lower bounds

Back to the Queue class. You saw that the previous definition of Queue[T] shown in Listing 18.4 cannot be made covariant in T because T appears as a type of a parameter of the enqueue method, and that's a negative position.

Fortunately, there's a way to get unstuck: you can generalize enqueue by making it polymorphic (*i.e.*, giving the enqueue method itself a type parameter) and using a *lower bound* for its type parameter. Listing 18.6 shows a new formulation of Queue that implements this idea.

```
class Queue[+T] (private val leading: List[T],
    private val trailing: List[T]):
  def enqueue[U >: T](x: U) =
    new Queue[U](leading, x :: trailing) // ...
```

Listing 18.6 · A type parameter with a lower bound.

The new definition gives enqueue a type parameter U, and with the syntax, "U >: T", defines T as the lower bound for U. As a result, U is required to be a supertype of T.[2] The parameter to enqueue is now of type U instead of type T, and the return value of the method is now Queue[U] instead of Queue[T].

For example, suppose there is a class Fruit with two subclasses, Apple and Orange. With the new definition of class Queue, it is possible to append an Orange to a Queue[Apple]. The result will be a Queue[Fruit].

---

[2]Supertype and subtype relationships are reflexive, which means a type is both a supertype and a subtype of itself. Even though T is a lower bound for U, you could still pass in a T to enqueue.

This revised definition of enqueue is type correct. Intuitively, if T is a more specific type than expected (for example, Apple instead of Fruit), a call to enqueue will still work because U (Fruit) will still be a supertype of T (Apple).[3]

The new definition of enqueue is arguably better than the old, because it is more general. Unlike the old version, the new definition allows you to append an arbitrary supertype U of the queue element type T. The result is then a Queue[U]. Together with queue covariance, this gives the right kind of flexibility for modeling queues of different element types in a natural way.

This shows that variance annotations and lower bounds play well together. They are a good example of *type-driven design*, where the types of an interface guide its detailed design and implementation. In the case of queues, it's likely you would not have thought of the refined implementation of enqueue with a lower bound. But you might have decided to make queues covariant, in which case, the compiler would have pointed out the variance error for enqueue. Correcting the variance error by adding a lower bound makes enqueue more general and queues as a whole more usable.

This observation is also the main reason that Scala prefers declaration-site variance over use-site variance as it is found in Java's wildcards. With use-site variance, you are on your own designing a class. It will be the clients of the class that need to put in the wildcards, and if they get it wrong, some important instance methods will no longer be applicable. Variance being a tricky business, users usually get it wrong, and they come away thinking that wildcards and generics are overly complicated. With definition-side variance, you express your intent to the compiler, and the compiler will double check that the methods you want available will indeed be available.

18.6 Contravariance

So far in this chapter, all examples you've seen were either covariant or non-variant. But there are also cases where contravariance is natural. For instance, consider the trait of output channels shown in Listing 18.7:

Here, OutputChannel is defined to be contravariant in T. So an output channel of AnyRefs, say, is a subtype of an output channel of Strings. Although it may seem non-intuitive, it actually makes sense. To see why, con-

---

[3]Technically, what happens is a flip occurs for lower bounds. The type parameter U is in a negative position (1 flip), while the lower bound (>: T) is in a positive position (2 flips).

```
trait OutputChannel[-T]:
  def write(x: T): Unit
```

Listing 18.7 · A contravariant output channel.

```
trait Function1[-S, +T]:
  def apply(x: S): T
```

Listing 18.8 · Covariance and contravariance of Function1s.

sider what you can do with an OutputChannel[String]. The only supported operation is writing a String to it. The same operation can also be done on an OutputChannel[AnyRef]. So it is safe to substitute an OutputChannel[AnyRef] for an OutputChannel[String]. By contrast, it would not be safe to substitute an OutputChannel[String] where an OutputChannel[AnyRef] is required. After all, you can send any object to an OutputChannel[AnyRef], whereas an OutputChannel[String] requires that the written values are all strings.

This reasoning points to a general principle in type system design: It is safe to assume that a type T is a subtype of a type U if you can substitute a value of type T wherever a value of type U is required. This is called the *Liskov Substitution Principle*. The principle holds if T supports the same operations as U, and all of T's operations require less and provide more than the corresponding operations in U. In the case of output channels, an OutputChannel[AnyRef] can be a subtype of an OutputChannel[String] because the two support the same write operation, and this operation requires less in OutputChannel[AnyRef] than in OutputChannel[String]. "Less" means the argument is only required to be an AnyRef in the first case, whereas it is required to be a String in the second case.

Sometimes covariance and contravariance are mixed in the same type. A prominent example is Scala's function traits. For instance, whenever you write the function type A => B, Scala expands this to Function1[A, B]. The definition of Function1 in the standard library uses both covariance and contravariance: the Function1 trait is contravariant in the function argument type S and covariant in the result type T, as shown in Listing 18.8. This satisfies the Liskov Substitution Principle because arguments are something that's required, whereas results are something that's provided.

As an example, consider the application shown in Listing 18.9. Here, class `Publication` contains one parametric field, `title`, of type `String`. Class `Book` extends `Publication` and forwards its string `title` parameter to the constructor of its superclass. The `Library` singleton object defines a set of books and a method `printBookList`, which takes a function, named `info`, of type `Book => AnyRef`. In other words, the type of the lone parameter to `printBookList` is a function that takes one `Book` argument and returns an `AnyRef`. The `Customer` application defines a method, `getTitle`, which takes a `Publication` as its lone parameter and returns a `String`, the title of the passed `Publication`.

```
class Publication(val title: String)
class Book(title: String) extends Publication(title)

object Library:
 val books: Set[Book] =
   Set(
     Book("Programming in Scala"),
     Book("Walden")
   )
 def printBookList(info: Book => AnyRef) =
   for book <- books do println(info(book))

object Customer:
 def getTitle(p: Publication): String = p.title
 def main(args: Array[String]): Unit =
   Library.printBookList(getTitle)
```

Listing 18.9 · Demonstration of function type parameter variance.

Now take a look at the last line in `Customer`. This line invokes `Library`'s `printBookList` method and passes `getTitle`, wrapped in a function value:

```
Library.printBookList(getTitle)
```

This line of code type checks even though `String`, the function's result type, is a subtype of `AnyRef`, the result type of `printBookList`'s `info` parameter. This code passes the compiler because function result types are declared to be covariant (the `+T` in Listing 18.8). If you look inside the body of `printBookList`, you can get a glimpse of why this makes sense.

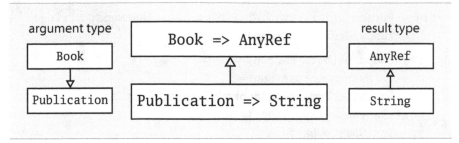

Figure 18.1 · Covariance and contravariance in function type parameters.

The `printBookList` method iterates through its book list and invokes the passed function on each book. It passes the `AnyRef` result returned by `info` to `println`, which invokes `toString` on it and prints the result. This activity will work with `String` as well as any other subclass of `AnyRef`, which is what covariance of function result types means.

Now consider the parameter type of the function being passed to the `printBookList` method. Although the `info` function's parameter type is declared as `Book`, the `getTitle` we're passing in takes a `Publication`, a *supertype* of `Book`. The reason this works is that since `printBookList`'s parameter type is `Book`, the body of the `printBookList` method will only be allowed to pass a `Book` into the function. And because `getTitle`'s parameter type is `Publication`, the body of that function will only be able to access on its parameter, p, members that are declared in class `Publication`. Because any method declared in `Publication` is also available on its subclass `Book`, everything should work, which is what contravariance of function parameter types means. You can see all this graphically in Figure 18.1.

The code in Listing 18.9 compiles because `Publication => String` is a subtype of `Book => AnyRef`, as shown in the center of the Figure 18.1. Because the result type of a `Function1` is defined as covariant, the inheritance relationship of the two result types, shown at the right of the diagram, is in the same direction as that of the two functions shown in the center. By contrast, because the parameter type of a `Function1` is defined as contravariant, the inheritance relationship of the two parameter types, shown at the left of the diagram, is in the opposite direction as that of the two functions.

381

```
class Person(val firstName: String, val lastName: String)
    extends Ordered[Person]:

  def compare(that: Person) =
    val lastNameComparison =
      lastName.compareToIgnoreCase(that.lastName)
    if lastNameComparison != 0 then
      lastNameComparison
    else
      firstName.compareToIgnoreCase(that.firstName)

  override def toString = s"$firstName $lastName"
```

Listing 18.10 · A Person class that mixes in the Ordered trait.

18.7   Upper bounds

In Listing 14.2 on page 286, we showed a merge sort function for lists that took a comparison function as a first argument and a list to sort as a second, curried argument. Another way you might want to organize such a sort function is by requiring the type of the list to mix in the Ordered trait. As mentioned in Section 11.2, by mixing Ordered into a class and implementing Ordered's one abstract method, compare, you enable clients to compare instances of that class with <, >, <=, and >=. For example, Listing 18.10 shows Ordered being mixed into a Person class.

As a result, you can compare two people like this:

```
val robert = new Person("Robert", "Jones")
val sally = new Person("Sally", "Smith")
robert < sally  // true
```

To require that the type of the list passed to your new sort function mixes in Ordered, you need to use an *upper bound*. An upper bound is specified similar to a lower bound, except instead of the >: symbol used for lower bounds, you use a <: symbol, as shown in Listing 18.11.

With the "T <: Ordered[T]" syntax, you indicate that the type parameter, T, has an upper bound, Ordered[T]. This means that the element type of the list passed to orderedMergeSort must be a subtype of Ordered. Thus, you could pass a List[Person] to orderedMergeSort because Person mixes in Ordered.

For example, consider this list:

```
val people = List(
  Person("Larry", "Wall"),
  Person("Anders", "Hejlsberg"),
  Person("Guido", "van Rossum"),
  Person("Alan", "Kay"),
  Person("Yukihiro", "Matsumoto")
)
```

Because the element type of this list, Person, mixes in (and is therefore a subtype of) Ordered[Person], you can pass the list to orderedMergeSort:

```
scala> val sortedPeople = orderedMergeSort(people)
val sortedPeople: List[Person] = List(Anders Hejlsberg,
  Alan Kay, Yukihiro Matsumoto, Guido van Rossum, Larry Wall)
```

Now, although the sort function shown in Listing 18.11 serves as a useful illustration of upper bounds, it isn't actually the most general way in Scala to design a sort function that takes advantage of the Ordered trait.

For example, you couldn't use the orderedMergeSort function to sort a list of integers, because class Int is not a subtype of Ordered[Int]:

```
def orderedMergeSort[T <: Ordered[T]](xs: List[T]): List[T] =
  def merge(xs: List[T], ys: List[T]): List[T] =
    (xs, ys) match
      case (Nil, _) => ys
      case (_, Nil) => xs
      case (x :: xs1, y :: ys1) =>
        if x < y then x :: merge(xs1, ys)
        else y :: merge(xs, ys1)
  val n = xs.length / 2
  if n == 0 then xs
  else
    val (ys, zs) = xs.splitAt(n)
    merge(orderedMergeSort(ys), orderedMergeSort(zs))
```

Listing 18.11 · A merge sort function with an upper bound.

383

```
scala> val wontCompile = orderedMergeSort(List(3, 2, 1))
<console>:5: error: inferred type arguments [Int] do
    not conform to method orderedMergeSort's type
      parameter bounds [T <: Ordered[T]]
        val wontCompile = orderedMergeSort(List(3, 2, 1))
                          ^
```

In Section 21.4, we'll show you how to use *given parameters* and *typeclasses* to achieve a more general solution.

18.8 Conclusion

In this chapter you saw several techniques for information hiding: private constructors, factory methods, type abstraction, and object private members. You also learned how to specify data type variance and what it implies for class implementation. Finally, you saw a technique that helps in obtaining flexible variance annotations: lower bounds for method type parameters. In the next chapter, we'll turn our attention to enums.

Chapter 19

Enums

Scala 3 introduced the enum construct to make the definition of sealed case class hierarchies more concise. Enums can be used to define the enumerated data types common in mainstream object-oriented languages such as Java, as well as algebraic data types found in functional languages such as Haskell. In Scala, these concepts are treated as two ends of the same spectrum, and are both defined with the enum construct. Both enumerated and algebraic data types will be described in this chapter.

19.1   Enumerated data types

An *enumerated data type*, or "EDT,"[1] is useful when you want a type that's restricted to a finite set of named values. These named values are called the *cases* of the EDT. For example, you could define an EDT to represent the four directions of the compass—north, east, south, and west—like this:

```
enum Direction:
  case North, East, South, West
```

This simple enum will generate a sealed class named Direction[2] with a companion object containing the four values declared as vals. The vals, named North, East, South, and West, will have type Direction. Given

---

[1] Although "enum" is a more common short name for enumerated data types, we will use EDT in this book because the enum construct in Scala is also used to define algebraic data types, which are called ADTs.

[2] The sealed class is called the "enum type."

385

this definition, you could, for example, define a method to invert a compass direction using a pattern match, as shown here:

```
import Direction.{North, South, East, West}

def invert(dir: Direction): Direction =
  dir match
    case North => South
    case East => West
    case South => North
    case West => East
```

Here are some example uses of the invert method:

```
invert(North) // South
invert(East)  // West
```

Enumerated data types are called "enumerated" because the compiler associates an Int ordinal to each case. The ordinal starts at 0 and increases by one for each case, in the order the cases are defined in the enum. You can access the ordinal via a method named ordinal, which the compiler generates for each EDT. For example:

```
North.ordinal // 0
East.ordinal  // 1
South.ordinal // 2
West.ordinal  // 3
```

The compiler also generates a method named values in the companion object for every EDT's enum type. This method returns an Array containing all of the EDT's cases, in declaration order. The array's element type is the enum type. For example, Direction.values will return an Array[Direction] containing, in order, North, East, South, and West:

```
Direction.values // Array(North, East, South, West)
```

Lastly, the compiler adds a method named valueOf to the companion object, which converts a string to an instance of the enum type—so long as the string exactly matches the name of one of the cases. If the given string does not match any of the cases, you will be rewarded by a thrown exception. Here are some examples of its use:

```
Direction.valueOf("North") // North
Direction.valueOf("East")  // East
Direction.valueOf("Up")
// IllegalArgumentException: enum case not found: Up
```

You can also give an EDT value parameters. Here's a new version of
Direction that captures an Int representing the angle at which the direction
appears on a compass:

```
enum Direction(val degrees: Int):
  case North extends Direction(0)
  case East extends Direction(90)
  case South extends Direction(180)
  case West extends Direction(270)
```

Because degrees is declared as a parametric field, you can access it on any
Direction instance. Here are some examples:

```
import Direction.*
North.degrees // 0
South.degrees // 180
```

You can also define your own methods on an enum type, by placing them
in the body of the enum. For example, you could redefine the invert method,
shown previously, such that is becomes a member of Direction, like this:

```
enum Direction(val degrees: Int):

  def invert: Direction =
    this match
      case North => South
      case East => West
      case South => North
      case West => East

  case North extends Direction(0)
  case East extends Direction(90)
  case South extends Direction(180)
  case West extends Direction(270)
```

Now you can politely ask a Direction to invert itself:

387

```
North.invert  // South
East.invert   // West
```

You can define a companion object for an EDT, in which case Scala will still fill in the `values` and `valueOf` methods if you don't provide them. For example, here's a companion object for `Direction` that defines a method that determines the nearest compass direction to the passed degrees:

```scala
object Direction:
  def nearestTo(degrees: Int): Direction =
    val rem = degrees % 360
    val angle = if rem < 0 then rem + 360 else rem
    val (ne, se, sw, nw) = (45, 135, 225, 315)
    angle match
      case a if a > nw || a <= ne => North
      case a if a > ne && a <= se => East
      case a if a > se && a <= sw => South
      case a if a > sw && a <= nw => West
```

This companion object offers both declared and generated methods. Here's an example function that uses both the declared `nearestTo` and the generated `values` methods of object `Direction`:

```scala
def allButNearest(degrees: Int): List[Direction] =
  val nearest = Direction.nearestTo(degrees)
  Direction.values.toList.filter(_ != nearest)
```

The `allButNearest` function returns a list containing all directions except the one nearest to the passed compass angle. Here's an example use:

```scala
allButNearest(42)  // List(East, South, West)
```

One restriction of enums is that you cannot define methods for the individual cases. Instead, you must declare any methods as members of the enum type itself, which will make those methods available on all of the enum's cases.[3] The primary purpose of an enum's cases is to provide a fixed set of different ways to construct instances of the enum type.

---

[3]You *could* define extension methods for the case types, but it might be better in that situation to just write out the sealed case class hierarchy by hand.

Integration with Java enums

To define a Java enum in Scala, simply make your Scala EDT extend
java.lang.Enum and give the Scala enum type as the type parameter.
Here's an example:

```
enum Direction extends java.lang.Enum[Direction]:
  case North, East, South, West
```

In addition to its usual Scala EDT features, this version of Direction
is also a java.lang.Enum. For example, you can use the compareTo
method, which is defined on java.lang.Enum:

```
Direction.East.compareTo(Direction.South)  // -1
```

19.2   Algebraic data types

An algebraic data type (ADT) is a data type composed of a finite set of
cases. ADTs are a natural way to express domain models in which you
model the data case by case. Each case represents one "data constructor,"
a particular way to construct an instance of the type. In Scala, a sealed
family of case classes forms an ADT so long as at least one of the cases
takes parameters.[4] For example, here's an ADT that represents one of three
possibilities: an expected value, the "good" type, an error value, the "bad"
type, or an exception, the "ugly" type:

```
enum Eastwood[+G, +B]:
  case Good(g: G)
  case Bad(b: B)
  case Ugly(ex: Throwable)
```

As you saw with EDTs, you cannot define methods for any of the specific
cases, Good, Bad, or Ugly, but you can define methods for their common
superclass, Eastwood. Here's an example of a map method that transforms
the Good value, if the Eastwood is a Good:

---

[4]By comparison, an EDT is a sealed family of case classes in which *none* of the cases
take parameters.

389

```
enum Eastwood[+G, +B]:

  def map[G2](f: G => G2): Eastwood[G2, B] =
    this match
      case Good(g) => Good(f(g))
      case Bad(b) => Bad(b)
      case Ugly(ex) => Ugly(ex)

  case Good(g: G)
  case Bad(b: B)
  case Ugly(ex: Throwable)
```

Here's an example of its use:

```
val eastWood = Good(41)
eastWood.map(n => n + 1) // Good(42)
```

The implementation of ADTs differs slightly from that of EDTs. For each case of an ADT that takes parameters, the compiler will generate a case class in the companion object of the enum type. Thus for Eastwood, the compiler would generate code similar to:

```
// Generated sealed trait (the "enum type")
sealed trait Eastwood[+G, +B]

object Eastwood: // Generated companion object

  // Generated case classes
  case class Good[+G, +B](g: G) extends Eastwood[G, B]
  case class Bad[+G, +B](b: B) extends Eastwood[G, B]
  case class Ugly[+G, +B](ex: Throwable) extends Eastwood[G, B]
```

Although the result type of the factory method created by the case classes will be the specific case class types, the compiler will widen those to the more general enum type. Here are some examples:

```
scala> Good(42)
val res0: Eastwood[Int, Nothing] = Good(42)

scala> Bad("oops")
val res1: Eastwood[Nothing, String] = Bad(oops)

scala> Ugly(new Exception)
val res2: Eastwood[Nothing, Nothing] = Ugly(java.lang.Exception)
```

If you need the more specific type for a case, you can construct an instance with new instead of the factory method. For example, although "Good(1)" will have type Eastwood[Int, Nothing], "new Good(1)" will have the more specific type, Good[Int, Nothing].

ADTs can be recursive. For example, a case could take an instance of the enum type as a parameter. A good example of such a recursive ADT is a linked list. You can define a linked list as a sealed type with two subtypes: a singleton object representing the empty list and a cons cell class that takes two parameters, an element (the head) and the rest of the list (the tail). Here's a linked list type whose empty list object is named Nada and whose cons cell class is named Yada:

```
enum Seinfeld[+E]:
  def ::[E2 >: E](o: E2): Seinfeld[E2] = Yada(o, this)
  case Yada(head: E, tail: Seinfeld[E])
  case Nada
```

The Seinfeld ADT is a recursive type because the Yada case takes another Seinfeld[E] as its tail parameter. Given Seinfeld declares a :: method, you can construct an instance similar to Scala's List, but starting with Nada instead of Nil:

```
scala> val xs = 1 :: 2 :: 3 :: Nada
val xs: Seinfeld[Int] = Yada(1,Yada(2,Yada(3,Nada)))
```

19.3 Generalized ADTs

Generalized algebraic data types (GADTs) are ADTs in which the sealed trait takes a type parameter that is filled in by the cases. Here's an example:

```
enum Literal[T]:
  case IntLit(value: Int) extends Literal[Int]
  case LongLit(value: Long) extends Literal[Long]
  case CharLit(value: Char) extends Literal[Char]
  case FloatLit(value: Float) extends Literal[Float]
  case DoubleLit(value: Double) extends Literal[Double]
  case BooleanLit(value: Boolean) extends Literal[Boolean]
  case StringLit(value: String) extends Literal[String]
```

The `Literal` enum represents a GADT because it takes a type parameter, T, which is specified by each of its cases in their extends clauses. For example, the `IntLit` case fixes T to Int by extending `Literal[Int]`.

This kind of sealed type hierarchy is given the special name "generalized ADT" because it presents special challenges to type checking and inference. Here's an illustrative example:

```
import Literal.*

def valueOfLiteral[T](lit: Literal[T]): T =
  lit match
    case IntLit(n) => n
    case LongLit(m) => m
    case CharLit(c) => c
    case FloatLit(f) => f
    case DoubleLit(d) => d
    case BooleanLit(b) => b
    case StringLit(s) => s
```

The `valueOfLiteral` method passes the type checker, despite none of its `match` alternatives resulting in the required result type, T. For example, the `case IntLit(n)` alternative results in n, which has type Int. The challenge is that Int is not type T, nor is Int a subtype of T. This type checks only because the compiler notices that for the `IntList` case, T can be none other than Int. The same is true for the other alternatives. Moreover, this more specific type is propagated back to the caller. Here are some examples:

```
valueOfLiteral(BooleanLit(true)) // true: Boolean
valueOfLiteral(IntLit(42))       // 42: Int
```

19.4   What makes ADTs algebraic

ADTs are called "algebraic" because they represent an application of algebraic theory to types. One way to observe this connection with mathematics is by mapping each type to its *cardinality*, a count of the *inhabitants* of that type. If you think of types as representing sets of values, then the cardinality of a type is the cardinality (the number of elements) of that corresponding set of values.

The fast track

This section provides insight into the mathematical properties of the data types you can define with an enum. If you prefer to learn about Scala collections now instead, it's safe to skip ahead to the next chapter.

For example, `Boolean` has two possible values, `true` and `false`. These are the two inhabitants of type `Boolean`. The cardinality of `Boolean`, therefore, is 2. The `Unit` type has just one possible value—the unit value, `()`—so its cardinality is 1. Type `Nothing` has zero possible values. It therefore has no inhabitants and a cardinality of 0.

You can find or define other types with cardinalities of 0, 1, or 2, but `Nothing`, `Unit`, and `Boolean` will suffice to illustrate the algebra. How about a type with a cardinality of 3? If no obvious candidates from the standard library come to mind, you could easily make one with an EDT:

```scala
enum TrafficLight:
  case Red, Yellow, Green
```

The `TrafficLight` type has three possible values: `Red`, `Yellow`, and `Green`. These three values comprise the three inhabitants of type `TrafficLight`, so its cardinality is 3.

Type cardinalities can get large quickly. The `Byte` type has 256 (2^8) possible values, ranging between `Byte.MinValue` and `Byte.MaxValue`, inclusive. These eight-bit integer values are the inhabitants of `Byte`, so its cardinality is 256. `Int` has 2^{32} inhabitants, so its cardinality is 2^{32}, or 42949672962. For many types, such as `String`, the set of possible values is unlimited. Such types have an infinite cardinality. The algebra works for infinite cardinalities too, but to illustrate the concepts here, we'll focus on types with relatively small, finite cardinalities.

You can combine types into a new, composite type such that their cardinalities follow the laws of addition. Such a composite type is called a *sum type*. In Scala, the most concise way to define a sum type is with an enum. Here's an example:

```scala
enum Hope[+T]:
  case Glad(o: T)
  case Sad
```

The `Hope` type will allow you to hope for the best, but prepare for the worst. `Hope` is like Scala's `Option` type, with `Glad` for `Some` and `Sad` for

None. How many inhabitants does Hope[T] have? Because it is a sum type, the cardinality of Hope[T] is equal to the *sum* of the cardinalities of its alternative types, Glad[T] and Sad.

Every Glad[T] instance wraps an instance of type T, so the cardinality of Glad[T] is equal to the cardinality of T. For example, because the cardinality of Boolean is 2, the cardinality of Glad[Boolean] is also 2. Its two inhabitants are Glad(true) and Glad(false). Sad is a singleton, like Unit, so its cardinality is 1. The cardinality for Hope[Boolean], therefore, is the sum of 2, the cardinality of Glad[Boolean], plus 1, the cardinality of Sad, which equals 3. Its three possible instances are Glad(true), Glad(false), and Sad. You can see other examples in Table 19.1.

Table 19.1 · The cardinality of Hope

Type	Total	Inhabitants
Hope[Nothing]	$0 + 1 = 1$	Sad
Hope[Unit]	$1 + 1 = 2$	Glad(()), Sad
Hope[Boolean]	$2 + 1 = 3$	Glad(true), Glad(false), Sad
Hope[TrafficLight]	$3 + 1 = 4$	Glad(Red), Glad(Yellow), Glad(Green), Sad
Hope[Byte]	$256 + 1 = 257$	Glad(Byte.MinValue), ... Glad(Byte.MaxValue), Sad

Now that you've seen addition, what about multiplication? As with addition, you can combine types into a new, composite type such that their cardinalities follow the laws of multiplication. Such a composite type is called a *product type*. In Scala, the most concise way to define a product type is with a case class: Here's an example:

```
case class Both[A, B](a: A, b: B)
```

The Both type allows you to gather together two values of types A and B, similar to Scala's Tuple2 type. How many inhabitants does Both[A, B] have? Because it is a product type, the cardinality of Both[A, B] is equal to the *product* of the cardinalities of its constituent types, A and B.

To enumerate all the inhabitants of Both[A, B], you must pair each inhabitant of type A with each inhabitant of type B. For example, because the cardinality of TrafficLight is 3 and the cardinality of Boolean is 2, the cardinality of Both[TrafficLight, Boolean] is 3 * 2, or 6. Its six possible instances are shown in Table 19.2, along with other examples.

Table 19.2 · The cardinality of Both

Type	Total	Inhabitants
Both[Nothing, Nothing]	0 * 0 = 0	*no inhabitants*
Both[Unit, Nothing]	1 * 0 = 0	*no inhabitants*
Both[Unit, Unit]	1 * 1 = 1	Both((), ())
Both[Boolean, Nothing]	2 * 0 = 0	*no inhabitants*
Both[Boolean, Unit]	2 * 1 = 2	Both(false, ())
		Both(true, ()),
Both[Boolean, Boolean]	2 * 2 = 4	Both(false, false),
		Both(false, true),
		Both(true, false),
		Both(true, true)
Both[TrafficLight, Nothing]	3 * 0 = 0	*no inhabitants*
Both[TrafficLight, Unit]	3 * 1 = 3	Both(Red, ())
		Both(Yellow, ())
		Both(Green, ())
Both[TrafficLight, Boolean]	3 * 2 = 6	Both(Red, false),
		Both(Red, true)
		Both(Yellow, false)
		Both(Yellow, true),
		Both(Green, false)
		Both(Green, true)
Both[TrafficLight, TrafficLight]	3 * 3 = 9	Both(Red, Red),
		Both(Red, Yellow)
		Both(Red, Green)
		Both(Yellow, Red)
		Both(Yellow, Yellow),
		Both(Yellow, Green),
		Both(Green, Red)
		Both(Green, Yellow)
		Both(Green, Green)

Generally, algebraic data types represent *sums of products*, where the cases form the alternatives of a sum type, and each case represents a product type that can be constructed from zero to many constituent types. An EDT is a special case of ADT where each product type is a singleton.

One of the benefits of understanding the algebraic properties of your data structures is that you can rely on the relevant mathematical laws to prove properties about your code. For example, you might be able to prove that certain refactorings will preserve the meaning of your program. ADT cardinalities obey laws regulating addition and multiplication, such as identity, commutativity, associativity, and distributivity. In general, functional programming often offers opportunities for you to gain insight into your code from branches of mathematics.

19.5   Conclusion

In this chapter, you learned about Scala's enums, a concise way to define sealed case class hierarchies that form enumerated and algebraic data types. You learned that in Scala, EDTs and ADTs form two ends of the same spectrum, and looked at the algebra of algebraic data types. Scala's enum construct makes a common idiom for functional data modeling concise, and indicates that EDTs and ADTs are important patterns.

Chapter 20

Abstract Members

A member of a class or trait is *abstract* if the member does not have a complete definition in the class. Abstract members are intended to be implemented in subclasses of the class in which they are declared. This idea is found in many object-oriented languages. For instance, Java lets you declare abstract methods. Scala also lets you declare such methods, as you saw in Section 10.2. But Scala goes beyond that and implements the idea in its full generality: Besides methods, you can declare abstract fields and even abstract types as members of classes and traits.

In this chapter we'll describe all four kinds of abstract member: `vals`, `vars`, methods, and types. Along the way we'll discuss trait parametric fields, lazy `vals`, and path-dependent types.

20.1 A quick tour of abstract members

The following trait declares one of each kind of abstract member: an abstract type (T), method (`transform`), val (`initial`), and var (`current`):

```
trait Abstract:
  type T
  def transform(x: T): T
  val initial: T
  var current: T
```

A concrete implementation of `Abstract` needs to fill in definitions for each of its abstract members. Here is an example implementation that provides these definitions:

```
class Concrete extends Abstract:
  type T = String
  def transform(x: String) = x + x
  val initial = "hi"
  var current = initial
```

The implementation gives a concrete meaning to the type name T by defining it as an alias of type String. The transform operation concatenates a given string with itself, and the initial and current values are both set to "hi".

This example gives you a rough first idea of the kinds of abstract members that exist in Scala. The remainder of the chapter will present the details and explain what the new forms of abstract members, as well as type members in general, are good for.

20.2 Type members

As you can see from the example in the previous section, the term *abstract type* in Scala means a type declared (with the "type" keyword) to be a member of a class or trait, without specifying a definition. Classes themselves may be abstract, and traits are by definition abstract, but neither of these are what are referred to as *abstract types* in Scala. An abstract type in Scala is always a member of some class or trait, such as type T in trait Abstract.

You can think of a non-abstract (or "concrete") type member, such as type T in class Concrete, as a way to define a new name, or *alias*, for a type. In class Concrete, for example, the type String is given the alias T. As a result, anywhere T appears in the definition of class Concrete, it means String. This includes the parameter and result types of transform, initial, and current, which mention T when they are declared in super-trait Abstract. Thus, when class Concrete implements these methods, those Ts are interpreted to mean String.

One reason to use a type member is to define a short, descriptive alias for a type whose real name is more verbose, or less obvious in meaning, than the alias. Such type members can help clarify the code of a class or trait. The other main use of type members is to declare abstract types that must be defined in subclasses. This use, which was demonstrated in the previous section, will be described in detail later in this chapter.

20.3   Abstract vals

An abstract val declaration has a form like:

```
val initial: String
```

It gives a name and type for a val, but not its value. This value has to be provided by a concrete val definition in a subclass. For instance, class Concrete implemented the val using:

```
val initial = "hi"
```

You use an abstract val declaration in a class when you do not know the correct value in the class, but you do know that the variable will have an unchangeable value in each instance of the class.

An abstract val declaration resembles an abstract parameterless method declaration such as:

```
def initial: String
```

Client code would refer to both the val and the method in exactly the same way (*i.e.*, obj.initial). However, if initial is an abstract val, the client is guaranteed that obj.initial will yield the same value every time it is referenced. If initial were an abstract method, that guarantee would not hold because, in that case, initial could be implemented by a concrete method that returns a different value every time it's called.

In other words, an abstract val constrains its legal implementation: Any implementation must be a val definition; it may not be a var or a def. Abstract method declarations, on the other hand, may be implemented by both concrete method definitions and concrete val definitions. Given the abstract class Fruit shown in Listing 20.1, class Apple would be a legal subclass implementation, but class BadApple would not.

20.4   Abstract vars

Like an abstract val, an abstract var declares just a name and a type, but not an initial value. For instance, Listing 20.2 shows a trait AbstractTime, which declares two abstract variables named hour and minute:

What is the meaning of abstract vars like hour and minute? You saw in Section 16.2 that vars declared as members of classes come equipped with

```
abstract class Fruit:
  val v: String // 'v' for value
  def m: String // 'm' for method
abstract class Apple extends Fruit:
  val v: String
  val m: String // OK to override a 'def' with a 'val'
abstract class BadApple extends Fruit:
  def v: String // ERROR: cannot override a 'val' with a 'def'
  def m: String
```

Listing 20.1 · Overriding abstract vals and parameterless methods.

```
trait AbstractTime:
  var hour: Int
  var minute: Int
```

Listing 20.2 · Declaring abstract vars.

getter and setter methods. This holds for abstract vars as well. If you declare an abstract var named hour, for example, you implicitly declare an abstract getter method, hour, and an abstract setter method, hour_=. There's no reassignable field to be defined—that will come in subclasses that define the concrete implementation of the abstract var. For instance, the definition of AbstractTime shown in Listing 20.2 is exactly equivalent to the definition shown in Listing 20.3.

```
trait AbstractTime:
  def hour: Int              // getter for 'hour'
  def hour_=(x: Int): Unit   // setter for 'hour'
  def minute: Int            // getter for 'minute'
  def minute_=(x: Int): Unit // setter for 'minute'
```

Listing 20.3 · How abstract vars are expanded into getters and setters.

20.5   Initializing abstract vals

Abstract vals sometimes play a role analogous to superclass parameters: they let you provide details in a subclass that are missing in a superclass. As an example, consider a reformulation of class Rational from Chapter 6, as shown in Listing 6.5 on page 109, as a trait:

```
trait RationalTrait:
  val numerArg: Int
  val denomArg: Int
```

The Rational class from Chapter 6 had two parameters: n for the numerator of the rational number, and d for the denominator. The RationalTrait trait given here defines instead two abstract vals: numerArg and denomArg. To instantiate a concrete instance of that trait, you need to implement the abstract val definitions. Here's an example:

```
new RationalTrait:
  val numerArg = 1
  val denomArg = 2
```

Here the keyword new appears in front of a trait name, RationalTrait, which is followed by a colon and indented class body. This expression yields an instance of an *anonymous class* that mixes in the trait and is defined by the body. This particular anonymous class instantiation has an effect analogous to the instance creation new Rational(1, 2).

The analogy is not perfect, however. There's a subtle difference concerning the order in which expressions are initialized. When you write:

```
new Rational(expr1, expr2)
```

the two expressions, expr1 and expr2, are evaluated before class Rational is initialized, so the values of expr1 and expr2 are available for the initialization of class Rational.

For traits, the situation is the opposite. When you write:

```
new RationalTrait:
  val numerArg = expr1
  val denomArg = expr2
```

401

the expressions, expr1 and expr2, are evaluated as part of the initialization of the anonymous class, but the anonymous class is initialized *after* the RationalTrait. So the values of numerArg and denomArg are not available during the initialization of RationalTrait (more precisely, a selection of either value would yield the default value for type Int, 0). For the definition of RationalTrait given previously, this is not a problem, because the trait's initialization does not make use of values numerArg or denomArg. However, it becomes a problem in the variant of RationalTrait shown in Listing 20.4, which defines normalized numerators and denominators.

```scala
trait RationalTrait:
  val numerArg: Int
  val denomArg: Int
  require(denomArg != 0)
  private val g = gcd(numerArg, denomArg)
  val numer = numerArg / g
  val denom = denomArg / g
  private def gcd(a: Int, b: Int): Int =
    if (b == 0) a else gcd(b, a % b)
  override def toString = s"$numer/$denom"
```

Listing 20.4 · A trait that uses its abstract vals.

If you try to instantiate this trait with some numerator and denominator expressions that are not simple literals, you'll get an exception:

```scala
scala> val x = 2
val x: Int = 2

scala> new RationalTrait:
         val numerArg = 1 * x
         val denomArg = 2 * x
java.lang.IllegalArgumentException: requirement failed
  at scala.Predef$.require(Predef.scala:280)
  at RationalTrait.$init$(<console>:4)
  ... 28 elided
```

The exception in this example was thrown because denomArg still had its default value of 0 when class RationalTrait was initialized, which caused the require invocation to fail.

This example demonstrates that initialization order is not the same for class parameters and abstract fields. A class parameter argument is evaluated *before* it is passed to the class constructor (unless the parameter is by-name). An implementing val definition in a subclass, by contrast, is evaluated only *after* the superclass has been initialized.

Now that you understand why abstract vals behave differently from parameters, it would be good to know what can be done about this. Is it possible to define a RationalTrait that can be initialized robustly, without fearing errors due to uninitialized fields? In fact, Scala offers two alternative solutions to this problem, *trait parametric fields* and *lazy vals*. They are presented in the remainder of this section.

Trait parametric fields

The first solution, trait parametric fields, lets you compute values for fields of a trait before the trait itself is initialized. To do this, define the fields as parametric fields—trait parameters annotated by val. An example is shown in Listing 20.5.

```scala
trait RationalTrait(val numerArg: Int, val denomArg: Int):
  require(denomArg != 0)
  private val g = gcd(numerArg, denomArg)
  val numer = numerArg / g
  val denom = denomArg / g
  private def gcd(a: Int, b: Int): Int =
    if (b == 0) a else gcd(b, a % b)
  override def toString = s"$numer/$denom"
```

Listing 20.5 · A trait that takes parametric fields.

You can create this as shown in Listing 20.6:

```scala
scala> new RationalTrait(1 * x, 2 * x) {}
val res1: RationalTrait = 1/2
```

Listing 20.6 · Trait parametric fields in an anonymous class expression.

Trait parametric fields are not restricted to anonymous classes; they can also be used in objects or named subclasses. Two examples are shown in

403

Listings 20.7 and 20.8. Class `RationalClass`, shown in Listing 20.8, exemplifies a general schema of how class parameters can be made available for the initialization of a supertrait.

```
object TwoThirds extends RationalTrait(2, 3)
```

Listing 20.7 · Trait parametric fields in an object definition.

```
class RationalClass(n: Int, d: Int) extends RationalTrait(n, d):
  def + (that: RationalClass) = new RationalClass(
    numer * that.denom + that.numer * denom,
    denom * that.denom
  )
```

Listing 20.8 · Trait parametric fields in a class definition.

Lazy vals

You can use trait parameters to simulate precisely the initialization behavior of class constructor arguments. Sometimes, however, you might prefer to let the system itself sort out how things should be initialized. This can be achieved by making your `val` definitions *lazy*. If you prefix a `val` definition with a `lazy` modifier, the initializing expression on the right-hand side will only be evaluated the first time the `val` is used.

For an example, define an object `Demo` with a `val` as follows:

```
object Demo:
  val x = { println("initializing x"); "done" }
```

Now, first refer to `Demo`, then to `Demo.x`:

```
scala> Demo
initializing x
val res0: Demo.type = Demo$@3002e397

scala> Demo.x
val res1: String = done
```

As you can see, the moment you use Demo, its x field becomes initialized. The initialization of x forms part of the initialization of Demo. The situation changes, however, if you define the x field to be lazy:

```
object Demo:
  lazy val x = { println("initializing x"); "done" }
```

```
scala> Demo
val res2: Demo.type = Demo$@24e5389c
```

```
scala> Demo.x
initializing x
val res3: String = done
```

Now, initializing Demo does not involve initializing x. The initialization of x will be deferred until the first time x is used. This is similar to the situation where x is defined as a parameterless method, using a def. However, unlike a def, a lazy val is never evaluated more than once. In fact, after the first evaluation of a lazy val the result of the evaluation is stored, to be reused when the same val is used subsequently.

Looking at this example, it seems that objects like Demo themselves behave like lazy vals, in that they are also initialized on demand, the first time they are used. This is correct. In fact an object definition can be seen as a shorthand for the definition of a lazy val with an anonymous class that describes the object's contents.

Using lazy vals, you could reformulate RationalTrait as shown in Listing 20.9. In the new trait definition, all concrete fields are defined lazy. Another change with respect to the previous definition of RationalTrait, shown in Listing 20.4, is that the require clause was moved from the body of the trait to the initializer of the private field, g, which computes the greatest common divisor of numerArg and denomArg. With these changes, there's nothing that remains to be done when LazyRationalTrait is initialized; all initialization code is now part of the right-hand side of a lazy val. Thus, it is safe to initialize the abstract fields of LazyRationalTrait after the class is defined.

Here's an example:

```
scala> val x = 2
val x: Int = 2
```

```
trait LazyRationalTrait:

  val numerArg: Int
  val denomArg: Int

  lazy val numer = numerArg / g
  lazy val denom = denomArg / g

  override def toString = s"$numer/$denom"

  private lazy val g =
    require(denomArg != 0)
    gcd(numerArg, denomArg)

  private def gcd(a: Int, b: Int): Int =
    if b == 0 then a else gcd(b, a % b)
```

Listing 20.9 · Initializing a trait with lazy vals.

```
scala> new LazyRationalTrait:
         val numerArg = 1 * x
         val denomArg = 2 * x

val res4: LazyRationalTrait = 1/2
```

No pre-computation is needed. It's instructive to trace the sequence of initializations that lead to the string 1/2 to be printed in the code above:

1. A fresh instance of LazyRationalTrait gets created and the initialization code of LazyRationalTrait is run. This initialization code is empty; none of the fields of LazyRationalTrait is initialized yet.

2. Next, the primary constructor of the anonymous subclass defined by the new expression is executed. This involves the initialization of numerArg with 2 and denomArg with 4.

3. Next, the toString method is invoked on the constructed object by the interpreter, so that the resulting value can be printed.

4. Next, the numer field is accessed for the first time by the toString method in trait LazyRationalTrait, so its initializer is evaluated.

5. The initializer of numer accesses the private field, g, so g is evaluated next. This evaluation accesses numerArg and denomArg, which were defined in Step 2.

6. Next, the toString method accesses the value of denom, which causes denom's evaluation. The evaluation of denom accesses the values of denomArg and g. The initializer of the g field is not re-evaluated, because it was already evaluated in Step 5.

7. Finally, the result string "1/2" is constructed and printed.

Note that the definition of g comes textually after the definitions of numer and denom in class LazyRationalTrait. Nevertheless, because all three values are lazy, g gets initialized before the initialization of numer and denom is completed.

This shows an important property of lazy vals: The textual order of their definitions does not matter because values get initialized on demand. Thus, lazy vals can free you as a programmer from having to think hard how to arrange val definitions to ensure that everything is defined when it is needed.

However, this advantage holds only as long as the initialization of lazy vals neither produces side effects nor depends on them. In the presence of side effects, initialization order starts to matter. And then it can be quite difficult to trace in what order initialization code is run, as the previous example has demonstrated. So lazy vals are an ideal complement to functional objects, where the order of initializations does not matter, as long as everything gets initialized eventually. They are less well suited for code that's predominantly imperative.

Lazy functional languages

Scala is by no means the first language to have exploited the perfect match of lazy definitions and functional code. In fact, there is a category of "lazy functional programming languages" in which *every* value and parameter is initialized lazily. The best known member of this class of languages is Haskell [SPJ02].

20.6 Abstract types

In the beginning of this chapter, you saw, "type T", an abstract type declaration. The rest of this chapter discusses what such an abstract type declaration means and what it's good for. Like all other abstract declarations, an
abstract type declaration is a placeholder for something that will be defined
concretely in subclasses. In this case, it is a type that will be defined further
down the class hierarchy. So T above refers to a type that is as yet unknown
at the point where it is declared. Different subclasses can provide different
realizations of T.

Here is a well-known example where abstract types show up naturally.
Suppose you are given the task of modeling the eating habits of animals. You
might start with a class Food and a class Animal with an eat method:

```
class Food
abstract class Animal:
  def eat(food: Food): Unit
```

You might then attempt to specialize these two classes to a class of Cows that
eat Grass:

```
class Grass extends Food
class Cow extends Animal:
  override def eat(food: Grass) = {} // This won't compile
```

However, if you tried to compile the new classes, you'd get the following
compilation errors:

```
2 |  class Cow extends Animal:
  |                 ^
  |class Cow needs to be abstract, since
  |def eat(food: Food): Unit is not defined (Note that Food
  |does not match Grass: class Grass is a subclass of class
  |Food, but method parameter types must match exactly.)
3 |    override def eat(food: Grass) = {} // This won't...
  |                      ^
  |      method eat has a different signature than the
  |      overridden declaration
```

What happened is that the eat method in class Cow did not override the eat method in class Animal because its parameter type is different: it's Grass in class Cow vs. Food in class Animal.

Some people have argued that the type system is unnecessarily strict in refusing these classes. They have said that it should be OK to specialize a parameter of a method in a subclass. However, if the classes were allowed as written, you could get yourself in unsafe situations very quickly.

For instance, the following script would pass the type checker:

```
class Food
abstract class Animal:
  def eat(food: Food): Unit

class Grass extends Food
class Cow extends Animal
  override def eat(food: Grass) = {} // This won't compile,
                                     // but if it did,...

class Fish extends Food
val bessy: Animal = new Cow
bessy.eat(new Fish)        // ...you could feed fish to cows.
```

The program would compile if the restriction were eased, because Cows are Animals and Animals do have an eat method that accepts any kind of Food, including Fish. But surely it would do a cow no good to eat a fish!

What you need to do instead is apply some more precise modeling. Animals do eat Food, but what kind of Food each Animal eats depends on the Animal. This can be neatly expressed with an abstract type, as shown in Listing 20.10:

```
class Food
abstract class Animal:
  type SuitableFood <: Food
  def eat(food: SuitableFood): Unit
```

Listing 20.10 · Modeling suitable food with an abstract type.

With the new class definition, an Animal can eat only food that's suitable. What food is suitable cannot be determined at the level of the Animal class. That's why SuitableFood is modeled as an abstract type. The type has an

409

upper bound, Food, which is expressed by the "<: Food" clause. This means that any concrete instantiation of SuitableFood (in a subclass of Animal) must be a subclass of Food. For example, you would not be able to instantiate SuitableFood with class IOException.

With Animal defined, you can now progress to cows, as shown in Listing 20.11. Class Cow fixes its SuitableFood to be Grass and also defines a concrete eat method for this kind of food.

```
class Grass extends Food
class Cow extends Animal:
  type SuitableFood = Grass
  override def eat(food: Grass) = {}
```

Listing 20.11 · Implementing an abstract type in a subclass.

These new class definitions compile without errors. If you tried to run the "cows-that-eat-fish" counterexample with the new class definitions, you would get the following compiler error:

```
class Fish extends Food
val bessy: Animal = new Cow

scala> bessy.eat(new Fish)
1 |bessy.eat(new Fish)
  |          ^^^^^^^^^
  |
  |          Found:    Fish
  |          Required: bessy.SuitableFood
```

20.7   Path-dependent types

Have a look at the last error message again. What's interesting about it is the type required by the eat method: bessy.SuitableFood. This type consists of an object reference, bessy, followed by a type field, SuitableFood, of the object. So this shows that objects in Scala can have types as members. The meaning of bessy.SuitableFood is "the type SuitableFood that is a member of the object referenced from bessy" or, alternatively, the type of food that's suitable for bessy.

A type like bessy.SuitableFood is called a *path-dependent type*. The word "path" here means a reference to an object. It could be a single name, such as bessy, or a longer access path, such as farm.barn.bessy, where each of farm, barn, and bessy are variables (or singleton object names) that refer to objects.

As the term "path-dependent type" implies, the type depends on the path; in general, different paths give rise to different types. For instance, say you defined classes DogFood and Dog, like this:

```
class DogFood extends Food
class Dog extends Animal:
  type SuitableFood = DogFood
  override def eat(food: DogFood) = {}
```

If you attempted to feed a dog with food fit for a cow, your code would not compile:

```
val bessy = new Cow
val lassie = new Dog

scala> lassie.eat(new bessy.SuitableFood)
1 |lassie.eat(new bessy.SuitableFood)
  |            ^^^^^^^^^^^^^^^^^^^^^^
  |             Found:    Grass
  |             Required: DogFood
```

The problem here is that the type of the SuitableFood object passed to the eat method, bessy.SuitableFood, is incompatible with the parameter type of eat, lassie.SuitableFood.

The case would be different for two Dogs. Because Dog's SuitableFood type is defined to be an alias for class DogFood, the SuitableFood types of two Dogs are in fact the same. As a result, the Dog instance named lassie could actually eat the suitable food of a different Dog instance (which we'll name bootsie):

```
val bootsie = new Dog
lassie.eat(new bootsie.SuitableFood)
```

A path-dependent type resembles the syntax for an inner class type in Java, but there is a crucial difference: a path-dependent type names an outer

411

object, whereas an inner class type names an outer *class*. Java-style inner class types can also be expressed in Scala, but they are written differently. Consider these two classes, `Outer` and `Inner`:

```
class Outer:
  class Inner
```

In Scala, the inner class is addressed using the expression `Outer#Inner` instead of Java's `Outer.Inner`. The '.' syntax is reserved for objects. For example, imagine you instantiate two objects of type `Outer`, like this:

```
val o1 = new Outer
val o2 = new Outer
```

Here `o1.Inner` and `o2.Inner` are two path-dependent types (and they are different types). Both of these types conform to (are subtypes of) the more general type `Outer#Inner`, which represents the `Inner` class with an *arbitrary* outer object of type `Outer`. By contrast, type `o1.Inner` refers to the `Inner` class with a *specific* outer object (the one referenced from `o1`). Likewise, type `o2.Inner` refers to the `Inner` class with a different, specific outer object (the one referenced from `o2`).

In Scala, as in Java, inner class instances hold a reference to an enclosing outer class instance. This allows an inner class, for example, to access members of its outer class. Thus you can't instantiate an inner class without in some way specifying an outer class instance. One way to do this is to instantiate the inner class inside the body of the outer class. In this case, the current outer class instance (referenced from `this`) will be used.

Another way is to use a path-dependent type. For example, because the type, `o1.Inner`, names a specific outer object, you can instantiate it:

```
new o1.Inner
```

The resulting inner object will contain a reference to its outer object, the object referenced from `o1`. By contrast, because the type `Outer#Inner` does not name any specific instance of `Outer`, you can't create an instance of it:

```
scala> new Outer#Inner
1 |new Outer#Inner
  |    ^^^^^^^^^^^
  |    Outer is not a valid class prefix, since it is
  |    not an immutable path
```

412

20.8 Refinement types

When a class inherits from another, the first class is said to be a *nominal* subtype of the other one. It's a *nominal* subtype because each type has a *name*, and the names are explicitly declared to have a subtyping relationship. Scala additionally supports *structural* subtyping, where you get a subtyping relationship simply because two types have compatible members. To get structural subtyping in Scala, use Scala's *refinement types*.

Nominal subtyping is usually more convenient, so you should try nominal types first with any new design. A name is a single short identifier and thus is more concise than an explicit listing of member types. Further, structural subtyping is often more flexible than you want. A widget can draw(), and a Western cowboy can draw(), but they aren't really substitutable. You'd typically prefer to get a compilation error if you tried to substitute a cowboy for a widget.

Nonetheless, structural subtyping has its own advantages. One is that sometimes there really is no more to a type than its members. For example, suppose you want to define a Pasture class that can contain animals that eat grass. One option would be to define a trait AnimalThatEatsGrass and mix it into every class where it applies. It would be verbose, however. Class Cow has already declared that it's an animal and that it eats grass, and now it would have to declare that it is also an animal-that-eats-grass.

Instead of defining AnimalThatEatsGrass, you can use a refinement type. Simply write the base type, Animal, followed by a sequence of members listed in curly braces. The members in the curly braces further specify— or refine, if you will—the types of members from the base class.

Here is how you write the type, "animal that eats grass":

```
Animal { type SuitableFood = Grass }
```

Given this type, you can now write the pasture class like this:

```
class Pasture:
  var animals: List[Animal { type SuitableFood = Grass }] = Nil
  // ...
```

20.9   Case study: Currencies

The rest of this chapter presents a case study that explains how abstract types can be used in Scala. The task is to design a class `Currency`. A typical instance of `Currency` would represent an amount of money in dollars, euros, yen, or some other currency. It should be possible to do some arithmetic on currencies. For instance, you should be able to add two amounts of the same currency. Or you should be able to multiply a currency amount by a factor representing an interest rate.

These thoughts lead to the following first design for a currency class:

```
// A first (faulty) design of the Currency class
abstract class Currency:
  val amount: Long
  def designation: String
  override def toString = s"$amount $designation"
  def + (that: Currency): Currency = ...
  def * (x: Double): Currency = ...
```

The `amount` of a currency is the number of currency units it represents. This is a field of type `Long` so that very large amounts of money, such as the market capitalization of Google or Apple, can be represented. It's left abstract here, waiting to be defined when a subclass talks about concrete amounts of money. The `designation` of a currency is a string that identifies it. The `toString` method of class `Currency` indicates an amount and a designation. It would yield results such as:

```
79 USD
11000 Yen
99 Euro
```

Finally, there are methods + for adding currencies and * for multiplying a currency with a floating-point number. You can create a concrete currency value by supplying concrete `amount` and `designation` values, like this:

```
new Currency:
  val amount = 79L
  def designation = "USD"
```

This design would be OK if all we wanted to model was a single currency, like only dollars or only euros. But it fails if we need to deal with several currencies. Assume that you model dollars and euros as two subclasses of class currency:

```
abstract class Dollar extends Currency:
  def designation = "USD"
```

```
abstract class Euro extends Currency:
  def designation = "Euro"
```

At first glance this looks reasonable. But it would let you add dollars to euros. The result of such an addition would be of type Currency. But it would be a funny currency that was made up of a mix of euros and dollars. What you want instead is a more specialized version of the + method. When implemented in class Dollar, it should take Dollar arguments and yield a Dollar result; when implemented in class Euro, it should take Euro arguments and yield a Euro result. So the type of the addition method would change depending on which class you are in. Nonetheless, you would like to write the addition method just once, not each time a new currency is defined.

In Scala, there's a simple technique to deal with situations like this. If something is not known at the point where a class is defined, make it abstract in the class. This applies to both values and types. In the case of currencies, the exact argument and result type of the addition method are not known, so it is a good candidate for an abstract type.

This would lead to the following sketch of class AbstractCurrency:

```
// A second (still imperfect) design of the Currency class
abstract class AbstractCurrency:
  type Currency <: AbstractCurrency
  val amount: Long
  def designation: String
  override def toString = s"$amount $designation"
  def + (that: Currency): Currency = ...
  def * (x: Double): Currency = ...
```

The only differences from the previous situation are that the class is now called AbstractCurrency, and that it contains an abstract type Currency, which represents the real currency in question. Each concrete subclass of

AbstractCurrency would need to fix the Currency type to refer to the concrete subclass itself, thereby "tying the knot."

For instance, here is a new version of class Dollar, which now extends class AbstractCurrency:

```
abstract class Dollar extends AbstractCurrency:
  type Currency = Dollar
  def designation = "USD"
```

This design is workable, but it is still not perfect. One problem is hidden by the ellipses that indicate the missing method definitions of + and * in class AbstractCurrency. In particular, how should addition be implemented in this class? It's easy enough to calculate the correct amount of the new currency as this.amount + that.amount, but how would you convert the amount into a currency of the right type?

You might try something like:

```
def + (that: Currency): Currency =
  new Currency:
    val amount = this.amount + that.amount
```

However, this would not compile:

```
7 |      new Currency:
  |          ^^^^^^^^
  |          AbstractCurrency.this.Currency is not a class type
8 |        val amount = this.amount + that.amount
  |                          ^
  |                          Recursive value amount needs type
```

One of the restrictions of Scala's treatment of abstract types is that you can neither create an instance of an abstract type nor have an abstract type as a supertype of another class. So the compiler would refuse the example code here that attempted to instantiate Currency.

However, you can work around this restriction using a *factory method*. Instead of creating an instance of an abstract type directly, declare an abstract method that does it. Then, wherever the abstract type is fixed to be some concrete type, you also need to give a concrete implementation of the factory method. For class AbstractCurrency, this would look as follows:

```
abstract class AbstractCurrency:
  type Currency <: AbstractCurrency // abstract type
  def make(amount: Long): Currency  // factory method
  ...                               // rest of class
```

A design like this could be made to work, but it looks rather suspicious.
Why place the factory method *inside* class `AbstractCurrency`? This looks
dubious for at least two reasons. First, if you have some amount of currency
(say, one dollar), you also hold in your hand the ability to make more of the
same currency, using code such as:

```
myDollar.make(100)  // here are a hundred more!
```

In the age of color copying this might be a tempting scenario, but hopefully
not one which you would be able to do for very long without being caught.
The second problem with this code is that you can make more `Currency`
objects if you already have a reference to a `Currency` object. But how do
you get the first object of a given `Currency`? You'd need another creation
method, which does essentially the same job as `make`. So you have a case of
code duplication, which is a sure sign of a code smell.

The solution, of course, is to move the abstract type and the factory
method outside class `AbstractCurrency`. You need to create another class
that contains the `AbstractCurrency` class, the `Currency` type, and the make
factory method.

We'll call this a `CurrencyZone`:

```
abstract class CurrencyZone:
  type Currency <: AbstractCurrency
  def make(x: Long): Currency
  abstract class AbstractCurrency:
    val amount: Long
    def designation: String
    override def toString = s"$amount $designation"
    def + (that: Currency): Currency =
      make(this.amount + that.amount)
    def * (x: Double): Currency =
      make((this.amount * x).toLong)
```

An example concrete `CurrencyZone` is the US, which could be defined as:

417

```
object US extends CurrencyZone:
  abstract class Dollar extends AbstractCurrency:
    def designation = "USD"

  type Currency = Dollar
  def make(x: Long) = new Dollar { val amount = x }
```

Here, US is an object that extends CurrencyZone. It defines a class Dollar, which is a subclass of AbstractCurrency. So the type of money in this zone is US.Dollar. The US object also fixes the type Currency to be an alias for Dollar, and it gives an implementation of the make factory method to return a dollar amount.

This is a workable design. There are only a few refinements to be added. The first refinement concerns subunits. So far, every currency was measured in a single unit: dollars, euros, or yen. However, most currencies have subunits: For instance, in the US, it's dollars and cents. The most straightforward way to model cents is to have the amount field in US.Currency represent cents instead of dollars. To convert back to dollars, it's useful to introduce a field CurrencyUnit into class CurrencyZone, which contains the amount of one standard unit in that currency:

```
abstract class CurrencyZone:
  ...
  val CurrencyUnit: Currency
```

As shown in Listing 20.12, The US object could define the quantities Cent, Dollar, and CurrencyUnit. This definition is just like the previous definition of the US object, except that it adds three new fields. The field Cent represents an amount of 1 US.Currency. It's an object analogous to a one-cent coin. The field Dollar represents an amount of 100 US.Currency. So the US object now defines the name Dollar in two ways. The *type* Dollar (defined by the abstract inner class named Dollar) represents the generic name of the Currency valid in the US currency zone. By contrast, the *value* Dollar (referenced from the val field named Dollar) represents a single US dollar, analogous to a one-dollar bill. The third field definition of CurrencyUnit specifies that the standard currency unit in the US zone is the Dollar (*i.e.*, the value Dollar, referenced from the field, not the type Dollar).

The toString method in class AbstractCurrency also needs to be adapted to take subunits into account. For instance, the sum of ten dollars and twenty three cents should print as a decimal number: 10.23 USD. To achieve this, you could implement AbstractCurrency's toString method as follows:

```
override def toString =
  ((amount.toDouble / CurrencyUnit.amount.toDouble)
    .formatted(s"%.${decimals(CurrencyUnit.amount)}f")
  + " " + designation)
```

Here, formatted is a method that Scala makes available on several classes, including Double.[1] The formatted method returns the string that results from formatting the original Double on which formatted was invoked according to a format string passed as the formatted method's right-hand operand. The syntax of format strings passed to formatted is the same as that of Java's String.format method.

```
object US extends CurrencyZone:
  abstract class Dollar extends AbstractCurrency:
    def designation = "USD"
  type Currency = Dollar
  def make(cents: Long) =
    new Dollar:
      val amount = cents
  val Cent = make(1)
  val Dollar = make(100)
  val CurrencyUnit = Dollar
```

Listing 20.12 · The US currency zone.

For instance, the format string %.2f formats a number with two decimal digits. The format string used in the toString shown previously is assembled by calling the decimals method on CurrencyUnit.amount. This method returns the number of decimal digits of a decimal power minus one. For instance, decimals(10) is 1, decimals(100) is 2, and so on. The decimals method is implemented by a simple recursion:

```
private def decimals(n: Long): Int =
  if n == 1 then 0 else 1 + decimals(n / 10)
```

---

[1] Scala uses rich wrappers, described in Section 5.10, to make formatted available.

Listing 20.13 shows some other currency zones. As another refinement, you can add a currency conversion feature to the model. First, you could write a `Converter` object that contains applicable exchange rates between currencies, as shown in Listing 20.14. Then, you could add a conversion method, `from`, to class `AbstractCurrency`, which converts from a given source currency into the current `Currency` object:

```
def from(other: CurrencyZone#AbstractCurrency): Currency =
  make(math.round(
    other.amount.toDouble * Converter.exchangeRate
      (other.designation)(this.designation)))
```

The `from` method takes an arbitrary currency as argument. This is expressed by its formal parameter type, `CurrencyZone#AbstractCurrency`, which indicates that the argument passed as `other` must be an `AbstractCurrency` type in some arbitrary and unknown `CurrencyZone`. It produces its result by multiplying the amount of the `other` currency with the exchange rate between the other and the current currency.[2]

The final version of the `CurrencyZone` class is shown in Listing 20.15. You can try the class out by typing commands into the Scala REPL. We'll assume that the `CurrencyZone` class and all concrete `CurrencyZone` objects are defined in a package `org.stairwaybook.currencies`. The first step is to import "`org.stairwaybook.currencies.*`" into the REPL. Then you can do some currency conversions:

```
scala> val yen = Japan.Yen.from(US.Dollar * 100)
val yen: Japan.Currency = 10470 JPY

scala> val euros = Europe.Euro.from(yen)
val euros: Europe.Currency = 85.03 EUR

scala> val dollars = US.Dollar.from(euros)
val dollars: US.Currency = 100.08 USD
```

The fact that we obtain almost the same amount after three conversions implies that these are some pretty good exchange rates! You can also add up values of the same currency:

---

[2]By the way, in case you think you're getting a bad deal on Japanese yen, the exchange rates convert currencies based on their `CurrencyZone` amounts. Thus, 1.211 is the exchange rate between US cents and Japanese yen.

```
object Europe extends CurrencyZone:
  abstract class Euro extends AbstractCurrency:
    def designation = "EUR"

  type Currency = Euro
  def make(cents: Long) =
    new Euro:
      val amount = cents

  val Cent = make(1)
  val Euro = make(100)
  val CurrencyUnit = Euro
object Japan extends CurrencyZone:
  abstract class Yen extends AbstractCurrency:
    def designation = "JPY"

  type Currency = Yen
  def make(yen: Long) =
    new Yen:
      val amount = yen

  val Yen = make(1)
  val CurrencyUnit = Yen
```

Listing 20.13 · Currency zones for Europe and Japan.

```
scala> US.Dollar * 100 + dollars
res3: US.Currency = 200.08 USD
```

On the other hand, you cannot add amounts of different currencies:

```
scala> US.Dollar + Europe.Euro
1 |US.Dollar + Europe.Euro
  |            ^^^^^^^^^^^
  |Found:    (Europe.Euro : Europe.Currency)
  |Required: US.Currency(2)
  |where:    Currency  is a type in object Europe which
  |          is an alias of Europe.Euro
  |          Currency(2) is a type in object US which is
  |          an alias of US.Dollar
```

```
object Converter:
  var exchangeRate =
    Map(
      "USD" -> Map("USD" -> 1.0, "EUR" -> 0.8498,
                   "JPY" -> 1.047, "CHF" -> 0.9149),
      "EUR" -> Map("USD" -> 1.177, "EUR" -> 1.0,
                   "JPY" -> 1.232, "CHF" -> 1.0765),
      "JPY" -> Map("USD" -> 0.9554, "EUR" -> 0.8121,
                   "JPY" -> 1.0, "CHF" -> 0.8742),
      "CHF" -> Map("USD" -> 1.093, "EUR" -> 0.9289,
                   "JPY" -> 1.144, "CHF" -> 1.0)
    )
```

Listing 20.14 · A converter object with an exchange rates map.

By preventing the addition of two values with different units (in this case, currencies), the type abstraction has done its job. It prevents us from performing calculations that are unsound. Failures to convert correctly between different units may seem like trivial bugs, but they have caused many serious systems faults. An example is the crash of the Mars Climate Orbiter spacecraft on September 23, 1999, which was caused because one engineering team used metric units while another used English units. If units had been coded in the same way as currencies are coded in this chapter, this error would have been detected by a simple compilation run. Instead, it caused the crash of the orbiter after a near ten-month voyage.

20.10   Conclusion

Scala offers systematic and very general support for object-oriented abstraction. It enables you to not only abstract over methods, but also over values, variables, and types. This chapter has shown how to take advantage of abstract members. They support a simple yet effective principle for systems structuring: when designing a class, make everything that is not yet known into an abstract member. The type system will then drive the development of your model, just as you saw with the currency case study. It does not matter whether the unknown is a type, method, variable or value. In Scala, all of these can be declared abstract.

```
abstract class CurrencyZone:

  type Currency <: AbstractCurrency
  def make(x: Long): Currency

  abstract class AbstractCurrency:

    val amount: Long
    def designation: String

    def + (that: Currency): Currency =
      make(this.amount + that.amount)
    def * (x: Double): Currency =
      make((this.amount * x).toLong)
    def - (that: Currency): Currency =
      make(this.amount - that.amount)
    def / (that: Double) =
      make((this.amount / that).toLong)
    def / (that: Currency) =
      this.amount.toDouble / that.amount

    def from(other: CurrencyZone#AbstractCurrency): Currency =
      make(math.round(
        other.amount.toDouble * Converter.exchangeRate
          (other.designation)(this.designation)))

    private def decimals(n: Long): Int =
      if (n == 1) 0 else 1 + decimals(n / 10)

    override def toString =
      ((amount.toDouble / CurrencyUnit.amount.toDouble)
        .formatted(s"%.${decimals(CurrencyUnit.amount)}f")
        + " " + designation)

  end AbstractCurrency

  val CurrencyUnit: Currency
end CurrencyZone
```

Listing 20.15 · The full code of class CurrencyZone.

Chapter 21

Givens

Often the behavior of a function depends on the context in which the function is called. For example, a function's behavior may depend on contextual data such as system properties, security permissions, an authenticated user, a database transaction, or a configured timeout. A function may also depend on contextual *behavior*—an algorithm that makes sense in the context where the function is called. For example, a sort function may rely on a comparison algorithm to determine how to order elements while sorting. Different contexts may call for different comparison algorithms.

Many techniques exist for getting such contextual information and behavior to a function, but functional programming has traditionally had one answer: pass everything as parameters. Although this approach works fine, it comes with a tradeoff: The more you parameterize a function with data and algorithms, the more general and useful the function becomes, but that generality requires more arguments to be specified at every invocation of the function. Unfortunately, passing everything in as parameters can quickly lead to repetitive, boilerplate code.

This chapter describes *context parameters*, which are often simply called "givens." This feature enables you to leave out certain arguments when you invoke functions, relying on the compiler to fill in appropriate values for each context based on the types.

21.1 How it works

The compiler will sometimes replace someCall(a) with someCall(a)(b), or new SomeClass(a) with new SomeClass(a)(b), thereby adding one or

425

more missing parameter lists to complete a function call. Entire curried parameter lists are supplied, not individual parameters. For example, if someCall's missing parameter list takes three parameters, the compiler can replace someCall(a) with someCall(a)(b, c, d). For this usage, the inserted identifiers, such as b, c, and d in (b, c, d), must be marked as given where they are defined, and the parameter list in someCall's or someClass's definition itself must begin with using.

As an example, suppose you have many methods that take a shell prompt string (such as, say "$ " or "> ") that is preferred by the current user. You can reduce boilerplate code by making the prompt a context parameter. The first step is to make a special type that encapsulates the preferred prompt string:

```
class PreferredPrompt(val preference: String)
```

Next, refactor each method that takes the prompt by placing the parameter into a separate parameter list marked with the using keyword. For example, the following Greeter object has a greet method that takes a PreferredPrompt as a context parameter:

```
object Greeter:
  def greet(name: String)(using prompt: PreferredPrompt) =
    println(s"Welcome, $name. The system is ready.")
    println(prompt.preference)
```

To enable the compiler to supply the context parameter implicitly, you must define a given instance of the expected type, in this case PreferredPrompt, using the given keyword. You could do this, for example, in a preferences object, like this:

```
object JillsPrefs:
  given prompt: PreferredPrompt =
    PreferredPrompt("Your wish> ")
```

The compiler can now supply this PreferredPrompt implicitly, but it will not do so unless it is in scope, as shown here:

```
scala> Greeter.greet("Jill")
1 |Greeter.greet("Jill")
  |                           ^
  |no implicit argument of type PreferredPrompt was found
  |for parameter prompt of method greet in object Greeter
```

Once you bring it into scope via an import, however, it will be used to supply the missing parameter list:

```
scala> import JillsPrefs.prompt

scala> Greeter.greet("Jill")
Welcome, Jill. The system is ready.
Your wish>
```

Because prompt is declared as a context parameter, if you try to pass the argument in explicitly in the usual way, it won't compile:

```
scala> Greeter.greet("Jill")(JillsPrefs.prompt)
1 |Greeter.greet("Jill")(JillsPrefs.prompt)
  |^^^^^^^^^^^^^^^^^^^^^^
  |method greet in object Greeter does not take more
  |parameters
```

You must instead indicate you want to fill in a context parameter explicitly with the using keyword at the call site, like this:

```
scala> Greeter.greet("Jill")(using JillsPrefs.prompt)
Welcome, Jill. The system is ready.
Your wish>
```

Note that the using keyword applies to an entire parameter list, not to individual parameters. Listing 21.1 shows an example in which the second parameter list of Greeter's greet method, which is again marked using, has two parameters: prompt (of type PreferredPrompt) and drink (of type PreferredDrink).

Singleton object JoesPrefs declares two given instances: prompt of type PreferredPrompt and drink of type PreferredDrink. As before, however, so long as these are not in scope as single identifiers, they won't be used to fill in a missing parameter list to greet:

```
scala> Greeter.greet("Joe")
1 |Greeter.greet("Joe")
  |                    ^
  |no implicit argument of type PreferredPrompt was found
  |for parameter prompt of method greet in object Greeter
```

```scala
class PreferredPrompt(val preference: String)
class PreferredDrink(val preference: String)

object Greeter:
  def greet(name: String)(using prompt: PreferredPrompt,
      drink: PreferredDrink) =

    println(s"Welcome, $name. The system is ready.")
    print("But while you work, ")
    println(s"why not enjoy a cup of ${drink.preference}?")
    println(prompt.preference)

object JoesPrefs:
  given prompt: PreferredPrompt =
    PreferredPrompt("relax> ")
  given drink: PreferredDrink =
    PreferredDrink("tea")
```

Listing 21.1 · An implicit parameter list with multiple parameters.

You can bring both givens into scope with an import:

```scala
scala> import JoesPrefs.{prompt, drink}
```

Because both `prompt` and `drink` are now in scope as single identifiers, you can use them to supply the last parameter list explicitly, like this:

```scala
scala> Greeter.greet("Joe")(using prompt, drink)
Welcome, Joe. The system is ready.
But while you work, why not enjoy a cup of tea?
relax>
```

And because all the rules for context parameters are now met, you can alternatively let the Scala compiler supply `prompt` and `drink` for you by leaving off that entire parameter list:

```scala
scala> Greeter.greet("Joe")
Welcome, Joe. The system is ready.
But while you work, why not enjoy a cup of tea?
relax>
```

428

One thing to note about the previous examples is that we didn't use String as the type of prompt or drink, even though ultimately it was a String that each of them provided through their preference fields. Because the compiler selects context parameters by matching types of parameters against types of given instances, context parameters should have "rare" or "special" enough types that accidental matches are unlikely. For example, the types PreferredPrompt and PreferredDrink in Listing 21.1 were defined solely to serve as context parameter types. As a result, it is unlikely that given instances of these types will exist if they aren't intended to be used as context parameters for methods like greet.

21.2 Parameterized given types

Context parameters are perhaps most often used to provide information about a type mentioned *explicitly* in an earlier parameter list, similar to the type classes of Haskell. This is an important way to achieve *ad hoc polymorphism* when writing functions in Scala: Your functions can be applied to values whose types make sense, but don't compile when applied to values of any other types. As an example, consider the two-line insertion sort shown in Listing 14.1 on page page 274. This definition of isort only works for a list of integers. To sort other types of lists, you need to make isort's argument type more general. To do that, the first step is to introduce a type parameter, T, and replace Ints with Ts in the List's parameter type, like this:

```
// Does not compile.
def isort[T](xs: List[T]): List[T] =
  if xs.isEmpty then Nil
  else insert(xs.head, isort(xs.tail))

def insert[T](x: T, xs: List[T]): List[T] =
  if xs.isEmpty || x <= xs.head then x :: xs
  else xs.head :: insert(x, xs.tail)
```

If you try to compile isort after this change, however, you will be greeted with the following compiler message:

```
6 |  if xs.isEmpty || x <= xs.head then x :: xs
  |                     ^^^^
  |                     value <= is not a member of T, ...
```

While the Int class defines a <= method that determines whether an integer is less than or equal to another integer, other types may require different comparison strategies, or may not be comparable at all. For isort to operate on lists with elements of types other than Int, it needs a bit more information to decide how to compare two elements.

To solve that problem, you can supply isort with a less-than-or-equal function suitable for the type of the List. That less-than-or-equal function must consume two instances of T and return a Boolean indicating whether the first T instance is less than or equal to the second instance:

```
def isort[T](xs: List[T])(lteq: (T, T) => Boolean): List[T] =
  if xs.isEmpty then Nil
  else insert(xs.head, isort(xs.tail)(lteq))(lteq)

def insert[T](x: T, xs: List[T])
    (lteq: (T, T) => Boolean): List[T] =
  if xs.isEmpty || lteq(x, xs.head) then x :: xs
  else xs.head :: insert(x, xs.tail)(lteq)
```

Instead of <=, the insert helper function now uses the lteq parameter to compare two elements during the sort. Passing the comparison function into isort makes it possible to sort a list of any type T so long as you provide a comparator function suitable for T. For example, you could use this version of isort to sort lists of Int, String, and the Rational class shown in Listing 6.5 on page 109, as shown here:

```
isort(List(4, -10, 10))((x: Int, y: Int) => x <= y)
// List(-10, 4, 10)

isort(List("cherry", "blackberry", "apple", "pear"))
    ((x: String, y: String) => x.compareTo(y) <= 0)
// List(apple, blackberry, cherry, pear)

isort(List(Rational(7, 8), Rational(5, 6), Rational(1, 2)))
    ((x: Rational, y: Rational) =>
        x.numer * y.denom <= x.denom * y.numer)
// List(1/2, 5/6, 7/8)
```

As described in Section 14.10, the Scala compiler infers parameter types one parameter list at a time, starting from left to right. Thus the compiler can infer the type of x and y, which are specified in a second parameter list, based on the element type T of the List[T] passed in the first parameter list:

```
isort(List(4, -10, 10))((x, y) => x <= y)
// List(-10, 4, 10)

isort(List("cherry", "blackberry", "apple", "pear"))
    ((x, y) => x.compareTo(y) < 1)
// List(apple, blackberry, cherry, pear)

isort(List(Rational(7, 8), Rational(5, 6), Rational(1, 2)))
    ((x, y) => x.numer * y.denom <= x.denom * y.numer)
// List(1/2, 5/6, 7/8)
```

The isort function is now more generally useful, but that generality comes at the cost of increased verbosity: At each invocation you need to supply the comparison function, and isort's definition must now pass that comparison function into every recursive invocation of isort, as well as into every invocation of the insert helper function. This isort is no longer the simple expression of a sort it once was.

If you make isort's comparison function a context parameter, you can reduce verbosity both in the implementation of isort and at its call sites. While you *could* make (Int, Int) => Boolean a context parameter, doing so would not be ideal, because the type is too general. Your program may have many functions that take two integers and return a boolean, for example, but which have nothing to do with sorting those integers. Since the lookup of given values occurs by type, you should try to ensure that the type of your given expresses the intent of the given.

Defining types specific to a purpose, such as sorting, is generally good practice, but as mentioned previously, specific types are especially important when using context parameters. In addition to ensuring that the correct given is used, carefully defined types can help you more clearly communicate intent. They also allow you to grow your programs incrementally, by enriching your type with more functionality without breaking existing contracts between types. You could define a type for the purpose of deciding the ordering of two elements as follows:

```
trait Ord[T]:
  def compare(x: T, y: T): Int
  def lteq(x: T, y: T): Boolean = compare(x, y) < 1
```

431

This trait implements a less-than-or-equal function in terms of a more general abstract `compare` method. The `compare`'s contract is that it returns 0 if the two parameters are equal, a positive integer if the first parameter is greater than the second, and a negative integer if the second parameter is greater. With this definition, you can now take an `Ord[T]` as a context parameter to specify a comparison strategy for T, as shown in Listing 21.2.

```
def isort[T](xs: List[T])(using ord: Ord[T]): List[T] =
  if xs.isEmpty then Nil
  else insert(xs.head, isort(xs.tail))

def insert[T](x: T, xs: List[T])
      (using ord: Ord[T]): List[T] =
  if xs.isEmpty || ord.lteq(x, xs.head) then x :: xs
  else xs.head :: insert(x, xs.tail)
```

Listing 21.2 · Context parameters passed with `using`.

As described previously, you designate parameters as being available for implicit passing by prefixing those parameters with `using`. With that in place, you no longer have to explicitly provide the parameters when invoking the function: If a `given` value of the required parameter type is available, the compiler will *use* that value and pass it into your function. To designate a value as the given value of a type, you declare it with the `given` keyword.

A good home for "natural" givens, which represent a natural way to do something with a type, such as sorting integers in forward numerical order, is the companion object of an "involved" type. For example, a good home for a natural given instance of `Ord[Int]` would be the companion object for either `Ord` or `Int`, the two types that are "involved" in type `Ord[Int]`. If the compiler does not find a given `Ord[Int]` in lexical scope, it will as a second step look in those two companion objects. Since you can't change the `Int` companion, the best home is in the `Ord` companion:

```
object Ord:
  // (Not yet idiomatic)
  given intOrd: Ord[Int] =
    new Ord[Int]:
      def compare(x: Int, y: Int) =
        if x == y then 0 else if x > y then 1 else -1
```

432

All of the examples of given declarations shown so far in this chapter are called *alias givens*. The name to the left of the equals sign is an alias for the value to the right. Because it is common to define an anonymous instance of a trait or class to the right of the equals sign when declaring an alias given, Scala offers a shorthand syntax that replaces the equals sign and the "new class name" portion of the alias given with just the keyword `with`.[1] Listing 21.3 shows `intOrd` defined using this more concise syntax.

```scala
object Ord:
  // This is idiomatic
  given intOrd: Ord[Int] with
    def compare(x: Int, y: Int) =
      if x == y then 0 else if x > y then 1 else -1
```

Listing 21.3 · Declaring a natural given in a companion.

With a given `Ord[Int]` defined in object `Ord`, sorting with `isort` becomes concise again:

```scala
isort(List(10, 2, -10))
// List(-10, 2, 10)
```

When you omit the second parameter to `isort`, the compiler looks for a given value it can pass as that second parameter based on the parameter's type. For sorting `Int`s, that parameter type is `Ord[Int]`. Although the compiler will first look in lexical scope for a given `Ord[Int]`, if it does not find any, it will look as a second step in the companion objects of the involved types `Ord` and `Int`. Because the given value `intOrd` in Listing 21.3 has that exact type, it will fill in the missing parameter list with `intOrd`.

To sort strings, all you have to do is provide a given value for the string comparison parameter:

```scala
// Added to object Ord
given stringOrd: Ord[String] with
  def compare(s: String, t: String) = s.compareTo(t)
```

With a given `Ord[String]` declared in the `Ord` companion, you can now use `isort` to sort lists of strings:

---

[1]This use of `with` differs from the one described in Chapter 11 for mixing together traits.

```
isort(List("mango", "jackfruit", "durian"))
// List(durian, jackfruit, mango)
```

If a given declaration does not take value parameters, then that given is initialized the first time it's accessed, similar to a lazy val. That initialization is performed in a thread-safe manner. If a given does take parameters, then a new given is created on every access, much like how a def behaves. Indeed, the Scala compiler transforms givens to lazy vals or defs, additionally marking them as being available for using parameters.

21.3 Anonymous givens

Although you can think of a given declaration as a special kind of lazy val or def, givens differ from these in an important aspect. When declaring a val, for example, you provide a term that refers to that val's value:

```
val age = 42
```

In this expression, the compiler must infer the type of age. Because age is initialized with 42, which the compiler knows is an Int, the compiler will decide the type of age is Int. In effect, you provide a *term*, age, and the compiler inferred the type of that term, Int.

With context parameters, it goes the other way: You provide a type, and the compiler synthesizes a term for you to represent that type, based on the available givens, and uses that term implicitly when the type is required. That is referred to as *term inference*, to distinguish it from type inference.

Because the compiler looks for givens by type, and you often don't need to refer to a given's term at all, you can declare your given value anonymously. Instead of:

```
given revIntOrd: Ord[Int] with
  def compare(x: Int, y: Int) =
    if x == y then 0 else if x > y then -1 else 1

given revStringOrd: Ord[String] with
  def compare(s: String, t: String) = -s.compareTo(t)
```

You can write:

```
given Ord[Int] with
  def compare(x: Int, y: Int) =
    if x == y then 0 else if x > y then -1 else 1
given Ord[String] with
  def compare(s: String, t: String) = -s.compareTo(t)
```

For these anonymous givens, the compiler would synthesize a name for you. In the isort function, the second parameter would be filled in with that synthesized value, which would then become available inside the function. Thus if all you care about is that a given will be provided implicitly as context parameters, you need not declare a term for it.

21.4 Parameterized givens as typeclasses

You can provide a given Ord[T] for any type T you wish to sort. You could, for example, enable lists of instances of the Rational class shown in Listing 6.5 to be sorted by defining a given Ord[Rational]. Because it represents a natural way to sort rational numbers, the Rational companion object would be a good home for this given instance:

```
object Rational:
  given rationalOrd: Ord[Rational] with
    def compare(x: Rational, y: Rational) =
      if x.numer * y.denom < x.denom * y.numer then -1
      else if x.numer * y.denom > x.denom * y.numer then 1
      else 0
```

Now you can sort lists of Rational:

```
isort(List(Rational(4, 5), Rational(1, 2), Rational(2, 3)))
// List(1/2, 2/3, 4/5)
```

According to the Liskov substitution principle, an object can be replaced with its subtype without altering the desirable properties of the program. That's at the core of object-oriented programming's subtype-supertype relationship. In the latest version of isort, shown in Listing 21.2, it appears that you can replace a list of Strings with a list of Ints or a list of Rationals, and isort still works as expected. That suggests that Ints, Rationals, and

435

Strings may share some common supertype, such as some "sortable" type.[2] However, they share no such common supertype: Moreover, defining a *new* supertype for types like Int or String would be impossible because they are part of the Java and Scala standard libraries.

Offering given instances of Ord[T] grants those specific types, T, membership into a set of "types that can be sorted," despite not sharing any common sortable supertype. This set of types is called a *typeclass*.[3] For example, at this point the Ord typeclass is comprised of three types—Int, String, and Rational—the set of types, T, for which given Ord[T] instances exist. Chapter 23 gives several more examples of typeclasses. Because the isort implementation shown in Listing 21.2 takes a context parameter of type Ord[T], it is an example of ad hoc polymorphism: isort can sort lists of certain types, T—the types for which given Ord[T] instances exist—and doesn't compile for any other types. Ad hoc polymorphism with typeclasses is an important, commonly used technique in idiomatic Scala programming.

Scala's standard library provides ready-made typeclasses for a variety of purposes, such as defining equality or specifying the ordering of elements when sorting. The Ord typeclass used in this chapter is a partial reimplementation of Scala's math.Ordering typeclass. The Scala library defines Ordering typeclass instances for common types, such as Ints and Strings.

A version of isort using the Scala Ordering typeclass is shown in Listing 21.4. Note that the context parameter for this version of isort does not have a parameter name. It is just the keyword using followed by the parameter type, Ordering[T]. This is called an *anonymous parameter*. Because the parameter is only used implicitly in the function (it is implicitly passed to insert and isort), Scala does not require that you give it a name.

As another example of ad hoc polymorphism, consider once again the orderedMergeSort method shown in Listing 18.11 on page 383. This sort method can sort lists of any type T so long as T is a subtype of Ordered[T]. This is called *subtyping polymorphism*, and as illustrated in Section 18.7, the upper bound of Ordered[T] means that you can't use orderedMergeSort on lists of Ints or Strings. By contrast, you can sort lists of Ints and Strings with the msort shown in Listing 21.5, because the Ordering[T] it requires forms a *separate* hierarchy distinct from T. Although you can't

---

[2] The Ordered trait described in Sections 11.2 and 18.7 is such a sortable type.

[3] In "typeclass," the word "class" does not refer to an object-oriented class. Instead, it refers to the set (or class, in the usual English sense of the word) of types for which given instances of a particular (object-oriented) class or trait exist.

```
def isort[T](xs: List[T])(using Ordering[T]): List[T] =
  if xs.isEmpty then Nil
  else insert(xs.head, isort(xs.tail))

def insert[T](x: T, xs: List[T])
    (using ord: Ordering[T]): List[T] =
  if xs.isEmpty || ord.lteq(x, xs.head) then x :: xs
  else xs.head :: insert(x, xs.tail)
```

Listing 21.4 · An insertion sort function that uses Ordering.

change Int to make it extend Ordered[Int], you can define and offer a given Ordering[Int].

Both the isort function shown in Listing 21.4 and the msort function shown in Listing 21.5 are examples of using a context parameter to provide more information about a type mentioned explicitly in an earlier parameter list. To be specific, the context parameter of type Ordering[T] provides more information about type T—in this case, how to order Ts. Type T is mentioned in List[T], the type of parameter xs, which appears in the earlier parameter list. Because xs must always be provided explicitly in any invocation of isort or msort, the compiler will know T at compile time and

```
def msort[T](xs: List[T])(using ord: Ordering[T]): List[T] =
  def merge(xs: List[T], ys: List[T]): List[T] =
    (xs, ys) match
      case (Nil, _) => ys
      case (_, Nil) => xs
      case (x :: xs1, y :: ys1) =>
        if ord.lt(x, y) then x :: merge(xs1, ys)
        else y :: merge(xs, ys1)
  val n = xs.length / 2
  if n == 0 then xs
  else
    val (ys, zs) = xs.splitAt(n)
    merge(msort(ys), msort(zs))
```

Listing 21.5 · A merge sort function that uses Ordering.

can therefore determine whether a given of type `Ordering[T]` is available. If so, it will pass in the second parameter list implicitly.

21.5   Given imports

Providing given values in the companion object of a class means that those givens will be available for lookup. That is a good practice for reasonable default behavior for a given that users would likely always want, such as providing a natural ordering for a type. Otherwise, it is good practice to place givens in singleton objects that will *not* be found automatically, thereby requiring users to invite these givens in with an import when they want them. To make it easier to discern where givens are coming from, Scala provides a special import syntax for givens.

Suppose you define an object as shown in Listing 21.6. In Chapter 12, you saw how to import all `vals` and `defs` with a wildcard import statement. However, the regular wildcard import syntax does not import givens:

```
// imports only favoriteColor and favoriteFood
import TomsPrefs.*
```

This statement imports all members of `TomsPrefs`, *except* given members. To import givens, one option is to import their names explicitly:

```
object TomsPrefs:
  val favoriteColor = "blue"
  def favoriteFood = "steak"
  given prompt: PreferredPrompt =
    PreferredPrompt("enjoy> ")
  given drink: PreferredDrink =
    PreferredDrink("red wine")
  given prefPromptOrd: Ordering[PreferredPrompt] with
    def compare(x: PreferredPrompt, y: PreferredPrompt) =
      x.preference.compareTo(y.preference)
  given prefDrinkOrd: Ordering[PreferredDrink] with
    def compare(x: PreferredDrink, y: PreferredDrink) =
      x.preference.compareTo(y.preference)
```

Listing 21.6 · A preferences object.

```
import TomsPrefs.prompt // imports prompt
```

If you want to import all givens, you can use a special *wildcard given import*:

```
// imports prompt, drink, prefPromptOrd, and prefDrinkOrd
import TomsPrefs.given
```

Because often the name of a given is not used explicitly in your source code, only its type, the given import mechanism also allows you to import a given by its type:[4]

```
// imports drink, because it is a given of
// type PreferredDrink
import TomsPrefs.{given PreferredDrink}
```

If you want to import both `prefPromptOrd` and `prefDrinkOrd` by type, you can mention them both explicitly by their type, preceded by `given`:

```
// imports prefPromptOrd and prefDrinkOrd
import TomsPrefs.{given Ordering[PreferredPrompt],
   given Ordering[PreferredDrink]}
```

Alternatively, you can use a question mark (?) for the type parameter to import them together, like this:

```
// imports prefPromptOrd and prefDrinkOrd
import TomsPrefs.{given Ordering[?]}
```

21.6 Rules for context parameters

Context parameters are those that are defined in a **using** clause. The compiler is allowed to insert context parameters to fix any errors due to missing parameter lists. For example, if `someCall(a)` does not type check, the compiler might change it to `someCall(a)(b)`, where the missing parameter list is marked with **using** and b is a given.[5] This change might fix a program so

---

[4]Because they don't have a name, anonymous givens, described in Section 21.3, can only be imported by type or via a wildcard given import.

[5]When the *compiler* does this rewrite internally, it need not prefix the explicitly passed parameter with using.

that it type checks and runs correctly. If passing b explicitly would amount to boilerplate code, then leaving it out of the source code can be a clarification.

Context parameters are governed by the following general rules:

Marking rule: Only definitions marked given are available. The `given` keyword is used to mark which declarations the compiler may use as context parameters. Here's an example of a given definition:

```
given amysPrompt: PreferredPrompt = PreferredPrompt("hi> ")
```

The compiler will change `greet("Amy")` to `greet("Amy")(amysPrompt)` only if `amysPrompt` is marked as `given`. This way, you avoid the confusion that would result if the compiler picked random values that happen to be in scope and inserted them implicitly. The compiler will only select among the definitions you have explicitly marked as given.

Visibility rule: An inserted given instance must be in scope as a single identifier, or be associated with a type that is involved in the parameter type. The Scala compiler will only consider givens that are "visible." To make a given available, therefore, you must in some way make it visible. Moreover, with one exception, the given must be visible in lexical scope *as a single identifier*. The compiler will not insert a given of the form `prefslib.AmysPrefs.amysPrompt`. For example, it will not expand `greet("Amy")` to `greet("Amy")(prefslib.AmysPrefs.amysPrompt)`. If you want to make `prefslib.AmysPrefs.amysPrompt` available as a given, you would need to import it, which would make it available as a single identifier. Once imported, the compiler would be free to apply it using a single identifier as `greet("Amy")(amysPrompt)`. In fact, it is common for libraries to include a `Preamble` object including a number of useful givens. Code that uses the library can then do a single "`import Preamble.given`" to access the library's givens.[6]

There's one exception to the "single identifier" rule. If the compiler does not find an applicable given in lexical scope, it will as a second step look for given definitions in the companion object of all the types involved in the context parameter type. For example, if you're attempting to invoke a method without explicitly specifying an argument for a context parameter of type

---

[6]The import of `Preamble.given` will also bring into lexical scope as single identifiers the synthesized names for any anonymous givens declared in `Preamble`.

Ordering[Rational], the compiler will look in the companion objects of Ordering, Rational, and the companion objects of their supertypes. You could, therefore, package such a given in the companion object of either class, Ordering or Rational. Given Ordering is part of the standard library, the best home for this given is the Rational companion object:

```
object Rational:
  given rationalOrdering: Ordering[Rational] with
    def compare(x: Rational, y: Rational) =
      if x.numer * y.denom < x.denom * y.numer then -1
      else if x.numer * y.denom > x.denom * y.numer then 1
      else 0
```

In this case, the given rationalOrdering is said to be *associated* to the type Rational. The compiler will find such an associated given every time it needs to synthesize a context parameter of type Ordering[Rational]. There's no need to import the given separately into your program.

The visibility rule helps with modular reasoning. When you read code in a file, the only things you need to consider from other files are those that are either imported or are explicitly referenced through a fully qualified name. This benefit is at least as important for givens as for explicitly written code. If givens took effect system-wide, then to understand a file you would have to know about every givens introduced anywhere in the program!

Explicits-first rule: Whenever code type checks as it is written, no givens are attempted. The compiler will not change code that already works. A corollary of this rule is that you can always replace implicitly supplied given identifiers by explicit ones with using, thus making the code longer but with less apparent ambiguity. You can trade between these choices on a case-by-case basis. Whenever you see code that seems repetitive and verbose, context parameters can help you decrease the tedium. Whenever code seems terse to the point of obscurity, you can pass arguments for context parameters explicitly with using. The amount of context parameters you leave the compiler to insert is ultimately a matter of style.

Naming a given

Givens can have arbitrary names. The name of a given matters only in two situations: If you want to write it explicitly with the using keyword when

441

passing it and for determining which givens are available at any place in the program. To illustrate the second point, say you want to make use of the `prefPromptOrd` given from the `TomsPrefs` singleton shown in Listing 21.6, but you don't want to use Tom's preferred drink, as is done by `prefDrinkOrd`. You can achieve this by importing only one given, but not the other:

```
import TomsPrefs.prefPromptOrd
```

In this example, it was useful that the givens had names, because that allows you to use its name to selectively import one and not the other.

21.7   When multiple givens apply

It can happen that multiple givens are in scope and each would work. For the most part, Scala refuses to fill in a context parameter in such a case. Context parameters work well when the parameter list left out is completely obvious and pure boilerplate. If multiple givens apply, then the choice isn't so obvious after all. As an example, take a look at Listing 21.7.

```
class PreferredPrompt(val preference: String)

object Greeter:
  def greet(name: String)(using prompt: PreferredPrompt) =
    println(s"Welcome, $name. The system is ready.")
    println(prompt.preference)

object JillsPrefs:
  given jillsPrompt: PreferredPrompt =
    PreferredPrompt("Your wish> ")

object JoesPrefs:
  given joesPrompt: PreferredPrompt =
    PreferredPrompt("relax> ")
```

Listing 21.7 · Multiple givens.

Both `JillsPrefs` and the `JoesPrefs` objects shown in Listing 21.7 offer a given `PreferredPrompt`. If you import both of these, there will be two different identifiers in lexical scope, `jillsPrompt` and `joesPrompt`:

```
scala> import JillsPrefs.jillsPrompt

scala> import JoesPrefs.joesPrompt
```

If you try to invoke `Greeter.greet` now, the compiler will refuse to choose between the two applicable givens.

```
scala> Greeter.greet("Who's there?")
1 |Greeter.greet("Who's there?")
  |                             ^
  |ambiguous implicit arguments: both given instance
  |joesPrompt in object JoesPrefs and given instance
  |jillsPrompt in object JillsPrefs match type
  |PreferredPrompt of parameter prompt of method
  |greet in object Greeter
```

The ambiguity here is real. Jill's preferred prompt is completely different from Joe's. In this case, the programmer should specify which one is intended and be explicit. Whenever multiple givens could be applied, the compiler will refuse to choose between them—unless one is more specific than the other. The situation is just as with method overloading. If you try to call `foo(null)` and there are two different `foo` overloads that accept `null`, the compiler will refuse. It will say that the method call's target is ambiguous.

If one of the available givens is strictly *more specific* than the others, however, then the compiler will choose the more specific one. The idea is that whenever there is a reason to believe a programmer would always choose one of the givens over the others, don't require the programmer to write it explicitly. After all, method overloading has the same relaxation. Continuing the previous example, if one of the available `foo` methods takes a `String` while the other takes an `Any`, then choose the `String` version. It's clearly more specific.

To be more precise, one given is *more specific* than another if one of the following applies:

- The type of the former is a subtype of the latter's.

- The enclosing class of the former extends the enclosing class of the latter.

443

If you have two givens that could be ambiguous, but for which there is an obvious first and second choice, you can place the second choice in a "LowPriority" trait and the first choice in a subclass or sub-object of that trait. The first choice will be taken by the compiler if it is applicable, even if the lower priority choice would otherwise be ambiguous. If the higher priority given is not applicable, but the lower priority given is, the compiler will use the lower priority given.

21.8   Debugging givens

Givens are a powerful feature in Scala, but one that's sometimes difficult to get right. This section contains a few tips for debugging givens.

Sometimes you might wonder why the compiler did not find a given that you think it should. In that case it helps to change the code to pass the given explicitly with using. If that also gives an error message, you then know why the compiler could not apply your given. On the other hand, it's also possible that inserting the given explicitly will make the error go away. In that case you know that one of the other rules (such as the visibility rule) was preventing the given from being used.

When you are debugging a program, it can sometimes help to see what givens the compiler is inserting. The -Xprint:typer option to the compiler is useful for this. If you run scalac with this option, the compiler will show you what your code looks like after all givens have been added by the type checker. An example is shown in Listing 21.8 and Listing 21.9. If you look at the last statement in each of these listings, you'll see that the second parameter list to enjoy, which was left off in the code in Listing 21.8, "enjoy("reader")," was inserted by the compiler, as shown in Listing 21.9:

```
Mocha.enjoy("reader")(Mocha.pref)
```

If you are brave, try scala -Xprint:typer to get an interactive shell that prints out the post-typing source code it uses internally. If you do so, be prepared to see an enormous amount of boilerplate surrounding the meat of your code.[7]

---

[7]IDEs such as IntelliJ and Metals have options to show inserted givens.

```
object Mocha:

  class PreferredDrink(val preference: String)

  given pref: PreferredDrink = new PreferredDrink("mocha")

  def enjoy(name: String)(using drink: PreferredDrink): Unit =
    print(s"Welcome, $name")
    print(". Enjoy a ")
    print(drink.preference)
    println("!")

  def callEnjoy: Unit = enjoy("reader")
```

Listing 21.8 · Sample code that uses a context parameter.

```
$ scalac -Xprint:typer Mocha.scala
package <empty> {
  final lazy module val Mocha: Mocha$ = new Mocha$()
    def callEnjoy: Unit = Mocha.enjoy("reader")(Mocha.pref)
  final module class Mocha$() extends Object() {
      this: Mocha.type =>
    // ...
    final lazy given val pref: Mocha.PreferredDrink =
      new Mocha.PreferredDrink("mocha")
    def enjoy(name: String)(using drink:
        Mocha.PreferredDrink): Unit = {
      print(
        _root_.scala.StringContext.apply(["Welcome,
            ","" : String]:String*).s([name : Any]:Any*)
      )
      print(". Enjoy a ")
      print(drink.preference)
      println("!")
    }
    def callEnjoy: Unit = Mocha.enjoy("reader")(Mocha.pref)
  }
}
```

Listing 21.9 · Sample code after type checking and insertion of givens.

445

21.9   Conclusion

Context parameters can make the signature of your functions easier on the reader: Instead of having to contend with boilerplate function arguments, the reader can focus on the true intent of your function, relegating to the function's context to supply those boilerplate arguments. The lookup of those context parameters also occurs at compile time, ensuring that values for those parameters will be available at runtime.

This chapter described the givens mechanism, which can pass data as arguments to functions implicitly. That reduces boilerplate, while also allowing functions to consume all the data they operate on as arguments. As you have seen, context parameter lookup is based on a funtion parameter's type: So long as a value of the appropriate parameter type is available for implicit passing, the compiler will use that value and pass it into the function. You also saw a few examples of using that mechanism for ad hoc polymorphism, as in the case of the `Ordering` typeclass. In the next chapter, you will learn how typeclasses can be used with extension methods, and in Chapter 23 you will see several examples of using givens for typeclasses.

Chapter 22

Extension Methods

If you are writing a function that works primarily with a particular class of object, you may be inclined to define that function as a member of the class. In an object-oriented language such as Scala, this approach may feel the most natural to the programmers who will be calling your function. Nevertheless, sometimes you can't change the class. Other times you may need to define the functionality on a given typeclass instance defined for the class. For such situations, Scala provides a mechanism for making it *appear* as if a function is defined as a method on a class, when it is really defined outside the class.

Scala 3 introduced a new mechanism for this, *extension methods*, which replaces the implicit classes approach of Scala 2. This chapter will show you how to create your own extension methods and how to use the extension methods provided by others.

22.1   The basics

Imagine you need to compare strings for equality, treating whitespace specially in two ways: First, you need to ignore whitespace on either end of the string. Second, you need to require that whitespace regions appearing internally in the strings correspond, while forgiving any differences in the corresponding regions. To accomplish this, you could trim whitespace from either end of both strings, change any consecutive whitespace characters internally to a single space, then compare the resulting strings for equality. Here's a function that will perform this transformation:

```
def singleSpace(s: String): String =
  s.trim.split("\\s+").mkString(" ")
```

The `singleSpace` function takes a string and transforms it into a form suitable for comparison with ==. First, it uses `trim` to remove whitespace from either end of the string. Next, it calls `split` to divide the trimmed string around consecutive regions of whitespace, yielding an array. Finally, it uses `mkString` to stitch the array of non-whitespace strings back together, separating each by a single space character. Here are some examples:

```
singleSpace("A  Tale\tof Two   Cities")
// "A Tale of Two Cities"
singleSpace("  It was  the\t\tbest\nof times. ")
// "It was the best of times."
```

You can use `singleSpace` to compare two strings for equality, forgiving differences in whitespace, like this:

```
val s = "One  Fish, Two\tFish "
val t = " One Fish,  Two Fish"
singleSpace(s) == singleSpace(t) // true
```

This design is perfectly reasonable. You could place the `singleSpace` method in an appropriate singleton object and move on to your next task. From the human interface perspective, however, you may feel that your users would prefer to invoke this method directly on `String`s, like this:

```
s.singleSpace == t.singleSpace // if only this were true
```

This syntax would make the use of this function feel more object-oriented. Because class `String` is part of the standard library, however, the easiest way to achieve this syntax for your users is by defining `singleSpace` as an extension method.[1] You can do so as shown in Listing 22.1.

```
extension (s: String)
  def singleSpace: String =
    s.trim.split("\\s+").mkString(" ")
```

Listing 22.1 · An extension method for `String`s.

---

[1] Your more challenging options are to add `singleSpace` to `String` using either the Java Community Process[SM] or Scala Improvement Process.

The `extension` keyword allows you to create the *illusion* that you've added a member function to a class without changing the class itself. In parentheses after `extension`, you place a single variable of the type to which you want to "add" the method. The object referenced by this variable is called the *receiver* of the extension method. In this case, the "(s: String)" means that you want to add the method to `String`. Following this preamble, you write a method like you would any other method, except that you can use the receiver, `s` in this case, in the method body.

Uses of an extension method are called *application*s. Here's an example in which `singleSpace` is applied twice to compare two strings:

```
s.singleSpace == t.singleSpace // It's true!
```

Although an extension method definition looks somewhat like the definition of an anonymous class that takes the receiver as its constructor parameter, thereby making the receiver object available to its methods, this is not the case. Instead, extension method definitions are rewritten *in place* to methods that take the receiver directly as a parameter. For example, the compiler will rewrite the extension method definition shown in Listing 22.1 to the form shown in Listing 22.2.

```
// With internal extension marker
def singleSpace(s: String): String =
  s.trim.split("\\s+").mkString(" ")
```

Listing 22.2 · An extension method as rewritten by the compiler.

The only special thing about the rewritten method is that the compiler gives it an internal marker identifying it as an extension method. The simplest way to make this extension method available is to bring the name of the rewritten method into lexical scope. Here's an example in the REPL:

```
scala> extension (s: String)
          def singleSpace: String =
            s.trim.split("\\s+").mkString(" ")
def singleSpace(s: String): String
```

Because `singleSpace` is now in lexical scope in this REPL session, and is internally marked as an extension method, it can be applied:

449

```
scala> s.singleSpace == t.singleSpace
val res0: Boolean = true
```

Because Scala rewrites extension methods in place, no unnecessary box-ing will occur when an extension method is applied. This was not always true of the implicit class approach used in Scala 2. Extension methods, therefore, give you "syntactic sugar without regret." An extension method invoked on a receiver, such as `s.singleSpace`, will always give you the same per-formance as passing the receiver to a corresponding non-extension method, such as `singleSpace(s)`.

22.2   Generic extensions

You can define extension methods that are generic. As an example, consider class `List`'s `head` method, which returns the first element in the list, but throws an exception if the list is empty:[2]

```
List(1, 2, 3).head // 1
List.empty.head    // throws NoSuchElementException
```

If you're not sure whether a list you have in hand is non-empty, you can instead use the `headOption` method, which will return the first element wrapped in a `Some` if the list is non-empty. Otherwise `headOption` will return `None`:

```
List(1, 2, 3).headOption // Some(1)
List.empty.headOption    // None
```

List also offers a `tail` method, which returns everything but the first element. Like `head`, `tail` throws an exception if invoked on an empty list:

```
List(1, 2, 3).tail // List(2, 3)
List.empty.tail    // throws NoSuchElementException
```

The `List` class does not, however, offer a safe alternative that returns the remainder of the list wrapped in an `Option`. If you desire such a method, you could provide it as a *generic extension*. To make an extension generic, you place one or more type parameters in square brackets after the extension

---

[2]The head method on List is described in Section 14.4.

keyword, before the parentheses containing the receiver. An example is shown in Listing 22.3.

```
extension [T](xs: List[T])
  def tailOption: Option[List[T]] =
    if xs.nonEmpty then Some(xs.tail) else None
```

Listing 22.3 · A generic extension method.

The `tailOption` extension method is generic in just one type, T. Here are some example uses of `tailOption` in which T is instantiated to either Int or String:

```
List(1, 2, 3).tailOption      // Some(List(2, 3))
List.empty[Int].tailOption    // None
List("A", "B", "C").tailOption // Some(List(B, C))
List.empty[String].tailOption  // None
```

Although you'd usually allow such a type parameter to be inferred, as is done in the previous examples, you can give it explicitly. To do so, you must call the method directly, *i.e.*, not as an extension method:

```
tailOption[Int](List(1, 2, 3))  // Some(List(2, 3))
```

22.3   Collective extensions

When you want to add multiple methods to the same type, you can define them together with a *collective extension*. For example, because many operations on Int can overflow, you may want to define some extension methods for Int that detect overflow.

The twos complement of an Int value is formed by inverting all its bits and adding one. This representation enables subtraction to be implemented as a twos-complement operation followed by an add. The representation also has just one zero value, rather than one positive and one negative zero value.[3] On the other hand, given there's no negative zero, there's one slot left over for another value. This extra value is placed at the far end of the negative

---

[3]The ones complement representation of integers has both a positive and negative zero, as does the IEEE 754 floating point format used by Float and Double.

integers. This is why the smallest expressible negative integer is one less than the negation of the largest expressible positive integer:

```
Int.MaxValue // 2147483647
Int.MinValue // -2147483648
```

Some methods on Int can overflow precisely because of this asymmetry between maximum and minimum values. For example, Int's abs method computes the absolute value of the integer. The absolute value of Int's minimum value is the 2147483648, but that integer is not expressible as an Int. Because Int's maximum value, 2147483647, is one less, invoking abs on Int.MinValue overflows and you get back the original MinValue:

```
Int.MinValue.abs // -2147483648 (overflow)
```

If you desire a method that returns the absolute value of an Int, but detects overflow, you could define an extension method, like this:

```
extension (n: Int)
  def absOption: Option[Int] =
    if n != Int.MinValue then Some(n.abs) else None
```

At Int.MinValue, where abs would overflow, absOption returns None. Otherwise, absOption returns the result of invoking abs, wrapped in a Some. Here are some examples using absOption:

```
42.absOption              // Some(42)
-42.absOption             // Some(42)
Int.MaxValue.absOption // Some(2147483647)
Int.MinValue.absOption // None
```

Another operation that can overflow at the minimum Int value is negation. At MinValue, the unary_- operation on Int returns again MinValue:[4]

```
-Int.MinValue // -2147483648 (overflow)
```

If you also wanted a safe variant of unary_-, you can define it together with absOption in a *collective extension*, as shown in Listing 22.4. This extension adds both absOption and negateOption methods to Int. Here are some usages of negateOption:

---

[4]As described in Section 5.4, the Scala compiler rewrites -Int.MinValue to an invocation of the unary_- method on Int.MinValue, *i.e.*, Int.MinValue.unary_-.

```
extension (n: Int)
  def absOption: Option[Int] =
    if n != Int.MinValue then Some(n.abs) else None
  def negateOption: Option[Int] =
    if n != Int.MinValue then Some(-n) else None
```

Listing 22.4 · A collective extension.

```
-42.negateOption              // Some(42)
42.negateOption               // Some(-42)
Int.MaxValue.negateOption // Some(-2147483647)
Int.MinValue.negateOption // None
```

The methods defined together in a collective extension are called *sibling methods*. From a method in a collective extension, you can invoke sibling methods as if they were members of the same class. For example, if you decided to add an isMinValue extension method to Ints as well, you could invoke it directly from the other two methods, absOption and negateOption, as shown in Listing 22.5.

In the collective extension shown in Listing 22.5, both absOption and negateOption invoke the sibling isMinValue method. In such cases, the compiler will rewrite the invocation as an invocation on the receiver. In the extension shown in Listing 22.5, for example, the compiler will rewrite the isMinValue invocations to n.isMinValue, as shown in Listing 22.6.

```
extension (n: Int)
  def isMinValue: Boolean = n == Int.MinValue
  def absOption: Option[Int] =
    if !isMinValue then Some(n.abs) else None
  def negateOption: Option[Int] =
    if !isMinValue then Some(-n) else None
```

Listing 22.5 · Invoking a sibling extension method.

453

```
// All with internal extension markers
def isMinValue(n: Int): Boolean = n == Int.MinValue
def absOption(n: Int): Option[Int] =
  if !n.isMinValue then Some(n.abs) else None
def negateOption(n: Int): Option[Int] =
  if !n.isMinValue then Some(-n) else None
```

Listing 22.6 · A collective extension as rewritten by the compiler.

22.4   Using a typeclass

The overflow detection for absolute value and negation operation makes sense for more types than just Int. Any integral type that is based on twos-complement arithmetic exhibits this same overflow issue:

```
Long.MinValue.abs   // -9223372036854775808 (overflow)
-Long.MinValue      // -9223372036854775808 (overflow)
Short.MinValue.abs  // -32768 (overflow)
-Short.MinValue     // -32768 (overflow)
Byte.MinValue.abs   // -128 (overflow)
-Byte.MinValue      // -128 (overflow)
```

If you would like safe alternatives to abs and unary_- for all of these types, you could define a separate collective extension for each, but the implementations would look the same. To avoid this code duplication, you could instead define an extension enabled by a typeclass. Such an *ad hoc extension* would work for any type with a given instance of that typeclass.

It is worth looking in the standard library to see if an appropriate typeclass trait already exists. Trait Numeric is too general, because given instances are provided for types such as Double and Float that are not based on twos-complement arithmetic. Trait Integral is also too general, because although no given instances are provided for Float and Double, a given instance is provided for BigInt, which does not overflow. Thus your best option is to define a new typeclass trait specifically for twos-complement integral types, such as the TwosComplement trait shown in Listing 22.7.

Next you would define given instances for the twos-complement types for which you want to enable the extension methods. The companion object is a good home for given instances that you expect users would always

```
trait TwosComplement[N]:

  def equalsMinValue(n: N): Boolean
  def absOf(n: N): N
  def negationOf(n: N): N

object TwosComplement:

  given tcOfByte: TwosComplement[Byte] with
    def equalsMinValue(n: Byte) = n == Byte.MinValue
    def absOf(n: Byte) = n.abs
    def negationOf(n: Byte) = (-n).toByte

  given tcOfShort: TwosComplement[Short] with
    def equalsMinValue(n: Short) = n == Short.MinValue
    def absOf(n: Short) = n.abs
    def negationOf(n: Short) = (-n).toShort

  given tcOfInt: TwosComplement[Int] with
    def equalsMinValue(n: Int) = n == Int.MinValue
    def absOf(n: Int) = n.abs
    def negationOf(n: Int) = -n

  given tcOfLong: TwosComplement[Long] with
    def equalsMinValue(n: Long) = n == Long.MinValue
    def absOf(n: Long) = n.abs
    def negationOf(n: Long) = -n
```

Listing 22.7 · A typeclass for twos-complement numbers.

want to be available.[5] In Listing 22.7, given TwosComplement instances are defined for Byte, Short, Int, and Long.

With these definitions, you could define a generic extension method as shown in Listing 22.8. Now you can use absOption and negateOption on the types for which it makes sense. Here are a few examples:

```
Byte.MaxValue.negateOption // Some(-127)
Byte.MinValue.negateOption // None
Long.MaxValue.negateOption // -9223372036854775807
Long.MinValue.negateOption // None
```

---

[5]Advice on where to define givens is given in Section 21.5.

455

```
extension [N](n: N)(using tc: TwosComplement[N])
  def isMinValue: Boolean = tc.equalsMinValue(n)
  def absOption: Option[N] =
    if !isMinValue then Some(tc.absOf(n)) else None
  def negateOption: Option[N] =
    if !isMinValue then Some(tc.negationOf(n)) else None
```

Listing 22.8 · Using a typeclass in an extension.

On the other hand, any attempt to use these extension methods on types for which it does *not* make sense will fail to compile:

```
BigInt(42).negateOption
1 |BigInt(42).negateOption
  |^^^^^^^^^^^^^^^^^^^^^^^^
  |value negateOption is not a member of BigInt.
  |An extension method was tried, but could not be
  |fully constructed:
  |
  |    negateOption[BigInt](BigInt.apply(42))(
  |      /* missing */summon[TwosComplement[BigInt]]
  |    )
```

As discussed in Section 21.4, typeclasses provide ad hoc polymorphism: functionality that can be used with certain specific types—those for which given typeclass instances exist—but will give a compiler error for any other type. In the case of extension methods, you can use typeclasses to enable the syntactic sugar of an extension method on certain specific types. Any attempts to use the extension method on other types will not compile.

22.5   Extension methods for givens

In the previous section, the purpose of the TwosComplement typeclass is to achieve the design goal of enabling extension methods on a specific set of types. Because the main goal is to offer extension methods for users, it should be easy for users to decide when and if to enable them. In such design scenarios, the best place for your extension is a singleton object. From the singleton object, your users can import the extension methods to bring them into lexical scope, which will make them applicable. You could, for example, place the collective extension for overflow detection into an object named TwosComplementOps, as shown in Listing 22.9.

```
object TwosComplementOps:
  extension [N](n: N)(using tc: TwosComplement[N])
    def isMinValue: Boolean = tc.equalsMinValue(n)
    def absOption: Option[N] =
      if !isMinValue then Some(tc.absOf(n)) else None
    def negateOption: Option[N] =
      if !isMinValue then Some(tc.negationOf(n)) else None
```

Listing 22.9 · Placing extension methods in a singleton.

Your users can then invite the syntactic sugar into their code with:

```
import TwosComplementOps.*
```

With this import, the extension methods will be applicable:

```
-42.absOption // Some(42)
```

In the TwosComplementOps case, the extension methods represent the main design goal and the typeclass plays a supporting role. But often it is the other way around: The typeclass is the main goal and extension methods play a supporting role of making the typeclass easier to use. In such situations, the best home for the extension methods is in the typeclass trait itself.

For example, in Chapter 21 an Ord typeclass is defined for the purpose of making an insertion sort method, isort, more general. Although this goal is achieved in the solutions shown in Chapter 21—the isort method can be used with any type T for which a given instance of Ord[T] is available—the addition of a few extension methods would make the Ord typeclass more pleasant to use.

Every typeclass trait takes a type parameter, because a typeclass instance knows how to do something with objects of that type. For example, an Ord[T] knows how to compare two instances of type T to determine whether one is greater than, less than, or equal to the other. Because the typeclass instance for T is a separate object from the instance or instances of T they operate on, the syntax when using typeclasses can be a bit cluttered. For example, in Listing 21.2 the insert method takes a given instance of Ord[T] and uses it to determine if an instance of T, is less than or equal to the head of an already-sorted list. Here's the insert method from that listing:

```
def insert[T](x: T, xs: List[T])(using ord: Ord[T]): List[T] =
  if xs.isEmpty || ord.lteq(x, xs.head) then x :: xs
  else xs.head :: insert(x, xs.tail)
```

There's nothing wrong with "ord.lteq(x, xs.head)", but a more natural, and arguably clearer, way to write this would be:

```
x <= xs.head // Ah, the clarity!
```

You could enable such <= syntactic sugar (along with <, >, and >=) with a collective extension. In this iteration, the extension methods are placed in a singleton object, OrdOps, as shown in Listing 22.10.

```
// (Not yet the best design)
object OrdOps:
  extension [T](lhs: T)(using ord: Ord[T])
    def < (rhs: T): Boolean = ord.lt(lhs, rhs)
    def <= (rhs: T): Boolean = ord.lteq(lhs, rhs)
    def > (rhs: T): Boolean = ord.gt(lhs, rhs)
    def >= (rhs: T): Boolean = ord.gteq(lhs, rhs)
```

Listing 22.10 · Placing extensions for Ord in a singleton.

Given the definition of OrdOps in Listing 22.10, users could invite the syntactic sugar into their code with an import, as shown here:

```
def insert[T](x: T, xs: List[T])(using Ord[T]): List[T] =
  import OrdOps.*
  if xs.isEmpty || x <= xs.head then x :: xs
  else xs.head :: insert(x, xs.tail)
```

Instead of "ord.leqt(x, xs.head)", you can write "x <= xs.head". In addition, you don't actually need a name for the Ord instance, because you don't use it anymore. As a result, "(using ord: Ord[T])" can be simplified to just "(using Ord[T])".

This approach works, but this syntactic sugar would be nice to have whenever an instance of Ord is available. Because this is often the case, Scala searches given instances for applicable extensions. Thus the best home for these extensions is not in a singleton object like OrdOps, but in the Ord typeclass trait itself. This placement will ensure these extension methods are applicable wherever an instance of the typeclass is already in scope. This would look as shown in Listing 22.11.

```
trait Ord[T]:

  def compare(x: T, y: T): Int
  def lt(x: T, y: T): Boolean = compare(x, y) < 0
  def lteq(x: T, y: T): Boolean = compare(x, y) <= 0
  def gt(x: T, y: T): Boolean = compare(x, y) > 0
  def gteq(x: T, y: T): Boolean = compare(x, y) >= 0

  // (This is the best design)
  extension (lhs: T)
    def < (rhs: T): Boolean = lt(lhs, rhs)
    def <= (rhs: T): Boolean = lteq(lhs, rhs)
    def > (rhs: T): Boolean = gt(lhs, rhs)
    def >= (rhs: T): Boolean = gteq(lhs, rhs)
```

Listing 22.11 · Placing an extension in a typeclass trait.

With this placement in the typeclass trait itself, the extension methods will be available wherever a given instance of the typeclass is being used. Inside the insert method, for example, the extension methods will "just work," with no need for an import, as shown in Listing 22.12.

```
def insert[T](x: T, xs: List[T])(using Ord[T]): List[T] =
  if xs.isEmpty || x <= xs.head then x :: xs
  else xs.head :: insert(x, xs.tail)
```

Listing 22.12 · Using an extension defined in a typeclass trait.

Because the import of "OrdOps.*" is no longer needed, the version of insert shown in Listing 22.12 is more concise than the previous version. Moreover, the extension itself has become simpler. Compare the implementations of the collective extension in Listing 22.10 with that of Listing 22.11.

Because the extension methods are part of the typeclass trait itself, it already has a reference to the typeclass instance, *i.e.*, the `this` reference. So you no longer need the "[T]" and "(using ord: Ord[T])" in the preamble, which is now simplified to "extension (lhs: T)". Also, since you no longer have the passed Ord[T] instance named ord, you can't use it to invoke the type-class's methods, such as `lt` and `lteq`, but you can invoke these on the `this` reference. Thus "ord.lt(lhs, rhs)" becomes just "lt(lhs, rhs)".

Because Scala rewrites extension methods in place, these methods will become members of the typeclass trait itself, as shown in Listing 22.13.

```
trait Ord[T]:

  def compare(x: T, y: T): Int
  def lt(x: T, y: T): Boolean = compare(x, y) < 0
  def lteq(x: T, y: T): Boolean = compare(x, y) <= 0
  def gt(x: T, y: T): Boolean = compare(x, y) > 0
  def gteq(x: T, y: T): Boolean = compare(x, y) >= 0

  // With internal extension markers:
  def < (lhs: T)(rhs: T): Boolean = lt(lhs, rhs)
  def <= (lhs: T)(rhs: T): Boolean = lteq(lhs, rhs)
  def > (lhs: T)(rhs: T): Boolean = gt(lhs, rhs)
  def >= (lhs: T)(rhs: T): Boolean = gteq(lhs, rhs)
```

Listing 22.13 · Typeclass extensions as rewritten by the compiler.

Scala will look inside given instances of Ord[T] when searching for extension methods to heal a candidate type error. The algorithm that the Scala compiler uses to search for extension methods is a bit involved. Those details are described next.

22.6   Where Scala looks for extension methods

When the compiler sees you are attempting to invoke a method on an object reference, it first checks to see if that method is defined on the object's class itself. If so, it selects that method and does not look for an extension method.[6] Otherwise, the method call is a candidate compiler error. Before

---

[6]This is a general rule: If any fragment of code compiles as is, the Scala compiler will not rewrite it to something else.

reporting an error, however, the compiler will search for an extension method or implicit conversion that will heal the candidate error.[7] The compiler will report an error only if it fails to find an extension method or implicit conversion that it can apply to heal the candidate error.

Scala divides extension method search into two phases. In the first phase the compiler looks in lexical scope. In the second phase it looks in three places: at the members of given instances in lexical scope; at the members of the companion objects of the receiver's class, superclasses, and supertraits; and at the members of given instances in those same companion objects. It also tries transforming the type of the receiver with an implicit conversion as part of phase two.

If the compiler finds more than one applicable extension method in either phase, it will choose one that is more specific, similar to the way it chooses an overloaded method among alternatives. If it finds two or more applicable extension methods at the same level of specificity, it will give a compiler error that includes a list of the ambiguous extensions.

A definition can appear in lexical scope in one of three ways: It can be being defined directly, imported, or inherited. For example, the following invocation of absOption on 88 compiles because the absOption extension method is imported as a single identifier prior to its use:

```
import TwosComplementOps.absOption
88.absOption // Some(88)
```

Thus the extension method search for absOption is resolved in phase one. By contrast, the search triggered by the use of <= in Listing 22.12 is resolved in phase two. The extension method applied is the <= method shown in Listing 22.11. It is invoked on the given Ord[T] passed as a using parameter.

22.7 Conclusion

Extension methods are a way to sprinkle syntactic sugar on code: They allow you to appear to invoke a function on an object, as if it is a method declared on that object's class, when really you are passing the object to the function. This chapter covered both how to define extension methods, and how to use extension methods defined by others. It showed how extension methods and

---

[7]Implicit conversions will be described in Chapter 23.

typeclasses complement each other, and how best to use them together. In the next chapter, we'll dive more deeply into typeclasses.

Chapter 23

Typeclasses

If you need to write a function that implements behavior useful for some types but not others, you have a few options in Scala. One option is to define overloaded methods. Another is to require that the class of any instance passed to your function mixes in a particular trait. A third, and more flexible, option is to define a typeclass and write your function to work with types for which a given instance of the typeclass trait is defined.

This chapter will compare and contrast these different approaches, then dive deeply into typeclasses. We will introduce the context bound syntax for typeclasses and give several examples of typeclasses from the standard library—for numeric literals, multiversal equality, implicit conversions, and main methods. We'll wrap up with an example that illustrates the use of a typeclass for JSON serialization.

23.1 Why typeclasses?

The word "typeclass" can be confusing in a Scala context, because although *type* refers to a Scala type in this word, *class* does not refer to a Scala class. Instead, class in the word typeclass is used in the regular English sense to mean a grouping or set of things. The name "typeclass," therefore, means a grouping or set of types.

As mentioned in Section 21.4, typeclasses support *ad hoc polymorphism*, which means that functions can be used with a particular, enumerated set of types. Any attempt to use such a function with a type not in its enumerated set will not compile. For example, the phrase ad hoc polymorphism was first used to describe the way that operators such as + or – can be used with

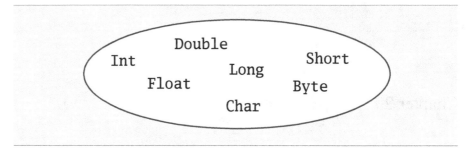

Figure 23.1 · Set of types accepted by Int's minus (–) methods.

certain types but not others in many programming languages.[1] In Scala, this is achieved by overloading methods. The interface of scala.Int, for instance, includes seven overloaded abstract methods named minus (–):

```
def -(x: Double): Double
def -(x: Float): Float
def -(x: Long): Long
def -(x: Int): Int
def -(x: Char): Int
def -(x: Short): Int
def -(x: Byte): Int
```

You can, therefore, pass instances of seven specific types to Int's minus method. You can think of these seven types as a grouping or set (or class, used in the regular English sense) of types accepted by the minus method. This is illustrated in Figure 23.1.

Another way to achieve polymorphism in Scala is with a class hierarchy. Here's an example that uses a sealed trait to define a family of colors:

```
sealed trait RainbowColor
class Red extends RainbowColor
class Orange extends RainbowColor
class Yellow extends RainbowColor
class Green extends RainbowColor
class Blue extends RainbowColor
class Indigo extends RainbowColor
class Violet extends RainbowColor
```

[1] Strachey, "Fundamental Concepts in Programming Languages." [Str00]

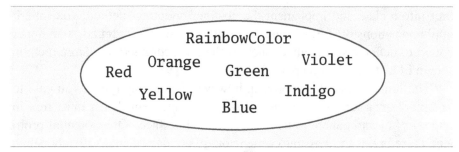

Figure 23.2 · Set of types accepted by the paint method.

With this hierarchy, you could define a method that accepts a RainbowColor as an argument:

```
def paint(rc: RainbowColor): Unit
```

Because RainbowColor is sealed, the paint method can be passed only arguments having one of the eight types shown in Figure 23.2. It won't compile for any other type. Although this approach could be viewed as ad hoc polymorphism, it is referred to as subtyping polymorphism to highlight an important difference: the classes of all the instances passed to the paint method must mix in trait RainbowColor and adhere any constraints established by its interface. By contrast, the types accepted by Int's minus (–) method, shown in Figure 23.1, need not adhere to any common interface other than that of Scala's top type, Any. In short, subtyping enables polymorphism of *related* types, whereas ad hoc polymorphism approaches such as overloading and typeclasses enable polymorphism of *unrelated* types.

Because of the interface constraints, subtyping works best when class hierarchies define small families of types focused on a single concept. Sealed hierarchies and enums are great examples. In such self-contained families of types it is straightforward to ensure the compatibility of interfaces. Subtyping can also be used to model larger, unsealed families that are focused on a single concept. A good example is the Scala collections library. However, when used to model behavior that is widely applicable to otherwise unrelated types, such as serialization or ordering, the subtyping approach becomes more cumbersome.

As an example, consider Scala's Ordered trait, which uses subtyping to model ordering. As shown in Sections 11.2 and 18.7, if you mix the Ordered

465

trait into a class and implement the abstract `compare` method, you inherit implementations of <, >, <=, and >=. You can also use `Ordered` as an upper bound to define a sort method, such as the the `orderedMergeSort` method shown in Listing 18.11 on page 383.

The limitation of this approach, however, is that any type T you pass to `orderedMergeSort` is constrained by the requirement that it must mix in `Ordered[T]` and adhere to the `Ordered[T]` interface. One potential problem, therefore, is the class into which you mix `Ordered` could already define methods whose names or contracts conflict with those in `Ordered`. Another potential problem is variance conflicts. Imagine you wanted to mix `Ordered` into the Hope enum shown in Section 19.4. You might hope you could implement the `compare` method by ordering the `Sad` object as the smallest Hope value, and ordering `Glads` based on the order of the objects they contain. Unfortunately, the compiler would reject your plan because Hope is covariant in its type parameter whereas `Ordered` is invariant:

```
class Hope[+T <: Ordered[T]] extends Ordered[Hope[T]]
1 |class Hope[+T <: Ordered[T]] extends Ordered[Hope[T]]
  |^^^^^^^^^^^^^^^^^^^^^^^^^^^^^^^^^^^^^^^^^^^^^^^^^^^^^^
  |covariant type T occurs in invariant position in type
  |Object with Ordered[Hope[T]] {...} of class Hope
```

Thus one potential problem with subtyping polymorphism is pre-existing interfaces that are incompatible. Another, more common problem is pre-existing compatible interfaces *that you can't change*. For example, you cannot use the `orderedMergeSort` shown in Listing 18.11 to sort a `List[Int]`, because `Int` does not extend `Ordered[Int]`—and you can't change that fact. In practice, the main difficulty with using subtyping for general concepts that apply to many, otherwise unrelated types is that very often some of those types are defined in libraries that you can't change.

Typeclasses solve this problem by defining a *separate* hierarchy focused on the general concept, using a type parameter to specify the type for which a service is being provided. Because this separate hierarchy is focused on just one concept, such as serialization or ordering, it is straightforward to ensure the compatibility of interfaces. Because a typeclass instance uses a type parameter to indicate the type for which it is providing a service, you need not change a type to provide the service for that type.[2] You can, therefore,

---

[2]Using a type parameter in this way is referred to as *universal polymorphism*.

easily define given typeclass instances for types that reside in libraries that you can't change.

A good example is Scala's `Ordering` typeclass, which defines a focused hierarchy devoted to ordering. This `Ordering` hierarchy of types is separate from the types being ordered. As a result, although you can't mix `Ordered` into `Hope`, you can define a given instance of `Ordering` for Hope. This works despite Hope being in a library you can't change, and despite the difference in variance between Hope, which is covariant, and `Ordering`, which is invariant. An implementation is shown in Listing 23.1.

```
import org.stairwaybook.enums_and_adts.hope.Hope

object HopeUtils:

  given hopeOrdering[T](using
      ord: Ordering[T]): Ordering[Hope[T]] with

    def compare(lh: Hope[T], rh: Hope[T]): Int =
      import Hope.{Glad, Sad}
      (lh, rh) match
        case (Sad, Sad) => 0
        case (Sad, _) => -1
        case (_, Sad) => +1
        case (Glad(lhv), Glad(rhv)) =>
          ord.compare(lhv, rhv)
```

Listing 23.1 · A given `Ordering` instance for `Hope[T]`.

The `Ordering` typeclass is the set of all types T for which given instances of `Ordering[T]` are defined. The standard library provides given instances of `Ordering` for many types, such as `Int` or `String`, which enlists these types as standard members of the `Ordering` typeclass. The hopeOrdering given shown in Listing 23.1 adds to the `Ordering` typeclass types of the form `Hope[T]` for all types T that are also members of the typeclass. The set of types that make up the `Ordering` typeclass is illustrated in Figure 23.3.

Typeclasses support ad hoc polymorphism, because you can write functions that can be used only with types for which given instances of a particular typeclass exists. Any attempt to use such a function with a type that lacks a given instance of the required typeclass will not compile. For example, you can pass a `List[T]` to the `msort` method shown in Listing 21.5 on page 437

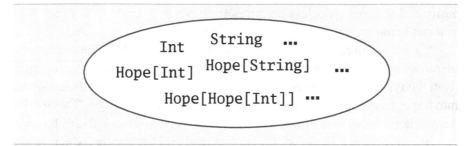

Figure 23.3 · Set of types T with given instances of `Ordering[T]`.

for any type T for which a given instance of `Ordering[T]` is defined. Because the standard library provides given instances of `Ordering[Int]` and `Ordering[String]`, therefore, you can pass `List[Int]` and `List[String]` to `msort`. Moreover, if you import the `hopeOrdering` given shown in Listing 23.1, you could also pass a `List[Hope[Int]]`, `List[Hope[String]]`, or `List[Hope[Hope[Int]]]`, *etc.*, to `msort`. On the other hand, any attempt to pass to `msort` a list with an element type for which no `Ordering` instance has been defined will not compile.

In summary, typeclasses address the problem that it is difficult, inconvenient, or impossible to jam all services involving a type into the class hierarchy of that type. In practice, not everything with which you want to perform a general service can implement an interface that brings it into a common hierarchy. The typeclass approach allows you to instead use a second, separate hierarchy focused just on providing the service.

23.2 Context bounds

Because typeclasses are such an important pattern in Scala, the language provides a shorthand syntax for them called *context bounds*. As an example, consider the `maxList` function shown in Listing 23.2, which returns the maximum element of the passed list. The `maxList` function takes a `List[T]` as its first argument, and in a subsequent argument list, takes an additional `using` argument of type `Ordering[T]`. In the body of `maxList`, the passed ordering is used in two places: a recursive call to `maxList` and an `if` expression that checks whether the head of the list is larger than the maximum element of the rest of the list.

```
def maxList[T](elements: List[T])
    (using ordering: Ordering[T]): T =
  elements match
    case List() =>
      throw new IllegalArgumentException("empty list!")
    case List(x) => x
    case x :: rest =>
      val maxRest = maxList(rest)(using ordering)
      if ordering.gt(x, maxRest) then x
      else maxRest
```

Listing 23.2 · A function with a using parameter.

The maxList function is an example of a using parameter used to provide more information about a type mentioned explicitly in an earlier parameter list. To be specific, the using parameter ordering, which has type Ordering[T], provides more information about type T—in this case, how to order Ts. Type T is mentioned in List[T], the type of parameter elements, which appears in the earlier parameter list. Because elements must always be provided explicitly in any invocation of maxList, the compiler will know T at compile time and can therefore determine whether a given definition of type Ordering[T] is available. If so, it can pass in the second parameter list, ordering, implicitly.

In the implementation of maxList shown in Listing 23.2, we passed ordering explicitly with using, but we didn't need to. When you specify using on a parameter, not only will the compiler try to *supply* that parameter with a given value, but the compiler will also *define* that parameter as an available given in the body of the method! Thus, the first use of ordering within the body of the method can be left out, as shown in Listing 23.3.

When the compiler examines the code in Listing 23.3, it will see that the types do not match up. The expression maxList(rest) only supplies one parameter list, but maxList requires two. Since the second parameter list is marked as using, the compiler does not give up type checking immediately. Instead, it looks for a given parameter of the appropriate type, which is Ordering[T]. In this case, it finds one and rewrites the call to maxList(rest)(using ordering), after which the code type checks.

There is also a way to eliminate the second use of ordering. It involves

```scala
def maxList[T](elements: List[T])
    (using ordering: Ordering[T]): T =
  elements match
    case List() =>
      throw new IllegalArgumentException("empty list!")
    case List(x) => x
    case x :: rest =>
      val maxRest = maxList(rest)        // Uses the given.
      if ordering.gt(x, maxRest) then x  // This ordering is
      else maxRest                       // still explicit.
```

Listing 23.3 · A function that uses a using parameter internally.

the following method defined in the standard library:

```scala
def summon[T](using t: T) = t
```

The effect of calling summon[Foo] is that the compiler will look for a given definition of type Foo. It will then call the summon method with that object, which returns the object right back. Thus you can write summon[Foo] whenever you want to find a given instance of type Foo in the current scope. For example, Listing 23.4 shows a use of summon[Ordering[T]] to retrieve the ordering parameter by its type.

Look closely at this last version of maxList. There is not a single mention of the ordering parameter in the text of the method. The second parameter could just as well be named "comparator":

```scala
def maxList[T](elements: List[T])
    (using comparator: Ordering[T]): T = // same body...
```

For that matter, this version works as well:

```scala
def maxList[T](elements: List[T])
    (using iceCream: Ordering[T]): T = ??? // same body...
```

Because this pattern is common, Scala lets you leave out the name of this parameter and shorten the method header with a *context bound*. Using a context bound, you would write the signature of maxList as shown in Listing 23.5. The syntax [T : Ordering] is the context bound, and it does

```
def maxList[T](elements: List[T])
    (using ordering: Ordering[T]): T =
  elements match
    case List() =>
      throw new IllegalArgumentException("empty list!")
    case List(x) => x
    case x :: rest =>
      val maxRest = maxList(rest)
      if summon[Ordering[T]].gt(x, maxRest) then x
      else maxRest
```

Listing 23.4 · A function that uses summon.

two things. First, it introduces a type parameter T as normal. Second, it adds a using parameter of type Ordering[T]. In previous versions of maxList, that parameter was called ordering, but when using a context bound you don't know what the parameter will be called. As shown earlier, you often don't need to know what the parameter is called.

Intuitively, you can think of a context bound as saying something *about* a type parameter. When you write [T <: Ordered[T]] you are saying that a T *is* an Ordered[T]. To contrast, when you write [T : Ordering] you are not so much saying what T is; rather, you are saying that there is some form of ordering associated with T.

Context bounds are essentially syntactic sugar for typeclasses. The fact that Scala provides this shorthand is a testament to the usefulness of type-classes in idiomatic Scala programming.

23.3   Main methods

As mentioned in Step 2 in Chapter 2, you can define a main method in Scala with the @main annotation. Here's an example:

```
// In file echoargs.scala
@main def echo(args: String*) =
  println(args.mkString(" "))
```

As illustrated in Chapter 2, you can execute this as a script by running scala and specifying the name of the source file, echoargs.scala:

471

```scala
def maxList[T : Ordering](elements: List[T]): T =
  elements match
    case List() =>
      throw new IllegalArgumentException("empty list!")
    case List(x) => x
    case x :: rest =>
      val maxRest = maxList(rest)
      if summon[Ordering[T]].gt(x, maxRest) then x
      else maxRest
```

Listing 23.5 · A function with a context bound.

```
$ scala echoargs.scala Running as a script
Running as a script
```

Alternatively, you can execute this as an application by compiling the source file then again invoking scala, but this time specifying the name of the *main method*, echo:

```
$ scalac echoargs.scala

$ scala echo Running as an application
Running as an application
```

Although all the main methods shown so far accept a single String* repeated parameters argument, that is not required. In Scala, main methods can actually accept any number and types of arguments. For example, here's a main method that expects a string and an integer:

```scala
// In file repeat.scala
@main def repeat(word: String, count: Int) =
  val msg =
    if count > 0 then
      val words = List.fill(count)(word)
      words.mkString(" ")
    else
      "Please enter a word and a positive integer count."
  println(msg)
```

472

Given this main method declaration, you must specify one string and one integer string on the command line when you run `repeat`:

```
$ scalac repeat.scala
```

```
$ scala repeat hello 3
hello hello hello
```

How does Scala know how to turn the command line string "3" into an `Int` 3? It uses a typeclass named `FromString`, which is a member of `scala.util.CommandLineParser`, defined as shown in Listing 23.6.

```
trait FromString[T]:
  def fromString(s: String): T
```

Listing 23.6 · The `FromString` typeclass trait.

The Scala standard library defines given `FromString` instances for several common types, including `String` and `Int`. These given instances are defined in the `FromString` companion object. If you want to write a main method that takes a custom type, you can do so by declaring a given instance of the `FromString` typeclass for the custom type.

For example, imagine you wanted to enhance the `repeat` main method with a third command line parameter that represents a "mood" that could be one of surprised, angry, or neutral. You might prefer to define an enum to represent Mood, as shown in Listing 23.7.

```
// In file moody.scala
enum Mood:
  case Surprised, Angry, Neutral
```

Listing 23.7 · A Mood enum.

With the enum defined, you could enhance the `repeat` main method to take a Mood as its third parameter, as shown in Listing 23.8.

The only remaining step is to teach the compiler how to transform a command line argument string into a Mood by defining a `FromString` instance for Mood. A good home for this is the Mood companion object, because the compiler will look there when searching for a given `FromString[Mood]`. One possible implementation is shown in Listing 23.9.

473

```
// In file moody.scala
val errmsg =
  "Please enter a word, a positive integer count, and\n" +
  "a mood (one of 'angry', 'surprised', or 'neutral')"

@main def repeat(word: String, count: Int, mood: Mood) =
  val msg =
    if count > 0 then
      val words = List.fill(count)(word.trim)
      val punc =
        mood match
          case Mood.Angry => "!"
          case Mood.Surprised => "?"
          case Mood.Neutral => ""
      val sep = punc + " "
      words.mkString(sep) + punc
    else errmsg
  println(msg)
```

Listing 23.8 · A main method that takes a custom type.

```
// In file moody.scala
object Mood:

  import scala.util.CommandLineParser.FromString

  given moodFromString: FromString[Mood] with
    def fromString(s: String): Mood =
      s.trim.toLowerCase match
        case "angry" => Mood.Angry
        case "surprised" => Mood.Surprised
        case "neutral" => Mood.Neutral
        case _ => throw new IllegalArgumentException(errmsg)
```

Listing 23.9 · A given FromString instance for Mood.

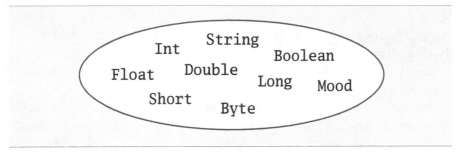

Figure 23.4 · Set of types T with given instances of FromString[T].

With the given `FromString[Mood]` definition, you can now run your moody `repeat` application:

```
$ scalac moody.scala
```

```
$ scala repeat hello 3 neutral
hello hello hello
```

```
$ scala repeat hello 3 surprised
hello? hello? hello?
```

```
$ scala repeat hello 3 angry
hello! hello! hello!
```

A typeclass-based design is a good choice for command line argument parsers for main methods because this service is needed only for certain types, which are otherwise unrelated to each other. In addition to `String` and `Int`, the `FromString` companion object defines given `FromString` instances for `Byte`, `Short`, `Long`, `Boolean`, `Float`, and `Double`. With the addition of the given `FromString[Mood]` defined in the Mood companion object in Listing 23.9, the set of types making up the `FromString` typeclass is as shown in Figure 23.4.

23.4 Multiversal equality

Scala 2 implemented *universal equality*, which allowed any two objects to be compared for equality with == and !=. This approach was simple for users to understand and worked well with Java's equals method, which allows any Object to be compared with any other Object. This approach also enabled

Scala 2 to support *cooperative equality*, whereby different types compare themselves for equality with other cooperating types. Cooperative equality allowed Scala 2, for example, to continue Java's tradition of performing equality comparisons between Int and Long without an explicit conversion from Int to Long.

Nevertheless, universal equality had one big downside: it masked bugs. For example, in Scala 2 you could compare a string and an option for equality. Here's an example:

```
scala> "hello" == Option("hello") // (in Scala 2)
val res0: Boolean = false
```

Although the answer Scala 2 gave at runtime is correct—the string "hello" is indeed unequal to Option("hello")—no string will ever equal any option. The result of such comparisons will always be false. Thus any equality comparison between a string and an option most likely represents a bug that was not caught by the Scala 2 compiler. This kind of bug can easily be introduced during refactoring: you change the type of a variable from String to Option[String], and you don't notice that elsewhere you are now comparing a String to an Option[String] for equality.

By contrast, attempting the same comparison in Scala 3 will give you an error at compile time:

```
scala> "hello" == Option("hello") // (in Scala 3)
1 |"hello" == Option("hello")
  |^^^^^^^^^^^^^^^^^^^^^^^^^^^
  |Values of types String and Option[String] cannot be
  | compared with == or !=
```

Scala 3 achieves this improvement in safety through a new feature called *multiversal equality*. Multiversal equality is a Scala 3 enhancement to the special compiler treatment given to the == and != methods in Scala 2. The definitions of == and !=, shown in Listing 23.10, are the same in Scala 3 as in Scala 2. Only the compiler treatment of == and != was changed in Scala 3 to transform universal equality into multiversal equality.

To understand multiversal equality in Scala 3, it is helpful to understand the details of how Scala 2 implemented universal equality. Here is how it worked on the JVM: When the Scala 2 compiler encountered an invocation of == or !=, it first checked whether the types being compared were Java

```
// On class Any:
final def ==(that: Any): Boolean
final def !=(that: Any): Boolean
```

Listing 23.10 · The == and != methods in both Scala 2 and 3.

primitive types. If so, the compiler emitted special Java bytecodes for efficient equality comparisons between those primitive types. Otherwise, if one side was a primitive type but the other side was not, it emitted code to box the primitive value. Now both operands were reference types. Next, the compiler emitted code that first determined whether the left operand was null. If so, the emitted code checked the right operand for null to determine a Boolean result, ensuring that invocations of == or != could never throw NullPointerException. Otherwise, the emitted code called equals on the left operand, which at this point was known to be non-null, passing in the right operand.

The Scala 3 compiler performs the exact same steps as Scala 2—after making sure the comparison should be allowed by looking for a given instance of a typeclass named CanEqual. Here's its definition:

```
sealed trait CanEqual[-L, -R]
```

The CanEqual trait takes two type parameters, L and R.[3] L is the type of the left operand of an equality comparison; R is the type of the right operand. CanEqual does not offer any method to actually compare two objects of types L and R for equality, because such comparisons are still achieved via the == and != methods in Scala 3. In short, rather than offering an equality comparison service for types L and R, as you would normally expect from a typeclass, CanEqual just *gives permission* to use == and != for an equality comparison of types L and R.

As described in Section 18.6, the minus sign next to the type parameters means that CanEqual is contravariant in both L and R. Because of this contravariance, the type CanEqual[Any, Any] is a *subtype* of any other

---

[3]Although "typeclass" usually refers to a set of types for which given instances of a trait that takes a *single* type parameter are available, you can think of the CanEqual trait as defining a set consisting of *pairs* of types. For example, an equality comparison between String and Option[String] does not compile in Scala 3 because type (String, Option[String]) is not in the set of types that comprise the CanEqual typeclass.

type, CanEqual[L, R], no matter the types L or R. As a result, an instance of CanEqual[Any, Any] could be used to give permission for any equality comparison between any two types. For example, if a given instance of CanEqual[Int, Int] is needed to permit an equality comparison of two Ints, a given instance of CanEqual[Any, Any] will suffice, because CanEqual[Any, Any] is a subtype of CanEqual[Int, Int]. Because of this fact, CanEqual is defined as a sealed trait with just one instance, which has the universally applicable type CanEqual[Any, Any]. This object is named "derived" and is declared in the CanEqual companion object:

```
object CanEqual:
  object derived extends CanEqual[Any, Any]
```

Therefore, to provide a given instance of CanEqual[L, R] no matter what types the L and R actually are, you must use CanEqual's one and only one instance, CanEqual.derived.

For backwards compatibility, the Scala 3 compiler by default allows some equality comparisons, even if a given CanEqual instance of the required type is *not* available. For an equality comparison between two types L and R, if the compiler finds no given instance of type CanEqual[L, R] it will still allow the comparison if any of the following conditions are true:

1. L and R are the same type.

2. Either L or R is a subtype of the other, after being *lifted*.[4]

3. No given *reflexive* CanEqual instance exists for either type L or R, where a reflexive instance is one that permits a type to be compared with itself, such as CanEqual[L, L].

The third rule ensures that as soon as you provide a given reflexive instance of CanEqual, enabling a type to be compared with itself, that type won't be comparable with any other type unless a given CanEqual instance exists that allows it. In essence, Scala 3, for backwards compatibility, drops back to universal equality by default for comparisons between types for which no reflexive CanEqual instances have been defined.

---

[4]To lift a type, the compiler replaces references to abstract types in covariant positions of the type by their upper bound and replaces refinement types in contravariant positions of the type by their parent.

Scala 3 provides given instances for several standard library types, including a reflexive instance for strings. This is why an equality comparison between `String` and `Option[String]` is disallowed by default. The given `CanEqual[String, String]` instance provided by the standard library is enough to cause the Scala 3 compiler, by default, to disallow the equality comparison between `String` and `Option[String]`.

This default behavior provides a smooth upgrade path from Scala 2 to Scala 3, because existing user code being ported from Scala 2 will not have any `CanEqual` instances for their types. For example, imagine your existing Scala 2 project contains a class `Apple`, defined like this:

```
case class Apple(size: Int)
```

And somewhere in your code you have been comparing two apples, like this:

```
val appleTwo = Apple(2)
val appleTwoToo = Apple(2)
appleTwo == appleTwoToo // true
```

This comparison would continue to compile and work under Scala 3 by default, because the left and right sides are the same type. However, because the Scala 3 compiler will also still by default allow comparisons of types for which no given reflexive `CanEqual` instances exist, the following undesirable equality comparison would still compile:

```
case class Orange(size: Int)
val orangeTwo = Orange(2)
appleTwo == orangeTwo // false
```

This comparison likely represents a bug, because the result of comparing any `Apple` to any `Orange` will always be false. To get full sanity checking of all equality comparisons in Scala 3, even if no reflexive instances have been defined for the involved types, you can enable "strict equality." You do so by either specifying a command line option to the compiler, `-language:strictEquality`, or including the following import in your source file:

```
import scala.language.strictEquality
```

With strict equality enabled, you will now get the desired compiler error when comparing apples and oranges:

```
scala> appleTwo == orangeTwo
1 |appleTwo == orangeTwo
  |^^^^^^^^^^^^^^^^^^^^^^
  |Values of types Apple and Orange cannot be
  |  compared with == or !=
```

Unfortunately, you will now also get an *undesired* compiler error for your desired comparison of apples to apples:

```
scala> appleTwo == appleTwoToo
1 |appleTwo == appleTwoToo
  |^^^^^^^^^^^^^^^^^^^^^^^
  |Values of types Apple and Apple cannot be
  |  compared with == or !=
```

To enable this comparison under strict equality, you will need to provide a `CanEqual` instance that gives permission for apples to be compared for equality with other apples. You could do that by providing an explicit given instance in the `Apple` companion object, as shown in Listing 23.11, though this is unidiomatic.

```
case class Apple(size: Int)
object Apple:
  given canEq: CanEqual[Apple, Apple] = CanEqual.derived
```

Listing 23.11 · An explicit `CanEqual` provider (not idiomatic).

A better way is to indicate you'd like an instance of the `CanEqual` typeclass *derived* for your `Apple` instance, as shown in Listing 23.12.

```
case class Apple(size: Int) derives CanEqual // idiomatic
```

Listing 23.12 · Offering `CanEqual` through a `derives` clause.

This idiomatic approach takes advantage of *typeclass derivation*, a feature that allows you to delegate the definition of a given typeclass instance to a member, named `derived`, in the typeclass's companion object. This derives clause will cause the compiler to insert a given provider in `Apple`'s companion object such as the one shown in Listing 23.11.

There is a lot more to the `derives` story, because most `derived` methods use compile-time metaprogramming to generate the typeclass instances. These more general techniques of typeclass derivation will be discussed in detail in *Advanced Programming in Scala*.

Now that you've defined a given instance of `CanEqual[Apple, Apple]` through a `derives` clause, the compiler will allow you to compare apples to apples under strict equality:

```
appleTwo == appleTwoToo // true too
```

23.5   Implicit conversions

Implicit conversions were the first implicit construct in Scala. Their purpose was to help make code more clear and concise by removing boilerplate type conversions. For example, Scala's standard library defines an implicit conversion from Int to Long. If you pass an Int to a method expecting a Long, the compiler will automatically coerce the Int type to Long without requiring you to invoke a conversion function, such as `toLong`, explicitly. Because any Int value can be safely converted to a Long value, and both types represent a twos-complement integer, this implicit conversion can make code easier to comprehend by eliminating boilerplate code.

Over time implicit conversions fell out of favor, however, because in addition to making code clearer by removing boilerplate, they could make code more obscure by removing explicitness. Other constructs were added to Scala that provide better alternatives to implicit conversions, such as extension methods and context parameters. As of Scala 3, only a few use cases remain for implicit conversions. Although they are still supported, you must import a feature flag to use them without a compiler warning.

Here's how they work: If the Scala compiler determines that a type does not match the expected type for that position, it will search for an implicit conversion that can heal the candidate type error. In other words, whenever the compiler sees an X, but needs a Y, it will look for an implicit conversion that converts X to Y. For example, if you had a tiny type[5] for the street portion of an address, such as:

```
case class Street(value: String)
```

---

[5]Tiny types were discussed in Section 17.4.

And you had an instance of this class, such as:

```
val street = Street("123 Main St")
```

You would not be able to initialize a variable of type string with a Street:

```
scala> val streetStr: String = street
1 |val streetStr: String = street
  |                        ^^^^^^
  |                        Found:    (street : Street)
  |                        Required: String
```

Instead, you would need to explicitly convert the Street to a String by invoking street.value:

```
val streetStr: String = street.value // 123 Main St
```

This code is clear, but you may feel that invoking value on a Street to convert it to String is boilerplate code that does not add much information. Because it is always safe to convert a Street to its underlying String, you might decide to offer an implicit conversion from Street to String. You accomplish this in Scala 3 by defining a given instance of type Conversion[Street, String],[6] which is a subtype of the function type, Street => String. It is defined like this:

```
abstract class Conversion[-T, +U] extends (T => U):
  def apply(x: T): U
```

Because trait Conversion has a single abstract method, you can often use a SAM function literal to define an instance.[7] You could, therefore, define an implicit conversion from Street to String like this:

```
given streetToString: Conversion[Street, String] = _.value
```

To use implicit conversions without compiler warnings, you must enable them, either globally with the -language:implicitConversions compiler option or locally with the following import:

---

[6]In Scala 3 you can also define an implicit conversion with an implicit def, for compatibility with Scala 2. This approach may be deprecated in the future.

[7]SAMs are described in Section 8.9.

482

```
import scala.language.implicitConversions
```

With implicit conversions enabled, and assuming the `streetToString` given is in scope as a single identifier, you could write:

```
val streetStr: String = street
```

What happens here is that the compiler sees a `Street` in a context that requires a `String`. So far, the compiler is looking at an ordinary type error. Before giving up, though, it searches for an implicit conversion from `Street` to `String`. In this case, it finds one, `streetToString`. The compiler then inserts an application of `streetToString` automatically. Behind the scenes, the code becomes:

```
val streetStr: String = streetToString(street)
```

This is literally an *implicit* conversion. You did not explicitly ask for conversion. Instead, you marked `streetToString` as an available implicit conversion by bringing it into scope as a given, and then the compiler automatically used it when it needed to convert from a `Street` to a `String`.

If you do define implicit conversions, make sure the conversion will always be appropriate. For example, converting `Doubles` to `Ints` implicitly would raise some eyebrows, because it's a dubious idea to have something that causes a loss in precision happen invisibly. So this is not really a conversion we recommend. It makes much more sense to go the other way, from some more constrained type to a more general one. For instance, an `Int` can be converted without loss of precision to a `Double`, so an implicit conversion from `Int` to `Double` makes sense. In fact, that's exactly what happens. The `scala.Predef` object, which is implicitly imported into every Scala program, defines implicit conversions that convert "smaller" numeric types to "larger" ones, including converting `Int` to `Double`.

That's why in Scala `Int` values can be stored in variables of type `Double`. There's no special rule in the type system for this; it's just an implicit conversion that gets applied.[8]

---

[8]The Scala compiler backend will treat the conversion specially, however, translating it to a special "i2d" bytecode. So the compiled image is the same as in Java.

23.6 Typeclass case study: JSON serialization

In Section 23.1, we mentioned serialization as an example of the kind of behavior that is widely applicable to otherwise unrelated types, and therefore a good fit for typeclasses. As a last example for this chapter, we'd like to illustrate using a typeclass to support serialization to JSON. To keep the example simple, we will only look at serialization, not deserialization, although normally both would be dealt with in the same library.

JSON is a commonly used interchange format between JavaScript clients and back-end servers.[9] It defines formats for representing strings, numbers, booleans, arrays, and objects. Anything you want to serialize to JSON must therefore be expressed in one of those five data types. A JSON string looks like a Scala string literal, such as "tennis". A JSON number representing an integer looks like a Scala Int literal, for example, 10. A JSON boolean is either true or false. A JSON object is a comma separated set of key value pairs enclosed in curly braces, where the key is a string name. A JSON array is a comma separated list of JSON data types enclosed in square brackets. Lastly, JSON also defines a null value. Here's a JSON object containing one member each of the other four JSON data types, plus a null member:

```
{
  "style": "tennis",
  "size": 10,
  "inStock": true,
  "colors": ["beige", "white", "blue"],
  "humor": null
}
```

In this case study, we will serialize Scala Strings as JSON strings, Ints and Longs as JSON numbers, Booleans as JSON booleans, Lists as JSON arrays, and a few other types as JSON objects. The need to serialize types from the Scala standard library, such as Int, highlights the difficulty of trying to tackle this problem with a trait you mix into each class you want to serialize. You could define such a trait, perhaps named JsonSerializable. It could offer a toJson method that produces the JSON text for that object. Although you could mix JsonSerializable into your own classes and im-

---

[9]JSON stands for "JavaScript Object Notation."

plement the toJson methods, you could not mix the trait into String, Int, Long, Boolean, or List, because you can't change those types.

A typeclass-based approach avoids that problem: You can define a class hierarchy focused entirely on serializing objects of an abstract type T to JSON, without requiring that the classes you want to serialize extend a common supertrait. Instead, you can define a given instance of the typeclass trait for each type you wish to serialize to JSON. Such a typeclass trait, named JsonSerializer, is shown in Listing 23.13. This trait takes one type parameter, T, and offers a serialize method that accepts a T and converts it to a JSON String.

```
trait JsonSerializer[T]:
  def serialize(o: T): String
```

Listing 23.13 · A JSON serializer typeclass.

To enable your users to invoke a toJson method on serializable classes, you can define an extension method. As discussed in Section 22.5, one good place to provide such an extension method is in the typeclass trait itself. By doing so, you ensure that the toJson method will be available on a type T wherever a given JsonSerializer[T] is in scope. Trait JsonSerializer enhanced with this extension method is shown in Listing 23.14.

```
trait JsonSerializer[T]:
  def serialize(o: T): String

  extension (a: T)
    def toJson: String = serialize(a)
```

Listing 23.14 · A JSON serializer typeclass with an extension method.

A reasonable next step is to define given typeclass instances for Strings, Ints, Longs, and Booleans. A good home for these given instances is in the JsonSerializer companion object, because the compiler will look there if it is unable to find a needed given instance in scope, as described in Section 21.2. These givens can be defined as shown in Listing 23.15.

```
object JsonSerializer:
  given stringSerializer: JsonSerializer[String] with
    def serialize(s: String) = s"\"$s\""

  given intSerializer: JsonSerializer[Int] with
    def serialize(n: Int) = n.toString

  given longSerializer: JsonSerializer[Long] with
    def serialize(n: Long) = n.toString

  given booleanSerializer: JsonSerializer[Boolean] with
    def serialize(b: Boolean) = b.toString
```

Listing 23.15 · JSON serializer companion object with givens.

Importing an extension method

It is useful to be able to import an extension method that adds a toJson method to any types T for which a JsonSerializer[T] is available. The extension method defined in Listing 23.14 does not achieve this, because it only makes toJson available for a type T if a given JsonSerializer[T] is in *scope*. If no JsonSerializer[T] is in scope, it will not work, even if there is a JsonSerializer[T] in the companion object for T. You can place an extension method in a singleton object, such as the one shown in Listing 23.16, so that it is easy to import. This extension method includes a using clause that requires that a given JsonSerializer[T] is available for the type T on which the extension method is applied.

```
object ToJsonMethods:
  extension [T](a: T)(using jser: JsonSerializer[T])
    def toJson: String = jser.serialize(a)
```

Listing 23.16 · An extension method for convenient importing.

With the ToJsonMethods object in place, you can try the serializers in the REPL. Here are some examples of their use:

```
import ToJsonMethods.*
"tennis".toJson // "tennis"
10.toJson // 10
true.toJson // true
```

It is instructive to compare the extension method in the ToJsonMethods object, shown in Listing 23.16, with the one in the JsonSerializer trait, shown in Listing 23.14. The extension method in ToJsonMethods takes a JsonSerializer[T] as a using parameter, but the extension method in JsonSerializers does not, because it is by definition already a *member* of a JsonSerializer[T]. Thus, whereas toJson in ToJsonMethods invokes serialize on the passed JsonSerializer reference, named jser, the toJson method in trait JsonSerializer invokes serialize on this.

Serializing domain objects

Next, imagine you need to serialize instances of certain classes from your domain model to JSON, including the address book shown in Listing 23.17. This address book contains a list of contacts. Each contact can have zero or more addresses and zero or more phones.[10]

```
case class Address(
  street: String,
  city: String,
  state: String,
  zip: Int
)
case class Phone(
  countryCode: Int,
  phoneNumber: Long
)
case class Contact(
  name: String,
  addresses: List[Address],
  phones: List[Phone]
)
case class AddressBook(contacts: List[Contact])
```

Listing 23.17 · Case classes for an address book.

---

[10]It would be better to define tiny types for the attributes of these classes, as described in Section 17.4. To keep this example simpler, though, we'll use Strings and Ints.

The JSON string for an address book is built up from the JSON strings of its nested objects. Generating the JSON string for an address book, therefore, requires that each of its nested objects can be transformed to a JSON representation. For example, each Contact in the contacts field must be transformed into the JSON representation of the contact. Each Address for a contact must be transformed into a JSON representation of that address. Serializing an AddressBook, therefore, requires serializing to JSON each constituent object of the address book. Thus it makes sense to define JSON serializers for all of the domain objects.

A good home for given JsonSerializers for your domain objects is in their companion objects. Listing 23.18 shows how you might, for example, define serializers for Address and Phone. In these serialize methods, we import and use the toJson extension method from the ToJsonMethods object, shown in Listing 23.16, but rename it to asJson. This renaming is necessary to avoid a conflict with the like-named toJson extension method inherited from JsonSerializer, shown in Listing 23.14.

```
object Address:
  given addressSerializer: JsonSerializer[Address] with
    def serialize(a: Address) =
      import ToJsonMethods.{toJson as asJson}
      s"""|{
          |   "street": ${a.street.asJson},
          |   "city": ${a.city.asJson},
          |   "state": ${a.state.asJson},
          |   "zip": ${a.zip.asJson}
          |}""".stripMargin

object Phone:
  given phoneSerializer: JsonSerializer[Phone] with
    def serialize(p: Phone) =
      import ToJsonMethods.{toJson as asJson}
      s"""|{
          |   "countryCode": ${p.countryCode.asJson},
          |   "phoneNumber": ${p.phoneNumber.asJson}
          |}""".stripMargin
```

Listing 23.18 · JSON serializers for Address and Phone.

Serializing lists

Both of the other domain objects, Contact and AddressBook, contain lists. To serialize these types, therefore, it would be helpful to have a general way to serialize Scala Lists to JSON arrays. Because a JSON array is a comma separated list of JSON data types enclosed in square brackets, it is possible to serialize a List[T] for any type T so long as a JsonSerializer[T] exists. Listing 23.19 shows a given JsonSerializer for lists that will produce a JSON array for a List, so long as a JsonSerializer exists for the list's element type.

```
object JsonSerializer:
  // givens for strings, ints, and booleans...
  given listSerializer[T](using
      JsonSerializer[T]): JsonSerializer[List[T]] with
    def serialize(ts: List[T]) =
      s"[${ts.map(t => t.toJson).mkString(", ")}]"
```

Listing 23.19 · Given JSON serializer for lists.

To express dependence on a serializer for the list's element type, the listSerializer given takes as a using parameter a serializer that can produce JSON for the element type. To serialize a List[Address] to a JSON array, for example, it is necessary to have a given serializer for Address itself available. If an Address serializer is not available, the program will not compile. For example, because a given JsonSerializer[Int] exists in the JsonSerializer companion object, it is possible to serialize a List[Int] to JSON. Here's an example:

```
import ToJsonMethods.*
List(1, 2, 3).toJson // [1, 2, 3]
```

On the other hand, because no JsonSerializer[Double] has yet been defined, an attempt to serialize a List[Double] to JSON will produce a compiler error:

```
scala> List(1.0, 2.0, 3.0).toJson
1 |List(1.0, 2.0, 3.0).toJson
  |^^^^^^^^^^^^^^^^^^^^^^^^^^^^
  |value toJson is not a member of List[Double].
  |An extension method was tried, but could not be fully
  |constructed:
  |
  |  ToJsonMethods.toJson[List[Double]](
  |    List.apply[Double]([1.0d,2.0d,3.0d : Double]*)
  |  )(JsonSerializer.listSerializer[T](
  |      /* missing */summon[JsonSerializer[Double]]))
  |  failed with
  |
  |    no implicit argument of type JsonSerializer[List[Double]]
  |    was found for parameter json of method toJson in
  |    object ToJsonMethods.
  |    I found:
  |
  |      JsonSerializer.listSerializer[T](
  |          /* missing */summon[JsonSerializer[Double]])
  |
  |    But no implicit values were found that match type
  |    JsonSerializer[Double].
```

This example illustrates a major benefit of using typeclasses to serialize Scala objects into JSON: Typeclasses allow the compiler to ensure that all the classes that make up the AddressBook can be serialized to JSON. If you fail to provide a given instance for Address, for example, your program will not compile. In Java, by contrast, if a deeply nested object does not implement Serializable, you will get an exception at runtime. The same mistake can happen in both cases, but whereas with Java serialization you get a runtime error, with typeclasses in Scala you get the error at compile time.

One last point worth noting is that the reason toJson can be invoked in the body of the function passed to map (the "toJson" in t => t.toJson) is because a given JsonSerializer[T] is in scope: the anonymous using parameter passed to listSerializer. The extension method used in this case, therefore, is the one declared in the JsonSerializer trait itself, shown in Listing 23.14.

Putting it all together

Now that you have a way to serialize lists, you can use that in the serializers for Contact and AddressBook. These are shown in Listing 23.20. As before we needed to rename toJson to asJson when importing the extension method to avoid a naming conflict.

```
object Contact:
  given contactSerializer: JsonSerializer[Contact] with
    def serialize(c: Contact) =
      import ToJsonMethods.{toJson as asJson}
      s"""|{
          |   "name": ${c.name.asJson},
          |   "addresses": ${c.addresses.asJson},
          |   "phones": ${c.phones.asJson}
          |}""".stripMargin

object AddressBook:
  given addressBookSerializer: JsonSerializer[AddressBook] with
    def serialize(a: AddressBook) =
      import ToJsonMethods.{toJson as asJson}
      s"""|{
          |   "contacts": ${a.contacts.asJson}
          |}""".stripMargin
```

Listing 23.20 · Given JSON serializers for Contact and AddressBook.

Now everything is in place to serialize an address book to JSON. As an example, consider the AddressBook instance shown in Listing 23.21, which is referenced from variable addressBook. So long as you have imported the toJson extension method from ToJsonMethods, you can serialize this address book with:

```
addressBook.toJson
```

The resulting JSON is shown in Listing 23.22.

A real world JSON library would, of course, be far more complicated than what you've seen here. One thing you would most likely want to do is use Scala's metaprogramming facilities to automate the generation of

```
val addressBook =
  AddressBook(
    List(
      Contact(
        "Bob Smith",
        List(
          Address(
            "12345 Main Street",
            "San Francisco",
            "CA",
            94105
          ),
          Address(
            "500 State Street",
            "Los Angeles",
            "CA",
            90007
          )
        ),
        List(
          Phone(
            1,
            5558881234
          ),
          Phone(
            49,
            5558413323
          )
        )
      )
    )
  )
```

Listing 23.21 · An AddressBook.

```
{
  "contacts": [{
    "name": "Bob Smith",
    "addresses": [{
      "street": "12345 Main Street",
      "city": "San Francisco",
      "state": "CA",
      "zip": 94105
    }, {
      "street": "500 State Street",
      "city": "Los Angeles",
      "state": "CA",
      "zip": 90007
    }],
    "phones": [{
      "countryCode": 1,
      "phoneNumber": 5558881234
    }, {
      "countryCode": 49,
      "phoneNumber": 5558413323
    }]
  }]
}
```

Listing 23.22 · JSON representation of an address book

JsonSerializer typeclass instances via typeclass derivation. We will cover this topic in *Advanced Programming in Scala*.

23.7 Conclusion

In this chapter, you learned about typeclasses and saw several examples. Typeclasses are a fundamental way to achieve ad hoc polymorphism in Scala. Scala's syntactic sugar for typeclasses, context bounds, is an indication of the importance of typeclasses as a design approach in Scala. You saw several applications of typeclasses: for main methods, safe equality comparisons, implicit conversions, and JSON serialization. These examples hopefully gave you a feel for the kind of use cases for which typeclasses are an appropriate design choice. In the next chapter, we will switch gears and take a more detailed look at Scala's collections library.

Chapter 24

Collections in Depth

Scala includes an elegant and powerful collection library. Even though the collections API is subtle at first glance, the changes it can provoke in your programming style can be profound. Quite often it's as if you work on a higher level with the basic building blocks of a program being whole collections instead of their elements. This new style of programming requires some adaptation. Fortunately, the adaptation is helped by several nice properties of Scala collections. They are easy to use, concise, safe, fast, and universal.

Easy to use: A small vocabulary of twenty to fifty methods is enough to solve most collection problems in a couple of operations. No need to wrap your head around complicated looping structures or recursions. Persistent collections and side-effect-free operations mean that you need not worry about accidentally corrupting existing collections with new data. Interference between iterators and collection updates is eliminated.

Concise: You can achieve with a single word what used to take one or several loops. You can express functional operations with lightweight syntax and combine operations effortlessly, so that the result feels like a custom algebra.

Safe: This one has to be experienced to sink in. The statically typed and functional nature of Scala's collections means that the overwhelming majority of errors you might make are caught at compile-time. The reason is that (1) the collection operations themselves are heavily used and therefore well tested. (2) the usages of the collection operation make inputs and output explicit as function parameters and results. (3) These explicit inputs and outputs are subject to static type checking. The bottom line is that the large majority of misuses will manifest themselves as type errors. It's not at all uncommon to have programs of several hundred lines run at first try.

Fast: Collection operations are tuned and optimized in the libraries. As a result, using collections is typically quite efficient. You might be able to do a little bit better with carefully hand-tuned data structures and operations, but you might also do a lot worse by making some suboptimal implementation decisions along the way. What's more, collections have been adapted to parallel execution on multi-cores. Parallel collections support the same operations as sequential ones, so no new operations need to be learned and no code needs to be rewritten. You can turn a sequential collection into a parallel one simply by invoking the par method.

Universal: Collections provide the same operations on any type where it makes sense to do so. So you can achieve a lot with a fairly small vocabulary of operations. For instance, a string is conceptually a sequence of characters. Consequently, in Scala collections, strings support all sequence operations. The same holds for arrays.

This chapter describes in depth the APIs of the Scala collection classes from a user perspective. You've already seen a quick tour of the collections library, in Chapter 15. This chapter takes you on a more detailed tour, showing all the collection classes and all the methods they define, so it includes everything you need to know to use Scala collections. *Advanced Programming in Scala* will look at the architecture and extensibility aspects of the collections library, for people implementing new collection types.

24.1   Mutable and immutable collections

As is now familiar to you, Scala collections systematically distinguish between mutable and immutable collections. A mutable collection can be updated or extended in place. This means you can change, add, or remove elements of a collection as a side effect. Immutable collections, by contrast, never change. You still have operations that simulate additions, removals, or updates, but those operations will in each case return a new collection and leave the old collection unchanged.

All collection classes are found in the package `scala.collection` or one of its subpackages: `mutable`, `immutable`, and `generic`. Most collection classes needed by client code exist in three variants, each of which has different characteristics with respect to mutability. The three variants are located in packages `scala.collection`, `scala.collection.immutable`, and `scala.collection.mutable`.

A collection in package `scala.collection.immutable` is guaranteed to be immutable for everyone. Such a collection will never change after it is created. Therefore, you can rely on the fact that accessing the same collection value repeatedly at different points in time will always yield a collection with the same elements.

A collection in package `scala.collection.mutable` is known to have some operations that change the collection in place. These operations let you write code to mutate the collection yourself. However, you must be careful to understand and defend against any updates performed by other parts of the code base.

A collection in package `scala.collection` can be either mutable or immutable. For instance, `scala.collection.IndexedSeq[T]` is a supertrait of both `scala.collection.immutable.IndexedSeq[T]` and its mutable sibling `scala.collection.mutable.IndexedSeq[T]`. Generally, the root collections in package `scala.collection` support transformation operations affecting the whole collection, such as `map` and `filter`. The immutable collections in package `scala.collection.immutable` typically add operations for adding and removing single values, and the mutable collections in package `scala.collection.mutable` add some side-effecting modification operations to the root interface.

Another difference between root collections and immutable collections is that clients of an immutable collection have a guarantee that nobody can mutate the collection, whereas clients of a root collection only know that they can't change the collection themselves. Even though the static type of such a collection provides no operations for modifying the collection, it might still be possible that the run-time type is a mutable collection that can be changed by other clients.

By default, Scala always picks immutable collections. For instance, if you just write `Set` without any prefix or without having imported anything, you get an immutable set, and if you write `Iterable` you get an immutable

497

iterable, because these are the default bindings imported from the `scala` package. To get the mutable default versions, you need to write explicitly `collection.mutable.Set`, or `collection.mutable.Iterable`.

The last package in the collection hierarchy is `collection.generic`. This package contains building blocks for abstracting over concrete collections. Everyday users of the collection framework should need to refer to classes in `generic` only in exceptional circumstances.

24.2 Collections consistency

The most important collection classes are shown in Figure 24.1. There is quite a bit of commonality shared by all these classes. For instance, every kind of collection can be created by the same uniform syntax, writing the collection class name followed by its elements:

```
Iterable("x", "y", "z")
Map("x" -> 24, "y" -> 25, "z" -> 26)
Set(Color.Red, Color.Green, Color.Blue)
SortedSet("hello", "world")
Buffer(x, y, z)
IndexedSeq(1.0, 2.0)
LinearSeq(a, b, c)
```

The same principle also applies for specific collection implementations:

```
List(1, 2, 3)
HashMap("x" -> 24, "y" -> 25, "z" -> 26)
```

The `toString` methods for all collections produce output written as above, with a type name followed by the elements of the collection in parentheses. All collections support the API provided by `Iterable`, but their methods all return their own class rather than the root class `Iterable`. For instance, the map method on `List` has a return type of `List`, whereas the map method on `Set` has a return type of `Set`. Thus the static return type of these methods is fairly precise:

```
Iterable
    Seq
        IndexedSeq
            ArraySeq
            Vector
            ArrayDeque (mutable)
            Queue (mutable)
            Stack (mutable)
            Range
            NumericRange
        LinearSeq
            List
            LazyList
            Queue (immutable)
        Buffer
            ListBuffer
            ArrayBuffer
    Set
        SortedSet
            TreeSet
        HashSet (mutable)
        LinkedHashSet
        HashSet (immutable)
        BitSet
        EmptySet, Set1, Set2, Set3, Set4
    Map
        SortedMap
            TreeMap
        HashMap (mutable)
        LinkedHashMap (mutable)
        HashMap (immutable)
        VectorMap (immutable)
        EmptyMap, Map1, Map2, Map3, Map4
```

Figure 24.1 · Collection hierarchy.

```
List(1, 2, 3).map(_ + 1) // List(2, 3, 4): List[Int]
Set(1, 2, 3).map(_ * 2)  // Set(2, 4, 6): Set[Int]
```

Equality is also organized uniformly for all collection classes; more on this in Section 24.12.

Most of the classes in Figure 24.1 exist in three variants: root, mutable, and immutable. The only exception is the `Buffer` trait, which only exists as a mutable collection.

In the remainder of this chapter, we will review these classes one by one.

24.3   Trait `Iterable`

At the top of the collection hierarchy is trait `Iterable[A]`, where A is the type of the collection's elements. All methods in this trait are defined in terms of an abstract method, `iterator`, which yields the collection's elements one by one.

```
def iterator: Iterator[A]
```

Collection classes implementing `Iterable` just need to define this single method; all other methods can be inherited from `Iterable`.

`Iterable` also defines many concrete methods, which are all listed in Table 24.1 on page 502. These methods fall into the following categories:

Iteration operations foreach, grouped, sliding, which iterate through the elements of the collection in the order defined by its iterator. The grouped and sliding methods return iterators that, rather than returning single elements, return subsequences of elements of the original collection. The maximal size of these subsequences is given as an argument to these methods. The grouped method chunks its elements into increments, whereas sliding yields a sliding window over the elements. The difference between the two should become clear by looking at the following code:

```
val xs = List(1, 2, 3, 4, 5)

val git = xs.grouped(3) // an Iterator[List[Int]]
git.next()              // List(1, 2, 3)
git.next()              // List(4, 5)
```

```
val sit = xs.sliding(3) // an Iterator[List[Int]]
sit.next()              // List(1, 2, 3)
sit.next()              // List(2, 3, 4)
sit.next()              // List(3, 4, 5)
```

Addition ++ (alias, concat), which appends two collections together, or appends all elements of an iterator to a collection.

Map operations map, flatMap, and collect, which produce a new collection by applying some function to collection elements.

Conversions toIndexedSeq, toIterable, toList, toMap, toSeq, toSet, and toVector, which turn an Iterable collection into an immutable collection. All these conversions return the receiver object if it already matches the demanded collection type. For instance, applying toList to a list will yield the list itself. The toArray and toBuffer methods return a new mutable collection, even if the receiver object already matches. The to method can be used to convert to any other collection.

Copying operations copyToArray. As its name implies, this copies collection elements to an array.

Size operations isEmpty, nonEmpty, size, knownSize, sizeCompare, and sizeIs, which deal with a collection's size. Computing the number of elements of a collection can require a traversal in some cases, such as List. In other cases the collection can have an infinite number of elements, for example, LazyList.from(0). The knownSize, sizeCompare, and sizeIs methods give information about the number of elements while traversing as few of the elements as possible.

Element retrieval operations head, last, headOption, lastOption, and find. These select the first or last element of a collection, or else the first element matching a condition. Note, however, that not all collections have a well-defined meaning of what "first" and "last" means. For instance, a hash set might store elements according to their hash keys, which might change from run to run. In that case, the "first" element of a hash set could also be different for different runs of a program. A collection is *ordered* if it always yields its elements in the same order. Most collections are ordered, but some (such as hash sets)

501

are not—dropping the ordering provides a little bit of extra efficiency. Ordering is often essential to give reproducible tests and help in debugging. That's why Scala collections provide ordered alternatives for all collection types. For instance, the ordered alternative for `HashSet` is `LinkedHashSet`.

Subcollection retrieval operations `takeWhile`, `tail`, `init`, `slice`, `take`, `drop`, `filter`, `dropWhile`, `filterNot`, and `withFilter`. These all return some subcollection identified by an index range or a predicate.

Subdivision operations `groupBy`, `groupMap`, `groupMapReduce`, `splitAt`, `span`, `partition`, and `partitionMap`, which split the elements of this collection into several subcollections.

Element tests `exists`, `forall`, and `count`, which test collection elements with a given predicate.

Folds `foldLeft`, `foldRight`, `reduceLeft`, `reduceRight`, which apply a binary operation to successive elements.

Specific folds `sum`, `product`, `min`, and `max`, which work on collections of specific types (numeric or comparable).

String operations `mkString` and `addString`, which offer alternative ways of converting a collection to a string.

View operation A view is a collection that's evaluated lazily. You'll learn more about views in Section 24.13.

Table 24.1 · Operations in trait `Iterable`

What it is	What it does
Abstract method:	
xs.iterator	An iterator that yields every element in xs.
Iteration:	
xs.foreach(f)	Executes function f for every element of xs. The invocation of f is done for its side effect only; in fact any function result of f is discarded by foreach.

Table 24.1 · continued

`xs.grouped(size)`	An iterator that yields fixed-sized "chunks" of this collection.
`xs.sliding(size)`	An iterator that yields a sliding fixed-sized window of elements in this collection.

Addition:

`xs ++ ys` (or `xs.concat(ys)`)	A collection consisting of the elements of both `xs` and `ys`. `ys` is an `IterableOnce` collection, *i.e.*, either an `Iterable` or an `Iterator`.

Maps:

`xs.map(f)`	The collection obtained from applying the function `f` to every element in `xs`.
`xs.flatMap(f)`	The collection obtained from applying the collection-valued function `f` to every element in `xs` and concatenating the results.
`xs.collect(f)`	The collection obtained from applying the partial function `f` to every element in `xs` for which it is defined and collecting the results.

Conversions:

`xs.toArray`	Converts the collection to an array.
`xs.toList`	Converts the collection to a list.
`xs.toIterable`	Converts the collection to an iterable.
`xs.toSeq`	Converts the collection to a sequence.
`xs.toIndexedSeq`	Converts the collection to an indexed sequence.
`xs.toSet`	Converts the collection to a set.
`xs.toMap`	Converts a collection of key/value pairs to a map.
`xs.to(SortedSet)`	Generic conversion operation that takes a collection factory as parameter.

Copying:

`xs.copyToArray(arr, s, len)`	Copies at most `len` elements to `arr`, starting at index `s`. The last two arguments are optional.

Size info:

`xs.isEmpty`	Tests whether the collection is empty.
`xs.nonEmpty`	Tests whether the collection contains elements.
`xs.size`	The number of elements in the collection.

Table 24.1 · continued

`xs.knownSize`	The number of elements if it can be computed in constant time, else −1.
`xs.sizeCompare(ys)`	Returns a negative value if xs is shorter than the ys collection, a positive value if it is longer, and 0 if they have the same size. Works even if the collection is infinite.
`xs.sizeIs < 42,` `xs.sizeIs != 42,` *etc.*	Compares the size of the collection with the given value while traversing as few elements as possible.

Element retrieval:

`xs.head`	The first element of the collection (or, some element, if no order is defined).
`xs.headOption`	The first element of xs in an option value, or None if xs is empty.
`xs.last`	The last element of the collection (or, some element, if no order is defined).
`xs.lastOption`	The last element of xs in an option value, or None if xs is empty.
`xs.find(p)`	An option containing the first element in xs that satisfies p, or None if no element qualifies.

Subcollections:

`xs.tail`	The rest of the collection except `xs.head`.
`xs.init`	The rest of the collection except `xs.last`.
`xs.slice(from, to)`	A collection consisting of elements in some index range of xs (from from, up to and excluding to).
`xs.take(n)`	A collection consisting of the first n elements of xs (or, some arbitrary n elements, if no order is defined).
`xs.drop(n)`	The rest of the collection except `xs.take(n)`.
`xs.takeWhile(p)`	The longest prefix of elements in the collection that all satisfy p.
`xs.dropWhile(p)`	The collection without the longest prefix of elements that all satisfy p.
`xs.takeRight(n)`	A collection consisting of the last n elements of xs (or, some arbitrary n elements, if no order is defined).

Table 24.1 · continued

`xs.dropRight(n)`	The rest of the collection except `xs.takeRight(n)`.
`xs.filter(p)`	The collection consisting of those elements of `xs` that satisfy the predicate p.
`xs.withFilter(p)`	A non-strict filter of this collection. All operations on the resulting filter will only apply to those elements of `xs` for which the condition p is true.
`xs.filterNot(p)`	The collection consisting of those elements of `xs` that do not satisfy the predicate p.

Zippers:

`xs.zip(ys)`	An iterable of pairs of corresponding elements from `xs` and `ys`.
`xs.lazyZip(ys)`	A value providing methods for manipulating the `xs` and `ys` collections element-wise. See Section 14.9.
`xs.zipAll(ys, x, y)`	An iterable of pairs of corresponding elements from `xs` and `ys`, where the shorter sequence is extended to match the longer one by appending elements x or y.
`xs.zipWithIndex`	An iterable of pairs of elements from `xs` with their indices.

Subdivisions:

`xs.splitAt(n)`	Splits `xs` at a position, giving the pair of collections (`xs.take(n)`, `xs.drop(n)`).
`xs.span(p)`	Splits `xs` according to a predicate, giving the pair of collections (`xs.takeWhile(p)`, `xs.dropWhile(p)`).
`xs.partition(p)`	Splits `xs` into a pair of collections; one with elements that satisfy the predicate p, the other with elements that do not, giving the pair of collections (`xs.filter(p)`, `xs.filterNot(p)`).
`xs.partitionMap(f)`	Transforms each element of `xs` into an `Either[X, Y]` value, and splits them into a pair of collections, one with elements contained in `Left`, the other with elements contained in `Right`.

Table 24.1 · continued

`xs.groupBy(f)`	Partitions xs into a map of collections according to a discriminator function f.
`xs.groupMap(f)(g)`	Partitions xs into a map of collections according to a discriminator function f, and applies the transformation function g to every element of each collection.
`xs.groupMapReduce(f)(g)(h)`	Partitions xs into a map of collections according to a discriminator function f, applies the transformation function g to every element of each collection, and reduces each collection to a single value by combining their elements with the h function.

Element conditions:

`xs.forall(p)`	A boolean indicating whether the predicate p holds for all elements of xs.
`xs.exists(p)`	A boolean indicating whether the predicate p holds for some element in xs.
`xs.count(p)`	The number of elements in xs that satisfy the predicate p.

Folds:

`xs.foldLeft(z)(op)`	Applies binary operation op between successive elements of xs, going left to right, starting with z.
`xs.foldRight(z)(op)`	Applies binary operation op between successive elements of xs, going right to left, starting with z.
`xs.reduceLeft(op)`	Applies binary operation op between successive elements of non-empty collection xs, going left to right.
`xs.reduceRight(op)`	Applies binary operation op between successive elements of non-empty collection xs, going right to left.

Specific folds:

`xs.sum`	The sum of the numeric element values of collection xs.
`xs.product`	The product of the numeric element values of collection xs.

506

Table 24.1 · continued

xs.min	The minimum of the ordered element values of collection xs.
xs.max	The maximum of the ordered element values of collection xs.

Strings:

xs.addString(b, start, sep, end)	Adds a string to StringBuilder b that shows all elements of xs between separators sep enclosed in strings start and end. start, sep, and end are all optional.
xs.mkString(start, sep, end)	Converts the collection to a string that shows all elements of xs between separators sep enclosed in strings start and end. start, sep, and end are all optional.

View:

xs.view	Produces a view over xs.

Subcategories of Iterable

In the inheritance hierarchy below Iterable you find three traits: Seq, Set, and Map. A common aspect of Seq and Map is that they both implement the PartialFunction trait[1] with its apply and isDefinedAt methods. However, the way each trait implements PartialFunction differs.

For sequences, apply is positional indexing, where elements are always numbered from 0. That is, Seq(1, 2, 3)(1) == 2. For sets, apply is a membership test. For instance, Set('a', 'b', 'c')('b') == true whereas Set()('a') == false. Finally for maps, apply is a selection. For instance, Map('a' -> 1, 'b' -> 10, 'c' -> 100)('b') == 10.

In the following three sections, we will explain each of the three kinds of collections in more detail.

24.4   The sequence traits Seq, IndexedSeq, and LinearSeq

The Seq trait represents sequences. A sequence is a kind of iterable that has a length and whose elements have fixed index positions, starting from 0.

---

[1]Partial functions were described in Section 13.7.

507

The operations on sequences, summarized in Table 24.2, fall into the following categories:

Indexing and length operations apply, isDefinedAt, length, indices, lengthCompare, and lengthIs. For a Seq, apply means indexing; hence a sequence of type Seq[T] is a partial function that takes an Int argument (an index) and yields a sequence element of type T. In other words Seq[T] extends PartialFunction[Int, T]. The elements of a sequence are indexed from zero up to the length of the sequence minus one. The length method on sequences is an alias of the size method of general collections. The lengthCompare method allows you to compare the lengths of two sequences even if one of the sequences has infinite length. The lengthIs method is an alias of the sizeIs method.

Index search operations indexOf, lastIndexOf, indexOfSlice, lastIndexOfSlice, indexWhere, lastIndexWhere, segmentLength, and prefixLength, which return the index of an element equal to a given value or matching some predicate.

Addition operations +: (alias, prepended), ++: (alias, prependedAll), :+ (alias, appended), :++ (alias, appendedAll), and padTo, which return new sequences obtained by adding elements at the front or the end of a sequence.

Update operations updated and patch, which return a new sequence obtained by replacing some elements of the original sequence.

Sorting operations sorted, sortWith, and sortBy, which sort sequence elements according to various criteria.

Reversal operations reverse and reverseIterator, which sequence or yield elements in reverse order, from last to first.

Comparison operations startsWith, endsWith, contains, corresponds containsSlice, and search, which relate two sequences or search an element in a sequence.

Multiset operations intersect, diff, distinct, and distinctBy, which perform set-like operations on the elements of two sequences or remove duplicates.

If a sequence is mutable, it offers in addition a side-effecting update method, which lets sequence elements be updated. Recall from Chapter 3 that syntax like seq(idx) = elem is just a shorthand for seq.update(idx, elem). Note the difference between update and updated. The update method changes a sequence element in place, and is only available for mutable sequences. The updated method is available for all sequences and always returns a new sequence instead of modifying the original.

Table 24.2 · Operations in trait Seq

What it is	**What it does**
Indexing and length:	
xs(i)	(or, written out, xs.apply(i)) The element of xs at index i.
xs.isDefinedAt(i)	Tests whether i is contained in xs.indices.
xs.length	The length of the sequence (same as size).
xs.lengthCompare(len)	Returns a negative Int if the length of xs is less than len, a positive Int if it is greater, and 0 if it is equal. Works even if xs is infinite.
xs.indices	The index range of xs, extending from 0 to xs.length − 1.
Index search:	
xs.indexOf(x)	The index of the first element in xs equal to x (several variants exist).
xs.lastIndexOf(x)	The index of the last element in xs equal to x (several variants exist).
xs.indexOfSlice(ys)	The first index of xs such that successive elements starting from that index form the sequence ys.
xs.lastIndexOfSlice(ys)	The last index of xs such that successive elements starting from that index form the sequence ys.
xs.indexWhere(p)	The index of the first element in xs that satisfies p (several variants exist).
xs.segmentLength(p, i)	The length of the longest uninterrupted segment of elements in xs, starting with xs(i), that all satisfy the predicate p.

Table 24.2 · continued

Additions:

x +: xs (or xs.prepended(x))	A new sequence consisting of x prepended to xs.
ys ++: xs (or xs.prependedAll(ys))	A new sequence consisting of all the elements of ys prepended to xs.
xs :+ x (or xs.appended(x))	A new sequence that consists of x appended to xs.
xs :++ ys (or xs.appendedAll(ys))	A new sequence that consists of all the elements of ys appended to xs. Same as xs ++ ys.
xs.padTo(len, x)	The sequence resulting from appending the value x to xs until length len is reached.

Updates:

xs.patch(i, ys, r)	The sequence resulting from replacing r elements of xs starting with i by the patch ys.
xs.updated(i, x)	A copy of xs with the element at index i replaced by x.
xs(i) = x	(or, written out, xs.update(i, x), only available for mutable.Seqs) Changes the element of xs at index i to y.

Sorting:

xs.sorted	A new sequence obtained by sorting the elements of xs using the standard ordering of the element type of xs.
xs.sortWith(lessThan)	A new sequence obtained by sorting the elements of xs, using lessThan as comparison operation.
xs.sortBy(f)	A new sequence obtained by sorting the elements of xs. Comparison between two elements proceeds by mapping the function f over both and comparing the results.

Reversals:

xs.reverse	A sequence with the elements of xs in reverse order.
xs.reverseIterator	An iterator yielding all the elements of xs in reverse order.

Table 24.2 · continued

Comparisons:

xs.sameElements(ys)	Tests whether xs and ys contain the same elements in the same order.
xs.startsWith(ys)	Tests whether xs starts with sequence ys (several variants exist).
xs.endsWith(ys)	Tests whether xs ends with sequence ys (several variants exist).
xs.contains(x)	Tests whether xs has an element equal to x.
xs.search(x)	Tests whether the sorted sequence xs has an element equal to x, in a possibly more efficient way than xs.contains(x).
xs.containsSlice(ys)	Tests whether xs has a contiguous subsequence equal to ys.
xs.corresponds(ys)(p)	Tests whether corresponding elements of xs and ys satisfy the binary predicate p.

Multiset operations:

xs.intersect(ys)	The multi-set intersection of sequences xs and ys that preserves the order of elements in xs.
xs.diff(ys)	The multi-set difference of sequences xs and ys that preserves the order of elements in xs.
xs.distinct	A subsequence of xs that contains no duplicated element.
xs.distinctBy(f)	A subsequence of xs that contains no duplicated element after applying the transforming function f.

Each Seq trait has two subtraits, LinearSeq and IndexedSeq, which offer different performance characteristics. A linear sequence has efficient head and tail operations, whereas an indexed sequence has efficient apply, length, and (if mutable) update operations. List is a frequently used linear sequence, as is LazyList. Two frequently used indexed sequences are Array and ArrayBuffer. The Vector class provides an interesting compromise between indexed and linear access. It has both effectively constant time indexing overhead and constant time linear access overhead. Because of this, vectors are a good foundation for mixed access patterns where both indexed and linear accesses are used. More on vectors in Section 24.7.

Mutable `IndexedSeq` adds operations for transforming its elements in place. These operations, shown in Table 24.3, contrast with operations such as `map` and `sort`, available on Seq, which return a new collection instance.

Table 24.3 · Operations in trait `mutable.IndexedSeq`

What it is	What it does
Transformations:	
`xs.mapInPlace(f)`	Transforms all the elements of xs by applying the function f to each of them.
`xs.sortInPlace()`	Sorts the elements of xs in place.
`xs.sortInPlaceBy(f)`	Sorts the elements of xs in place according to an ordering defined on the result of the application of the function f to each element.
`xs.sortInPlaceWith(c)`	Sorts the elements of xs in place according to the comparison function c.

Buffers

An important sub-category of mutable sequences is buffers. Buffers allow not only updates of existing elements but also element insertions, element removals, and efficient additions of new elements at the end of the buffer. The principal new methods supported by a buffer are += (alias, `append`) and ++= (alias, `appendAll`) for element addition at the end, +=: (alias, `prepend`) and ++=: (alias, `prependAll`) for addition at the front, `insert` and `insertAll` for element insertions, and `remove`, -= (alias, `subtractOne`) and --= (alias, `subtractAll`) for element removal. These operations are summarized in Table 24.4.

Two `Buffer` implementations that are commonly used are `ListBuffer` and `ArrayBuffer`. As the name implies, a `ListBuffer` is backed by a `List` and supports efficient conversion of its elements to a `List`, whereas an `ArrayBuffer` is backed by an array, and can be quickly converted into one. You saw a glimpse of the implementation of `ListBuffer` in Section 2.2.

Table 24.4 · Operations in trait Buffer

What it is	What it does
Additions:	
buf += x (or buf.append(x))	Appends element x to buffer buf, and returns buf itself as result.
buf ++= xs (or buf.appendAll(xs))	Appends all elements in xs to buffer.
x +=: buf (or buf.prepend(x))	Prepends element x to buffer.
xs ++=: buf (or buf.prependAll(xs))	Prepends all elements in xs to buffer.
buf.insert(i, x)	Inserts element x at index i in buffer.
buf.insertAll(i, xs)	Inserts all elements in xs at index i in buffer..
buf.padToInPlace(n, x)	Appends element x to buffer until it has n elements in total.
Removals:	
buf -= x (or buf.subtractOne(x))	Removes element x from buffer.
buf --= xs (or buf.subtractAll(xs))	Removes elements in xs from buffer.
buf.remove(i)	Removes element at index i from buffer.
buf.remove(i, n)	Removes n elements starting at index i from buffer.
buf.trimStart(n)	Removes first n elements from buffer.
buf.trimEnd(n)	Removes last n elements from buffer.
buf.clear()	Removes all elements from buffer.
Replacement:	
buf.patchInPlace(i, xs, n)	Replaces (at most) n elements of buffer by elements in xs, starting from index i in buffer.
Cloning:	
buf.clone()	A new buffer with the same elements as buf.

24.5 Sets

Sets are `Iterable`s that contain no duplicate elements. The operations on sets are summarized in Table 24.5 for general sets, Table 24.6 for immutable sets, and Table 24.7 for mutable sets. They fall into the following categories:

Tests `contains`, `apply`, and `subsetOf`. The `contains` method indicates whether a set contains a given element. The `apply` method for a set is the same as `contains`, so `set(elem)` is the same as `set contains elem`. That means sets can also be used as test functions that return true for the elements they contain. For example:

```
val fruit = Set("apple", "orange", "peach", "banana")
fruit("peach")  // true
fruit("potato") // false
```

Additions `+` (alias, `incl`) and `++` (alias, `concat`), which add one or more elements to a set, yielding a new set as a result.

Removals `-` (alias, `excl`) and `--` (alias, `removedAll`), which remove one or more elements from a set, yielding a new set.

Set operations for union, intersection, and set difference. These set operations exist in two forms: alphabetic and symbolic. The alphabetic versions are `intersect`, `union`, and `diff`, whereas the symbolic versions are `&`, `|`, and `&~`. The `++` that `Set` inherits from `Iterable` can be seen as yet another alias of `union` or `|`, except that `++` takes an `IterableOnce` argument whereas `union` and `|` take sets.

Table 24.5 · Operations in trait `Set`

What it is	**What it does**
Tests:	
`xs.contains(x)`	Tests whether x is an element of xs.
`xs(x)`	Same as xs contains x.
`xs.subsetOf(ys)`	Tests whether xs is a subset of ys.

Table 24.5 · continued

Removals:

xs.empty	An empty set of the same class as xs.

Binary operations:

xs & ys (or xs.intersect(ys))	The set intersection of xs and ys.
xs | ys (or xs.union(ys))	The set union of xs and ys.
xs &~ ys (or xs.diff(ys))	The set difference of xs and ys.

Immutable sets offer methods to add or remove elements by returning new Sets, as summarized in Table 24.6:

Table 24.6 · Operations in trait `immutable.Set`

What it is	What it does
Additions:	
xs + x (or xs.incl(x))	The set containing all elements of xs as well as x.
xs ++ ys (or xs.concat(ys))	The set containing all elements of xs as well as all elements of ys.
Removals:	
xs – x (or xs.excl(x))	The set containing all elements of xs except x.
xs -- ys (or xs.removedAll(ys))	The set containing all elements of xs except the elements of ys.

Mutable sets have methods that add, remove, or update elements, which are summarized in Table 24.7.

Table 24.7 · Operations in trait `mutable.Set`

What it is	What it does
Additions:	
xs += x (or xs.addOne(x))	Adds element x to set xs as a side effect and returns xs itself.

515

Table 24.7 · continued

xs ++= ys (or xs.addAll(ys))	Adds all elements in ys to set xs as a side effect and returns xs itself.
xs.add(x)	Adds element x to xs and returns true if x was not previously contained in the set, false if it was previously contained.

Removals:

xs -= x (or xs.subtractOne(x))	Removes element x from set xs as a side effect and returns xs itself.
xs --= ys (or xs.subtractAll(ys))	Removes all elements in ys from set xs as a side effect and returns xs itself.
xs.remove(x)	Removes element x from xs and returns true if x was previously contained in the set, false if it was not previously contained.
xs.filterInPlace(p)	Keeps only those elements in xs that satisfy predicate p.
xs.clear()	Removes all elements from xs.

Update:

xs(x) = b	(or, written out, xs.update(x, b)) If boolean argument b is true, adds x to xs, otherwise removes x from xs.

Cloning:

xs.clone()	A new mutable set with the same elements as xs.

The operation s += elem adds elem to the set s as a side effect, and returns the mutated set as a result. Likewise, s -= elem removes elem from the set, and returns the mutated set as a result. Besides += and -= there are also the bulk operations ++= and --= which add or remove all elements of an iterable or an iterator.

The choice of the method names += and -= means that very similar code can work with either mutable or immutable sets. Consider first the following interaction that uses an immutable set s:

```
var s = Set(1, 2, 3)
s += 4
s -= 2
s // Set(1, 3, 4)
```

516

In this example, we used += and -= on a var of type immutable.Set. As was explained in Step 10 in Chapter 3, a statement such as s += 4 is an abbreviation for s = s + 4. So this invokes the addition method + on the set s and then assigns the result back to the s variable. Consider now an analogous interaction with a mutable set:

```
val s = collection.mutable.Set(1, 2, 3)
s += 4 // Set(1, 2, 3, 4)
s -= 2 // Set(1, 3, 4)
s      // Set(1, 3, 4)
```

The end effect is very similar to the previous interaction; we start with a Set(1, 2, 3) and end up with a Set(1, 3, 4). However, even though the statements look the same as before, they do something different. The s += 4 statement now invokes the += method on the mutable set value s, changing the set in place. Likewise, the s -= 2 statement now invokes the -= method on the same set.

Comparing the two interactions shows an important principle. You often can replace a mutable collection stored in a val by an immutable collection stored in a var, and *vice versa*. This works at least as long as there are no alias references to the collection through which you can observe whether it was updated in place or a new collection was created.

Mutable sets also provide add and remove as variants of += and -=. The difference is that add and remove return a boolean result indicating whether the operation had an effect on the set.

The current default implementation of a mutable set uses a hash table to store the set's elements. The default implementation of an immutable set uses a representation that adapts to the number of elements of the set. An empty set is represented by just a singleton object. Sets of sizes up to four are represented by a single object that stores all elements as fields. Beyond that size, immutable sets are implemented as compressed hash-array mapped prefix-trees.[2]

A consequence of these representation choices is that for sets of small sizes, up to about four, immutable sets are more compact and more efficient than mutable sets. So if you expect the size of a set to be small, try to make it immutable.

---

[2]Compressed hash-array mapped prefix-trees are described in Section 24.7.

517

24.6 Maps

Maps are `Iterables` of key-value pairs (also named *mappings* or *associations*). Scala's `Predef` object offers an implicit conversion that lets you write `key -> value` as an alternate syntax for `(key, value)`. Thus, the initialization expression, `Map("x" -> 24, "y" -> 25, "z" -> 26)`, means exactly the same as `Map(("x", 24), ("y", 25), ("z", 26))`, but reads better.

The fundamental operations on maps, summarized in Table 24.8, are similar to those on sets. Immutable maps support additional operations to add and remove mappings by returning new maps, as shown in Table 24.9. Mutable maps additionally support the operations shown in Table 24.10. Map operations fall into the following categories:

Lookups `apply`, `get`, `getOrElse`, `contains`, and `isDefinedAt`. These operations turn maps into partial functions from keys to values. The fundamental lookup method for a map is:

```
def get(key): Option[Value]
```

The operation "`m.get(key)`" tests whether the map contains an association for the given key. If so, it returns the associated value in a `Some`. If no key is defined in the map, `get` returns `None`. Maps also define an `apply` method that returns the value associated with a given key directly, without wrapping it in an `Option`. If the key is not defined in the map, an exception is raised.

Additions and updates `+` (alias, `updated`), `++` (alias, `concat`), `updateWith`, and `updatedWith`, which let you add new bindings to a map or change existing bindings.

Removals `-` (alias, `removed`) and `--` (alias, `removedAll`), which remove bindings from a map.

Subcollection producers `keys`, `keySet`, `keysIterator`, `valuesIterator`, and `values`, which return a map's keys and values separately in various forms.

Transformations `filterKeys` and `mapValues`, which produce a new map by filtering and transforming bindings of an existing map.

Table 24.8 · Operations in trait Map

What it is	What it does
Lookups:	
ms.get(k)	The value associated with key k in map ms as an option, or None if not found
ms(k)	(or, written out, ms apply k) The value associated with key k in map ms, or a thrown exception if not found
ms.getOrElse(k, d)	The value associated with key k in map ms, or the default value d if not found
ms.contains(k)	Tests whether ms contains a mapping for key k
ms.isDefinedAt(k)	Same as contains
Subcollections:	
ms.keys	An iterable containing each key in ms
ms.keySet	A set containing each key in ms
ms.keysIterator	An iterator yielding each key in ms
ms.values	An iterable containing each value associated with a key in ms
ms.valuesIterator	An iterator yielding each value associated with a key in ms
Transformation:	
ms.view.filterKeys(p)	A map view containing only those mappings in ms where the key satisfies predicate p
ms.view.mapValues(f)	A map view resulting from applying function f to each value associated with a key in ms

Table 24.9 · Operations in trait immutable.Map

What it is	What it does
Additions and updates:	
ms + (k -> v) (or ms.updated(k, v))	The map containing all mappings of ms as well as the mapping k -> v from key k to value v
ms ++ kvs (or ms.concat(kvs))	The map containing all mappings of ms as well as all key/value pairs of kvs

519

Table 24.9 · continued

`ms.updatedWith(k)(f)`	The map with a binding added, updated, or removed for the key k. The function f takes as a parameter the value currently associated with the key k (or None if there was no such binding) and returns the new value (or None to remove the binding).

Removals:

`ms - k` (or `ms.removed(k)`)	The map containing all mappings of `ms` except for any mapping of key k
`ms -- ks` (or `ms.removedAll(ks)`)	The map containing all mappings of `ms` except for any mapping with a key in `ks`

Table 24.10 · Operations in trait `mutable.Map`

What it is	**What it does**
Additions and updates:	
`ms(k) = v`	(or, written out, `ms.update(k, v)`) Adds mapping from key k to value v to map ms as a side effect, overwriting any previous mapping of k
`ms += (k -> v)`	Adds mapping from key k to value v to map ms as a side effect and returns ms itself
`ms ++= kvs`	Adds all mappings in kvs to ms as a side effect and returns ms itself
`ms.put(k, v)`	Adds mapping from key k to value v to ms and returns any value previously associated with k as an option
`ms.getOrElseUpdate(k, d)`	If key k is defined in map ms, returns its associated value. Otherwise, updates ms with the mapping k -> d and returns d
`ms.updateWith(k)(f)`	Adds, updates, or removes a binding for the key k. The function f takes as a parameter the value currently associated with the key k (or None if there was no such binding) and returns the new value (or None to remove the binding).
Removals:	
`ms -= k`	Removes mapping with key k from ms as a side effect and returns ms itself

Table 24.10 · continued

ms --= ks	Removes all keys in ks from ms as a side effect and returns ms itself
ms.remove(k)	Removes any mapping with key k from ms and returns any value previously associated with k as an option
ms.filterInPlace(p)	Keeps only those mappings in ms that have a key satisfying predicate p.
ms.clear()	Removes all mappings from ms
Transformation and cloning:	
ms.mapValuesInPlace(f)	Transforms all associated values in map ms with function f
ms.clone()	Returns a new mutable map with the same mappings as ms

The addition and removal operations for maps mirror those for sets. An immutable map can be transformed with operations such as +, -, and updated. A mutable map, by contrast, m can be updated "in place" using the two variants m(key) = value and m += (key -> value). Mutable maps also offer the variant m.put(key, value), which returns an Option value that contains the value previously associated with key, or None if the key did not exist in the map before.

The getOrElseUpdate is useful for accessing maps that act as caches. Say you have an expensive computation triggered by invoking a function f:

```
def f(x: String) =
  println("taking my time.")
  Thread.sleep(100)
  x.reverse
```

Assume further that f has no side-effects, so invoking it again with the same argument will always yield the same result. In that case you could save time by storing previously computed bindings of argument and results of f in a map, and only computing the result of f if a result of an argument was not found there. You could say the map is a *cache* for the computations of the function f.

```
val cache = collection.mutable.Map[String, String]()
```

You can now create a more efficient caching version of the f function:

```
scala> def cachedF(s: String) = cache.getOrElseUpdate(s, f(s))
def cachedF(s: String): String

scala> cachedF("abc")
taking my time.
val res16: String = cba

scala> cachedF("abc")
val res17: String = cba
```

Note that the second argument to getOrElseUpdate is "by-name," so the computation of f("abc") above is only performed if getOrElseUpdate requires the value of its second argument, which is precisely if its first argument is not found in the cache map. You could also have implemented cachedF directly, using just basic map operations, but it would have taken more code to do so:

```
def cachedF(arg: String) =
  cache.get(arg) match
    case Some(result) => result
    case None =>
      val result = f(arg)
      cache(arg) = result
      result
```

24.7   Concrete immutable collection classes

Scala provides many concrete immutable collection classes for you to choose from. They differ in the traits they implement (maps, sets, sequences), whether they can be infinite, and the speed of various operations. We'll start by reviewing the most common immutable collection types.

Lists

Lists are finite immutable sequences. They provide constant-time access to their first element as well as the rest of the list, and they have a constant-time cons operation for adding a new element to the front of the list. Many other operations take linear time. See Chapters 14 and 2 for extensive discussions about lists.

LazyLists

A lazy list is a list whose elements are computed lazily. Only those elements requested will be computed. A lazy list can, therefore, be infinitely long. Otherwise, lazy lists have the same performance characteristics as lists.

Whereas lists are constructed with the :: operator, lazy lists are constructed with the similar-looking #::. Here is a simple example of a lazy list containing the integers 1, 2, and 3:

```
scala> val str = 1 #:: 2 #:: 3 #:: LazyList.empty
val str: scala.collection.immutable.LazyList[Int] =
  LazyList(<not computed>)
```

The head of this lazy list is 1, and the tail of it has 2 and 3. None of the elements are printed here, though, because the list hasn't been computed yet! Lazy lists are specified to compute lazily, and the toString method of a lazy list is careful not to force any extra evaluation.

Below is a more complex example. It computes a lazy list that contains a Fibonacci sequence starting with the given two numbers. A Fibonacci sequence is one where each element is the sum of the previous two elements in the series:

```
scala> def fibFrom(a: Int, b: Int): LazyList[Int] =
          a #:: fibFrom(b, a + b)
def fibFrom: (a: Int, b: Int)LazyList[Int]
```

This function is deceptively simple. The first element of the sequence is clearly a, and the rest of the sequence is the Fibonacci sequence starting with b followed by a + b. The tricky part is computing this sequence without causing an infinite recursion. If the function used :: instead of #::, then every call to the function would result in another call, thus causing an infinite recursion. Since it uses #::, though, the right-hand side is not evaluated until it is requested.

Here are the first few elements of the Fibonacci sequence starting with two ones:

```
scala> val fibs = fibFrom(1, 1).take(7)
val fibs: scala.collection.immutable.LazyList[Int] =
  LazyList(<not computed>)
```

```
scala> fibs.toList
val res23: List[Int] = List(1, 1, 2, 3, 5, 8, 13)
```

Immutable ArraySeqs

Lists are very efficient if you use algorithms that work exclusively at the front of the list. Accessing, adding, and removing the head of a list takes constant time. Accessing or modifying elements deeper in the list, however, takes time linear in the depth into the list. As a result, a list may not be the best choice for algorithms that don't limit themselves to processing just the front of the sequence.

ArraySeq is an immutable sequence type, backed by a private Array, that addresses the inefficiency of random access on lists. ArraySeqs allow you to access any element of the collection in constant time. As a result, you need not worry about accessing just the head of an ArraySeq. Because you can access elements at arbitrary locations in contant time, ArraySeqs can be more efficient than lists for some algorithms.

On the other hand, since ArraySeqs are backed by an Array, prepending to an ArraySeq requires linear time, not constant time as with list. Moreover, any addition or update of a single element requires linear time on ArraySeq, because the entire underlying array must be copied.

Vectors

List and ArraySeq are efficient data structures for some use cases but inefficient for others. For example, prepending an element is constant time for List, but linear time for ArraySeq. Conversely, indexed access is constant time for ArraySeq, but linear time for List.

Vector provides good performance for all its operations. Access and update to any elements of a vector takes only "effectively constant time," as defined below. It's a larger constant than for access to the head of a list or for reading an element of an ArraySeq, but it's a constant nonetheless. As a result, algorithms using vectors do not have to be careful about accessing or updating just the head of the sequence. They can access and update elements at arbitrary locations, and thus they can be much more convenient to write.

Vectors are built and modified just like any other sequence:

```
val vec = scala.collection.immutable.Vector.empty
val vec2 = vec :+ 1 :+ 2 // Vector(1, 2)
val vec3 = 100 +: vec2    // Vector(100, 1, 2)
vec3(0)                   // 100
```

Vectors are represented as broad, shallow trees. Every tree node contains up to 32 elements of the vector or contains up to 32 other tree nodes. Vectors with up to 32 elements can be represented in a single node. Vectors with up to 32 * 32 = 1024 elements can be represented with a single indirection. Two hops from the root of the tree to the final element node are sufficient for vectors with up to 2^{15} elements, three hops for vectors with 2^{20}, four hops for vectors with 2^{25} elements and five hops for vectors with up to 2^{30} elements. So for all vectors of reasonable size, an element selection involves up to five primitive array selections. This is what we meant when we wrote that element access is "effectively constant time."

Vectors are immutable, so you cannot change an element of a vector in place. However, with the updated method you can create a new vector that differs from a given vector only in a single element:

```
val vec = Vector(1, 2, 3)
vec.updated(2, 4) // Vector(1, 2, 4)
vec               // Vector(1, 2, 3)
```

As the last line above shows, a call to updated has no effect on the original vector vec. Like selection, functional vector updates are also "effectively constant time." Updating an element in the middle of a vector can be done by copying the node that contains the element, and every node that points to it, starting from the root of the tree. This means that a functional update creates between one and five nodes that each contain up to 32 elements or subtrees. This is certainly more expensive than an in-place update in a mutable array, but still a lot cheaper than copying the whole vector.

Because vectors strike a good balance between fast random selections and fast random functional updates, they are currently the default implementation of immutable indexed sequences:

```
collection.immutable.IndexedSeq(1, 2, 3) // Vector(1, 2, 3)
```

Immutable queues

A queue is a first-in-first-out sequence. A simplified implementation of immutable queues was discussed in Chapter 18. Here's how you can create an empty immutable queue:

```
val empty = scala.collection.immutable.Queue[Int]()
```

You can append an element to an immutable queue with enqueue:

```
val has1 = empty.enqueue(1) // Queue(1)
```

To append multiple elements to a queue, call enqueueAll with a collection as its argument:

```
val has123 = has1.enqueueAll(List(2, 3)) // Queue(1, 2, 3)
```

To remove an element from the head of the queue, use dequeue:

```
scala> val (element, has23) = has123.dequeue
val element: Int = 1
has23: scala.collection.immutable.Queue[Int] = Queue(2, 3)
```

Note that dequeue returns a pair consisting of the element removed and the rest of the queue.

Ranges

A range is an ordered sequence of integers that are equally spaced apart. For example, "1, 2, 3" is a range, as is "5, 8, 11, 14." To create a range in Scala, use the predefined methods to and by. Here are some examples:

```
1 to 3       // Range(1, 2, 3)
5 to 14 by 3 // Range(5, 8, 11, 14)
```

If you want to create a range that is exclusive of its upper limit, use the convenience method until instead of to:

```
1 until 3    // Range(1, 2)
```

Ranges are represented in constant space, because they can be defined by just three numbers: their start, their end, and the stepping value. Because of this representation, most operations on ranges are extremely fast.

Compressed hash-array mapped prefix-trees

Hash tries[3] are a standard way to implement immutable sets and maps efficiently. Compressed hash-array mapped prefix-trees[4] are a design for hash tries on the JVM that improves locality and makes sure the trees remain in a canonical and compact representation. Their representation is similar to vectors in that they are also trees where every node has 32 elements or 32 subtrees, but selection is done based on a hash code. For instance, to find a given key in a map, you use the lowest five bits of the hash code of the key to select the first subtree, the next five bits the next subtree, and so on. Selection stops once all elements stored in a node have hash codes that differ from each other in the bits that are selected so far. Thus, not all the bits of the hash code are necessarily used.

Hash tries strike a nice balance between reasonably fast lookups and reasonably efficient functional insertions (+) and deletions (-). That's why they underlie Scala's default implementations of immutable maps and sets. In fact, Scala has a further optimization for immutable sets and maps that contain less than five elements. Sets and maps with one to four elements are stored as single objects that just contain the elements (or key/value pairs in the case of a map) as fields. The empty immutable set and empty immutable map is in each case a singleton object—there's no need to duplicate storage for those because an empty immutable set or map will always stay empty.

Red-black trees

Red-black trees are a form of balanced binary trees where some nodes are designated "red" and others "black." Like any balanced binary tree, operations on them reliably complete in time logarithmic to the size of the tree.

Scala provides implementations of sets and maps that use a red-black tree internally. You access them under the names TreeSet and TreeMap:

```
val set = collection.immutable.TreeSet.empty[Int]
set + 1 + 3 + 3 // TreeSet(1, 3)
```

---

[3]"Trie" comes from the word "retrieval" and is pronounced *tree* or *try*.

[4]Steindorfer, *et al.*, "Optimizing hash-array mapped tries for fast and lean immutable JVM collections." [Ste15]

Red-black trees are also the standard implementation of SortedSet in Scala, because they provide an efficient iterator that returns all elements of the set in sorted order.

Immutable bit sets

A bit set represents a collection of small integers as the bits of a larger integer. For example, the bit set containing 3, 2, and 0 would be represented as the integer 1101 in binary, which is 13 in decimal.

Internally, bit sets use an array of 64-bit Longs. The first Long in the array is for integers 0 through 63, the second is for 64 through 127, and so on. Thus, bit sets are very compact so long as the largest integer in the set is less than a few hundred or so.

Operations on bit sets are very fast. Testing for inclusion takes constant time. Adding an item to the set takes time proportional to the number of Longs in the bit set's array, which is typically a small number. Here are some simple examples of the use of a bit set:

```
val bits = scala.collection.immutable.BitSet.empty
val moreBits = bits + 3 + 4 + 4 // BitSet(3, 4)
moreBits(3) // true
moreBits(0) // false
```

Vector maps

A VectorMap represents a map using both a Vector of keys and a HashMap. It provides an iterator that returns all the entries in their insertion order.

```
import scala.collection.immutable.VectorMap
val vm = VectorMap.empty[Int, String]
val vm1 = vm + (1 -> "one")  // VectorMap(1 -> one)
val vm2 = vm1 + (2 -> "two") // VectorMap(1 -> one, 2 -> two)
vm2 == Map(2 -> "two", 1 -> "one") // true
```

The first lines show that the content of the VectorMap keeps the insertion order, and the last line shows that VectorMaps are comparable with other maps, and that this comparison does not take the order of elements into account.

List maps

A list map represents a map as a linked list of key-value pairs. In general, operations on a list map might have to iterate through the entire list. Thus, operations on a list map take time linear in the size of the map. In fact there is little usage for list maps in Scala because standard immutable maps are almost always faster. The only possible difference is if the map is for some reason constructed in such a way that the first elements in the list are selected much more often than the other elements.

```
val map = collection.immutable.ListMap(1 -> "one", 2 -> "two")
map(2) // "two"
```

24.8   Concrete mutable collection classes

Now that you've seen the most commonly used immutable collection classes that Scala provides in its standard library, take a look at the mutable collection classes.

Array buffers

You've already seen array buffers in Section 15.1. An array buffer holds an array and a size. Most operations on an array buffer have the same speed as an array, because the operations simply access and modify the underlying array. Additionally, array buffers can have data efficiently added to the end. Appending an item to an array buffer takes amortized constant time. Thus, array buffers are useful for efficiently building up a large collection whenever the new items are always added to the end. Here are some examples:

```
val buf = collection.mutable.ArrayBuffer.empty[Int]
buf += 1     // ArrayBuffer(1)
buf += 10    // ArrayBuffer(1, 10)
buf.toArray // Array(1, 10)
```

List buffers

You've also already seen list buffers in Section 15.1. A list buffer is like an array buffer except that it uses a linked list internally instead of an array. If you plan to convert the buffer to a list once it is built up, use a list buffer instead of an array buffer. Here's an example:[5]

```
val buf = collection.mutable.ListBuffer.empty[Int]
buf += 1   // ListBuffer(1)
buf += 10  // ListBuffer(1, 10)
buf.toList // List(1, 10)
```

String builders

Just like an array buffer is useful for building arrays, and a list buffer is useful for building lists, a string builder is useful for building strings. String builders are so commonly used that they are already imported into the default namespace. Create them with a simple new StringBuilder, like this:

```
val buf = new StringBuilder
buf += 'a'        // a
buf ++= "bcdef" // abcdef
buf.toString    // abcdef
```

ArrayDeque

An ArrayDeque is a mutable sequence that supports efficient addition of elements in the front and in the end. Internally it uses a resizable array. If you need to append and prepend elements to a buffer, use an ArrayDeque instead of an ArrayBuffer.

---

[5]The "buf.type" that appears in the interpreter responses in this and several other examples in this section is a *singleton type*. As will be explained in Section 7.6, buf.type means the variable holds exactly the object referred to by buf.

Queues

Scala provides mutable queues in addition to immutable ones. You use a mutable queue similarly to the way you use an immutable one, but instead of enqueue, you use the += and ++= operators to append. Also, on a mutable queue, the dequeue method will just remove the head element from the queue and return it. Here's an example:

```
val queue = new scala.collection.mutable.Queue[String]
queue += "a"              // Queue(a)
queue ++= List("b", "c") // Queue(a, b, c)
queue                     // Queue(a, b, c)
queue.dequeue             // a
queue                     // Queue(b, c)
```

Stacks

Scala provides a mutable Stack. Here's an example:

```
val stack = new scala.collection.mutable.Stack[Int]
stack.push(1) // Stack(1)
stack         // Stack(1)
stack.push(2) // Stack(2, 1)
stack         // Stack(2, 1)
stack.top     // 2
stack         // Stack(2, 1)
stack.pop     // 2
stack         // Stack(1)
```

Note that Scala does not offer an immutable stack, because List provides the same functions. A push on an immutable stack is the same as a :: on a list. A pop is the same as calling both head and tail on list.

Mutable ArraySeqs

Array sequences are mutable sequences of fixed size that store their elements internally in an Array[AnyRef]. They are implemented in Scala by class ArraySeq.

You would typically use an ArraySeq if you want an array for its performance characteristics, but you also want to create generic instances of the

531

sequence where you do not know the type of the elements and do not have a `ClassTag` to provide it at run-time. You will find out about these issues with arrays shortly, in Section 24.9.

Hash tables

A hash table stores its elements in an underlying array, placing each item at a position in the array determined by the hash code of that item. Adding an element to a hash table takes only constant time, so long as there isn't already another element in the array that has the same hash code. Hash tables are thus very fast so long as the objects placed in them have a good distribution of hash codes. As a result, the default mutable map and set types in Scala are based on hash tables.

Hash sets and maps are used just like any other set or map. Here are some simple examples:

```
val map = collection.mutable.HashMap.empty[Int,String]
map += (1 -> "make a web site")
                // Map(1 -> make a web site)
map += (3 -> "profit!")
                // Map(1 -> make a web site, 3 -> profit!)
map(1)          // make a web site
map.contains(2) // false
```

Iteration over a hash table is not guaranteed to occur in any particular order. Iteration simply proceeds through the underlying array in whichever order it happens to be. To get a guaranteed iteration order, use a *linked* hash map or set instead of a regular one. A linked hash map or set is just like a regular hash map or set except that it also includes a linked list of the elements in the order they were added. Iteration over such a collection is always in the same order that the elements were initially added.

Weak hash maps

A weak hash map is a special kind of hash map in which the garbage collector does not follow links from the map to the keys stored in it. This means that a key and its associated value will disappear from the map if there is no other reference to that key. Weak hash maps are useful for tasks such as caching, where you want to re-use an expensive function's result if the function is called again on the same key. If keys and function results are stored in a regular hash map, the map could grow without bounds, and no key would ever become garbage. Using a weak hash map avoids this problem. As soon as a key object becomes unreachable, its entry is removed from the weak hash map. Weak hash maps in Scala are implemented as a wrapper of an underlying Java implementation, `java.util.WeakHashMap`.

Concurrent maps

A concurrent map can be accessed by several threads at once. In addition to the usual `Map` operations, it provides the following atomic operations:

Table 24.11 · Operations in trait `concurrent.Map`

What it is	What it does
m.putIfAbsent(k, v)	Adds key/value binding k -> v unless k is already defined in m
m.remove(k, v)	Removes entry for k if it is currently mapped to v
m.replace(k, old, new)	Replaces value associated with key k to new, if it was previously bound to old
m.replace(k, v)	Replaces value associated with key k to v, if it was previously bound to some value

The `scala.concurrent.Map` trait defines an interface for mutable maps that allow concurrent access. The standard library offers two implementations of this trait. The first is `java.util.concurrent.ConcurrentMap`, which can be converted automatically to a Scala map using the standard Java/Scala collection conversions. (These conversions will be described in Section 24.16.) The second is `TrieMap`, a lock-free implementation of a hash array mapped trie.

Mutable bit sets

A mutable bit set is just like an immutable one, except that it can be modified in place. Mutable bit sets are slightly more efficient at updating than immutable ones, because they don't have to copy around Longs that haven't changed. Here is an example:

```
val bits = scala.collection.mutable.BitSet.empty
bits += 1 // BitSet(1)
bits += 3 // BitSet(1, 3)
bits      // BitSet(1, 3)
```

24.9 Arrays

Arrays are a special kind of collection in Scala. On the one hand, Scala arrays correspond one-to-one to Java arrays. That is, a Scala array `Array[Int]` is represented as a Java `int[]`, an `Array[Double]` is represented as a Java `double[]` and an `Array[String]` is represented as a Java `String[]`. But at the same time, Scala arrays offer much more than their Java analogues. First, Scala arrays can be *generic*. That is, you can have an `Array[T]`, where T is a type parameter or abstract type. Second, Scala arrays are compatible with Scala sequences—you can pass an `Array[T]` where a `Seq[T]` is required. Finally, Scala arrays also support all sequence operations. Here's an example of this in action:

```
val a1 = Array(1, 2, 3)
val a2 = a1.map(_ * 3)        // Array(3, 6, 9)
val a3 = a2.filter(_ % 2 != 0) // Array(3, 9)
a3.reverse                     // Array(9, 3)
```

Given that Scala arrays are represented just like Java arrays, how can these additional features be supported in Scala?

The answer lies in systematic use of implicit conversions. An array cannot pretend to *be* a sequence, because the data type representation of a native array is not a subtype of Seq. Instead, whenever an array would be used as a Seq, implicitly wrap it in a subclass of Seq. The name of that subclass is `scala.collection.mutable.ArraySeq`. Here you see it in action:

```
val seq: collection.Seq[Int] = a1 // ArraySeq(1, 2, 3)
val a4: Array[Int] = seq.toArray  // Array(1, 2, 3)
a1 eq a4 // false
```

This interaction demonstrates that arrays are compatible with sequences, because there's an implicit conversion from `Array` to `ArraySeq`. To go the other way, from an `ArraySeq` to an `Array`, you can use the `toArray` method defined in `Iterable`. The last interpreter line above shows that wrapping then unwrapping with `toArray` produces a copy of the original array.

There is yet another implicit conversion that gets applied to arrays. This conversion simply "adds" all sequence methods to arrays but does not turn the array itself into a sequence. "Adding" means that the array is wrapped in another object of type `ArrayOps`, which supports all sequence methods. Typically, this `ArrayOps` object is short-lived; it will usually be inaccessible after the call to the sequence method and its storage can be recycled. Modern VMs often avoid creating this object entirely.

The difference between the two implicit conversions on arrays is demonstrated here:

```
val seq: collection.Seq[Int] = a1 // ArraySeq(1, 2, 3)
seq.reverse // ArraySeq(3, 2, 1)
val ops: collection.ArrayOps[Int] = a1 // Array(1, 2, 3)
ops.reverse // Array(3, 2, 1)
```

You see that calling `reverse` on `seq`, which is an `ArraySeq`, will give again an `ArraySeq`. That's logical, because `ArraySeqs` are `Seqs`, and calling `reverse` on any `Seq` will give again a `Seq`. On the other hand, calling `reverse` on the `ops` value, which has type `ArrayOps`, will result in an `Array`, not a `Seq`.

The `ArrayOps` example above was quite artificial, intended only to show the difference to `ArraySeq`. Normally, you'd never define a value of class `ArrayOps`. You'd just call a `Seq` method on an array:

```
a1.reverse // Array(3, 2, 1)
```

The `ArrayOps` object gets inserted automatically by the implicit conversion. So the line above is equivalent to the following line, where `intArrayOps` was the conversion that was implicitly inserted previously:

```
intArrayOps(a1).reverse // Array(3, 2, 1)
```

This raises the question how the compiler picked `intArrayOps` over the other implicit conversion to `ArraySeq` in the line above. After all, both conversions map an array to a type that supports a `reverse` method, which is what the input specified. The answer to that question is that the two implicit conversions are prioritized. The `ArrayOps` conversion has a higher priority than the `ArraySeq` conversion. The first is defined in the `Predef` object whereas the second is defined in a class `scala.LowPriorityImplicits`, which is a superclass of `Predef`. Implicits in subclasses and subobjects take precedence over implicits in base classes. So if both conversions are applicable, the one in `Predef` is chosen. A very similar scheme, which was described in Section 21.7, works for strings.

So now you know how arrays can be compatible with sequences and how they can support all sequence operations. What about genericity? In Java you cannot write a `T[]` where `T` is a type parameter. How then is Scala's `Array[T]` represented? In fact a generic array like `Array[T]` could be at run time any of Java's eight primitive array types `byte[]`, `short[]`, `char[]`, `int[]`, `long[]`, `float[]`, `double[]`, `boolean[]`, or it could be an array of objects. The only common run-time type encompassing all of these types is `AnyRef` (or, equivalently `java.lang.Object`), so that's the type to which the Scala compiler maps `Array[T]`. At run-time, when an element of an array of type `Array[T]` is accessed or updated there is a sequence of type tests that determine the actual array type, followed by the correct array operation on the Java array. These type tests slow down array operations somewhat. You can expect accesses to generic arrays to be three to four times slower than accesses to primitive or object arrays. This means that if you need maximal performance, you should prefer concrete over generic arrays.

Representing the generic array type is not enough, however, there must also be a way to *create* generic arrays. This is an even harder problem, which requires a little bit of help from you. To illustrate the problem, consider the following attempt to write a generic method that creates an array:

```
// This is wrong!
def evenElems[T](xs: Vector[T]): Array[T] =
  val arr = new Array[T]((xs.length + 1) / 2)
  for i <- 0 until xs.length by 2 do
    arr(i / 2) = xs(i)
  arr
```

The evenElems method returns a new array that consists of all elements of the argument vector xs that are at even positions in the vector. The first line of the body of evenElems creates the result array, which has the same element type as the argument. So depending on the actual type parameter for T, this could be an `Array[Int]`, or an `Array[Boolean]`, or an array of some of the other primitive types in Java, or an array of some reference type. But these types all have different runtime representations, so how is the Scala runtime going to pick the correct one? In fact, it can't do that based on the information it is given, because the actual type that corresponds to the type parameter T is erased at runtime. That's why you will get the following error message if you attempt to compile the code above:

```
2 |    val arr = new Array[T]((xs.length + 1) / 2)
  |                                              ^
  |                           No ClassTag available for T
```

What's required here is that you help the compiler by providing a runtime hint of what the actual type parameter of evenElems is. This runtime hint takes the form of a *class tag* of type `scala.reflect.ClassTag`. A class tag describes the *runtime class* of a given type, which is all the information needed to construct an array of that type.

In many cases the compiler can generate a class tag on its own. Such is the case for a concrete type like `Int` or `String`. It's also the case for certain generic types, like `List[T]`, where enough information is known to predict the runtime class; in this example the runtime class would be `List`.

For fully generic cases, the usual idiom is to pass the class tag using a context bound, as discussed in Section 23.2. Here is how the above definition could be fixed by using a context bound:

```
// This works
import scala.reflect.ClassTag
def evenElems[T: ClassTag](xs: Vector[T]): Array[T] =
  val arr = new Array[T]((xs.length + 1) / 2)
  for i <- 0 until xs.length by 2 do
    arr(i / 2) = xs(i)
  arr
```

In this new definition, when the `Array[T]` is created, the compiler looks for a class tag for the type parameter T, that is, it will look for an implicit value of type `ClassTag[T]`. If such a value is found, the class tag is used to construct the right kind of array. Otherwise, you'll see an error message like the one shown previously.

Here is an interaction that uses the evenElems method:

```
evenElems(Vector(1, 2, 3, 4, 5)) // Array(1, 3, 5)
```

```
evenElems(Vector("this", "is", "a", "test", "run"))
  // Array(this, a, run)
```

In both cases, the Scala compiler automatically constructed a class tag for the element type (first Int, then String) and passed it to the implicit parameter of the evenElems method. The compiler can do that for all concrete types, but not if the argument is itself another type parameter without its class tag. For instance, the following fails:

```
scala> def wrap[U](xs: Vector[U]) = evenElems(xs)
1 |def wrap[U](xs: Vector[U]) = evenElems(xs)
  |                                      ^
  |                       No ClassTag available for U
```

What happened here is that the evenElems demands a class tag for the type parameter U, but none was found. The solution in this case is, of course, to demand another implicit class tag for U. So the following works:

```
def wrap[U: ClassTag](xs: Vector[U]) = evenElems(xs)
```

This example also shows that the context bound in the definition of U is just a shorthand for an implicit parameter named here evidence$1 of type ClassTag[U].

24.10 Strings

Like arrays, strings are not directly sequences, but they can be converted to them, and they also support all sequence operations. Here are some examples of operations you can invoke on strings:

```
val str = "hello"
str.reverse              // olleh
str.map(_.toUpper)       // HELLO
str.drop(3)              // lo
str.slice(1, 4)          // ell
val s: Seq[Char] = str // hello
```

These operations are supported by two implicit conversions, which were explained in Section 23.5. The first, low-priority conversion maps a String to a WrappedString, which is a subclass of immutable.IndexedSeq. This conversion was applied in the last line of the previous example in which a string was converted into a Seq. The other, high-priority conversion maps a string to a StringOps object, which adds all methods on immutable sequences to strings. This conversion was implicitly inserted in the method calls of reverse, map, drop, and slice in the previous example.

24.11 Performance characteristics

As the previous explanations have shown, different collection types have different performance characteristics. That's often the primary reason for picking one collection type over another. You can see the performance characteristics of some common operations on collections summarized in two tables, Table 24.12 and Table 24.13.

	head	tail	apply	update	prepend	append	insert
immutable							
List	C	C	L	L	C	L	-
LazyList	C	C	L	L	C	L	-
ArraySeq	C	L	C	L	L	L	-
Vector	eC	eC	eC	eC	eC	eC	-
Queue	aC	aC	L	L	L	C	-
Range	C	C	C	-	-	-	-
String	C	L	C	L	L	L	-
mutable							
ArrayBuffer	C	L	C	C	L	aC	L
ListBuffer	C	L	L	L	C	C	L
StringBuilder	C	L	C	C	L	aC	L
Queue	C	L	L	L	C	C	L
ArraySeq	C	L	C	C	-	-	-
Stack	C	L	L	L	C	L	L
Array	C	L	C	C	-	-	-
ArrayDeque	C	L	C	C	aC	aC	L

Table 24.12 · Performance characteristics of sequence types

	lookup	add	remove	min
immutable				
HashSet/HashMap	eC	eC	eC	L
TreeSet/TreeMap	Log	Log	Log	Log
BitSet	C	L	L	eC[a]
VectorMap	eC	eC	aC	L
ListMap	L	L	L	L
mutable				
HashSet/HashMap	eC	eC	eC	L
WeakHashMap	eC	eC	eC	L
BitSet	C	aC	C	eC[a]

Table 24.13 · Performance characteristics of set and map types

[a]Assuming bits are densely packed.

The entries in these two tables are explained as follows:

C   The operation takes (fast) constant time.

eC   The operation takes effectively constant time, but this might depend on some assumptions such as the maximum length of a vector or the distribution of hash keys.

aC   The operation takes amortized constant time. Some invocations of the operation might take longer, but if many operations are performed on average only constant time per operation is taken.

Log   The operation takes time proportional to the logarithm of the collection size.

L   The operation is linear, that is it takes time proportional to the collection size.

-   The operation is not supported.

Table 24.12 treats sequence types—both immutable and mutable—with the following operations:

head Selecting the first element of the sequence.

tail Producing a new sequence that consists of all elements except the first one.

apply Indexing.

update Functional update (with `updated`) for immutable sequences, side-effecting update (with `update`) for mutable sequences.

prepend Adding an element to the front of the sequence. For immutable sequences, this produces a new sequence. For mutable sequences it modifies the existing sequence.

append Adding an element at the end of the sequence. For immutable sequences, this produces a new sequence. For mutable sequences it modifies the existing sequence.

insert Inserting an element at an arbitrary position in the sequence. This is only supported directly for mutable sequences.

Table 24.13 treats mutable and immutable sets and maps with the following operations:

lookup Testing whether an element is contained in set, or selecting a value associated with a key.

add Adding a new element to a set or a new key/value pair to a map.

remove Removing an element from a set or a key from a map.

min The smallest element of the set, or the smallest key of a map.

24.12   Equality

The collection libraries have a uniform approach to equality and hashing. The idea is, first, to divide collections into sets, maps, and sequences. Collections in different categories are always unequal. For instance, Set(1, 2, 3) is unequal to List(1, 2, 3) even though they contain the same elements. On the other hand, within the same category, collections are equal if and only if they have the same elements (for sequences: the same elements in the same order). For example, List(1, 2, 3) == Vector(1, 2, 3), and HashSet(1, 2) == TreeSet(2, 1).

It does not matter for the equality check whether a collection is mutable or immutable. For a mutable collection, equality simply depends on the current elements at the time the equality test is performed. This means that a mutable collection might be equal to different collections at different times, depending what elements are added or removed. This is a potential trap when using a mutable collection as a key in a hash map. For example:

```
import collection.mutable.{HashMap, ArrayBuffer}
val buf = ArrayBuffer(1, 2, 3)
val map = HashMap(buf -> 3) // Map((ArrayBuffer(1, 2, 3),3))
map(buf) // 3
buf(0) += 1
map(buf)
  // java.util.NoSuchElementException: key not found:
  //   ArrayBuffer(2, 2, 3)
```

In this example, the selection in the last line will most likely fail because the hash code of the array xs has changed in the second-to-last line. Therefore, the hash-code-based lookup will look at a different place than the one in which xs was stored.

24.13 Views

Collections have quite a few methods that construct new collections. Some examples are map, filter, and ++. We call such methods *transformers* because they take at least one collection as their receiver object and produce another collection in their result.

Transformers can be implemented in two principal ways: strict and non-strict (or lazy). A strict transformer constructs a new collection with all of its elements. A non-strict, or lazy, transformer constructs only a proxy for the result collection, and its elements are constructed on demand.

As an example of a non-strict transformer, consider the following implementation of a lazy map operation:

```
def lazyMap[T, U](col: Iterable[T], f: T => U) =
  new Iterable[U]:
    def iterator = col.iterator.map(f)
```

Note that `lazyMap` constructs a new `Iterable` without stepping through all elements of the given collection `coll`. The given function `f` is instead applied to the elements of the new collection's `iterator` as they are demanded.

Scala collections are by default strict in all their transformers, except for `LazyList`, which implements all its transformer methods lazily. However, there is a systematic way to turn every collection into a lazy one and *vice versa*, which is based on collection views. A *view* is a special kind of collection that represents some base collection, but implements all of its transformers lazily.

To go from a collection to its view, you can use the `view` method on the collection. If `xs` is some collection, then `xs.view` is the same collection, but with all transformers implemented lazily. To get back from a view to a strict collection, you can use the `to` conversion operation with a strict collection factory as parameter.

As an example, say you have a vector of `Int`s over which you want to map two functions in succession:

```
val v = Vector((1 to 10)*)
  // Vector(1, 2, 3, 4, 5, 6, 7, 8, 9, 10)
v.map(_ + 1).map(_ * 2)
  // Vector(4, 6, 8, 10, 12, 14, 16, 18, 20, 22)
```

In the last statement, the expression `v.map(_ + 1)` constructs a new vector that is then transformed into a third vector by the second call to `map(_ * 2)`. In many situations, constructing the intermediate result from the first call to `map` is a bit wasteful. In the pseudo example, it would be faster to do a single `map` with the composition of the two functions `(_ + 1)` and `(_ * 2)`. If you have the two functions available in the same place you can do this by hand. But quite often, successive transformations of a data structure are done in different program modules. Fusing those transformations would then undermine modularity. A more general way to avoid the intermediate results is by turning the vector first into a view, applying all transformations to the view, and finally forcing the view to a vector:

```
(v.view.map(_ + 1).map(_ * 2)).toVector
  // Vector(4, 6, 8, 10, 12, 14, 16, 18, 20, 22)
```

We'll do this sequence of operations again, one by one:

```
scala> val vv = v.view
val vv: scala.collection.IndexedSeqView[Int] =
  IndexedSeqView(<not computed>)
```

The application `v.view` gives you an `IndexedSeqView`, a lazily evaluated `IndexedSeq`. As with `LazyList`, `toString` on views does not force the view elements. That's why the vv's elements are displayed as `not computed`.

Applying the first `map` to the view gives you:

```
scala> vv.map(_ + 1)
val res13: scala.collection.IndexedSeqView[Int] =
  IndexedSeqView(<not computed>)
```

The result of the `map` is another `IndexedSeqView[Int]` value. This is in essence a wrapper that *records* the fact that a `map` with function `(_ + 1)` needs to be applied on the vector v. It does not apply that map until the view is forced, however. We'll now apply the second `map` to the last result.

```
scala> res13.map(_ * 2)
val res14: scala.collection.IndexedSeqView[Int] =
  IndexedSeqView(<not computed>)
```

Finally, forcing the last result gives:

```
scala> res14.toVector
val res15: Seq[Int] =
      Vector(4, 6, 8, 10, 12, 14, 16, 18, 20, 22)
```

Both stored functions, `(_ + 1)` and `(_ * 2)`, get applied as part of the execution of the `to` operation and a new vector is constructed. That way, no intermediate data structure is needed.

Transformation operations applied to views don't build a new data structure. Instead, they return an iterable whose iterator is the result of applying the transformation operation to the underlying collection's iterator.

The main reason for using views is performance. You have seen that by switching a collection to a view the construction of intermediate results can be avoided. These savings can be quite important. As another example, consider the problem of finding the first palindrome in a list of words. A palindrome is a word that reads backwards the same as forwards. Here are the necessary definitions:

```
def isPalindrome(x: String) = x == x.reverse
def findPalindrome(s: Iterable[String]) = s.find(isPalindrome)
```

Now, assume you have a very long sequence, words, and you want to find a palindrome in the first million words of that sequence. Can you re-use the definition of findPalindrome? Of course, you could write:

```
findPalindrome(words.take(1000000))
```

This nicely separates the two aspects of taking the first million words of a sequence and finding a palindrome in it. But the downside is that it always constructs an intermediary sequence consisting of one million words, even if the first word of that sequence is already a palindrome. So potentially, 999,999 words are copied into the intermediary result without being inspected at all afterwards. Many programmers would give up here and write their own specialized version of finding palindromes in some given prefix of an argument sequence. But with views, you don't have to. Simply write:

```
findPalindrome(words.view.take(1000000))
```

This has the same nice separation of concerns, but instead of a sequence of a million elements it will only construct a single lightweight view object. This way, you do not need to choose between performance and modularity.

After having seen all these nifty uses of views you might wonder why have strict collections at all? One reason is that performance comparisons do not always favor lazy over strict collections. For smaller collection sizes the added overhead of forming and applying closures in views is often greater than the gain from avoiding the intermediary data structures. A possibly more important reason is that evaluation in views can be very confusing if the delayed operations have side effects.

Here's an example that bit a few users of versions of Scala before 2.8. In these versions the Range type was lazy, so it behaved in effect like a view. People were trying to create a number of actors[6] like this:

---

[6]The Scala actors library has been deprecated, but this historical example is still relevant.

```
val actors = for i <- 1 to 10 yield actor { ??? }
```

They were surprised that none of the actors were executing afterwards, even though the `actor` method should create and start an actor from the code that's enclosed in the braces following it. To explain why nothing happened, remember that the `for` expression above is equivalent to an application of the `map` method:

```
val actors = (1 to 10).map(i => actor { ??? })
```

Since previously the range produced by (1 to 10) behaved like a view, the result of the `map` was again a view. That is, no element was computed, and, consequently, no actor was created! Actors would have been created by forcing the range of the whole expression, but it's far from obvious that this is what was required to make the actors do their work.

To avoid surprises like this, the Scala collections gained more regular rules in version 2.8. All collections except lazy lists and views are strict. The only way to go from a strict to a lazy collection is via the `view` method. The only way to go back is via `to`. So the `actors` definition above would behave as expected in Scala 2.8 in that it would create and start ten actors. To get back the surprising previous behavior, you'd have to add an explicit `view` method call:

```
val actors = for i <- (1 to 10).view yield actor { ??? }
```

In summary, views are a powerful tool to reconcile concerns of efficiency with concerns of modularity. But in order not to be entangled in aspects of delayed evaluation, you should restrict views to purely functional code where collection transformations do not have side effects. What's best avoided is a mixture of views and operations that create new collections while also having side effects.

24.14 Iterators

An iterator is not a collection, but rather a way to access the elements of a collection one by one. The two basic operations on an iterator `it` are `next` and `hasNext`. A call to `it.next()` will return the next element of the iterator and advance the state of the iterator. Calling `next` again on the same iterator will then yield the element one beyond the one returned previously. If there are no more elements to return, a call to next will throw a NoSuchElementException. You can find out whether there are more elements to return using Iterator's hasNext method.

The most straightforward way to "step through" all the elements returned by an iterator is to use a while loop:

```
while it.hasNext do
  println(it.next())
```

Iterators in Scala also provide analogues of most of the methods that you find in the Iterable and Seq traits. For instance, they provide a foreach method that executes a given procedure on each element returned by an iterator. Using foreach, the loop above could be abbreviated to:

```
it.foreach(println)
```

As always, for expressions can be used as an alternate syntax for expressions involving foreach, map, filter, and flatMap, so yet another way to print all elements returned by an iterator would be:

```
for elem <- it do println(elem)
```

There's an important difference between the foreach method on iterators and the same method on iterable collections: When called on an iterator, foreach will leave the iterator at its end when it is done. So calling next again on the same iterator will fail with a NoSuchElementException. By contrast, when called on a collection, foreach leaves the number of elements in the collection unchanged (unless the passed function adds or removes elements, but this is discouraged, because it can easily lead to surprising results).

The other operations that Iterator has in common with Iterable have the same property of leaving the iterator at its end when done. For instance, iterators provide a map method, which returns a new iterator:

```
val it = Iterator("a", "number", "of", "words")
val lit = it.map(_.length)
it.hasNext // true
lit.foreach(println) // prints 1, 6, 2, 5
it.hasNext // false
```

As you can see, after the call to map, the it iterator hasn't advanced to its end, but traversing the iterator resulting from the call to it.map also traverses it and advances it to its end.

Another example is the dropWhile method, which can be used to find the first element of an iterator that has a certain property. For instance, to find the first word in the iterator shown previously that has at least two characters, you could write:

```
val it = Iterator("a", "number", "of", "words")
val dit = it.dropWhile(_.length < 2)
dit.next() // number
it.next()  // of
```

Note again that it has changed by the call to dropWhile: it now points to the second word "number" in the list. In fact, it and the result dit returned by dropWhile will return exactly the same sequence of elements.

There is only one standard operation, duplicate, which allows you to re-use the same iterator:

```
val (it1, it2) = it.duplicate
```

The call to duplicate gives you *two* iterators, which each return exactly the same elements as the iterator it. The two iterators work independently; advancing one does not affect the other. By contrast the original iterator, it, is advanced to its end by duplicate and is thus rendered unusable.

In summary, iterators behave like collections *if you never access an iterator again after invoking a method on it*. The Scala collection libraries make this explicit with an abstraction called IterableOnce, which is a common supertrait of Iterable and Iterator. As the name implies, IterableOnce objects can be traversed at least once but the state of that object after the traversal is not specified. If the IterableOnce object is in fact an Iterator, it will be at its end after the traversal, but if it is an Iterable, it will still exist as before. A common use case of IterableOnce is as an argument type for methods that can take either an iterator or an iterable as argument. An example is the appending method ++ in trait Iterable. It takes a IterableOnce parameter, so you can append elements coming from either an iterator or an iterable collection.

All operations on iterators are summarized in Table 24.14.

Table 24.14 · Operations in trait `Iterator`

What it is	What it does
Abstract methods:	
`it.next()`	Returns the next element in the iterator and advances past it.
`it.hasNext`	Returns `true` if `it` can return another element.
Variations:	
`it.buffered`	A buffered iterator returning all elements of `it`.
`it.grouped(size)`	An iterator that yields the elements returned by `it` in fixed-sized sequence "chunks."
`it.sliding(size)`	An iterator that yields the elements returned by `it` in sequences representing a sliding fixed-sized window.
Copying:	
`it.copyToArray(arr, s, l)`	Copies at most `l` elements returned by `it` to array `arr` starting at index `s`. The last two arguments are optional.
Duplication:	
`it.duplicate`	A pair of iterators that each independently return all elements of `it`.
Additions:	
`it ++ jt`	An iterator returning all elements returned by iterator `it`, followed by all elements returned by iterator `jt`.
`it.padTo(len, x)`	The iterator that returns all elements of `it` followed by copies of `x` until length `len` elements are returned overall.
Maps:	
`it.map(f)`	The iterator obtained from applying the function `f` to every element returned from `it`.
`it.flatMap(f)`	The iterator obtained from applying the iterator-valued function `f` to every element in `it` and appending the results.
`it.collect(f)`	The iterator obtained from applying the partial function `f` to every element in `it` for which it is defined and collecting the results.

549

Table 24.14 · continued

Conversions:

`it.toArray`	Collects the elements returned by `it` in an array.
`it.toList`	Collects the elements returned by `it` in a list.
`it.toIterable`	Collects the elements returned by `it` in an iterable.
`it.toSeq`	Collects the elements returned by `it` in a sequence.
`it.toIndexedSeq`	Collects the elements returned by `it` in an indexed sequence.
`it.toSet`	Collects the elements returned by `it` in a set.
`it.toMap`	Collects the key/value pairs returned by `it` in a map.
`it to SortedSet`	Generic conversion operation that takes a collection factory as parameter.

Size info:

`it.isEmpty`	Tests whether the iterator is empty (opposite of `hasNext`).
`it.nonEmpty`	Tests whether the collection contains elements (alias of `hasNext`).
`it.size`	The number of elements returned by `it`. Note: `it` will be at its end after this operation!
`it.length`	Same as `it.size`.
`it.knownSize`	The number of elements, if it is known without modifying the iterator's state, otherwise −1.

Element retrieval index search:

`it.find(p)`	An option containing the first element returned by `it` that satisfies `p`, or `None` if no element qualifies. Note: The iterator advances to just after the element, or, if none is found, to the end.
`it.indexOf(x)`	The index of the first element returned by `it` that equals `x`. Note: The iterator advances past the position of this element.
`it.indexWhere(p)`	The index of the first element returned by `it` that satisfies `p`. Note: The iterator advances past the position of this element.

550

Table 24.14 · continued

Subiterators:

it.take(n)	An iterator returning of the first n elements of it. Note: it will advance to the position after the n'th element, or to its end, if it contains less than n elements.
it.drop(n)	The iterator that starts with the (n + 1)'th element of it. Note: it will advance to the same position.
it.slice(m, n)	The iterator that returns a slice of the elements returned from it, starting with the m'th element and ending before the n'th element.
it.takeWhile(p)	An iterator returning elements from it as long as condition p is true.
it.dropWhile(p)	An iterator skipping elements from it as long as condition p is true, and returning the remainder.
it.filter(p)	An iterator returning all elements from it that satisfy the condition p.
it.withFilter(p)	Same as it.filter(p). Needed so that iterators can be used in for expressions.
it.filterNot(p)	An iterator returning all elements from it that do not satisfy the condition p.
it.distinct	An iterator returning the elements from it without duplicates.

Subdivisions:

it.partition(p)	Splits it into a pair of two iterators; one returning all elements from it that satisfy the predicate p, the other returning all elements from it that do not.

Element conditions:

it.forall(p)	A boolean indicating whether the predicate p holds for all elements returned by it.
it.exists(p)	A boolean indicating whether the predicate p holds for some element in it.
it.count(p)	The number of elements in it that satisfy the predicate p.

551

Table 24.14 · continued

Folds:

`it.foldLeft(z)(op)`	Applies binary operation op between successive elements returned by it, going left to right, starting with z.
`it.foldRight(z)(op)`	Applies binary operation op between successive elements returned by it, going right to left, starting with z.
`it.reduceLeft(op)`	Applies binary operation op between successive elements returned by non-empty iterator it, going left to right.
`it.reduceRight(op)`	Applies binary operation op between successive elements returned by non-empty iterator it, going right to left.

Specific folds:

`it.sum`	The sum of the numeric element values returned by iterator it.
`it.product`	The product of the numeric element values returned by iterator it.
`it.min`	The minimum of the ordered element values returned by iterator it.
`it.max`	The maximum of the ordered element values returned by iterator it.

Zippers:

`it zip jt`	An iterator of pairs of corresponding elements returned from iterators it and jt.
`it.zipAll(jt, x, y)`	An iterator of pairs of corresponding elements returned from iterators it and jt, where the shorter iterator is extended to match the longer one by appending elements x or y.
`it.zipWithIndex`	An iterator of pairs of elements returned from it with their indices.

Update:

`it.patch(i, jt, r)`	The iterator resulting from it by replacing r elements starting with i by the patch iterator jt.

Table 24.14 · continued

Comparison:

it.sameElements(jt)	A test whether iterators it and jt return the same elements in the same order. Note: Both it and jt should be discarded after this operation.

Strings:

it.addString(b, start, sep, end)	Adds a string to StringBuilder b that shows all elements returned by it between separators sep enclosed in strings start and end. start,sep, and end are all optional.
it.mkString(start, sep, end)	Converts the iterator to a string that shows all elements returned by it between separators sep enclosed in strings start and end. start, sep, and end are all optional.

Buffered iterators

Sometimes you want an iterator that can "look ahead" so that you can inspect the next element to be returned without advancing past that element. Consider, for instance, the task to skip leading empty strings from an iterator that returns a sequence of strings. You might be tempted to write something like the following method:

```
// This won't work
def skipEmptyWordsNOT(it: Iterator[String]) =
  while it.next().isEmpty do {}
```

But looking at this code more closely, it's clear that this is wrong: the code will indeed skip leading empty strings, but it will also advance it past the first non-empty string!

The solution to this problem is to use a buffered iterator, an instance of trait BufferedIterator. BufferedIterator is a subtrait of Iterator, which provides one extra method, head. Calling head on a buffered iterator will return its first element, but will not advance the iterator. Using a buffered iterator, skipping empty words can be written like this:

```
def skipEmptyWords(it: BufferedIterator[String]) =
  while it.head.isEmpty do it.next()
```

Every iterator can be converted to a buffered iterator by calling its `buffered` method. Here's an example:

```
val it = Iterator(1, 2, 3, 4)
val bit = it.buffered
bit.head   // 1
bit.next() // 1
bit.next() // 2
```

Note that calling `head` on the buffered iterator, `bit`, did not advance it. Therefore, the subsequent call, `bit.next()`, returned again the same value as `bit.head`.

24.15   Creating collections from scratch

You have already seen syntax like `List(1, 2, 3)`, which creates a list of three integers, and `Map('A' -> 1, 'C' -> 2)`, which creates a map with two bindings. This is actually a universal feature of Scala collections. You can take any collection name and follow it by a list of elements in parentheses. The result will be a new collection with the given elements. Here are some more examples:

```
Iterable()              // An empty collection
List()                  // The empty list
List(1.0, 2.0)          // A list with elements 1.0, 2.0
Vector(1.0, 2.0)        // A vector with elements 1.0, 2.0
Iterator(1, 2, 3)       // An iterator returning three integers.
Set(dog, cat, bird)     // A set of three animals
HashSet(dog, cat, bird) // A hash set of the same animals
Map('a' -> 7, 'b' -> 0) // A map from characters to integers
```

"Under the covers" each of the above lines is a call to the `apply` method of some object. For instance, the third line above expands to:

```
List.apply(1.0, 2.0)
```

So this is a call to the `apply` method of the companion object of the `List` class. That method takes an arbitrary number of arguments and constructs a list from them. Every collection class in the Scala library has a companion object with such an `apply` method. It does not matter whether the collection class represents a concrete implementation, like `List`, `LazyList`, or `Vector`, or whether it is a trait such as `Seq`, `Set`, or `Iterable`. In the latter case, calling `apply` will produce some default implementation of the trait. Here are some examples:

```scala
scala> List(1, 2, 3)
val res17: List[Int] = List(1, 2, 3)

scala> Iterable(1, 2, 3)
val res18: Iterable[Int] = List(1, 2, 3)

scala> mutable.Iterable(1, 2, 3)
val res19: scala.collection.mutable.Iterable[Int] =
  ArrayBuffer(1, 2, 3)
```

Besides `apply`, every collection companion object also defines a member `empty`, which returns an empty collection. So instead of `List()` you could write `List.empty`, instead of `Map()`, `Map.empty`, and so on.

Descendants of `Seq` and `Set` traits also provide other factory operations in their companion objects. These are summarized in Table 24.15. In short, there's:

concat, which concatenates an arbitrary number of collections together,

fill and tabulate, which generate single or multi-dimensional collections of given dimensions initialized by some expression or tabulating function,

range, which generates integer collections with some constant step length, and

iterate and unfold, which generate a collection resulting from repeated application of a function to a start element or state.

Table 24.15 · Factory methods for Seqs and Sets

What it is	What it does
C.empty	The empty collection
C(x, y, z)	A collection consisting of elements x, y, and z

Table 24.15 · continued

`C.concat(xs, ys, zs)`	The collection obtained by concatenating the elements of xs, ys, and zs
`C.fill(n)(e)`	A collection of length n where each element is computed by expression e
`C.fill(m, n)(e)`	A collection of collections of dimension $m \times n$ where each element is computed by expression e (exists also in higher dimensions)
`C.tabulate(n)(f)`	A collection of length n where the element at each index i is computed by $f(i)$
`C.tabulate(m, n)(f)`	A collection of collections of dimension $m \times n$ where the element at each index (i, j) is computed by $f(i, j)$ (exists also in higher dimensions)
`C.range(start, end)`	The collection of integers start … end – 1
`C.range(start, end, step)`	The collection of integers starting with start and progressing by step increments up to, and excluding, the end value
`C.iterate(x, n)(f)`	The collection of length n with elements x, f(x), f(f(x)), …
`C.unfold(init)(f)`	A collection that uses a function f to compute its next element and state, starting from the init state.

24.16 Conversions between Java and Scala collections

Like Scala, Java has a rich collections library. There are many similarities between the two. For instance, both libraries know iterators, iterables, sets, maps, and sequences. But there are also important differences. In particular, the Scala libraries put much more emphasis on immutable collections, and provide many more operations that transform a collection into a new one.

Sometimes you might need to convert from one collection framework to the other. For instance, you might want to access an existing Java collection, as if it were a Scala collection. Or you might want to pass one of Scala's collections to a Java method that expects the Java counterpart. It is quite easy to do this, because Scala offers convenient conversions between all the major collection types in the `CollectionConverters` object. In particular, you will find bidirectional conversions between the following types:

```
Iterator         ⇔    java.util.Iterator
Iterator         ⇔    java.util.Enumeration
Iterable         ⇔    java.lang.Iterable
Iterable         ⇔    java.util.Collection
mutable.Buffer   ⇔    java.util.List
mutable.Set      ⇔    java.util.Set
mutable.Map      ⇔    java.util.Map
```

To enable these conversions, simply import like this:

```
scala> import jdk.CollectionConverters.*
```

This enables conversions between Scala collections and their corresponding Java collections via extension methods asScala and asJava:

```
scala> import collection.mutable.*

scala> val jul: java.util.List[Int] = ArrayBuffer(1, 2, 3).asJava
val jul: java.util.List[Int] = [1, 2, 3]

scala> val buf: Seq[Int] = jul.asScala
val buf: scala.collection.mutable.Seq[Int] = ArrayBuffer(1, 2, 3)

scala> val m: java.util.Map[String, Int] =
         HashMap("abc" -> 1, "hello" -> 2).asJava
m: java.util.Map[String,Int] = {hello=2, abc=1}
```

Internally, these conversions work by setting up a "wrapper" object that forwards all operations to the underlying collection object. So collections are never copied when converting between Java and Scala. An interesting property is that if you do a round-trip conversion from, say, a Java type to its corresponding Scala type, and back to the same Java type, you end up with the identical collection object you started with.

Some other common Scala collections exist that can also be converted to Java types, but for which no corresponding conversion exists in the other direction. These are:

```
Seq            ⇒    java.util.List
mutable.Seq    ⇒    java.util.List
Set            ⇒    java.util.Set
Map            ⇒    java.util.Map
```

557

Because Java does not distinguish between mutable and immutable collections in their type, a conversion from, say, `collection.immutable.List` will yield a `java.util.List`, on which all attempted mutation operations will throw an `UnsupportedOperationException`. Here's an example:

```
scala> val jul: java.util.List[Int] = List(1, 2, 3)
val jul: java.util.List[Int] = [1, 2, 3]

scala> jul.add(7)
java.lang.UnsupportedOperationException
        at java.util.AbstractList.add(AbstractList.java:131)
```

24.17 Conclusion

You've now seen how to use Scala's collection in great detail. Scala's collections take the approach of giving you powerful building blocks rather than a number of ad hoc utility methods. Putting together two or three such building blocks allows you to express an enormous number of useful computations. This style of library is especially effective due to Scala having a light syntax for function literals, and due to it providing many collection types that are persistent and immutable. In the next and final chapter, we'll turn our attention to assertions and unit testing.

Chapter 25

Assertions and Tests

Assertions and tests are two important ways you can check that the software you write behaves as you expect. In this chapter, we'll show you several options you have in Scala to write and run them.

25.1 Assertions

Assertions in Scala are written as calls of a predefined method assert.[1] The expression assert(condition) throws an AssertionError if condition does not hold. There's also a two-argument version of assert: The expression assert(condition, explanation) tests condition and, if it does not hold, throws an AssertionError that contains the given explanation. The type of explanation is Any, so you can pass any object as the explanation. The assert method will call toString on it to get a string explanation to place inside the AssertionError. For example, in the method named "above" of class Element, shown in Listing 10.13 on page 196, you might place an assert after the calls to widen to make sure that the widened elements have equal widths. This is shown in Listing 25.1.

Another way you might choose to do this is to check the widths at the end of the widen method, right before you return the value. You can accomplish this by storing the result in a val, performing an assertion on the result, then mentioning the val last so the result is returned if the assertion succeeds. However, you can do this more concisely with a convenience method in Predef named ensuring, as shown in Listing 25.2.

---

[1]The assert method is defined in the Predef singleton object, whose members are automatically imported into every Scala source file.

```
def above(that: Element): Element =
  val this1 = this widen that.width
  val that1 = that widen this.width
  assert(this1.width == that1.width)
  elem(this1.contents ++ that1.contents)
```

Listing 25.1 · Using an assertion.

The ensuring method can be used with any result type because of an implicit conversion. Although it looks in this code as if we're invoking ensuring on widen's result, which is type Element, we're actually invoking ensuring on a type to which Element is implicitly converted. The ensuring method takes one argument, a predicate function that takes a result type and returns Boolean, and passes the result to the predicate. If the predicate returns true, ensuring will return the result; otherwise, ensuring will throw an AssertionError.

In this example, the predicate is "w <= _.width". The underscore is a placeholder for the one argument passed to the predicate, the Element result of the widen method. If the width passed as w to widen is less than or equal to the width of the result Element, the predicate will result in true, and ensuring will result in the Element on which it was invoked. Because this is the last expression of the widen method, widen itself will then result in the Element.

Assertions can be enabled and disabled using the JVM's -ea and -da command-line flags. When enabled, each assertion serves as a little test that uses the actual data encountered as the software runs. In the remainder of

```
private def widen(w: Int): Element =
  if w <= width then
    this
  else {
    val left = elem(' ', (w - width) / 2, height)
    var right = elem(' ', w - width - left.width, height)
    left beside this beside right
  } ensuring (w <= _.width)
```

Listing 25.2 · Using ensuring to assert a function's result.

this chapter, we'll focus on the writing of external tests, which provide their own test data and run independently from the application.

25.2 Testing in Scala

You have many options for testing in Scala, from established Java tools, such as JUnit and TestNG, to tools written in Scala, such as ScalaTest, specs2, and ScalaCheck. For the remainder of this chapter, we'll give you a quick tour of these tools. We'll start with ScalaTest.

ScalaTest is the most flexible Scala test framework: it can be easily customized to solve different problems. ScalaTest's flexibility means teams can use whatever testing style fits their needs best. For example, for teams familiar with JUnit, the AnyFunSuite style will feel comfortable and familiar. Listing 25.3 shows an example.

```
import org.scalatest.funsuite.AnyFunSuite
import Element.elem

class ElementSuite extends AnyFunSuite:

  test("elem result should have passed width") {
    val ele = elem('x', 2, 3)
    assert(ele.width == 2)
  }
```

Listing 25.3 · Writing tests with AnyFunSuite.

The central concept in ScalaTest is the *suite*, a collection of tests. A *test* can be anything with a name that can start and either succeed, fail, be pending, or canceled. Trait Suite is the central unit of composition in Scala-Test. Suite declares "lifecycle" methods defining a default way to run tests, which can be overridden to customize how tests are written and run.

ScalaTest offers *style traits* that extend Suite and override lifecycle methods to support different testing styles. It also provides *mixin traits* that override lifecycle methods to address particular testing needs. You define test classes by composing Suite style and mixin traits, and define test suites by composing Suite instances.

AnyFunSuite, which is extended by the test class shown in Listing 25.3, is an example of a testing style. The "Fun" in AnyFunSuite stands for func-

561

tion; "test" is a method defined in AnyFunSuite, which is invoked by the primary constructor of ElementSuite. You specify the name of the test as a string between the parentheses and the test code itself between curly braces. The test code is a function passed as a by-name parameter to test, which registers it for later execution.

ScalaTest is integrated into common build tools (such as sbt and Maven) and IDEs (such as IntelliJ IDEA and Eclipse). You can also run a Suite directly via ScalaTest's Runner application or from the Scala interpreter simply by invoking execute on it. Here's an example:

```
scala> (new ElementSuite).execute()
ElementSuite:
- elem result should have passed width
```

All ScalaTest styles, including AnyFunSuite, are designed to encourage the writing of focused tests with descriptive names. In addition, all styles generate specification-like output that can facilitate communication among stakeholders. The style you choose dictates only how the declarations of your tests will look. Everything else in ScalaTest works consistently the same way no matter what style you choose.[2]

25.3 Informative failure reports

The test in Listing 25.3 attempts to create an element of width 2 and asserts that the width of the resulting element is indeed 2. Were this assertion to fail, the failure report would include the filename and line number of the offending assertion, and an informative error message:

```
scala> val width = 3
width: Int = 3

scala> assert(width == 2)
org.scalatest.exceptions.TestFailedException:
    3 did not equal 2
```

To provide descriptive error messages when assertions fail, ScalaTest analyzes the expressions passed to each assert invocation at compile time.

---

[2]More detail on ScalaTest is available from https://www.scalatest.org/.

If you prefer to see even more detailed information about assertion failures, you can use ScalaTest's Diagrams, assertions whose error messages display a diagram of the expression passed to assert:

```
scala> assert(List(1, 2, 3).contains(4))
org.scalatest.exceptions.TestFailedException:

  assert(List(1, 2, 3).contains(4))
         |    | | |    |        |
         |    1 2 3    false    4
         List(1, 2, 3)
```

ScalaTest's assert methods do not differentiate between the actual and expected result in error messages. They just indicate that the left operand did not equal the right operand, or show the values in a diagram. If you wish to emphasize the distinction between actual and expected, you can alternatively use ScalaTest's assertResult method, like this:

```
assertResult(2) {
  ele.width
}
```

With this expression you indicate that you expect the code between the curly braces to result in 2. Were the code between the braces to result in 3, you'd see the message, "Expected 2, but got 3" in the test failure report.

If you want to check that a method throws an expected exception, you can use ScalaTest's assertThrows method, like this:

```
assertThrows[IllegalArgumentException] {
  elem('x', -2, 3)
}
```

If the code between the curly braces throws a different exception than expected, or throws no exception, assertThrows will complete abruptly with a TestFailedException. You'll get a helpful error message in the failure report, such as:

```
Expected IllegalArgumentException to be thrown,
  but NegativeArraySizeException was thrown.
```

On the other hand, if the code completes abruptly with an instance of the passed exception class, `assertThrows` will return normally. If you wish to inspect the expected exception further, you can use `intercept` instead of `assertThrows`. The `intercept` method works the same as `assertThrows`, except if the expected exception is thrown, `intercept` returns it:

```
val caught =
  intercept[ArithmeticException] {
    1 / 0
  }
assert(caught.getMessage == "/ by zero")
```

In short, ScalaTest's assertions work hard to provide useful failure messages that will help you diagnose and fix problems in your code.

25.4 Tests as specifications

In the *behavior-driven development* (BDD) testing style, the emphasis is on writing human-readable specifications of the expected behavior of code and accompanying tests that verify the code has the specified behavior. ScalaTest includes several traits that facilitate this style of testing. An example using one such trait, `AnyFlatSpec`, is shown in Listing 25.4.

In an `AnyFlatSpec`, you write tests as *specifier clauses*. You start by writing a name for the *subject* under test as a string ("A UniformElement" in Listing 25.4), then `should` (or `must` or `can`), then a string that specifies a bit of behavior required of the subject, then `in`. In the curly braces following `in`, you write code that tests the specified behavior. In subsequent clauses you can write `it` to refer to the most recently given subject. When a `AnyFlatSpec` is executed, it will run each specifier clause as a ScalaTest test. `AnyFlatSpec` (and ScalaTest's other specification traits) generate output that reads like a specification when run. For example, here's what the output will look like if you run `ElementSpec` from Listing 25.4 in the interpreter:

```
scala> (new ElementSpec).execute()
A UniformElement
- should have a width equal to the passed value
- should have a height equal to the passed value
- should throw an IAE if passed a negative width
```

```
import org.scalatest.flatspec.AnyFlatSpec
import org.scalatest.matchers.should.Matchers
import Element.elem

class ElementSpec extends AnyFlatSpec, Matchers:

  "A UniformElement" should
      "have a width equal to the passed value" in {
    val ele = elem('x', 2, 3)
    ele.width should be (2)
  }

  it should "have a height equal to the passed value" in {
    val ele = elem('x', 2, 3)
    ele.height should be (3)
  }

  it should "throw an IAE if passed a negative width" in {
    an [IllegalArgumentException] should be thrownBy {
      elem('x', -2, 3)
    }
  }
}
```

Listing 25.4 · Specifying and testing behavior with an AnyFlatSpec.

Listing 25.4 also illustrates ScalaTest's *matchers* domain-specific language (DSL). By mixing in trait Matchers, you can write assertions that read more like natural language. ScalaTest provides many matchers in its DSL, and also enables you to define new matchers with custom failure messages. The matchers shown in Listing 25.4 include the "should be" and "an [...] should be thrownBy { ... } " syntax. You can alternatively mix in MustMatchers if you prefer must to should. For example, mixing in MustMatchers would allow you to write expressions such as:

```
result must be >= 0
map must contain key 'c'
```

If the last assertion failed, you'd see an error message similar to:

```
Map('a' -> 1, 'b' -> 2) did not contain key 'c'
```

The specs2 testing framework, an open source tool written in Scala by Eric Torreborre, also supports the BDD style of testing but with a different syntax. For example, you could use specs2 to write the test shown in Listing 25.5:

```
import org.specs2.*
import Element.elem

object ElementSpecification extends Specification:
  "A UniformElement" should {
    "have a width equal to the passed value" in {
      val ele = elem('x', 2, 3)
      ele.width must be_==(2)
    }
    "have a height equal to the passed value" in {
      val ele = elem('x', 2, 3)
      ele.height must be_==(3)
    }
    "throw an IAE if passed a negative width" in {
      elem('x', -2, 3) must
        throwA[IllegalArgumentException]
    }
  }
```

Listing 25.5 · Specifying and testing behavior with the specs2 framework.

Like ScalaTest, specs2 provides a matchers DSL. You can see some examples of specs2 matchers in action in Listing 25.5 in the lines that contain "must be_==" and "must throwA".[3] You can use specs2 standalone, but it is also integrated with ScalaTest and JUnit, so you can run specs2 tests with those tools as well.

One of the big ideas of BDD is that tests can be used to facilitate communication between the people who decide what a software system should do, the people who implement the software, and the people who determine whether the software is finished and working. Although any of ScalaTest's or specs2's styles can be used in this manner, ScalaTest's AnyFeatureSpec in particular is designed for it. Listing 25.6 shows an example:

---

[3] You can download specs2 from http://specs2.org/.

```
import org.scalatest.*
import org.scalatest.featurespec.AnyFeatureSpec

class TVSetSpec extends AnyFeatureSpec, GivenWhenThen:

  Feature("TV power button") {
    Scenario("User presses power button when TV is off") {
      Given("a TV set that is switched off")
      When("the power button is pressed")
      Then("the TV should switch on")
      pending
    }
  }
```

Listing 25.6 · Using tests to facilitate communication among stakeholders.

AnyFeatureSpec is designed to guide conversations about software requirements: You must identify specific *features*, then specify those features in terms of *scenarios*. The Given, When, and Then methods (provided by trait GivenWhenThen) can help focus the conversation on the specifics of individual scenarios. The pending call at the end indicates that neither the test nor the actual behavior has been implemented—just the specification. Once all the tests and specified behavior have been implemented, the tests will pass and the requirements can be deemed to have been met.

25.5 Property-based testing

Another useful testing tool for Scala is ScalaCheck, an open source framework written by Rickard Nilsson. ScalaCheck enables you to specify properties that the code under test must obey. For each property, ScalaCheck will generate data and execute assertions that check whether the property holds. Listing 25.7 shows an example of using ScalaCheck from a ScalaTest AnyWordSpec that mixes in trait ScalaCheckPropertyChecks.

AnyWordSpec is a ScalaTest style class. The PropertyChecks trait provides several forAll methods that allow you to mix property-based tests with traditional assertion-based or matcher-based tests. In this example, we check a property that the elem factory should obey. ScalaCheck properties are expressed as function values that take as parameters the data needed by

```
import org.scalatest.wordspec.AnyWordSpec
import org.scalatestplus.scalacheck.ScalaCheckPropertyChecks
import org.scalatest.matchers.must.Matchers.*
import Element.elem

class ElementSpec extends AnyWordSpec,
        ScalaCheckPropertyChecks:
  "elem result" must {
    "have passed width" in {
      forAll { (w: Int) =>
        whenever (w > 0) {
          elem('x', w % 100, 3).width must equal (w % 100)
        }
      }
    }
  }
```

Listing 25.7 · Writing property-based tests with ScalaCheck.

the property's assertions. This data will be generated by ScalaCheck. In the property shown in Listing 25.7, the data is an integer named w that represents a width. Inside the body of the function, you see this code:

```
whenever (w > 0) {
  elem('x', w % 100, 3).width must equal (w % 100)
}
```

The whenever clause indicates that whenever the left hand expression is true, the expression on the right must hold true. Thus in this case, the expression in the block must hold true whenever w is greater than 0. The right-hand expression in this case will yield true if the width passed to the elem factory is the same as the width of the Element returned by the factory.

With this small amount of code, ScalaCheck will generate several values for w and test each one, looking for a value for which the property doesn't hold. If the property holds true for every value ScalaCheck tries, the test will pass. Otherwise, the test will throw a TestFailedException that contains information including the value that caused the failure.

25.6 Organizing and running tests

Each framework mentioned in this chapter provides some mechanism for organizing and running tests. In this section, we'll give a quick overview of ScalaTest's approach. To get the full story on any of these frameworks, however, you'll need to consult their documentation.

In ScalaTest, you organize large test suites by nesting `Suites` inside `Suites`. When a `Suite` is executed, it will execute its nested `Suites` as well as its tests. The nested `Suites` will in turn execute their nested `Suites`, and so on. A large test suite, therefore, is represented as a tree of `Suite` objects. When you execute the root `Suite` in the tree, all `Suites` in the tree will be executed.

You can nest suites manually or automatically. To nest manually, you either override the `nestedSuites` method on your `Suites` or pass the `Suites` you want to nest to the constructor of class `Suites`, which ScalaTest provides for this purpose. To nest automatically, you provide package names to ScalaTest's `Runner`, which will discover `Suites` automatically, nest them under a root `Suite`, and execute the root `Suite`.

You can invoke ScalaTest's `Runner` application from the command line or via a build tool, such as sbt or maven. The most common way people run ScalaTest is most likely through sbt.[4] To run the test class shown in Listing 25.6 with sbt, create a new directory, place the test class in a file named `TVSetSpec.scala` in the `src/test/scala` subdirectory, and add the following `build.sbt` file in the new directory:

```
name := "ThankYouReader!"

scalaVersion := "3.0.0"

libraryDependencies += "org.scalatest" %% "scalatest" %
    "3.2.9" % "test"
```

You can then enter the sbt shell by typing sbt:

```
$ sbt
[info] welcome to sbt 1.5.2 (AdoptOpenJDK Java 1.8.0_262)
...
sbt:ThankYouReader!>
```

---

[4]To install sbt, visit `https://www.scala-sbt.org/`.

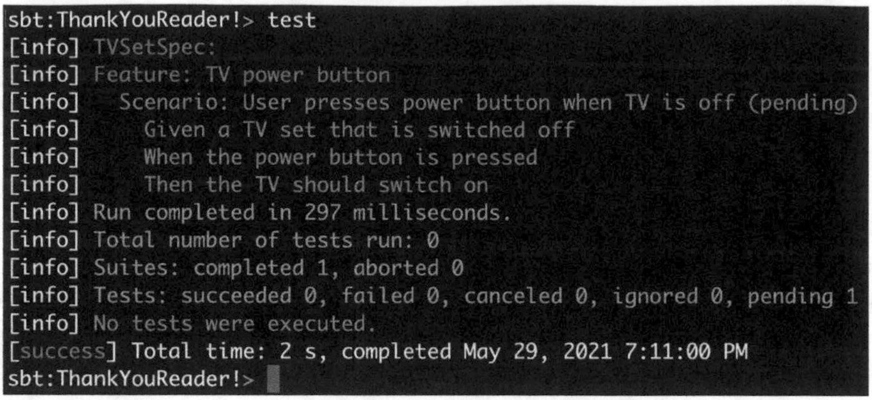

```
sbt:ThankYouReader!> test
[info] TVSetSpec:
[info] Feature: TV power button
[info]    Scenario: User presses power button when TV is off (pending)
[info]      Given a TV set that is switched off
[info]      When the power button is pressed
[info]      Then the TV should switch on
[info] Run completed in 297 milliseconds.
[info] Total number of tests run: 0
[info] Suites: completed 1, aborted 0
[info] Tests: succeeded 0, failed 0, canceled 0, ignored 0, pending 1
[info] No tests were executed.
[success] Total time: 2 s, completed May 29, 2021 7:11:00 PM
sbt:ThankYouReader!>
```

Figure 25.1 · The output of `org.scalatest.run`.

You will be given a prompt that indicates the name of the project, in this case `ThankYouReader!`. If you type `test`, it will compile and run the test class. The result is shown in Figure 25.1.

25.7 Conclusion

In this chapter you saw examples of mixing assertions directly in production code, as well as writing them externally in tests. You saw that as a Scala programmer, you can take advantage of popular testing tools from the Java community, such as JUnit, as well as newer tools designed explicitly for Scala, such as ScalaTest, ScalaCheck, and specs2. Both in-code assertions and external tests can help you achieve your software quality goals.

Glossary

algebraic data type A type defined by providing several alternatives, each of which comes with its own constructor. It usually comes with a way to decompose the type through pattern matching. The concept is found in specification languages and functional programming languages. Algebraic data types can be emulated in Scala with case classes.

alternative A branch of a `match` expression. It has the form "case *pattern* => *expression*." Another name for alternative is *case*.

annotation An *annotation* appears in source code and is attached to some part of the syntax. Annotations are computer processable, so you can use them to effectively add an extension to Scala.

anonymous class An anonymous class is a synthetic subclass generated by the Scala compiler from a new expression in which the class or trait name is followed by curly braces. The curly braces contains the body of the anonymous subclass, which may be empty. However, if the name following new refers to a trait or class that contains abstract members, these must be made concrete inside the curly braces that define the body of the anonymous subclass.

anonymous function Another name for function literal.

apply You can *apply* a method, function, or closure *to* arguments, which means you invoke it on those arguments.

argument When a function is invoked, an *argument* is passed for each parameter of that function. The parameter is the variable that refers to the argument. The argument is the object passed at invocation time. In addition, applications can take (command line) arguments that show up in the `Array[String]` passed to `main` methods of singleton objects.

assign You can *assign* an object *to* a variable. Afterwards, the variable will refer to the object.

auxiliary constructor Extra constructors defined inside the curly braces of the class definition, which look like method definitions named `this`, but with no result type.

block One or more expressions and declarations surrounded by curly braces. When the block evaluates, all of its expressions and declarations are processed in order, and then the block returns the value of the last expression as its own value. Blocks are commonly used as the bodies of functions, `for` expressions, `while` loops, and any other place where you want to group a number of statements together. More formally, a block is an encapsulation construct for which you can only see side effects and a result value. The curly braces in which you define a class or object do not, therefore, form a block, because fields and methods (which are defined inside those curly braces) are visible from the outside. Such curly braces form a *template*.

bound variable A *bound variable* of an expression is a variable that's both used and defined inside the expression. For instance, in the function literal expression `(x: Int) => (x, y)`, both variables x and y are used, but only x is bound, because it is defined in the expression as an `Int` and the sole argument to the function described by the expression.

by-name parameter A parameter that is marked with a `=>` in front of the parameter type, *e.g.*, `(x: => Int)`. The argument corresponding to a by-name parameter is evaluated not before the method is invoked, but each time the parameter is referenced *by name* inside the method. If a parameter is not by-name, it is *by-value*.

by-value parameter A parameter that is *not* marked with a `=>` in front of the parameter type, *e.g.*, `(x: Int)`. The argument corresponding to a by-value parameter is evaluated before the method is invoked. By-value parameters contrast with *by-name* parameters.

class Defined with the `class` keyword, a *class* may either be abstract or concrete, and may be parameterized with types and values when instantiated. In "`new Array[String](2)`", the class being instantiated is Array and the type of the value that results is Array[String]. A class that takes type parameters is called a *type constructor*. A type can be said to have a class as well, as in: the class of type Array[String] is Array.

closure A function object that captures free variables, and is said to be "closed" over the variables visible at the time it is created.

companion class A class that shares the same name with a singleton object defined in the same source file. The class is the singleton object's companion class.

companion object A singleton object that shares the same name with a class defined in the same source file. Companion objects and classes have access to each other's private members. In addition, any implicit conversions defined in the companion object will be in scope anywhere the class is used.

contravariant A *contravariant* annotation can be applied to a type parameter of a class or trait by putting a minus sign (–) before the type parameter. The class or trait then subtypes contravariantly with—in the opposite direction as—the type annotated parameter. For example, Function1 is contravariant in its first type parameter, and so Function1[Any, Any] is a subtype of Function1[String, Any].

covariant A *covariant* annotation can be applied to a type parameter of a class or trait by putting a plus sign (+) before the type parameter. The class or trait then subtypes covariantly with—in the same direction as—the type annotated parameter. For example, List is covariant in its type parameter, so List[String] is a subtype of List[Any].

currying A way to write functions with multiple parameter lists. For instance def f(x: Int)(y: Int) is a curried function with two parameter lists. A curried function is applied by passing several arguments lists, as in: f(3)(4). However, it is also possible to write a *partial application* of a curried function, such as f(3).

declare You can *declare* an abstract field, method, or type, which gives an entity a name but not an implementation. The key difference between declarations and definitions is that definitions establish an implementation for the named entity, declarations do not.

define To *define* something in a Scala program is to give it a name and an implementation. You can define classes, traits, singleton objects, fields, methods, local functions, local variables, *etc.* Because definitions always involve some kind of implementation, abstract members are *declared* not defined.

direct subclass A class is a *direct subclass* of its direct superclass.

direct superclass The class from which a class or trait is immediately derived, the nearest class above it in its inheritance hierarchy. If a class `Parent` is mentioned in a class `Child`'s optional extends clause, then `Parent` is the direct superclass of `Child`. If a trait is mentioned in `Child`'s extends clause, the trait's direct superclass is the `Child`'s direct superclass. If `Child` has no extends clause, then `AnyRef` is the direct superclass of `Child`. If a class's direct superclass takes type parameters, for example `class Child extends Parent[String]`, the direct superclass of `Child` is still `Parent`, not `Parent[String]`. On the other hand, `Parent[String]` would be the direct *supertype* of `Child`. See *supertype* for more discussion of the distinction between class and type.

equality When used without qualification, *equality* is the relation between values expressed by '=='. See also *reference equality*.

expression Any bit of Scala code that yields a result. You can also say that an expression *evaluates to* a result or *results in* a value.

filter An `if` followed by a boolean expression in a `for` expression. In `for(i <- 1 to 10; if i % 2 == 0)`, the filter is "`if i % 2 == 0`". The value to the right of the `if` is the *filter expression*.

filter expression A *filter expression* is the boolean expression following an `if` in a `for` expression. In `for(i <- 1 to 10; if i % 2 == 0)`, the filter expression is "`i % 2 == 0`".

first-class function Scala supports *first-class functions*, which means you can express functions in *function literal* syntax, *i.e.*, `(x: Int) => x + 1`, and that functions can be represented by objects, which are called *function values*.

for comprehension Another name for `for` *expression*.

free variable A *free variable* of an expression is a variable that's used inside the expression but not defined inside the expression. For instance, in the function literal expression (x: Int) => (x, y), both variables x and y are used, but only y is a free variable, because it is not defined inside the expression.

function A *function* can be *invoked* with a list of arguments to produce a result. A function has a parameter list, a body, and a result type. Functions that are members of a class, trait, or singleton object are called *methods*. Functions defined inside other functions are called *local functions*. Functions with the result type of Unit are called *procedures*. Anonymous functions in source code are called *function literals*. At run time, function literals are instantiated into objects called *function values*.

function literal A function with no name in Scala source code, specified with function literal syntax. For example, (x: Int, y: Int) => x + y.

function value A function object that can be invoked just like any other function. A function value's class extends one of the FunctionN traits (*e.g.*, Function0, Function1) from package scala, and is usually expressed in source code via *function literal* syntax. A function value is "invoked" when its apply method is called. A function value that captures free variables is a *closure*.

functional style The *functional style* of programming emphasizes functions and evaluation results and deemphasizes the order in which operations occur. The style is characterized by passing function values into looping methods, immutable data, methods with no side effects. It is the dominant paradigm of languages such as Haskell and Erlang, and contrasts with the *imperative style*.

generator A *generator* defines a named val and assigns to it a series of values in a for expression. For example, in for(i <- 1 to 10), the generator is "i <- 1 to 10". The value to the right of the <- is the *generator expression*.

generator expression A *generator expression* generates a series of values in a for expression. For example, in for(i <- 1 to 10), the generator expression is "1 to 10".

generic class A class that takes type parameters. For example, because scala.List takes a type parameter, scala.List is a generic class.

generic trait A trait that takes type parameters. For example, because trait scala.collection.Set takes a type parameter, it is a generic trait.

helper function A function whose purpose is to provide a service to one or more other functions nearby. Helper functions are often implemented as local functions.

helper method A helper function that's a member of a class. Helper methods are often private.

immutable An object is *immutable* if its value cannot be changed after it is created in any way visible to clients. Objects may or may not be immutable.

imperative style The *imperative style* of programming emphasizes careful sequencing of operations so that their effects happen in the right order. The style is characterized by iteration with loops, mutating data in place, and methods with side effects. It is the dominant paradigm of languages such as C, C++, C# and Java, and contrasts with the *functional style*.

initialize When a variable is defined in Scala source code, you must *initialize* it with an object.

instance An *instance*, or class instance, is an object, a concept that exists only at run time.

instantiate To *instantiate* a class is to make a new object from the class, an action that happens only at run time.

invariant *Invariant* is used in two ways. It can mean a property that always holds true when a data structure is well-formed. For example, it is an invariant of a sorted binary tree that each node is ordered before its right subnode, if it has a right subnode. *Invariant* is also sometimes used as a synonym for nonvariant: "class `Array` is invariant in its type parameter."

invoke You can *invoke* a method, function, or closure *on* arguments, meaning its body will be executed with the specified arguments.

JVM The *JVM* is the Java Virtual Machine, or *runtime*, that hosts a running Scala program.

literal 1, "One", and (x: Int) => x + 1 are examples of *literals*. A literal is a shorthand way to describe an object, where the shorthand exactly mirrors the structure of the created object.

local function A *local function* is a `def` defined inside a block. To contrast, a `def` defined as a member of a class, trait, or singleton object is called a *method*.

local variable A *local variable* is a `val` or `var` defined inside a block. Although similar to local variables, parameters to functions are not referred to as local variables, but simply as parameters or "variables" without the "local."

member A *member* is any named element of the template of a class, trait, or singleton object. A member may be accessed with the name of its owner, a dot, and its simple name. For example, top-level fields and methods defined in a class are members of that class. A trait defined inside a class is a member of its enclosing class. A type defined with the `type` keyword in a class is a member of that class. A class is a member of the package in which is it defined. By contrast, a local variable or local function is not a member of its surrounding block.

meta-programming Meta-programming software is software whose input is itself software. Compilers are meta-programs, as are tools like `scaladoc`. Meta-programming software is required in order to do anything with an *annotation*.

method A *method* is a function that is a member of some class, trait, or singleton object.

mixin *Mixin* is what a trait is called when it is being used in a mixin composition. In other words, in "trait Hat," Hat is just a trait, but in "new Cat extends AnyRef with Hat," Hat can be called a mixin. When used as a verb, "mix in" is two words. For example, you can *mix* traits *in*to classes or other traits.

mixin composition The process of mixing traits into classes or other traits. *Mixin composition* differs from traditional multiple inheritance in that the type of the super reference is not known at the point the trait is defined, but rather is determined anew each time the trait is mixed into a class or other trait.

modifier A keyword that qualifies a class, trait, field, or method definition in some way. For example, the private modifier indicates that a class, trait, field, or method being defined is private.

multiple definitions The same expression can be assigned in *multiple definitions* if you use the syntax val *v1*, *v2*, *v3* = *exp*.

nonvariant A type parameter of a class or trait is by default *nonvariant*. The class or trait then does not subtype when that parameter changes. For example, because class Array is nonvariant in its type parameter, Array[String] is neither a subtype nor a supertype of Array[Any].

operation In Scala, every *operation* is a method call. Methods may be invoked in *operator notation*, such as b + 2, and when in that notation, + is an *operator*.

parameter Functions may take zero to many *parameters*. Each parameter has a name and a type. The distinction between parameters and arguments is that arguments refer to the actual objects passed when a function is invoked. Parameters are the variables that refer to those passed arguments.

parameterless function A function that takes no parameters, which is defined without any empty parentheses. Invocations of parameterless functions may not supply parentheses. This supports the *uniform access principle*, which enables the def to be changed into a val without requiring a change to client code.

parameterless method A *parameterless method* is a parameterless function that is a member of a class, trait, or singleton object.

parametric field A field defined as a class parameter.

partially applied function A function that's used in an expression and that misses some of its arguments. For instance, if function f has type Int => Int => Int, then f and f(1) are *partially applied functions*.

path-dependent type A type like swiss.cow.Food. The swiss.cow part is a *path* that forms a reference to an object. The meaning of the type is sensitive to the path you use to access it. The types swiss.cow.Food and fish.Food, for example, are different types.

pattern In a match expression alternative, a *pattern* follows each case keyword and precedes either a *pattern guard* or the => symbol.

pattern guard In a match expression alternative, a *pattern guard* can follow a *pattern*. For example, in "case x if x % 2 == 0 => x + 1", the pattern guard is "if x % 2 == 0". A case with a pattern guard will only be selected if the pattern matches and the pattern guard yields true.

predicate A *predicate* is a function with a Boolean result type.

primary constructor The main constructor of a class, which invokes a superclass constructor, if necessary, initializes fields to passed values, and executes any top-level code defined between the curly braces of the class. Fields are initialized only for value parameters not passed to the superclass constructor, except for any that are not used in the body of the class and can therefore be optimized away.

procedure A *procedure* is a function with result type of Unit, which is therefore executed solely for its side effects.

reassignable A variable may or may not be *reassignable*. A var is reassignable while a val is not.

receiver The *receiver* of a method call is the variable, expression, or object on which the method is invoked.

recursive A function is *recursive* if it calls itself. If the only place the function calls itself is the last expression of the function, then the function is *tail recursive*.

reference A *reference* is the Java abstraction of a pointer, which uniquely identifies an object that resides on the JVM's heap. Reference type variables hold references to objects, because reference types (instances of AnyRef) are implemented as Java objects that reside on the JVM's heap. Value type variables, by contrast, may sometimes hold a reference (to a boxed wrapper type) and sometimes not (when the object is being represented as a primitive value). Speaking generally, a Scala variable *refers* to an object. The term "refers" is more abstract than "holds a reference." If a variable of type scala.Int is currently represented as a primitive Java int value, then that variable still refers to the Int object, but no reference is involved.

reference equality *Reference equality* means that two references identify the very same Java object. Reference equality can be determined, for reference types only, by calling eq in AnyRef. (In Java programs, reference equality can be determined using == on Java reference types.)

reference type A *reference type* is a subclass of AnyRef. Instances of reference types always reside on the JVM's heap at run time.

referential transparency A property of functions that are independent of temporal context and have no side effects. For a particular input, an invocation of a referentially transparent function can be replaced by its result without changing the program semantics.

refers A variable in a running Scala program always *refers* to some object. Even if that variable is assigned to null, it conceptually refers to the Null object. At runtime, an object may be implemented by a Java object or a value of a primitive type, but Scala allows programmers to think at a higher level of abstraction about their code as they imagine it running. See also *reference*.

refinement type A type formed by supplying a base type a number of members inside curly braces. The members in the curly braces refine the types that are present in the base type. For example, the type of "animal that eats grass" is Animal { type SuitableFood = Grass }.

result An expression in a Scala program yields a *result*. The result of every expression in Scala is an object.

result type A method's *result type* is the type of the value that results from calling the method. (In Java, this concept is called the return type.)

return A function in a Scala program *returns* a value. You can call this value the *result* of the function. You can also say the function *results in* the value. The result of every function in Scala is an object.

runtime The Java Virtual Machine, or JVM, that hosts a running Scala program. *Runtime* encompasses both the virtual machine, as defined by the Java Virtual Machine Specification, and the runtime libraries of the Java API and the standard Scala API. The phrase *at run time* (with a space between *run* and *time*) means when the program is running, and contrasts with compile time.

runtime type The type of an object at run time. To contrast, a *static type* is the type of an expression at compile time. Most runtime types are simply bare classes with no type parameters. For example, the runtime type of "Hi" is String, and the runtime type of (x: Int) => x + 1 is Function1. Runtime types can be tested with isInstanceOf.

script A file containing top level definitions and statements, which can be run directly with scala without explicitly compiling. A script must end in an expression, not a definition.

selector The value being matched on in a match expression. For example, in "s match { case _ => }", the selector is s.

self type A *self type* of a trait is the assumed type of this, the receiver, to be used within the trait. Any concrete class that mixes in the trait must ensure that its type conforms to the trait's self type. The most common use of self types is for dividing a large class into several traits as described in Chapter 7.

semi-structured data XML data is semi-structured. It is more structured than a flat binary file or text file, but it does not have the full structure of a programming language's data structures.

serialization You can *serialize* an object into a byte stream which can then be saved to files or transmitted over the network. You can later *deserialize* the byte stream, even on different computer, and obtain an object that is the same as the original serialized object.

shadow A new declaration of a local variable *shadows* one of the same name in an enclosing scope.

signature *Signature* is short for *type signature*.

singleton object An object defined with the `object` keyword. Each singleton object has one and only one instance. A singleton object that shares its name with a class, and is defined in the same source file as that class, is that class's *companion object*. The class is its *companion class*. A singleton object that doesn't have a companion class is a *standalone object*.

standalone object A singleton object that has no companion class.

statement An expression, definition, or import, *i.e.*, things that can go into a template or a block in Scala source code.

static type See *type*.

subclass A class is a *subclass* of all of its superclasses and supertraits.

subtrait A trait is a *subtrait* of all of its supertraits.

subtype The Scala compiler will allow any of a type's *subtypes* to be used as a substitute wherever that type is required. For classes and traits that take no type parameters, the subtype relationship mirrors the subclass relationship. For example, if class `Cat` is a subclass of abstract class `Animal`, and neither takes type parameters, type `Cat` is a subtype of type `Animal`. Likewise, if trait `Apple` is a subtrait of trait `Fruit`, and neither takes type parameters, type `Apple` is a subtype of type `Fruit`. For classes and traits that take type parameters, however, variance comes into play. For example, because abstract class `List` is declared to be covariant in its lone type parameter (*i.e.*, List is declared List[+A]), List[Cat] is a subtype of List[Animal], and List[Apple] a subtype of List[Fruit]. These subtype relationships exist even though the class of each of these types is List. By contrast, because Set is not declared to be covariant in its type parameter (*i.e.*, Set is declared Set[A] with no plus sign), Set[Cat] is *not* a subtype of Set[Animal]. A subtype should correctly implement the contracts of its supertypes, so that the Liskov Substitution Principle applies, but the compiler only verifies this property at the level of type checking.

superclass A class's *superclasses* include its direct superclass, its direct superclass's direct superclass, and so on, all the way up to Any.

supertrait A class's or trait's *supertraits*, if any, include all traits directly mixed into the class or trait or any of its superclasses, plus any supertraits of those traits.

supertype A type is a *supertype* of all of its subtypes.

synthetic class A *synthetic class* is generated automatically by the compiler rather than being written by hand by the programmer.

tail recursive A function is *tail recursive* if the only place the function calls itself is the last operation of the function.

target typing *Target typing* is a form of type inference that takes into account the type that's expected. In nums.filter((x) => x > 0), for example, the Scala compiler infers type of x to be the element type of nums, because the filter method invokes the function on each element of nums.

template A *template* is the body of a class, trait, or singleton object definition. It defines the type signature, behavior, and initial state of the class, trait, or object.

trait A *trait*, which is defined with the trait keyword, is like an abstract class that cannot take any value parameters and can be "mixed into" classes or other traits via the process known as *mixin composition*. When a trait is being mixed into a class or trait, it is called a *mixin*. A trait may be parameterized with one or more types. When parameterized with types, the trait constructs a type. For example, Set is a trait that takes a single type parameter, whereas Set[Int] is a type. Also, Set is said to be "the trait of" type Set[Int].

type Every variable and expression in a Scala program has a *type* that is known at compile time. A type restricts the possible values to which a variable can refer, or an expression can produce, at run time. A variable or expression's type can also be referred to as a *static type* if necessary to differentiate it from an object's *runtime type*. In other words, "type" by itself means static type. Type is distinct from class because a class that takes type parameters can construct many types. For example, List is a class, but not a type. List[T] is a type with a free type parameter. List[Int] and List[String] are also types (called *ground types* because they have no free type parameters). A type can have a "class" or "trait." For example, the class of type List[Int] is List. The trait of type Set[String] is Set.

type constraint Some annotations are *type constraints*, meaning that they add additional limits, or constraints, on what values the type includes. For example, @positive could be a type constraint on the type Int, limiting the type of 32-bit integers down to those that are positive. Type constraints are not checked by the standard Scala compiler, but must instead be checked by an extra tool or by a compiler plugin.

type constructor A class or trait that takes type parameters.

type parameter A parameter to a generic class or generic method that must be filled in by a type. For example, class List is defined as "class List[T] { ...", and method identity, a member of object Predef, is defined as "def identity[T](x:T) = x". The T in both cases is a type parameter.

type signature A method's *type signature* comprises its name, the number, order, and types of its parameters, if any, and its result type. The type signature of a class, trait, or singleton object comprises its name, the type signatures of all of its members and constructors, and its declared inheritance and mixin relations.

uniform access principle The *uniform access principle* states that variables and parameterless functions should be accessed using the same syntax. Scala supports this principle by not allowing parentheses to be placed at call sites of parameterless functions. As a result, a parameterless function definition can be changed to a val, or *vice versa*, without affecting client code.

unreachable At the Scala level, objects can become *unreachable*, at which point the memory they occupy may be reclaimed by the runtime. Unreachable does not necessarily mean unreferenced. Reference types (instances of AnyRef) are implemented as objects that reside on the JVM's heap. When an instance of a reference type becomes unreachable, it indeed becomes unreferenced, and is available for garbage collection. Value types (instances of AnyVal) are implemented as both primitive type values and as instances of Java wrapper types (such as java.lang.Integer), which reside on the heap. Value type instances can be boxed (converted from a primitive value to a wrapper object) and unboxed (converted from a wrapper object to a primitive value) throughout the lifetime of the variables that refer to them. If a value type instance currently represented as a wrapper object on the JVM's heap becomes unreachable, it indeed becomes unreferenced, and is available for garbage collection. But if a value type currently represented as a primitive value becomes unreachable, then it does not become unreferenced, because it does not exist as an object on the JVM's heap at that point in time. The runtime may reclaim memory occupied by unreachable objects, but if an Int, for example, is implemented at run time by a primitive Java int that occupies some memory in the stack frame of an executing method, then the memory for that object is "reclaimed" when the stack frame is popped as the method completes. Memory for reference types, such as Strings, may be reclaimed by the JVM's garbage collector after they become unreachable.

unreferenced See *unreachable*.

value The result of any computation or expression in Scala is a *value*, and in Scala, every value is an object. The term value essentially means the image of an object in memory (on the JVM's heap or stack).

value type A *value type* is any subclass of AnyVal, such as Int, Double, or Unit. This term has meaning at the level of Scala source code. At runtime, instances of value types that correspond to Java primitive types may be implemented in terms of primitive type values or instances of wrapper types, such as java.lang.Integer. Over the lifetime of a value type instance, the runtime may transform it back and forth between primitive and wrapper types (*i.e.*, to box and unbox it).

variable A named entity that refers to an object. A variable is either a val or a var. Both vals and vars must be initialized when defined, but only vars can be later reassigned to refer to a different object.

variance A type parameter of a class or trait can be marked with a *variance* annotation, either *covariant* (+) or *contravariant* (-). Such variance annotations indicate how subtyping works for a generic class or trait. For example, the generic class List is covariant in its type parameter, and thus List[String] is a subtype of List[Any]. By default, *i.e.*, absent a + or - annotation, type parameters are *nonvariant*.

wildcard type A wildcard type includes references to type variables that are unknown. For example, Array[_] is a wildcard type. It is an array where the element type is completely unknown.

yield An expression can *yield* a result. The yield keyword designates the result of a for expression.

Bibliography

[Abe96] Abelson, Harold and Gerald Jay Sussman. *Structure and Interpretation of Computer Programs*. The MIT Press, second edition, 1996.

[Aho86] Aho, Alfred V., Ravi Sethi, and Jeffrey D. Ullman. *Compilers: Principles, Techniques, and Tools*. Addison-Wesley Longman Publishing Co., Inc., Boston, MA, USA, 1986. ISBN 0-201-10088-6.

[Bay72] Bayer, Rudolf. "Symmetric binary B-Trees: Data structure and maintenance algorithms." *Acta Informatica*, 1(4):290–306, 1972.

[Blo08] Bloch, Joshua. *Effective Java Second Edition*. Addison-Wesley, 2008.

[DeR75] DeRemer, Frank and Hans Kron. "Programming-in-the large versus programming-in-the-small." In *Proceedings of the international conference on Reliable software*, pages 114–121. ACM, New York, NY, USA, 1975. doi:http://doi.acm.org/10.1145/800027.808431.

[Dij70] Dijkstra, Edsger W. "Notes on Structured Programming.", April 1970. Circulated privately. Available at http://www.cs.utexas.edu /users/EWD/ewd02xx/EWD249.PDF as EWD249 (accessed June 6, 2008).

[Eck98] Eckel, Bruce. *Thinking in Java*. Prentice Hall, 1998.

[Emi07] Emir, Burak, Martin Odersky, and John Williams. "Matching Objects With Patterns." In *Proc. ECOOP*, Springer LNCS, pages 273–295. July 2007.

[Eva03] Evans, Eric. *Domain-Driven Design: Tackling Complexity in the Heart of Software*. Addison-Wesley Professional, 2003.

[Fow04] Fowler, Martin. "Inversion of Control Containers and the Dependency Injection pattern." January 2004. Available on the web at http://martinfowler.com/articles/injection.html (accesssed August 6, 2008).

[Gam95] Gamma, Erich, Richard Helm, Ralph Johnson, and John Vlissides. *Design Patterns : Elements of Reusable Object-Oriented Software*. Addison-Wesley, 1995.

[Goe06] Goetz, Brian, Tim Peierls, Joshua Bloch, Joseph Bowbeer, David Homes, and Doug Lea. *Java Concurrency in Practice*. Addison Wesley, 2006.

[Jav] *The Java Tutorials: Creating a GUI with JFC/Swing*. Available on the web at http://java.sun.com/docs/books/tutorial/uiswing.

[Kay96] Kay, Alan C. "The Early History of Smalltalk." In *History of programming languages—II*, pages 511–598. ACM, New York, NY, USA, 1996. ISBN 0-201-89502-1. doi:http://doi.acm.org/10.1145/234286.1057828.

[Kay03] Kay, Alan C. An email to Stefan Ram on the meaning of the term "object-oriented programming", July 2003. The email is published on the web at http://www.purl.org/stefan_ram/pub/doc_kay_oop_en (accesssed June 6, 2008).

[Kri19] Krikava, Filip, Heather Miller, and Jan Vitek. "Scala implicits are everywhere: a large-scale study of the use of Scala implicits in the wild." In *Proceedings of the ACM on Programming Languages*, volume 3. ACM, 2019. doi:https://doi.org/10.1145/3360589.

[Lan66] Landin, Peter J. "The Next 700 Programming Languages." *Communications of the ACM*, 9(3):157–166, 1966.

[Mey91] Meyers, Scott. *Effective C++*. Addison-Wesley, 1991.

[Mey00] Meyer, Bertrand. *Object-Oriented Software Construction*. Prentice Hall, 2000.

588

[Mor68] Morrison, Donald R. "PATRICIA—Practical Algorithm To Retrieve Information Coded in Alphanumeric." *J. ACM*, 15(4):514–534, 1968. ISSN 0004-5411. doi:http://doi.acm.org/10.1145/321479.321481.

[Ode03] Odersky, Martin, Vincent Cremet, Christine Röckl, and Matthias Zenger. "A Nominal Theory of Objects with Dependent Types." In *Proc. ECOOP'03*, Springer LNCS, pages 201–225. July 2003.

[Ode05] Odersky, Martin and Matthias Zenger. "Scalable Component Abstractions." In *Proceedings of OOPSLA*, pages 41–58. October 2005.

[Ode11] Odersky, Martin. *The Scala Language Specification, Version 2.9*. EPFL, May 2011. Available on the web at http://www.scala-lang.org/docu/manuals.html (accessed April 20, 2014).

[Ray99] Raymond, Eric. *The Cathedral & the Bazaar: Musings on Linux and Open Source by an Accidental Revolutionary*. O'Reilly, 1999.

[Rum04] Rumbaugh, James, Ivar Jacobson, and Grady Booch. *The Unified Modeling Language Reference Manual (2nd Edition)*. Addison-Wesley, 2004.

[SPJ02] Simon Peyton Jones, et.al. "Haskell 98 Language and Libraries, Revised Report." Technical report, http://www.haskell.org/onlinereport, 2002.

[Ste99] Steele, Jr., Guy L. "Growing a Language." *Higher-Order and Symbolic Computation*, 12:221–223, 1999. Transcript of a talk given at OOPSLA 1998.

[Ste15] Steindorfer, Michael J and Jurgen J Vinju. "Optimizing hash-array mapped tries for fast and lean immutable JVM collections." In *ACM SIGPLAN Notices*, volume 50, pages 783–800. ACM, 2015.

[Str00] Strachey, Christopher. "Fundamental Concepts in Programming Languages." *Higher-Order and Symbolic Computation*, 13:11–49, 2000.

[Vaz07] Vaziri, Mandana, Frank Tip, Stephen Fink, and Julian Dolby. "Declarative Object Identity Using Relation Types." In *Proc. ECOOP 2007*, pages 54–78. 2007.

About the Authors

Martin Odersky is the creator of the Scala language. He is a professor at EPFL in Lausanne, Switzerland, and a founder of Lightbend, Inc. He works on programming languages and systems, more specifically on the topic of how to combine object-oriented and functional programming. Since 2001 he has concentrated on designing, implementing, and refining Scala. Previously, he has influenced the development of Java as a co-designer of Java generics and as the original author of the current `javac` reference compiler. He is a fellow of the ACM.

Lex Spoon is a software engineer at Square, Inc., which provides easy to use business software and mobile payments. In addition to Scala, he has helped develop a wide variety of programming languages, including the dynamic language Smalltalk, the scientific language X10, and the logic language CodeQL.

Bill Venners is president of Artima, Inc., publisher of the Artima website (www.artima.com) and provider of Scala consulting, training, books, and tools. He is author of the book, *Inside the Java Virtual Machine*, a programmer-oriented survey of the Java platform's architecture and internals. His popular columns in JavaWorld magazine covered Java internals, object-oriented design, and Jini. Bill is a community representative on the Scala Center advisory board, and is the lead developer and designer of the ScalaTest test framework and the Scalactic library for functional, object-oriented programming.

Frank Sommers is founder and president of Autospaces, Inc, a company providing workflow automation solutions to the financial services industry. Frank has been an active Scala user for over twelve years, and has worked with the language daily ever since.

591

Index

If you liked this book, you'll like this book...
in electronic form!

A comprehensive step-by-step guide

Programming in

Scala

Fifth Edition

Updated for Scala 3.0

Martin Odersky
Lex Spoon
Bill Venners
Frank Sommers

artima

The PDF eBook is a great companion to the paper book, because it is easy to carry around on your laptop, shows code with color syntax highlighting, lets you copy and paste Scala code directly into the interpreter, is quickly searchable and extensively hyperlinked. You can also download the book in mobi (for the Kindle) or epub formats.

Get your PDF, mobi, and epub version today at:

https://www.artima.com/shop/programming_in_scala_5ed

Printed in the USA
CPSIA information can be obtained
at www.ICGtesting.com
LVHW080954211024
794351LV00001B/1

9 780997 148008